ASP.NET

Tips & Techniques

Greg Buczek

McGraw-Hill/Osborne

New York   Chicago   San Francisco
Lisbon   London   Madrid   Mexico City
Milan   New Delhi   San Juan
Seoul   Singapore   Sydney   Toronto

McGraw-Hill/Osborne
2600 Tenth Street
Berkeley, California 94710
U.S.A.

To arrange bulk purchase discounts for sales promotions, premiums, or fund-raisers, please contact
McGraw-Hill/Osborne at the above address. For information on translations or book distributors outside the
U.S.A., please see the International Contact Information page immediately following the index of this book.

ASP.NET Tips & Techniques

1234567890 FGR FGR 0198765432

ISBN 0-07-222514-9

Publisher	Brandon A. Nordin
Vice President & Associate Publisher	Scott Rogers
Acquisitions Editor	Jim Schachterle
Project Editor	Janet Walden
Acquisitions Coordinator	Timothy Madrid
Technical Editor	Michael Adams
Copy Editor	Claire Splan
Proofreader	Pam Vevea
Indexer	David Heiret
Computer Designers	Carie Abrew, Tara A. Davis
Illustrators	Michael Mueller, Lyssa Wald
Series Designer	Roberta Steele
Cover Series Design	Greg Scott

This book was composed with Corel VENTURA™ Publisher.

I wish to dedicate this book to independent, free-thinking journalists and documentarians around the world who risk their lives to shed light on the darkest acts that take place. When we want to look the other way, they bring our attention back and remind so many of us how good life is and how hard we need to work to improve the lives of those less fortunate. I thank them for performing this difficult task and hope they will continue to do so in a world that seems to build new separatist walls every day.

About the Author

Greg Buczek is a Microsoft Certified Solutions Developer working as an independent consultant in Flagstaff, Arizona, in addition to being the author of eight previous titles. He has created and managed numerous Web sites where he strives to bring dynamic, data-driven content to the Internet. In his role as Webmaster, Greg has extensive experience with ASP.NET. Greg also has extensive ASP, Visual Basic, SQL Server, and Access experience. He has developed numerous Visual Basic applications, ActiveX Components, and ActiveX Controls. As a trainer, Greg has taught and developed curriculum for the MCSD courses. Greg's previous titles include *ASP.NET Developer's Guide*, *Instant ASP.NET Applications*, *Instant ASP Scripts Edition 1*, *Instant ASP Scripts Edition 2*, *Instant Access Databases*, *Instant SQL Server 2000 Applications*, *Instant ASP Components*, and *ASP Developer's Guide*.

You can e-mail Greg at books@netstats2000.com. When e-mailing, please include the title and edition of the book, do not send attachments, and, to avoid the spreading of viruses, please do not add him to your e-mail address list.

Contents at a Glance

Contents

Acknowledgements

First, I wish to thank Michael Adams, my technical editor on this book. I have known Mike for years, and he has been my technical editor for many of my books. His critical reviews are always helpful and provide me with additional confidence in the statements that I make.

I wish to thank the professionals that I work with at my publisher, McGraw-Hill/Osborne. In particular, I wish to thank Jim Schachterle, my acquisitions editor, for providing me the opportunity to write this title, and Tim Madrid, my acquisitions coordinator, for always being there to answer my questions and queries. And I wish to thank Janet Walden and her crew for their outstanding review and layout of this book. One of the many things they did for this book was to take this paragraph and make it more readable by correcting my grammar and punctuation. I know I killed this paragraph, so thanks for fixing it!

Introduction

The developmental approach of ASP.NET makes the process of creating dynamic Web applications a whole new technique. In some ways that technique is easier; in others, it has become more complex. But regardless of the difficulty with which you find learning ASP.NET, hopefully you will find that it allows you to create Web applications that are better able to meet your business needs. Whether it is through the approach of using controls, sending e-mail from your Web pages, or creating a Web service, ASP.NET allows you to expand the possibilities of what you can do through your Web site.

This book can be used as a tool to understand how ASP.NET can help you with the development of your site. As you are trying to solve a problem using ASP.NET, browse through the tips and techniques presented here and if they do not address your problem directly, think about how you can adjust the code to suit your needs. Remember that the developers who are able to complete the task at hand are the ones who are aware of their resources and rarely build a page without copying and pasting from other pages.

Book Structure

This book contains hundreds of tips and techniques that show you how to use ASP.NET and relating technologies. The tips and techniques are presented as individual units. In other words, to use and understand a tip or technique, you don't have to rely on a previous tip or technique.

Each tip and technique is presented in the same format. After the title of the tip or technique, a brief description of the item is presented. That is followed by the code or steps you need to take to complete the task. Most of the tips and techniques have an accompanying ASP.NET page that contains the code reviewed in the item. Therefore, you will often be able to copy and paste from the ASP.NET page right into your application. (See "Downloading Book Files" later in this Introduction for more information.)

The tips and techniques are grouped together with similar tips and techniques into a chapter. The next section briefly describes the tips and techniques presented in each chapter.

Chapter 1: Basic ASP.NET Page Issues   In the first chapter, tips and techniques related to page structure are presented. These items will show you the structure of a page and how to define compiler options on ASP.NET pages.

Chapter 2: HTML Controls   One of the most basic control libraries provided by ASP.NET is defined through the HTMLControls namespace. The controls in this library allow you to define elements that mirror closely the basic HTML elements. This chapter presents tips and techniques that show you how to use those controls.

Chapter 3: Basic Web Controls   Probably the most important library that comes with ASP.NET, and the one you will likely use the most, is the WebControls namespace. The tips and techniques presented in this chapter show you how to use one-dimensional, basic controls contained in this library.

Chapter 4: List Web Controls   This chapter continues the presentation of tips and techniques using the WebControls namespace. The items presented in this chapter relate to controls that let you list repeating data, such as the DataGrid control and the Repeater control.

Chapter 5: Validation Web Controls   ASP.NET contains a slew of controls that make it easy to validate visitor input. These controls allow you to make sure that visitors enter data into a field, check the data type of data entered, or check to see if data entered matches a pattern. This chapter presents tips and techniques that show you how to use those controls.

Chapter 6: Other Web Controls   This chapter presents tips and techniques for controls from the WebControls namespace that are more advanced or specialized. The controls discussed include the Calendar control, the AdRotator control, the Panel control, and the Table control.

Chapter 7: Internet Explorer Web Controls   An additional and very helpful library of controls that you can download from Microsoft is the Internet Explorer Web Controls namespace. This namespace includes controls like the Multipage control, the TabStrip control, Toolbar control, and the TreeView control. Tips and techniques presented in this chapter show you how to use these controls.

Chapter 8: Creating Your Own Controls   A very nice capability provided by ASP.NET is the ability to create your own controls. Doing this allows you to encapsulate functionality that you wish to use over and over again into a single source. This chapter presents tips and techniques that show you how to create and use your own controls.

Chapter 9: E-mail   Your ASP.NET applications won't get very complex before you find that you need to send e-mail through one of your ASP.NET pages. You can do that through ASP.NET. The tips and techniques presented in this chapter show you how to work with e-mail from your ASP.NET pages.

Chapter 10: Application Issues   Once you get beyond single-page development with ASP.NET, you will want to group your pages together into an ASP.NET application. This chapter presents tips and techniques that show you how to work with applications within ASP.NET.

Chapter 11: Code-Behind Files   ASP.NET provides a technique that allows you to split the code from the design interface. Doing this allows you to have one developer who works on the code and one who designs the page. Each developer has his or her own file to work with. This chapter presents tips and techniques that show you how to separate the code from the page.

Chapter 12: Working with IIS   If you create ASP.NET pages or applications, knowledge of how to use IIS will make your work much easier. This chapter presents tips and techniques that show you how to perform a variety of tasks within IIS.

Chapter 13: Database Code   As the complexity of your Web site grows, you will want to provide dynamic content that comes from a database. This chapter presents tips and techniques that show you how to connect to, retrieve data from, and manipulate data in a database through ASP.NET.

Chapter 14: Web Services   Web services provide a way for you to encapsulate functionality that can be used by other pages and sites on your server or by other developers on different servers. This chapter presents tips and techniques that show you how to create, compile, and consume Web services.

Chapter 15: Mobile Internet Toolkit   One of the changes in Internet access is that visitors are starting to come to your site through a mobile device like a mobile phone. You may find that you wish to create specialized pages and sites for visitors connecting to you through mobile devices. You can do this using the Mobile Internet Toolkit. This chapter presents tips and techniques that show you how to create Mobile ASP.NET pages.

Chapter 16: Page Samples   In the final chapter of the book, page samples are presented. These samples combine controls used throughout the book to create more complex pages.

Downloading Book Files

Most of the tips and techniques presented in this book have an ASP.NET page or file that contains the code presented with the topic. You can download this code by navigating to this location

   http://www.osborne.com

and clicking on the link for free code and samples. On that page, you should see this book's title under the "Source Code" heading. Click on that link to download the book files.

   Unzip the files to the desired location on your computer. You will see that the files are organized by chapter number. Within each chapter folder, you will find files that have titles that are similar to the names of the tips and techniques from that chapter.

CHAPTER 1

Basic ASP.NET Page Issues

TIPS IN THIS CHAPTER

W hen you create an ASP.NET page it can contain certain items and those items need to be defined in an expected way. To get the most out of your ASP.NET development work, you need to be familiar with this structure. This chapter presents tips and techniques that show you how to effectively define an ASP.NET page. In addition, tips and techniques are presented with regards to the Page object, which is the underlying class that all ASP.NET pages are based on.

Coding the Basic ASP.NET Page Structure

When you create an ASP.NET page, that page needs to include certain tags and have an expected structure to it. This tip defines the basic structure of an ASP.NET page.

USE IT The page created for this tip contains the basic structure of an ASP.NET page. At the top of that page, you will find these directives:

```
<%@ Page Language=VB Debug=true %>
<%@ Import Namespace="System.Web.Mail" %>
```

Directives are instructions to the compiler that tell it how the page should be run. In this case, the Page directive is used to indicate the code language on the page. The Import directive indicates a namespace that should be compiled with this page.

That is followed by your page code, which is placed within Script tags:

```
<script runat=server>
Private A as Integer
Sub Page_Load(ByVal Sender as Object, ByVal E as EventArgs)

End Sub
Sub SubmitBtn_Click(Sender As Object, E As EventArgs)

End Sub
</script>
```

Notice that the Script tag includes the parameter RunAt with a value of Server. That means that this code is server-side code and should be used by the compiler when the page loads or is posted back for processing.

Within the Script tags, you define the procedures for the page. These procedures can be made up of event procedures that fire when something happens on the page, such as when a button is clicked or the page loads. These procedures can also be made up of your own procedures that are called from other event-driven procedures.

After defining the code for your page, you can start including the HTML tags for the page structure:

```
<HTML>
<HEAD>
<TITLE>Coding the Basic ASP.NET Page Structure</TITLE>
</HEAD>
<Body LEFTMARGIN="40">
```

That is typically followed by an opening ASP.NET Form tag:

```
<form runat="server">
```

Within the Form tag, you define your ASP.NET controls mixed in with standard HTML elements:

```
<asp:label
    id="lblDataEntered"
    runat="server"
/>
<BR><BR>
Enter your Name:<BR>
<asp:textbox
    id="txtName"
    columns="25"
    maxlength="30"
    runat=server
/>
<BR><BR>
<asp:button
    id="butOK"
    text="  OK  "
    onclick="SubmitBtn_Click"
    runat="server"
/>
```

Here, a Label control, a TextBox control, and a Button control are defined. Notice that between the control definitions, HTML elements are defined.

Once you define the controls and other content on the page, you need to close the ASP.NET Form control:

```
</Form>
</BODY>
</HTML>
```

Notice that the HTML tags are also closed.

Using the Load Event of the Page Object

Frequently, you need to include code on your page that fires when the page loads. This type of code is used to set up the items on your page. For example, if you wanted to display a list of products, you would need to retrieve those products from a database when visitors view the page. You do this by creating a Load event procedure for the Page object. This technique shows you how to create that procedure.

 USE IT The page created for this technique displays to visitors text through two Label controls. The text in these controls is set in code when the page loads.

The Label controls are defined within the form on the ASP.NET page. The first Label control has this definition:

```
<asp:label
    id="lblFixed"
    runat="server"
/>
```

The other Label control has this definition:

```
<asp:label
    id="lblStatic"
    runat="server"
/>
```

When the page loads, the following code runs:

```
Sub Page_Load(ByVal Sender as Object, ByVal E as EventArgs)
    lblFixed.Text = "Welcome to the page!"
    lblStatic.Text = "The current time on the server is " _
        & TimeOfDay()
End Sub
```

Notice that the name of the procedure is Page_Load:

```
Sub Page_Load(ByVal Sender as Object, ByVal E as EventArgs)
```

If you want the code to run whenever the page loads, you must give the procedure this name. Also, notice that two parameters are passed into this procedure. If you do not supply these two parameters, your page will not run and an error will be returned.

Within the procedure, you define code that you want to run every time the page loads:

```
lblFixed.Text = "Welcome to the page!"
lblStatic.Text = "The current time on the server is " _
    & TimeOfDay()
```

In this case, fixed text is displayed in the first Label control and the current system time is displayed in the other Label control.

You then need to close the procedure's definition:

```
End Sub
```

Using the Unload Event of the Page Object

Another event procedure of the Page object that you can provide code for is the Unload event. This event fires when the page is finished processing and is being removed from memory. You can use this procedure to write any final clean-up code such as closing connections to databases or storing any closing statistical values. Note though that you cannot change the controls on the page during this event because they already will have been rendered. This technique shows you how to use the Unload event.

USE IT   The page created for this technique displays text to visitors when the page loads. Then, when the page is done processing, the time that the page finished is stored in a persistent variable.

Defined within the ASP.NET page are these three Label controls:

```
<asp:label
    id="lblFixed"
    runat="server"
/>
<BR><BR>
<asp:label
    id="lblStatic"
    runat="server"
/>
<BR><BR>
<asp:label
    id="lblDone"
    runat="server"
/>
```

When the page loads, this code fires:

```
Sub Page_Load(ByVal Sender as Object, ByVal E as EventArgs)
    lblFixed.Text = "Welcome to the page!"
    lblStatic.Text = "The current time on the server is " _
        & TimeOfDay()
    lblDone.Text = Session("FinalText")
End Sub
```

Notice that the text in the third Label control is set to a value in a Session variable. That variable gets its value in the Unload event, so the first time the page loads, this Label will not display any text. But on subsequent calls, the Label control will display the time the page finished processing.

That Session variable has its value set in the Unload event:

```
Sub Page_Unload(ByVal Sender as Object, ByVal E as EventArgs)
    Session("FinalText")  = "During last load, the " _
        & "page finished processing at: " & TimeOfDay()
End Sub
```

Therefore, when the page is done processing, the Session variable is set to the system time.

Redirecting Visitors When an Unhandled Error Occurs

Your code may, on occasion, produce results that cause an error to occur. When that happens, you can choose to simply let visitors see the error message on the page. But you could choose to redirect visitors to another page when an unhandled error occurs. On such a page, you could display friendly help telling them to retry at a later time or to contact your company for support. You can do this on an ASP.NET page through the use of the Error event. This tip shows you how to use that event.

USE IT   The page created for this technique produces an error. The error occurs in the Load event of the Page object:

```
Sub Page_Load(ByVal Sender as Object, ByVal E as EventArgs)
    Dim I as Boolean
    I = "hello"
End Sub
```

Notice that the variable "I" is declared as a Boolean. Therefore, it should be assigned a True/False value. But in this procedure, it is set to a string. That will cause an error.

Typically, visitors to this page would see the standard error page. But this page includes an Error event procedure:

```
Sub Page_Error(Sender as Object, e as EventArgs)
    Response.Redirect("./errorshappen.aspx")
End Sub
```

The effect of this procedure is that when an error occurs on this page that is not handled, the code in this procedure fires. In this case, visitors are sent to another page. You would then supply that other page and let visitors see a friendlier message with regards to the problem that occurred.

Using the IsPostBack Property of the Page Object

Frequently, you will have code on your ASP.NET page that you want to run when the page loads. But you will only want the code to run the first time the page loads. When visitors submit the page for processing, you would not want the code to run again. This technique shows you how to do that.

USE IT   The page created for this technique defines two Label controls. One Label control is assigned the current time every time the page loads. The other Label control is assigned the current time only the first time the page loads.

The Label controls have this definition:

```
<asp:label
    id="lblFirstTime"
    runat="server"
/>
<BR><BR>
<asp:label
    id="lblOtherTimes"
    runat="server"
/>
```

Also defined on the page is a Button control that allows subsequent calls to the page to be performed:

```
<asp:button
    id="butOK"
    text="  OK  "
    onclick="SubmitBtn_Click"
    runat="server"
/>
```

The following code fires every time the page loads:

```
Sub Page_Load(ByVal Sender as Object, ByVal E as EventArgs)
    If Not Page.IsPostBack Then
        lblFirstTime.Text = "The page first loaded at: " _
            & TimeOfDay()
    End If
    lblOtherTimes.Text = "The last page load fired at " _
        & TimeOfDay()
End Sub
```

Notice the use of the IsPostBack property of the Page object:

```
If Not Page.IsPostBack Then
```

That property returns True if the page has been returned for processing. In other words, the property is set to True when visitors click the Button control. But it is set to False the first time the page loads.

When it is the first load of the page, one of the Label controls is assigned the current system time:

```
lblFirstTime.Text = "The page first loaded at: " _
    & TimeOfDay()
```

The other Label control will have its value assigned regardless of whether the page is initially loading or not:

```
lblOtherTimes.Text = "The last page load fired at " _
    & TimeOfDay()
```

Creating Your Own Procedures

In addition to writing event procedures on your page that fire when an event such as a page loading occurs, you can create your own procedures. You call these procedures from the event procedures. You will find doing this is helpful as your ASP.NET pages become more complex and you are repeating code within event procedures. This technique shows you how to create your own procedures.

USE IT   The page created for this technique prompts the visitor for two numbers. Those numbers are added when the page is submitted. The page includes two user-defined procedures that are called from two event procedures. One of the procedures is a Function, so it returns a value. The other procedure does not return a value, since it is a Sub.

Defined on the page is this Label control, which will display page instructions to visitors:

```
<asp:label
    id="lblInstructions"
    runat="server"
/>
```

Next, two TextBox controls are defined for entering the two numbers that will be added:

```
<asp:textbox
    id="txtNumber1"
    runat=server
/>
<asp:textbox
    id="txtNumber2"
    runat=server
/>
```

After those controls a Button control is defined:

```
<asp:button
    id="butOK"
    text="Add"
    onclick="SubmitBtn_Click"
    runat="server"
/>
```

A second Label control is defined that will display the result of adding the numbers:

```
<asp:label
    id="lblResult"
    runat="server"
/>
```

The first procedure defined on the page is called DisplayInstructions:

```
Sub DisplayInstructions(Mode as String)
    If Mode = "Initial" Then
      lblInstructions.Text = "Enter two numbers that " _
          & "you want to add."
    Else
      lblInstructions.Text = "The results are " _
          & "below."
    End If
End Sub
```

This procedure displays different information into the Label control, based on whether the page is in initial load mode or a subsequent posting. The procedure is called from the Load event:

```
Sub Page_Load(ByVal Sender as Object, ByVal E as EventArgs)
    If IsPostBack Then
        DisplayInstructions("Final")
    Else
        DisplayInstructions("Initial")
    End If
End Sub
```

Notice that the IsPostBack property is used to determine whether the page is in its initial load or whether the page is loading because the form on the page was posted.

The other procedure defined on this page is called AddNums:

```
Function AddNums(Num1 as Single, Num2 as Single) as Single
   AddNums = Num1 + Num2
End Function
```

This procedure requires two parameters to be passed in. Those are the numbers to be added. The procedure returns the result of adding those two numbers.

That procedure is called when the Button control is clicked:

```
Sub SubmitBtn_Click(Sender As Object, E As EventArgs)
    lblResult.Text = "Result: " & AddNums( _
        txtNumber1.Text, txtNumber2.Text)
End Sub
```

Notice that the two numbers entered into the TextBox controls by visitors is passed into the procedure call.

Using the Page Directive

Directives are instructions that you supply to the compiler to indicate how a page should be compiled. One of the directives that you are likely to include on every page is the Page directive. This technique shows you how to define that directive.

 The ASP.NET page created for this technique uses the Page directive to set a variety of options. The Page directive, used on that page, has this syntax:

```
<%@ Page
    Language=VB
    EnableSessionState=false
    Debug=true
    Buffer=true
    Explicit=true
    Strict=false
    Description="Sample Page directive page."
%>
```

You start by indicating the name of the directive:

```
<%@ Page
```

Notice the specific characters used to open a directive.

Then within the Page directive you can start setting its parameters. One of those is the Language parameter:

```
Language=VB
```

This parameter is set to the name of the programming language you are using on the page.

Next, the EnableSessionState parameter is set:

```
EnableSessionState=false
```

A value of True in this parameter means that Session variables can be created and they will persist. A value of False means that these variables cannot be used on this page. The parameter can also be set to ReadOnly, which means that Session variables can be read but not changed.

The next parameter set is the Debug parameter:

```
Debug=true
```

Setting this parameter to True sometimes provides you with more information when an error occurs.

► **QUICK TIP**

Set the Debug parameter to False when you move your page to a production machine. This will reduce page overhead.

Next, the Buffer parameter is set:

```
Buffer=true
```

If this parameter is set to True, the page will be sent after all the processing is complete. If the parameter is set to False, the page is sent as it is processed.

The next parameter, Explicit, is only used with Visual Basic.NET:

```
Explicit=true
```

When you set this parameter to True, you must declare all your variables.

The Strict parameter also is only used by Visual Basic.NET:

```
Strict=false
```

Setting this parameter to False means that the compiler will allow you to place a value of one data type into another data type without throwing an error.

The last parameter set is the Description parameter:

```
Description="Sample Page directive page."
```

This parameter is just for you. It provides a place for you to define the description of the page.

Using the Import Directive

To instantiate objects of a class, the compiler needs to know where the definitions for those classes can be found. In .NET architecture those definitions can be found within a namespace. To indicate to the compiler that you want to use classes in a namespace on your ASP.NET page, you use the Import directive. This tip shows you how to do that.

USE IT   The page created for this tip imports three namespaces. It does this using the Import directive. Those directives are defined towards the top of the ASP.NET page:

```
<%@ Import
    Namespace="System.Web.Mail"
%>
<%@ Import
    Namespace="System.Data"
%>
<%@ Import
    Namespace="System.Data.OLEDB"
%>
```

Only one parameter is used with the Import directive. That is the Namespace parameter. You place into that parameter the name of the namespace that you wish to include in the compilation of your page. Notice that each namespace is imported through a separate Import directive.

Using the OutputCache Directive

The OutputCache directive provides a way for you to have your page only be processed at specific time intervals. This is helpful when you have a resource-intensive page that does not change frequently. For example, if you had a page that lists all the employees at your company through a DataGrid control, you really don't need this page to grab fresh data from the database every time the page is loaded. You would use the OutputCache parameter to indicate how frequently you want the page to refresh. This tip shows you how to do that.

USE IT   The page created for this tip displays the current time to visitors when the page loads. But since the OutputCache directive is used, the time displayed is only updated after 30 seconds have elapsed.

Defined within the page is this Label control:

```
<asp:label
    id="lbl1"
    runat="server"
/>
```

That control has its Text property set when the page loads:

```
Sub Page_Load(ByVal Sender as Object, ByVal E as EventArgs)
    lbl1.Text = "The current time on the server is " _
        & TimeOfDay()
End Sub
```

But the text will not be set every time the page is loaded because of this OutputCache directive:

```
<%@ OutputCache
    Duration=30
    VaryByParam=none
%>
```

The Duration parameter is set to the number of seconds that the page will be cached. After that time elapses, the page will run again.

Notice the use of the VaryByParam parameter. You must include this parameter. You can use this parameter to have caching be based on a value passed in through the Get or Post methods. You can set this parameter to None if you want caching to occur regardless of how the page loads.

CHAPTER 2
HTML Controls

One of the main namespaces that comes with ASP.NET is the System.Web.UI.HTMLControls namespace. That namespace contains controls that you render through your ASP.NET pages that are very similar to HTML elements. These controls are helpful because of their basic nature. They are easy to employ and relate more directly with their HTML element counterparts. The tips and techniques presented in this chapter show you how to use many of the controls in that namespace.

Using the HTMLAnchor Control

The HTMLAnchor control provides a way for you to create an Anchor tag through your ASP.NET page. The control contains properties that allow you to define in code or through the control's definition the text displayed on the control and where visitors will be taken to when they select a link. This technique shows you how to define a basic HTMLAnchor control.

USE IT   The page created for this technique contains two HTMLAnchor controls. Both take visitors to another site when they are clicked.

The first HTMLAnchor control has this definition:

```
<a
    id="Anchor1"
    runat=server
    target="_blank"
    href = "http://www.google.com"
>
</a>
```

You can give the control a name through the ID property. If you do that, you can manipulate the control in code. After supplying the name for the control, you indicate that it should run on the server end.

The Target property is used to indicate what browser window should be used when displaying the page resulting from the link. Here it is set to "_blank", which indicates that a new browser window should be opened and used. The HREF property of the HTMLAnchor control indicates the Web site visitors should be taken to when they select the link. Notice that no text is supplied for this link. That is because it is set in code.

The other HTMLAnchor control has this definition:

```
<a
    id="Anchor2"
    runat=server
    taget="_self"
    href = "http://www.google.com"
    title="Don't forget to click me!"
>
```

```
<I>Another Link</I>
</a>
```

Notice that the Target property for this control is set to "_self". That means that the current browser window will be used to display the page resulting from clicking on the link.

The Title property is set to whatever text that you want to appear when visitors hover their mouse over the link. You can use this property to provide additional information about the link that is not displayed with the text.

The text that will be displayed in this HTMLAnchor control is set between the opening and closing tags. Notice that the text itself contains the HTML italics tag. You can use most basic HTML tags within the text displayed through a HTMLAnchor control.

The text displayed in the first HTMLAnchor control is set in code when the page loads:

```
Sub Page_Load(ByVal Sender as Object, ByVal E as EventArgs)
    Anchor1.InnerHTML = "<B>Click Me Anchor1 in Bold</B>"
End Sub
```

Notice that the InnerHTML property is used to indicate the text that you want to display in the link.

▶ **QUICK TIP**

The HTMLAnchor control also contains an InnerText property. If you use that property instead of the InnerHTML property, you cannot place HTML tags in the text that is to be displayed.

Creating an HTMLAnchor Control That Is a Button

One way that you can use an HTMLAnchor control is as a basic anchor that links visitors to another page. Another way that you can use the HTMLAnchor control is as a button. Doing that allows you to supply code to run when visitors select the HTMLAnchor control. This technique shows you how to do that.

USE IT The page created for this technique displays an HTMLAnchor control. When visitors click on the link, code runs that changes the text that is displayed on the link.

The HTMLAnchor control has this definition:

```
<a
    id="Anchor1"
    onserverclick="Anchor_Click"
    runat=server
>
Click Me
</a>
```

The name of the control is set through the ID property. You indicate the name of the procedure that you want to run when the link is selected through the OnServerClick property.

In code, you must create a procedure that has that exact name and has the parameters like the ones in this procedure:

```
Sub Anchor_Click(Source As Object, E as EventArgs)
    Anchor1.InnerHtml = "<B>Thanks for clicking " _
        & "the link!</B>"
End Sub
```

The code uses the InnerHTML property to change the text that is displayed in the HTMLAnchor control.

Using the HTMLButton Control

The HTMLButton control provides a way for you to allow visitors to submit the information that they entered on the form of your ASP.NET pages. You then supply code that runs on the submitted data. This technique shows you how to do that.

USE IT   The ASP.NET page created for this technique prompts visitors for their name. Visitors then click the HTMLButton control defined on the page to submit their name. Then, they see their name echoed back to them through a Span tag.

The first control defined on the page is this Span control:

```
<Span
    id="MyMessage"
    runat=server
>
</Span>
```

Notice that it does not have any initial text. It will contain visitors' names after they submit the page for processing.

The next control defined on the page allows visitors to enter their name:

```
<Input
    id="YourName"
    runat="server"
    type="text"
>
```

The other control defined on the page is the HTMLButton control:

```
<button
    id="Button1"
```

```
    runat="server"
    onserverclick="SubmitBtn_Click"
>
Submit
</button>
```

You set the name of the HTMLButton control through the ID property. Then you must indicate that the server will render the control. You do this by setting the RunAt property to "Server."

Next, you need to specify the name of the procedure that will run when the button is clicked. You do that through the OnServerClick property. The text that is displayed on the face of the button is set between the opening and closing tags of the control.

The only code on the page fires when the HTMLButton control is clicked:

```
Sub SubmitBtn_Click(Source As Object, E as EventArgs)
    MyMessage.InnerHTML = "Hello " & YourName.Value
End Sub
```

Notice that this procedure name matches the name of the procedure specified in the OnServerClick property. Within the procedure, the name that visitors entered is echoed back to them through the Span control.

Displaying a Graphic on an HTMLButton Control

In addition to displaying text on the face of an HTMLButton control, you can display an image. This technique shows you how to do that.

USE IT The ASP.NET page created for this technique prompts visitors for their name. That name is echoed back to visitors through a Span control. Visitors submit their name by clicking an HTMLButton control. That control is defined with an image on its face instead of text.

The first control defined on the page is the Span control:

```
<Span
    id="MyMessage"
    runat=server
>
</Span>
```

That control will display visitors' names after they submit the page.

The next control defined on the page is an Input control:

```
<Input
    id="YourName"
    runat="server"
```

```
        type="text"
>
```

The control is rendered as a text box, which visitors use to enter their name.

  The third control defined on the page is the HTMLButton control:

```
<button
    id="Button1"
    runat="server"
    onserverclick="SubmitBtn_Click"
>
    <img
        src="./button.gif"
    />
</button>
```

  You specify the name of the control through the ID property. You specify the name of the procedure that should run when the control is clicked through the OnServerClick property.

  Normally, between the opening and closing tags of the control you would place the text that you want to appear on its face. But in this case, you want a picture to appear on the button's face. Therefore, an HTML Image tag is defined within the HTMLButton control. This has the affect of displaying an image on the face of the button control.

  The only code on the page fires when the HTMLButton control is clicked:

```
Sub SubmitBtn_Click(Source As Object, E as EventArgs)
    MyMessage.InnerHTML = "Hello " & YourName.Value
End Sub
```

  The procedure echoes visitors' names back to them through the Span control.

Defining a Basic Span Control

If you are using the controls from the HTMLControls namespace, you will likely find that you want to display text on your ASP.NET page that you wish to manipulate through code. You can do that by defining Span controls. This technique shows you how to do that.

  USE IT   The ASP.NET page created for this technique displays text through four Span controls. The properties of the control are used to show you how you can use the control in different ways.

  The first Span control defined on the page has this definition:

```
<span
    id="Span1"
    runat=server
```

```
>
<B>This text will appear in bold.</B>
</span>
```

The name of the control is set through the ID property. You must set the RunAt property to "Server" to indicate that your server should process the control.

Then between the opening and closing tags of the control, you specify the text that you want displayed. As is done here, the text can include basic HTML tags like bold and italics.

The second Span control has this definition:

```
<span
    id="Span2"
    runat=server
>
</span>
```

Notice that no text is supplied for this control. Instead, the text that is displayed through this control is set when the page loads.

The third Span control has this definition:

```
<span
    id="Span3"
    runat=server
    disabled="True"
>
This text will appear disabled.
</span>
```

The control used the Disabled property, which is set to True. That means that the text in the Span control will be displayed in a grayed-out state.

The fourth Span control has this definition:

```
<span
    id="Span4"
    runat=server
    visible="False"
>
This text will not appear.
</span>
```

Notice that the Visible property is set to False. That means that the control will not be visible to visitors. This is a technique that you can employ if you wish to have information that you do not want displayed on the page sent back to the page for processing.

The only code on the page fires when the page loads:

```
Sub Page_Load(ByVal Sender as Object, ByVal E as EventArgs)
    Span2.InnerText = "<B>This text will not " _
        & "appear in bold.</B>"
End Sub
```

When that happens, the text is set for the second Span control. But notice that the InnerText property is used. That means that the bold tags placed into this property will not be interpreted. Take a look at the screenshot from this page.

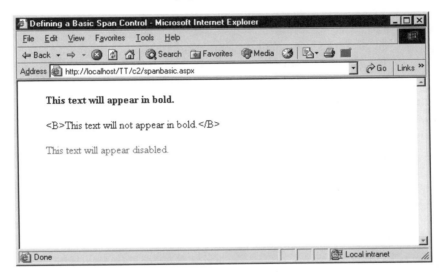

Notice that the bold tags are interpreted in the first Span control but not in the second. Also notice that the fourth Span tag is not displayed at all.

Using an HTMLForm Control

On almost all of the ASP.NET pages that you create, you will add an HTMLForm control. The control is typically the foundation onto which you add other controls. With an HTMLForm control, visitors can interact with a page by submitting it for processing. This technique shows you how to define an HTMLForm control.

USE IT You can only define one HTMLForm control on each ASP.NET page. The definition of the control and its contents looks like this:

```
<form
    runat="server"
    id="MyForm"
    method="Post"
```

```
    disabled="False"
    visible="True"
>
'Define other controls.
</form>
```

First, you need to indicate that the control should be processed by the server:

```
<form
    runat="server"
```

You can supply a name for the control through the ID property:

```
id="MyForm"
```

Doing so isn't required, but if you want to add controls dynamically to the form, you would need to do this.

You can optionally set the method by which the page is returned to the server for processing:

```
method="Post"
```

By default, this method is set to Post. You can also set the property to Get. If you do that, be aware that you may lose values in some of your controls since you may exceed the byte limitation of the Get method.

You can disable a form, which disables all the controls defined within the form:

```
disabled="False"
```

You can also hide the form through the Visible property:

```
visible="True"
```

Between the opening and closing tags of the HTMLForm control, you define your other controls:

```
'Define other controls.
```

and after defining those controls, you need to close the HTMLForm control's definition:

```
</form>
```

Displaying an Image Through the HTMLImage Control

An HTMLImage control provides the mechanism for you to display a simple HTML Image tag that you can manipulate in code. This is helpful when you need to programmatically control the image displayed to visitors. For example, on a product page you may want to display a picture of the product. But that image would need to change based on the product visitors select. This technique shows you how to define an HTMLImage control.

USE IT   The page created for this technique displays three images through HTMLImage controls. The definitions demonstrate the use of the HTMLImage control.
The first HTMLImage control has this definition:

```
<img
    id="Image1"
    runat="Server"
    src="button.gif"
>
```

You can specify a name for the control through the ID property:

```
id="Image1"
```

You then need to indicate that the control should be processed by the server:

```
runat="Server"
```

You use the Src property to indicate the name of the file that you want to display in the HTMLImage control:

```
src="button.gif"
```

In this case, the image must be located in the same folder as the ASP.NET page. But you can specify a full path through this property.
The second HTMLImage control has this definition:

```
<img
    id="Image2"
    runat="Server"
    src="button.gif"
    alt="Picture of a button."
    border="4"
>
```

Notice the use of the Alt property:

```
alt="Picture of a button."
```

This is the text that visitors see if the image does not load or when they hover their mouse over the image.
The Border property is set to the width of the border you want displayed around the image:

```
border="4"
```

The third Image control uses the Height and Width properties:

```
<img
    id="Image3"
    runat="Server"
    src="button.gif"
    width="300"
    height="300"
>
```

When you use these properties, the image will be stretched or shrunk to meet these dimensions.

Using the HTMLInputText Control

If you use the HTMLControls namespace to define the controls on the forms in your ASP.NET pages, you will often want to use the HTMLInputText control. Using that control, you can define a page where visitors can enter text or passwords. This tip shows you how to define an HTMLInputText control.

 The tip created for this page defines four HTMLInputText controls that show the versatility of the control. The first HTMLInputText control has this definition:

```
<input
    id="Text1"
    runat="server"
    type="text"
    maxlength=50
    size=30
    value="Basic Text Box"
>
```

You indicate the name of the control through the ID property:

```
<input
    id="Text1"
```

Then, you need to specify that the server should process the control:

```
runat="server"
```

This control will allow visitors to enter text:

```
type="text"
```

The MaxLength property is set to the number of characters that can be entered into the control:

```
maxlength=50
```

The Size property is set to the width of the control:

```
size=30
```

and the Value property is set to the text displayed in the control:

```
value="Basic Text Box"
```

This property would be used by you, in code, to determine the text entered by visitors.

The second HTMLInputText control has this definition:

```
<input
    id="Text2"
    runat="server"
    type="password"
    value="Basic Password Text Box"
>
```

In this case, the control allows for the entry of a password. You do this by setting the Type property to the value Password.

The third HTMLInputText control has this definition:

```
<input
    id="Text3"
    runat="server"
    type="text"
    disabled="True"
    value="Disabled Text Box"
>
```

Visitors will not be able to change the value in this text box. This is because the Disabled property is set to True.

The fourth HTMLInputText control has this definition:

```
<input
    id="Text4"
    runat="server"
    type="text"
    visible="False"
    value="Hidden Text Box"
>
```

This HTMLInputText control will be hidden from visitors because the Visible property is set to False.

Using the HTMLInputCheckBox Control

The HTMLInputCheckBox control provides a way for you to display a check box to visitors so that they can select a Boolean type of option. For example, you could use this type of control to ask visitors a yes or no question. This technique shows you how to define a HTMLInputCheckBox control.

USE IT   The page created for this technique prompts visitors to answer two yes/no questions through HTMLInputCheckBox controls. When visitors submit the page, they see text based on their responses.

The first control defined on the page is a Span control:

```
<Span
    id="MyMessage"
    runat=server
>
</Span>
```

That control will display text back to visitors after they submit the page.

The next control is an HTMLInputCheckBox control:

```
<Input
    id="chkDrawing"
    runat="server"
    type="checkbox"
>
Enter free drawing?
```

This control will display a check box to visitors with a question after the check box.

The other HTMLInputCheckBox control on the page asks visitors another question:

```
<Input
    id="chkContact"
    runat="server"
    type="checkbox"
    checked
>
Be added to our contact list?
```

Notice that this check box will initially be checked because of the use of the Checked keyword.

The other control defined on the page is a Button control:

```
<button
    id="Button1"
```

```
        runat="server"
        onserverclick="SubmitBtn_Click"
>
Submit
</button>
```

Visitors click this button to submit the page for processing. When they do that, this code block fires:

```
Sub SubmitBtn_Click(Source As Object, E as EventArgs)
    MyMessage.InnerHTML = ""
    If chkDrawing.Checked = True Then
        MyMessage.InnerHTML = "You have entered the " _
            & "drawing.<BR>"
    End If
    If chkContact.Checked = True Then
        MyMessage.InnerHTML = MyMessage.InnerHTML _
            & "You are on our contact " _
            & "list.<BR>"
    End If
End Sub
```

The code uses the Checked property of the HTMLInputCheckBox control to determine which check boxes have been checked. Based on those checks, text is displayed to visitors through the Span control.

Uploading Files with the HTMLInputFile Control

On occasion, you may need to create a page that allows visitors to upload files to your server. For example, maybe you offer an image manipulation service. Through your service, visitors upload images that you process. Or maybe you have a shareware site. Developers would need to upload their files to you. This technique shows you how to create a page that allows file upload through the use of the HTMLInputFile control.

USE IT The page created for this technique prompts visitors for the name of the file to upload and the name that they want to save the file as. Then when the page is submitted, the file is transferred from visitors' machines to the server.

The HTMLInputFile control allows visitors to enter in the name of the file to be uploaded:

```
Enter the name and path of the file to upload:
<BR>
<input
    id="MyFile"
```

```
    type="file"
    runat="server"
>
```

Through most browsers, visitors will see a text box control where they can enter the path and name of the file to be uploaded. Visitors will also see a Browse button that they can click to browse to the file that they wish to upload.

The next control defined on the page prompts visitors for the name that they want the file to be uploaded as:

```
Enter the name only to save the file as: <BR>
<input
    id="txtFileSaveAs"
    type="text"
    runat="server"
>
```

Also defined on the page is this Button control:

```
<input
    runat="server"
    type=button
    value="Upload"
    OnServerClick="SubmitButton_Click"
>
```

When that button is clicked, this code block fires:

```
Sub SubmitButton_Click(Source As Object, e As EventArgs)
    MyFile.PostedFile.SaveAs("c:\upload\" & txtFileSaveAs.Value)
    TheMessage.InnerHTML = "File uploaded!"
End Sub
```

The SaveAs method of the HTMLInputFile control is used to save the file to the local server. Visitors then see a message that lets them know that the file was successfully uploaded.

Placing Values on a Form Through the HTMLInputHidden Control

On occasion, you may find that you need to store a value that is passed back to a page when it is posted. The value may not be something you would want to display to visitors but you would need it to process the page. One way that you can pass this type of information is through an HTMLInputHidden control. This tip shows you how to define a control of that type and how to reference its value.

USE IT   The page created for this technique defines an HTMLInputHidden control. The value placed into that control is echoed into a Span control when the page loads. The HTMLInputHidden control has this definition:

```
<input
    id="Hidden1"
    runat="server"
    type="hidden"
    value="22"
>
```

You place the name for the control into the ID property:

```
<input
    id="Hidden1"
```

You then need to indicate that the server should process the control:

```
runat="server"
```

You need to indicate that this control should be rendered as an HTML Hidden element:

```
type="hidden"
```

And you place the value that you want to store with the control into the Value property:

```
value="22"
```

The other control defined on this page is this Span control:

```
<span
    id="Span1"
    runat=server
/>
```

A value is placed into that control when the code on the page runs:

```
Sub Page_Load(ByVal Sender as Object, ByVal E as EventArgs)
    Span1.InnerText = "The value in the hidden " _
        & "element is: " & Hidden1.Value
End Sub
```

Notice that the Value property of the HTMLInputHidden control is used to retrieve the value hidden into that control.

Using the HTMLInputImage Control

The HTMLInputImage control provides a way for you to allow visitors to submit a form for processing by clicking on an image instead of clicking a button. This tip shows you how to define and write a click event procedure for the HTMLInputImage control.

 The page created for this tip prompts visitors for their names. Visitors submit the name they enter by clicking on an HTMLInputImage control that submits the page for processing. Visitors' names are echoed back to them through a Span control.

Visitors enter their name through a text box control:

```
<input
    id="YourName"
    runat="server"
    type="text"
>
```

Visitors see their name echoed back to them through this Span control:

```
<span
    id="MyMessage"
    runat=server
>
</span>
```

The form is submitted for processing by clicking on this HTMLInputImage control:

```
<input
    id="ImageButton1"
    runat="server"
    type="image"
    src="button.gif"
    onserverclick="SubmitBtn_Click"
>
```

When using the HTMLInputImage control, you supply a name for the control through the ID property:

```
<input
    id="ImageButton1"
```

You also need to indicate that the control should be processed by the server:

```
runat="server"
```

Next, you indicate that this is an HTMLInputImage control:

```
type="image"
```

The path to the image displayed on the button is specified through the Src property:

```
src="button.gif"
```

You also need to specify the name of the procedure that you want to run when the image button is clicked:

```
    onserverclick="SubmitBtn_Click"
>
```

That procedure needs to have a definition like this one:

```
Sub SubmitBtn_Click(Source As Object, _
    E as ImageClickEventArgs)
    MyMessage.InnerHTML = "Hello " & YourName.Value
End Sub
```

Notice the parameters in this procedure. When you use an HTMLInputImage control, the parameters must match these exactly.

Retrieving Clicked Coordinates Through the HTMLInputImage Control

One of the ways that the HTMLInputImage control can be used is as a mechanism to prompt an action based on where visitors click on an image. For example, maybe you display an image of a country through the HTMLInputImage control. Based on where the visitor clicks on the image, you would take the visitor to a different page. This technique shows you how to retrieve the coordinates visitors click on through an HTMLInputImage control.

USE IT The ASP.NET page created for this technique displays to visitors an image. When visitors click on the image, the coordinates that they clicked at are displayed to them. Those coordinates are displayed through this Span control:

```
<span
    id="MyMessage"
    runat=server
>
</span>
```

```
<input
    id="ImageButton1"
    runat="server"
    type="image"
    src="button.gif"
    onserverclick="SubmitBtn_Click"
>
```

When visitors click on the HTMLInputImage control, this procedure runs:

```
Sub SubmitBtn_Click(Source As Object, _
    E as ImageClickEventArgs)
    MyMessage.InnerHTML = "Coordinates Clicked<BR><BR>" _
        & "X: " & E.X & "<BR>" _
        & "Y: " & E.Y
End Sub
```

Within the procedure, the X and Y properties of the ImageClickEventArgs parameter are used to retrieve the coordinates that visitors clicked on. Those values are displayed to visitors through the Span control.

Allowing Input Through the HTMLInputRadioButton Control

Frequently, you need visitors to provide a response to a question that has a small number of answers and that they must select one and only one of the answers to the question. One of the ways that you can implement a control like this is through the HTMLInputRadioButton control. This technique shows you how to use that control.

USE IT The HTMLInputRadioButton control is rendered as a radio button. You group together radio button items so that visitors must select one item from a group. But visitors can select another item from another group.

The page created for this technique displays to visitors a question with three possible answers. Visitors submit their choice by clicking a button. Then, text is displayed based on the choice they made.

The text displayed back to visitors is displayed through this Span control:

```
<Span
    id="MyMessage"
    runat=server
>
</Span>
```

Raw text and three HTMLInputRadioButton controls are used to prompt visitors with a question and answers:

```
Which is your favorite meal?
<BR>
<Input
    id="radBreakfast"
    runat="server"
    type="radio"
    Checked
    name="Meal"
/>
Breakfast
<BR>
<Input
    id="radLunch"
    runat="server"
    type="radio"
    name="Meal"
/>
Lunch
<BR>
<Input
    id="radDinner"
    runat="server"
    type="radio"
    name="Meal"
/>
Dinner
```

Notice that each of the HTMLInputRadioButton controls has the same value in the Name property. This is how you group together HTMLInputRadioButton controls. Each HTMLInputRadioButton control with the same value in the Name property can only have one item selected by visitors.

Notice that the Type property is set to the value Radio. Also notice that the first HTMLInputRadioButton control includes the Checked keyword in its definition. This means that this HTMLInputRadioButton control is initially checked.

Visitors submit their choice by clicking this button:

```
<button
    id="Button1"
    runat="server"
    onserverclick="SubmitBtn_Click"
>
Submit
</button>
```

When the button is clicked, this code fires:

```
Sub SubmitBtn_Click(Source As Object, E as EventArgs)
    MyMessage.InnerHTML = ""
    If radBreakfast.Checked = True Then
        MyMessage.InnerHTML = "You selected " _
            & "breakfast.<BR>"
    ElseIf radLunch.Checked = True Then
        MyMessage.InnerHTML = "You selected " _
            & "lunch.<BR>"
    Else
        MyMessage.InnerHTML = "You selected " _
            & "dinner.<BR>"
    End If
End Sub
```

The code checks to see which of the HTMLInputRadioButton controls was selected by visitors. Based on their choice, different text is displayed to them through the Span control.

Using the HTMLSelect Control

The HTMLSelect control provides a way for you to offer items to visitors in the form of a list. That list can be either a drop-down list or as a standard list control, which displays items vertically. This technique shows you how to define and retrieve the selected item in an HTMLSelect control.

USE IT The page created for this technique asks visitors a question that they answer by selecting an item in an HTMLSelect control. Visitors then see the text of the item they selected echoed back to them through a Span control.

Within the form on the ASP.NET page, this Span control will display visitors' selections:

```
<Span
    id="MyMessage"
    runat=server
>
</Span>
```

Visitors answer the question through this HTMLSelect control:

```
<select
    id="meal"
    runat="Server"
    multiple="False"
    size=1
>
```

```
<option>Breakfast</option>
<option>Lunch</option>
<option>Dinner</option>
</select>
```

The name of the HTMLSelect control is entered through the ID property:

```
<select
    id="meal"
```

You also must include the RunAt property and indicate that the Server should process the control:

```
runat="Server"
```

The Multiple property is used to indicate whether the visitor can select more than one item in the list:

```
multiple="False"
```

The size property is used to indicate how many items are displayed at one time through the control. A value of one indicates that this is a drop-down list control:

```
    size=1
>
```

Any other numeric value would render this control as a list.

You place items into the list of the HTMLSelect control through Option controls:

```
<option>Breakfast</option>
<option>Lunch</option>
<option>Dinner</option>
```

After the Option controls, you need to close the HTMLSelect control's definition:

```
</select>
```

The other control defined on this page is a Button control:

```
<button
    id="Button1"
    runat="server"
    onserverclick="SubmitBtn_Click"
>
Submit
</button>
```

When it is clicked, this code block fires:

```
Sub SubmitBtn_Click(Source As Object, E as EventArgs)
    MyMessage.InnerHTML = "You selected as your " _
        & "favorite meal: " & Meal.Value
End Sub
```

The procedure uses the Value property of the HTMLSelect control to display the choice made by visitors back to them through the Span control.

Using the HTMLTextArea Control

Often you need to allow visitors to enter free-flowing text information. For example, maybe you have a page where visitors supply you with a comment related to your site. You would want to provide them with a large area in which to enter their comment. You can allow for this through the HTMLTextArea control. This technique shows you how to define and retrieve the value placed into an HTMLTextArea control.

USE IT The page created for this technique prompts visitors for a text message. That message is echoed back to visitors when the page is submitted for processing.

Defined on the page is this Span tag:

```
<span
    id="MyMessage"
    runat=server
>
</span>
```

That control will contain the echoed message back to visitors.

Visitors enter their message through this HTMLTextArea control:

```
<textarea
    id="txtMessage"
    runat="Server"
    rows=5
    cols=40
    value="Enter message here!"
/>
```

You can give the control a name through the ID property:

```
<textarea
    id="txtMessage"
```

You need to indicate that the control needs to be processed by the server:

```
runat="Server"
```

You use the Rows property to indicate the height of the HTMLTextArea control on the rendered page:

```
rows=5
```

The Cols property is set to the width, in characters, for the control:

```
cols=40
```

You can enter the initial text that is displayed in the control through the Value property:

```
value="Enter message here!"
```

The other control defined on the page is a Button control:

```
<button
    id="Button1"
    runat="server"
    onserverclick="SubmitBtn_Click"
>
Submit
</button>
```

This code fires when that Button control is clicked:

```
Sub SubmitBtn_Click(Source As Object, E as EventArgs)
    MyMessage.InnerHTML = "You entered: " _
        & txtMessage.Value
End Sub
```

The code uses the Value property of the HTMLTextArea control to echo the choice made by visitors back to them.

Displaying Information Through the HTMLTable Control

Frequently, you need to display data back to visitors in the form of rows and columns. One of the ways that you can do this is through the HTMLTable control. The HTMLTable control renders itself as HTML table elements. But as an ASP.NET control, you can configure its properties in code or through its definition just like any other control. This technique shows you how to create a basic HTMLTable control.

USE IT   The ASP.NET page created for this technique displays to visitors a table of information
through an HTMLTable control. The table contains different colors in rows and cells to
demonstrate the use of the control.

The definition of the control starts with the opening portion of the HTMLTable control:

```
<table
    id="Table1"
    runat=server
    bgcolor="Gray"
    border=1
    bordercolor="Red"
    cellpadding=2
    cellspacing=2
    align="Left"
>
```

You give the control a name through the ID property. Then, you can supply color and other
formatting properties of the control. The Align property is used to indicate the horizontal position
of the table within the page. This property can be set to Left, Right, or Center.

Then within the HTMLTable definition, you can add rows and cells to those rows. The first row
has this definition:

```
<tr
        id="Row11"
        runat=server
        bgcolor="Yellow"
        valign="Top"
    >
        <TD id="Cell111" runat=Server>Cell 1</TD>
        <TD id="Cell112" runat=Server
            bgcolor="Pink">Cell 2</TD>
        <TD id="Cell113" runat=Server>Cell 3</TD>
    </tr>
```

Notice that the row can override the color specifications defined at the table level. The same is true
for each cell within a row. The VAlign property sets the vertical position of the text within the row.

The second row in the HTMLTable has this definition:

```
<tr
        id="Row12"
        runat=server
        valign="Bottom"
    >
        <TD id="Cell121" runat=Server>The second row</TD>
        <TD id="Cell122" runat=Server
```

```
            BGColor="Pink" Disabled=True>
            Disabled Cell
      </TD>
      <TD id="Cell123" runat=Server>Cell 3</TD>
      <TD id="Cell124" runat=Server Visible=False>
          Should not see this cell
      </TD>
   </tr>
```

Notice that this row has a disabled cell. That cell will be displayed but the text will appear grayed-out. Also notice that the row contains a cell that will not be seen because its Visible property is set to False.

The third row of the table has this definition:

```
<tr
    id="Row13"
    runat=server
    valign="Bottom"
>
    <TD id="Cell131" runat=Server colspan=3>
        The text of a long cell that spans all three columns.
    </TD>
</tr>
```

Notice that this row just contains a single cell. But that cell sets the ColSpan property to 3. That means that the text in this cell can extend past its own boundaries and occupy a total of three cells.

After defining the rows and the cells, you need to close the table's definition:

```
</table>
```

Adding Rows and Cells to an HTMLTable Control Through Code

In addition to defining the rows and cells of an HTMLTable control directly on the form of the page, you can add rows and cells directly in code. This technique shows you how to do that.

USE IT The page created for this technique displays an HTMLTable to the visitor. Properties for the table, as well as rows and cells displayed in the HTMLTable control, are defined in code when the page loads.

The HTMLTable control has this definition:

```
<Table
    id="Table1"
```

```
    runat=server
>
```

When the page loads, the following code block populates the HTMLTable control:

```
Sub Page_Load(ByVal Sender as Object, ByVal E as EventArgs)
    Dim MyRow as new HTMLTableRow
    Dim MyCell as new HTMLTableCell
    Dim i as Integer
    Dim j as Integer
    Table1.BGColor="Ivory"
    Table1.Border=2
    Table1.BorderColor="LawnGreen"
    Table1.CellPadding=4
    Table1.CellSpacing=3
    Table1.Align="Center"
    MyCell.InnerText = "Column 1"
    MyRow.Cells.Add(MyCell)
    MyCell = New HTMLTableCell
    MyCell.InnerText = "Column 2"
    MyRow.Cells.Add(MyCell)
    Table1.Rows.Add(MyRow)
    For i = 2 to 6
        MyRow = New HTMLTableRow
        For j = 1 to 2
            MyCell = New HTMLTableCell
            MyCell.InnerText = "Cell " & i & ", " & j
            MyRow.Cells.Add(MyCell)
        Next
        Table1.Rows.Add(MyRow)
    Next
End Sub
```

Within the procedure, you need to define a row and a cell object:

```
Dim MyRow as new HTMLTableRow
Dim MyCell as new HTMLTableCell
```

You also need to define two numbers that will be used within For code blocks:

```
Dim i as Integer
Dim j as Integer
```

First, you set color and border properties of the table:

```
Table1.BGColor="Ivory"
Table1.Border=2
Table1.BorderColor="LawnGreen"
Table1.CellPadding=4
Table1.CellSpacing=3
Table1.Align="Center"
```

Next, you place text into the first header column:

```
MyCell.InnerText = "Column 1"
```

That cell is placed into the Row object:

```
MyRow.Cells.Add(MyCell)
```

and a second header cell is added to that row:

```
MyCell = New HTMLTableCell
MyCell.InnerText = "Column 2"
MyRow.Cells.Add(MyCell)
```

That row is then added to the HTMLTable control:

```
Table1.Rows.Add(MyRow)
```

Next, you enter two For code blocks so that rows and columns can be added to the HTMLTable. The outer loop adds Rows:

```
For i = 2 to 6
    MyRow = New HTMLTableRow
```

The inner loop adds columns to the rows:

```
For j = 1 to 2
    MyCell = New HTMLTableCell
    MyCell.InnerText = "Cell " & i & ", " & j
    MyRow.Cells.Add(MyCell)
Next
```

After adding the cells to the row, the row is added to the table:

```
    Table1.Rows.Add(MyRow)
Next
```

The process is repeated until the table is designed so that it contains a single column header row followed by five data rows. Each cell displays its coordinates in the table as its text.

CHAPTER 3

Basic Web Controls

The tips and techniques presented in this chapter are based on some of the controls that you will use on a majority of your ASP.NET pages. These controls are the basic foundation of an ASP.NET page. The tips and techniques presented are for controls like the Button, TextBox, Label, Image, HyperLink, and many more. So keep the code from this chapter handy. You may find that you often refer to it to copy and paste the control definitions into your ASP.NET applications.

Creating a Basic TextBox Control

You will find that almost all of your ASP.NET pages that ask visitors for information will include a basic TextBox control. A basic TextBox control allows visitors to enter textual data up to a maximum number of characters that you specify.

When ASP.NET renders a TextBox control to the visitor's browser, it creates an HTML Input tag like this one:

```
<input
    name="txtName"
    type="text"
    value="Michelle Harrison"
    maxlength="30"
    size="25"
    id="txtName"
/>
```

Notice that it renders the control as a "Text" type of input control. Also note that the name and ID given to the control are the same as the name of the control that you supply to it when the control is defined.

USE IT   Although a Basic TextBox control can be very basic and simple to define, you can also format the font and color of the control so that it appears very specialized to visitors. This technique defines three TextBox controls; one contains a very basic definition but the other two contain formatting elements. These controls prompt visitors to enter their name, e-mail address, and phone number. Here is the ASP.NET form for that page:

```
<form runat="server">
<asp:label
    id="lblDataEntered"
    runat="server"
/>
<BR><BR>
Enter your Name:<BR>
<asp:textbox
    id="txtName"
    columns="25"
    maxlength="30"
    text="Your Name Here"
    runat=server
/>
<BR><BR>
Enter your Email Address:<BR>
<asp:textbox
    id="txtEmail"
    columns="35"
    maxLength="50"
    text="@mycompany.com"
    backcolor="LightYellow"
    font-name="Comic Sans MS"
    font-size="9pt"
    font-bold="True"
    tooltip="Remember to include your full email address!"
    runat=server
/>
<BR><BR>
Enter your Phone Number:<BR>
<asp:textbox
    id="txtPhone"
    columns="15"
    maxlength="15"
    text="() -"
    accesskey="P"
    backcolor="DarkRed"
    borderwidth="3"
    bordercolor="DarkBlue"
    borderctyle="Dashed"
    forecolor="Yellow"
    tooltip="No Extensions!"
```

```
        runat=server
/>
<BR><BR>
<asp:button
    id="butOK"
    text="OK"
    type="Submit"
    onclick="SubmitBtn_Click"
    runat="server"
/>
</form>
```

The first TextBox control is given the name txtName:

```
<asp:textbox
    id="txtName"
```

You set the visible width of the control using the Columns property:

```
    columns="25"
```

The maximum number of characters that visitors can enter into the control is set through the MaxLength property. With this first TextBox control, visitors can enter up to 30 characters:

```
    maxlength="30"
```

Use the Text property to indicate the initial value for the control:

```
    text="Your Name Here"
    runat=server
/>
```

The second TextBox control allows visitors to enter their e-mail address. The control is given the name txtEmail:

```
<asp:textbox
    id="txtEmail"
    columns="35"
    maxLength="50"
    text="@mycompany.com"
```

The control uses formatting properties to add flair to how it is rendered. The background color of the control is set to light yellow:

```
    backcolor="LightYellow"
```

► **QUICK TIP**

When setting the color for a control, you can use any of the standard HTML named colors.

Next, the name, size, and weight of the font used for the text in the control are set:

```
font-name="Comic Sans MS"
font-size="9pt"
font-bold="True"
```

You can use the ToolTip property to provide additional information about the data that should be entered into the TextBox. The value in this property is displayed to visitors when they hover their mouse over the control:

```
tooltip="Remember to include your full email address!"
runat=server
/>
```

The third TextBox control allows visitors to enter their phone number:

```
<asp:textbox
    id="txtPhone"
    columns="15"
    maxlength="15"
    text="() -"
```

The TextBox control has a property called AccessKey that here is set to the letter "P." This means that when visitors press the alternate key along with P, the focus on the page will shift to this control:

```
accesskey="P"
```

This control also sets the background color for the control:

```
backcolor="DarkRed"
```

But the border properties are also set. First the size of the border is set:

```
borderwidth="3"
```

then the color of the border:

```
bordercolor="DarkBlue"
```

and the style of the border:

```
borderctyle="Dashed"
forecolor="Yellow"
tooltip="No Extensions!"
runat=server
/>
```

When visitors click the OK button on the page, this code echoes their entries back to them through a Label control defined on the page:

```
Sub SubmitBtn_Click(Sender As Object, E As EventArgs)
    lblDataEntered.Text = "You entered:<BR>" _
        & txtName.Text & "<BR>" _
        & txtEmail.Text & "<BR>" _
        & txtPhone.Text
End Sub
```

The output of this page is shown here:

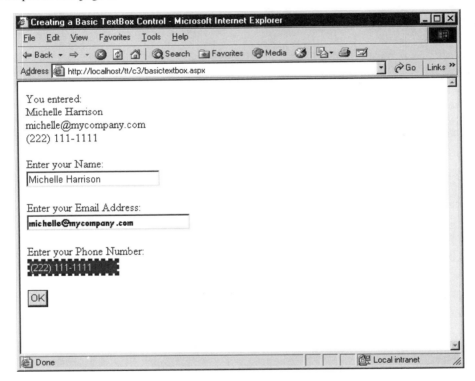

Notice the difference in the style for each of these basic TextBox controls. By simply changing the colors and font properties of a TextBox control you can dramatically affect its appearance on the overall page.

Using a TextBox Control for Passwords

In addition to letting visitors supply you with basic information, you will frequently want them to enter data, specifically passwords, that anyone looking over their shoulders should not be able to see.

ASP.NET allows you to use a TextBox control as a special control for entering passwords. As visitors type into this control, the value they enter is replaced by the "*" character. But in code you can still retrieve the value they entered.

When you create a password TextBox control in ASP.NET, it is rendered to the visitor's browser like this:

```
<input
    name="txtPassword"
    type="password"
    maxlength="30"
    size="25"
    id="txtPassword"
/>
```

Notice that the control is defined as an HTML Input tag with the Type parameter set to "Password."

USE IT   The following ASP.NET page prompts visitors for their name and password. If the values entered match a specific value, they gain entry. Otherwise, visitors are denied entry.
Here are the controls defined on that page:

```
<form runat="server">
<asp:label
    id="lblMessage"
    runat="server"
/>
<BR><BR>
Enter your Name:<BR>
<asp:textbox
    id="txtName"
    columns="25"
    maxlength="30"
    backcolor="LightYellow"
    font-name="Comic Sans MS"
    font-size="9pt"
    tooltip="Contact your administrator for a new log-in"
    runat=server
/>
<BR><BR>
Enter your Password:<BR>
<asp:textbox
    id="txtPassword"
    textmode="Password"
    columns="25"
    maxlength="30"
```

```
        backcolor="LightYellow"
        font-name="Comic Sans MS"
        font-size="9pt"
        tooltip="Passwords a case-sensitve"
        runat=server
/>
<BR><BR>
<asp:button
    id="butOK"
    text="OK"
    type="Submit"
    onclick="SubmitBtn_Click"
    runat="server"
/>
</form>
```

The first TextBox control on the page is just a basic formatted TextBox control that prompts visitors for their name:

```
<asp:textbox
    id="txtName"
    columns="25"
    maxlength="30"
    backcolor="LightYellow"
    font-name="Comic Sans MS"
    font-size="9pt"
    tooltip="Contact your administrator for a new log-in"
    runat=server
/>
```

The second TextBox control prompts visitors for their password:

```
<asp:textbox
    id="txtPassword"
```

Notice the TextMode property. This is how you indicate that the control should be rendered as a password TextBox control:

```
    textmode="Password"
    columns="25"
    maxlength="30"
    backcolor="LightYellow"
    font-name="Comic Sans MS"
    font-size="9pt"
```

Also notice the use of the ToolTip property, which will display the following text when visitors hover their mouse over the control:

```
    tooltip="Passwords a case-sensitve"
    runat=server
/>
```

When the OK button is clicked, the following code checks the name and password entered by the visitors:

```
Sub SubmitBtn_Click(Sender As Object, E As EventArgs)
    If txtName.Text = "Admin" and txtPassword.Text = "me" Then
        lblMessage.Text = "Access approved."
    Else
        lblMessage.Text = "Access denied"
    End If
End Sub
```

If the visitors were to provide a valid user name and password, you would likely store their user name and pass them onto the main menu of your ASP.NET application.

Creating a Multiline TextBox Control

A third way that a TextBox control can be used is as a multiline TextBox control. This means that the control appears in the visitor's browser across more than one page. You would use a control of this type to solicit comments or other lengthy textual information from the visitor.

When you create an ASP.NET page that contains a multiline TextBox control, it is rendered in the visitor's browser as an HTML TextArea tag like this one:

```
<textarea
    name="txtComment1"
    rows="5"
    cols="25"
    id="txtComment1">
</textarea>
```

 This next ASP.NET page uses the TextBox control to display two multiline TextBox controls to the visitor. The following controls are defined on that page:

```
<form runat="server">
Enter your comment:<BR>
<asp:textbox
    id="txtComment1"
```

```
        textmode="MultiLine"
        columns="25"
        rows="5"
        wrap="True"
        backcolor="LightYellow"
        font-name="Comic Sans MS"
        font-size="9pt"
        runat=server
/>
<BR><BR>
Enter your comment:<BR>
<asp:textbox
        id="txtComment2"
        textmode="MultiLine"
        columns="25"
        rows="10"
        wrap="False"
        backcolor="LightYellow"
        font-name="Comic Sans MS"
        font-size="9pt"
        runat=server
/>
<BR><BR>
</Form>
```

The first TextBox control is called txtComment1:

```
<asp:textbox
        id="txtComment1"
```

Notice that the TextMode property is set to MultiLine. This is how you indicate that you want a multiline TextBox control:

```
textmode="MultiLine"
```

As with any other type of TextBox control, you set the width of the control through the Columns property:

```
columns="25"
```

Additionally, you can set the Rows property to the height of the control. In other words, you set the number of rows of text that appear within the code.

```
rows="5"
```

> ▶ **QUICK TIP**
>
> *The MaxLength property is ignored when you use a multiline TextBox control. Use a basic or password TextBox control if you need to control the number of characters entered by the visitor.*

Another property that you can use just with the multiline type of TextBox control is the Wrap property. This property determines whether the text entered by visitors wraps from line to line or whether the text scrolls off the right-edge of the control as visitors type their information. In this control the text will wrap:

```
    wrap="True"
    backcolor="LightYellow"
    font-name="Comic Sans MS"
    font-size="9pt"
    runat=server
/>
```

But in the other TextBox control the text does not wrap:

```
<asp:textbox
    id="txtComment2"
    textmode="MultiLine"
    columns="25"
    rows="10"
    wrap="False"
    backcolor="LightYellow"
    font-name="Comic Sans MS"
    font-size="9pt"
    runat=server
/>
```

The output from this page is shown here:

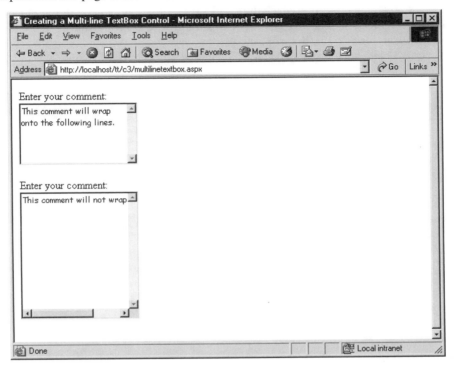

Notice in this illustration the effect of the Wrap property. The first TextBox control has the text wrapping from line to line. But the other control has the text scrolling off the edge of the control.

Adding a TextBox Control Dynamically Through Code

On occasion you may find that you need to add an unknown number of TextBox controls to a page. For example, maybe you want to create a reusable Request for More Information page and the number of fields that appear on the different copies of the page can range from five to ten fields. Therefore, you would want to be able to create an unknown number of TextBox controls on the page.

Or maybe you have a quiz page that presents a question and prompts visitors for a written answer. You don't know how many questions each quiz will have, since that value is stored in a database, but you do know that each will need a TextBox control for the answer. Again, you would need to create an unknown number of TextBox controls.

The technique presented here shows you how to do that.

USE IT This example prompts visitors for a number. When visitors click the OK button, that number is used to generate additional TextBox controls.

The form on the page has the following definition:

```
<form
    id="frmMyPage"
    runat="server"
>
Enter the number of TextBox controls you want:<BR>
<asp:TextBox
    id="txtNumber"
    columns="25"
    maxlength="3"
    runat=server
/>
<BR><BR>
<asp:button
    id="butOK"
    text="OK"
    type="Submit"
    onclick="SubmitBtn_Click"
    runat="server"
/>
</form>
```

Notice that the Form is given a name:

```
<form
    id="frmMyPage"
    runat="server"
>
```

This is needed so that we have a parent object to dynamically add TextBox controls to.

Within the form, we define a standard TextBox control that prompts visitors for a number:

```
<asp:TextBox
    id="txtNumber"
    columns="25"
    maxlength="3"
```

```
    runat=server
/>
```

Also defined on the page is a Button control that has the code that dynamically adds the TextBox controls.

```
<asp:button
    id="butOK"
    text="OK"
    type="Submit"
    onclick="SubmitBtn_Click"
    runat="server"
/>
```

When that button is clicked, this code runs:

```
Sub SubmitBtn_Click(Sender As Object, E As EventArgs)
    Dim I as Integer
    For I = 1 to txtNumber.Text
        Dim MyTextBox = New TextBox
        MyTextBox.ID = "txtDynamic" & I
        MyTextBox.Text = "Control Number: " & I
        frmMyPage.Controls.Add(MyTextBox)
        Dim MyLiteral = New LiteralControl
        MyLiteral.Text = "<BR><BR>"
        frmMyPage.Controls.Add(MyLiteral)
    Next
End Sub
```

Within the procedure, you need a variable for a loop:

```
Dim I as Integer
```

You then set up a For Next block that will run for the number of controls indicated by the visitor:

```
For I = 1 to txtNumber.Text
```

Next, a TextBox control is dynamically created:

```
Dim MyTextBox = New TextBox
```

The control is given a name and a value for the Text property. You could also add values for the control's other properties:

```
MyTextBox.ID = "txtDynamic" & I
MyTextBox.Text = "Control Number: " & I
```

The Add method of the Controls collection of the Form object is used to add the TextBox control to the page:

```
frmMyPage.Controls.Add(MyTextBox)
```

You also would want to define a LiteralControl:

```
Dim MyLiteral = New LiteralControl
```

so that you could dynamically display line breaks or other HTML between each TextBox control:

```
MyLiteral.Text = "<BR><BR>"
```

That control is also added to the Form through the Add method:

```
frmMyPage.Controls.Add(MyLiteral)
```

The code then loops back up to the top of the block until the number of controls has been created:

```
    Next
```

The output of this page is shown here:

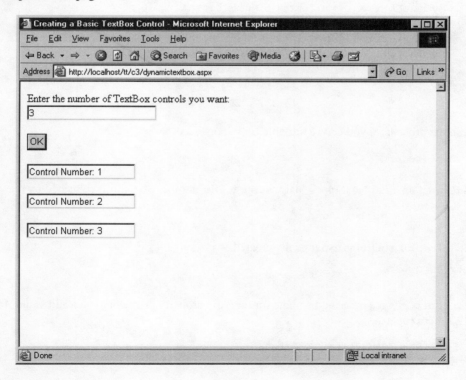

Notice the number of additional TextBox controls on the page. Also notice the effect of the LiteralControl, which provides spaces between the TextBox controls.

Writing Code That Fires When Text in a TextBox Control Changes

You may find that you sometimes want code to run whenever text in a TextBox control changes from what it was when visitors first entered the control. For example, maybe you want to take visitors to a search results page, based on the text that they entered, without having to click a button. Or maybe you want to change the case of the text visitors entered.

The TextBox control contains an event called TextChanged that allows you to do that. This tip demonstrates that event.

 This ASP.NET page defines a single TextBox control. When visitors press the ENTER key or when they leave the TextBox control, the text they entered is automatically converted to uppercase.

The following is the form definition for that page:

```
<form runat="server">
Enter your Name:<BR>
<asp:TextBox
    id="txtName"
    AutoPostBack=True
    OnTextChanged="txtName_TextChanged"
    Columns="25"
    MaxLength="30"
    Font-Name="Comic Sans MS"
    Font-Size="9pt"
    runat=server
/>
```

The TextBox control is defined like a standard TextBox control with the addition of **two properties** being set. The first is the AutoPostBack property being set to True:

```
AutoPostBack=True
```

When the property is set in that way, the page is submitted back to the server when the contents of the control change or when the ENTER key is pressed.

Also set is the OnTextChanged property:

```
OnTextChanged="txtName_TextChanged"
```

This property is set to the name of the procedure that you want to run when the text in the TextBox control changes.

The name placed in that property must be defined within your code like this:

```
Sub txtName_TextChanged(Sender As Object, E As EventArgs)
    txtName.Text = UCase(txtName.Text)
End Sub
```

Within the procedure, the text entered into the TextBox control is changed to uppercase.

Creating a Basic Label Control

One of the most basic controls that you will add to almost all of your ASP.NET pages is the Label control. The Label control provides a method for you to display formatted text back to visitors. That text can be simply raw text or it can contain HTML tags.

When the control is rendered to the visitors' browser, it appears like this:

```
<span
    id="lblMessage1"
    title="Mouse hovering text."
    Welcome to our site.
</span>
```

As you can see, the control is rendered as an HTML Span tag. The tag is given an ID matching the name that you give the control when you define it and it contains the text that you enter into the control.

USE IT Although the Label control is a very basic control, it is also very versatile, as shown next:

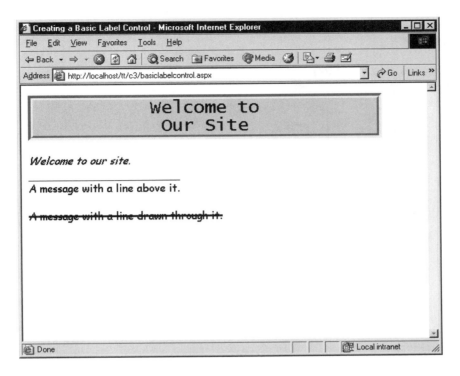

You can see that the control can be used to create a title box. It can also be used to vary the look of the messages through its font, border, and color properties.

These four Label controls were defined to create the page displayed in the previous illustration:

```
<form runat="server">
<asp:label
    id="lblTitle"
    backcolor="LightGreen"
    borderwidth="7px"
    borderstyle=6
    width="90%"
    font-size="20pt"
    font-name="Lucida Console"
    text="<CENTER>Welcome to<BR>Our Site</CENTER>"
    runat="server"
/>
```

```
<BR><BR>
<asp:label
    id="lblMessage1"
    backcolor="LightYellow"
    font-name="Comic Sans MS"
    font-size="12pt"
    font-italic="True"
    tooltip="Mouse hovering text."
    text="Welcome to our site."
    runat="server"
/>
<BR><BR>
<asp:label
    id="lblMessage2"
    font-name="Comic Sans MS"
    font-size="12pt"
    font-overline="True"
    text="A message with a line above it."
    runat="server"
/>
<BR><BR>
<asp:label
    id="lblMessage3"
    font-name="Comic Sans MS"
    font-size="12pt"
    font-strikeout="True"
    text="A message with a line drawn through it."
    runat="server"
/>
</form>
```

The first Label control is given the name lblTitle:

```
<asp:label
    id="lblTitle"
```

Notice the formatting done to its background, border, and font that give it the appearance of a title box:

```
backcolor="LightGreen"
borderwidth="7px"
borderstyle=6
```

```
width="90%"
font-size="20pt"
font-name="Lucida Console"
```

A Label control can contain raw text, but as you can see here, you can also embed HTML tags directly into the text of the Label control:

```
    text="<CENTER>Welcome to<BR>Our Site</CENTER>"
    runat="server"
/>
```

The second Label control displays a simple text message:

```
<asp:label
    id="lblMessage1"
```

The control has a different background color than the message label and uses different font values:

```
    backcolor="LightYellow"
    font-name="Comic Sans MS"
    font-size="12pt"
    font-italic="True"
```

The text placed into the ToolTip property will appear when visitors hover their mouse over the control:

```
    tooltip="Mouse hovering text."
    text="Welcome to our site."
    runat="server"
/>
```

The third Label control demonstrates that the text in a Label control can have a line that appears above the text. You do this by setting the Font-OverLine property to True:

```
<asp:label
    id="lblMessage2"
    font-name="Comic Sans MS"
    font-size="12pt"
    font-overline="True"
    text="A message with a line above it."
    runat="server"
/>
```

The last Label control demonstrates that the text in a Label can have a line drawn through it. You do this by setting the Font-StrikeOut property to True:

```
<asp:label
    id="lblMessage3"
    font-name="Comic Sans MS"
    font-size="12pt"
    font-strikeout="True"
    text="A message with a line drawn through it."
    runat="server"
/>
```

Manipulating a Label Control in Code

Many of the Label controls that you add to an ASP.NET page will need to have their text set in code. For example, you may want to have a Label control display the current visitor's name. Or maybe you want to display the total number of matching records found in a search. This technique shows you how to set the Text property of a Label control in code.

 This very basic ASP.NET page uses a Label control to dynamically set the Text property of the control to today's date. Only one control, a Label control called lblMessage1, is defined on the page:

```
<form runat="server">
<BR><BR>
<asp:label
    id="lblMessage1"
    tooltip="Today's server date."
    runat="server"
/>
<BR><BR>
</form>
```

When the page opens, the following code runs since it is placed in the Page_Load event:

```
Sub Page_Load(ByVal Sender as Object, ByVal E as EventArgs)
    lblMessage1.Text = Today()
End Sub
```

The Today method is used to return the current server date. That value is placed into the Text property of the Label control:

```
lblMessage1.Text = Today()
```

Displaying a Basic RadioButton Control

A RadioButton control provides a way for you to present the visitor with a limited number of options that are not mutually exclusive. In other words, you use the control to provide a list of options from which the visitor can select only one.

You group together controls that provide the list of options to the visitor. But you can create more than one group of RadioButton controls.

When you place a RadioButton control on your ASP.NET page, the compiler renders an HTML tag like this one:

```
<span
    style="font-family:Comic Sans MS;font-size:12pt;"
>
    <input
        id="rdoColorBlue"
        type="radio"
        name="rgColors"
        value="rdoColorBlue"
    />
    <label
        for="rdoColorBlue">
        Blue
    </label>
</span>
```

As you can see, to properly display the control, three HTML tags are generated. A Span tag is used for formatting properties. Then a Radio Input HTML tag is defined for the RadioButton control. And finally an HTML Label tag is generated. That tag contains whatever text you supply to go with the control.

USE IT The controls defined on this ASP.NET page show you how you can create a RadioButton control on your ASP.NET page:

```
form runat="server">
<BR><BR>
Select your favorite Color:<BR>
<asp:radiobutton
    id="rdoColorBlue"
    text="Blue"
    font-size="12pt"
    font-name="Comic Sans MS"
```

```
    groupname="rgColors"
    runat="server"
/>
<BR>
<asp:radiobutton
    id="rdoColorGreen"
    text="Green"
    font-size="12pt"
    font-name="Comic Sans MS"
    groupname="rgColors"
    checked="True"
    textalign="Left"
    runat="server"
/>
<BR>
<asp:radiobutton
    id="rdoColorYellow"
    text="Yellow"
    font-size="12pt"
    font-name="Comic Sans MS"
    groupname="rgColors"
    textalign="Right"
    runat="server"
/>
</form>
```

The page contains three RadioButton controls. The first is called rdoColorBlue:

```
<asp:radiobutton
    id="rdoColorBlue"
```

Placed into the Text property is the text that the visitor sees on the page for the control:

```
text="Blue"
font-size="12pt"
font-name="Comic Sans MS"
```

Notice the GroupName property. Each of the controls that have the same value in the GroupName property are linked together and the visitor can only select one of those RadioButton controls:

```
    groupname="rgColors"
    runat="server"
/>
```

A RadioButton control can be defined to have the text appear before the button or after the button. You determine that position through the TextAlign property. Notice that the second RadioButton has this property set to Left:

```
<asp:radiobutton
    id="rdoColorGreen"
    text="Green"
    font-size="12pt"
    font-name="Comic Sans MS"
    groupname="rgColors"
    checked="True"
    textalign="Left"
    runat="server"
/>
```

That means that the text will appear before the button. The other value of Right for this property is the default and causes the button to appear before the text.

Also notice that the Checked property for this particular RadioButton control is set to True. That means that, by default, this item in the Group is checked.

Setting and Retrieving the Selected Item in a RadioButton Control Group

When you produce an ASP.NET page that contains a series of RadioButton controls you will need code that sets the initial value of a RadioButton control and determines which control was selected by visitors when they submit a page for processing. One way to check the value is by creating a large If statement where you check to see if each button has been selected in turn.

But if you have a large number of RadioButton controls, your code block may be unnecessarily long. The technique presented in this section shows you how you can iterate through all the RadioButton controls on a page to determine which one has been selected.

USE IT   The ASP.NET presented with this technique allows visitors to select one of three RadioButton controls. The text of the RadioButton control that they select is echoed back to them through a Label control.

The page contains the following controls:

```
<form
    id="frmMainForm"
    runat="server"
>
<BR><BR>
```

```
<asp:Label
    id="lblColorSelected"
    runat="server"
/>
<BR>
Select your favorite Color:<BR>
<asp:radiobutton
    id="rdoColorBlue"
    text="Blue"
    font-size="12pt"
    font-name="Comic Sans MS"
    groupname="rgColors"
    runat="server"
/>
<BR>
<asp:radiobutton
    id="rdoColorGreen"
    text="Green"
    font-size="12pt"
    font-name="Comic Sans MS"
    groupname="rgColors"
    checked="True"
    textalign="Left"
    runat="server"
/>
<BR>
<asp:radiobutton
    id="rdoColorYellow"
    text="Yellow"
    font-size="12pt"
    font-name="Comic Sans MS"
    groupname="rgColors"
    textalign="Right"
    runat="server"
/>
<BR><BR>
<asp:button
    id="butOK"
    text="OK"
    Type="Submit"
    OnClick="SubmitBtn_Click"
    runat="server"
/>
</form>
```

Notice that the page contains three RadioButton controls, all belonging to the same group. Therefore, visitors can select only one of these controls. Notice also that none of the controls has been selected by default.

Instead this code fires when the page first loads:

```
Sub Page_Load(ByVal Sender as Object, ByVal E as EventArgs)
    If Not IsPostBack Then
        rdoColorYellow.Checked = True
    End If
End Sub
```

The code checks the rdoColorYellow control as the default one checked when the page first loads.

The next procedure fires when visitors click the Button control on the page:

```
Sub SubmitBtn_Click(Sender As Object, E As EventArgs)
    Dim MyControl as Control
    Dim MyRadioButton as RadioButton
    For Each MyControl in frmMainForm.Controls
        If MyControl.GetType().FullName = _
                "System.Web.UI.WebControls.RadioButton" Then
            MyRadioButton = MyControl
            If MyRadioButton.GroupName = "rgColors" then
                If MyRadioButton.Checked = "True" Then
                    lblColorSelected.Text = "You selected the color " _
                        & MyRadioButton.Text
                End If
            End If
        End If
    Next
End Sub
```

This procedure iterates through all the controls to determine which RadioButton has been selected. Within the procedure a generic control is defined:

```
Dim MyControl as Control
```

as is a RadioButton control:

```
Dim MyRadioButton as RadioButton
```

A loop is set up so that each control on the page can be processed:

```
For Each MyControl in frmMainForm.Controls
```

Within that loop, you need to determine if the control that you are currently examining is a RadioButton control:

```
If MyControl.GetType().FullName = _
    "System.Web.UI.WebControls.RadioButton" Then
```

If that is the case, you assign it to your specific RadioButton control in code:

```
MyRadioButton = MyControl
```

You can then check to see if the RadioButton control is part of the group that you are currently testing:

```
If MyRadioButton.GroupName = "rgColors" then
```

If that is the case, you need to check and see if it has been checked:

```
If MyRadioButton.Checked = "True" Then
```

If that control has been selected, the text from that control is placed into the Label control:

```
lblColorSelected.Text = "You selected the color " _
    & MyRadioButton.Text
```

After that, the code loops back up to check the next control on this ASP.NET page.

Writing Code That Fires When Selection Changes in a RadioButton Control

Sometimes you may find that you need code that fires automatically when visitors select one of the RadioButton controls in a group. For example, you may want to redirect visitors to a page based on the item that they select. You can provide such a procedure by setting the OnCheckedChanged property of the TextBox control.

USE IT This ASP.NET page shows you how to use the CheckedChanged event of the RadioButton control. The page prompts visitors for the type of shipping that they prefer. When they select one of the shipping options, implemented as RadioButton controls, the value is stored for future reference in a Session variable and the choice is echoed back to them.

The following controls are defined on the page:

```
<form runat="server">
<BR><BR>
<asp:Label
    id="lblShipSelected"
    runat="server"
/>
<BR>
Select Shipping Type:
```

```
<BR>
<asp:radiobutton
    id="rdoUPS"
    text="UPS"
    autopostback="True"
    oncheckedchanged="rgShipping_Clicked"
    groupname="rgShipping"
    runat="server"
/>
<BR>
<asp:radiobutton
    id="rdoUSPS"
    text="United States Postal Service"
    autopostback="True"
    oncheckedchanged="rgShipping_Clicked"
    groupname="rgShipping"
    runat="server"
/>
<BR>
<asp:radiobutton
    id="rdoFedEx"
    text="FedEx"
    autopostback="True"
    oncheckedchanged="rgShipping_Clicked"
    groupname="rgShipping"
    runat="server"
/>
<BR>
</form>
```

▶ **QUICK TIP**

If you need a control that allows visitors to select more than one item in a group, try the CheckBox control.

Notice that all three of the RadioButton controls belong to the same group. Therefore, visitors can only select one of the RadioButton controls.

To allow code to run when any of the RadioButton controls are selected, you need to do two things. First you must set the AutoPostBack property to True:

```
autopostback="True"
```

When you do that, the page is posted back to the server for processing when any of the items change.

The other thing you need to do is indicate the event procedure that you would like to run when an item changes:

```
oncheckedchanged="rgShipping_Clicked"
```

You then need to define a procedure in your code that matches that name, like this one:

```
Sub rgShipping_Clicked(Sender As Object, E As EventArgs)
    If rdoUPS.Checked = True Then
        Session("ShippingMethod") = "UPS"
    ElseIf rdoUSPS.Checked = True Then
        Session("ShippingMethod") = "USPS"
    Else
        Session("ShippingMethod") = "FedEx"
    End If
    lblShipSelected.Text = Session("ShippingMethod")
End Sub
```

Within this procedure, the type of shipping visitors select is stored in a Session variable so that it can be referenced from another page. The value is also echoed back to visitors on the page through the Text property of a Label control.

Displaying a Basic CheckBox Control

The CheckBox control provides a mechanism for you to gather a True/False or Yes/No type of response from visitors. Each CheckBox control is mutually exclusive from any other CheckBox control. So checking one box has no effect on checking another box.

When you create a CheckBox control on an ASP.NET page it renders three HTML tags like these:

```
<span
    style="background-color:LightYellow;">
    <label for="chkMailingList">
        Would you like to be on our mailing list?
    </label>
    <input
        id="chkMailingList"
        type="checkbox"
        name="chkMailingList"
        checked="checked"
    />
</span>
```

Two of the HTML tags are embedded within a Span tag. The Span tag contains the style element of the control. The text you associated with a CheckBox control is placed within a Label tag and the box portion of the CheckBox control is rendered through a CheckBox Input tag.

USE IT   The following ASP.NET page demonstrates the use of a CheckBox control. Visitors to the page indicate how they would like to be contacted. Then, based on their selection, they will see a message box with their selections after submitting the page for processing.

The following controls are defined on the page:

```
<form runat="server">
<BR><BR>
<asp:checkbox
    id="chkMailingList"
    text="Would you like to be on our mailing list?"
    checked="true"
    backcolor="LightYellow"
    bordercolor="DarkRed"
    borderwidth=3
    font-size="12pt"
    font-name="Comic Sans MS"
    textalign="Left"
    runat="server"
/>
<BR><BR>
<asp:checkbox
    id="chkContact"
    text="Would you like us to contact you by phone?"
    checked="false"
    backcolor="LightYellow"
    bordercolor="DarkRed"
    borderwidth=3
    font-size="12pt"
    font-name="Comic Sans MS"
    textalign="Right"
    runat="server"
/>
<BR><BR>
<asp:button
    id="butOK"
    text="OK"
    Type="Submit"
    OnClick="SubmitBtn_Click"
    runat="server"
/>
</form>
```

As with other controls, you supply the name of a CheckBox control through the ID property:

```
<asp:checkbox
    id="chkMailingList"
```

You set the Text property to the label that you would like generated with the CheckBox control:

```
text="Would you like to be on our mailing list?"
```

By default, a CheckBox control is not checked. You can check it or uncheck it through the Checked property:

```
checked="true"
```

The CheckBox control contains color, border, and font properties, providing you with the mechanism to create a unique-looking interface:

```
backcolor="LightYellow"
bordercolor="DarkRed"
borderwidth=3
font-size="12pt"
font-name="Comic Sans MS"
```

You can have the text appear before the box of the CheckBox control or after the box. You set this through the TextAlign property. A value of Left places the text before the box and a value of Right for this property places the text after the box:

```
    textalign="Left"
    runat="server"
/>
```

The button on the page submits the page for processing. When that occurs, the following code block runs:

```
Sub SubmitBtn_Click(Sender As Object, E As EventArgs)
    If chkMailingList.Checked = "True" Then
        Response.Write ("<SCRIPT LANGUAGE=""JavaScript"">" _
            & Chr(13) & "<!--" & Chr(13) _
            & "alert('You have been added to " _
            & "our mailing list')" & Chr(13) _
            & "--><" & "/" & "SCRIPT>")
    End If
    If chkContact.Checked = "True" Then
        Response.Write ("<SCRIPT LANGUAGE=""JavaScript"">" _
            & Chr(13) & "<!--" & Chr(13) _
            & "alert('We will contact you " _
```

```
            & "by phone')" & Chr(13) _
            & "--><" & "/" & "SCRIPT>")
      End If
End Sub
```

Notice what this procedure does. First, you check to see if the CheckBox control has been checked:

```
If chkMailingList.Checked = "True" Then
```

If it has, you write JavaScript code directly to the visitors' browser. This code displays a message box confirming to visitors that their request has been processed:

```
Response.Write ("<SCRIPT LANGUAGE=""JavaScript"">" _
    & Chr(13) & "<!--" & Chr(13) _
    & "alert('You have been added to " _
    & "our mailing list')" & Chr(13) _
    & "--><" & "/" & "SCRIPT>")
```

The same action is then performed for the other CheckBox control.

Writing Code That Runs When a CheckBox Control Is Checked

ASP.NET provides a way for you to have a procedure fire whenever the value of the check in a CheckBox control changes. You do that by writing your own event procedure and linking to that procedure through the OnCheckedChanged property of the CheckBox control.

USE IT This next technique presents a CheckBox control which, when checked, automatically sends the visitor to Google.com. Just one control is defined within the body of this ASP.NET page—the CheckBox control itself:

```
<form runat="server">
<BR><BR>
<asp:checkbox
    id="chkGoogle"
    text="Would you like to go to Google.com?"
    autopostback="True"
    oncheckedchanged="chkGoogle_Clicked"
    runat="server"
/>
</form>
```

First, notice that the AutoPostBack property is set to True:

```
autopostback="True"
```

This means that the page will be sent back to the server for processing whenever the value in the CheckBox control changes. You then indicate the procedure that you want to run through the OnCheckedChanged property:

```
oncheckedchanged="chkGoogle_Clicked"
```

Then, in code, you need to define a procedure with that same name:

```
Sub chkGoogle_Clicked(Sender As Object, E As EventArgs)
    if chkGoogle.Checked = True Then
        Response.Redirect("http://www.google.com")
    End If
End Sub
```

In this procedure, you check to see if the CheckBox control has been checked:

```
if chkGoogle.Checked = True Then
```

If it has, the visitor is redirected to Google.com:

```
Response.Redirect("http://www.google.com")
```

Creating a Basic HyperLink Control

A HyperLink control provides a way for you to dynamically add a link to your ASP.NET page. For example, maybe you have an e-commerce site and on the product page you want to provide a link to a large picture of a product. The HyperLink control is an ideal candidate for that task since you can set its properties in code.

 This next ASP.NET page shows you how to create a basic text HyperLink control. Just that one control is defined within the body of the page:

```
<form runat="server">
<asp:HyperLink
    id="hypMS"
    runat="server"
    text="Click to connect to Microsoft"
    navigateurl="http://www.microsoft.com"
    target="_blank"
    borderwidth="7px"
    borderstyle=7
```

```
/>
</form>
```

The name of the control is set through the ID property:

```
<asp:HyperLink
    id="hypMS"
    runat="server"
```

The value you place in the Text property appears to visitors in their browser as the text for the HyperLink:

```
text="Click to connect to Microsoft"
```

You set the location that you want visitors to go to through the NavigateURL property:

```
navigateurl="http://www.microsoft.com"
```

QUICK TIP

You can set the NavigateURL property to a relative location. For example, if you wanted to link to an image in a sub-folder called Images, you would place this value in the property: "./images/someimage.gif"

Next, you can set the browser target for the link through the Target property. If you set the property to "_blank"

```
target="_blank"
```

a new browser window would open. By default, the link opens in the current browser window. But you can also set the Target property to "_parent". This will cause the link to occupy the container frame for the current frame if the current page is frame-based.

Additionally, you can set the style properties for the HyperLink control:

```
    borderwidth="7px"
    borderstyle=7
/>
```

Displaying a Graphic on a HyperLink Control

The HyperLink control is rendered in one of two ways. It is either rendered as a simple text anchor tag or it is rendered as an image tag embedded within an anchor tag. This tip shows you how to create a HyperLink control that displays a graphical link.

The form on this tip's ASP.NET page contains a single control definition:

```
<form runat="server">
<asp:HyperLink
    id="hypMS"
    runat="server"
    text="Click to connect to Microsoft"
    imageurl="./button.gif"
    navigateurl="http://www.microsoft.com"
    target="_blank"
/>
</form>
```

You start by supplying a name for the HyperLink control through the ID property:

```
<asp:HyperLink
    id="hypMS"
    runat="server"
```

You can use the Text property to supply text that is displayed to visitors when they hover their mouse over the link:

```
text="Click to connect to Microsoft"
```

You then set the ImageURL property to the location of the graphic that you want to display for the link:

```
imageurl="./button.gif"
```

> ### QUICK TIP
>
> *In this example, the graphic is located in the same folder as the ASP.NET page. But you can also put the full address to the graphic in this property, which would allow you to display a graphic that was on an entirely different server.*

You also need to supply the location that you want visitors to go to when they click the image. You do that through the NavigateURL property:

```
navigateurl="http://www.microsoft.com"
```

You can also indicate that you want the link to appear in a new browser window:

```
    target="_blank"
/>
```

Creating a Basic LinkButton Control

A LinkButton control has attributes similar to a Button control and a HyperLink control. Its appearance is like a textual HyperLink control. Visitors see a link to click on. But as with a Button control, the page is posted back to the server for processing when the link is clicked.

When you add a LinkButton control to an ASP.NET page, the control is rendered like this to the visitors' browser:

```
<a
    id="lnkbutOK"
    type="Submit"
    href="javascript:__doPostBack('lnkbutOK','')">
    Click to Submit
</a>
```

So an Anchor tag is rendered. But the URL for the link is a JavaScript procedure that the compiler places in your rendered ASP.NET page. That procedure submits the page to the server for processing.

 USE IT   The LinkButton control can be used as either a Command button or a standard Submit button. This tip shows you how to use the control as a Submit button.

The sample page allows visitors to enter some personal information, which is echoed back to them when they click the LinkButton control. The following controls are defined on the page:

```
<form runat="server">
<asp:label
    id="lblDataEntered"
    runat="server"
/>
<BR><BR>
Enter your Name:<BR>
<asp:textbox
    id="txtName"
    columns="25"
    maxlength="30"
    runat=server
/>
<BR><BR>
Enter your Email Address:<BR>
<asp:textbox
    id="txtEmail"
    columns="35"
    maxlength="50"
    runat=server
/>
<BR><BR>
```

```
Enter your Phone Number:<BR>
<asp:textbox
    id="txtPhone"
    columns="15"
    maxlength="15"
    runat=server
/>
<BR><BR>
<asp:linkbutton
    id="lnkbutOK"
    text="Click to Submit"
    onclick="SubmitBtn_Click"
    runat="server"
/>
</form>
```

The Label control will display back to visitors what they have entered. The three TextBox controls allow them to enter their personal information.

The LinkButton control is given a name through the ID property:

```
<asp:linkbutton
    id="lnkbutOK"
```

The text that we want to display in the rendered link is placed into the Text property:

```
text="Click to Submit"
```

We also need to specify the name of the procedure that we want to run when visitors click the link. We do that through the OnClick property:

```
    onclick="SubmitBtn_Click"
    runat="server"
/>
```

Then, in code, we need to create an event procedure like this one that has the same name as the one we specified in that property:

```
Sub SubmitBtn_Click(Sender As Object, E As EventArgs)
    lblDataEntered.Text = "You entered:<BR>" _
        & txtName.Text & "<BR>" _
        & txtEmail.Text & "<BR>" _
        & txtPhone.Text
End Sub
```

Within that procedure you would place whatever code you needed to run to process the page. In this case, we simply echo the selections visitors made back to them through the Label control.

Using a LinkButton Control as a Command Button

You may find the need to have a series of LinkButton controls on an ASP.NET page. Each one would process the data on the page differently. For example, you may have a search results page and, based on the button clicked by the visitor, you would sort the results in a different way or start a new search.

One of the ways you can achieve this functionality is by defining a series of LinkButton controls as command buttons. Like a standard Submit button, when a Command button is clicked it submits the page for processing. But the big difference is that when the page is submitted and the procedure fires, the procedure passes information about the button that was clicked.

 USE IT   This technique demonstrates how to define a LinkButton control as a command button and how to determine which button was clicked. Information about the button clicked is echoed back to the visitor through a Label control.

The following controls are defined on the page:

```
<form runat="server">
<asp:label
    id="lblButtonPressed"
    runat="server"
/>
<BR><BR>
<asp:linkbutton
    id="lnkbutSortName"
    text="Sort By Name"
    oncommand="CommandButton_Click"
    commandname="Sort"
    commandargument="By Name"
    runat="server"
/>
<BR><BR>
<asp:linkbutton
    id="lnkbutSortPrice"
    text="Sort By Price"
    oncommand="CommandButton_Click"
    commandname="Sort"
    commandargument="By Price"
    runat="server"
/>
<BR><BR>
<asp:linkbutton
    id="lnkbutNewSearch"
    text="New Search"
    oncommand="CommandButton_Click"
    commandname="New Search"
```

```
    commandargument="None"
    runat="server"
/>
</Form>
```

Take a look at how the LinkButton controls are defined. The ID is set to the name of the control:

```
<asp:linkbutton
    id="lnkbutSortName"
```

And the Text property is set to the text that you want to appear on the button in the visitors' browser:

```
text="Sort By Name"
```

But, you specify the name of the procedure that you want to run through the OnCommand property:

```
oncommand="CommandButton_Click"
```

You can pass two pieces of information on to that procedure. The first is the internal name that you give the control:

```
commandname="Sort"
```

And the second is any accompanying information that you want passed into the procedure:

```
    commandargument="By Name"
    runat="server"
/>
```

▶ **QUICK TIP**

You are not required to supply a value for either of the extra command properties. You may find it useful to just give the command a name and use that within the called procedure.

Notice that all three of the LinkButton controls call the same procedure but pass to it different values in the CommandName and CommandArgument properties.

Next, you need to define a procedure that matches the name you placed in the OnCommand property:

```
Sub CommandButton_Click(Sender As Object, E As CommandEventArgs)
    lblButtonPressed.Text = "You pressed: " _
        & E.CommandName & "<BR>With this argument: " _
        & E.CommandArgument & "<BR>"
End Sub
```

Notice that the procedure has passed into it CommandEventArgs instead of the EventArgs passed in through a submit button call. Within the procedure you can retrieve the name and argument passed in by the button clicked through the properties of the CommandEventArgs parameter:

```
lblButtonPressed.Text = "You pressed: " _
    & E.CommandName & "<BR>With this argument: " _
    & E.CommandArgument & "<BR>"
```

Creating a Basic Image Control

The Image control in ASP.NET provides a way for you to dynamically display an image on a page. For example, you may have a products page on which you wish to display the product's image. Or you may have an employee page where you want to display the picture of the employee selected by the visitor. Both of these examples would require a dynamic way of displaying an image. The Image control provides that functionality.

USE IT The following ASP.NET page allows visitors to select an image from a list of names in a DropDownList control. When an item is selected, an Image control is used to display the image selected.

The page defines the following controls:

```
<form runat="server">
<BR><BR>
Select an image to display:<BR>
<asp:dropdownlist
    id="ddlImages"
    runat=server
>
    <asp:listitem text="Image 1" value="./button.gif"/>
    <asp:listitem text="Image 2" value="./button2.gif"/>
    <asp:listitem text="Image 3" value="./button3.gif"/>
</asp:dropdownlist>
<BR>
<asp:linkbutton
    id="lnkbutOK"
    text="View Image"
    onclick="SubmitBtn_Click"
    runat="server"
/>
<BR><BR>
<asp:image
    id="imgToView"
```

```
        runat="server"
/>
</form>
```

The DropDownList control contains three items. Each item has a text value displayed to visitors as well as a value that indicates the path to the image to be displayed. A LinkButton control submits the visitors' request. And an Image control is defined just by specifying its name. The other properties are set in code.

When the page first loads, the following code runs:

```
Sub Page_Load(ByVal Sender as Object, ByVal E as EventArgs)
    If Not IsPostBack Then
        imgToView.AlternateText = "Image 1"
        imgToView.ImageUrl = "./button3.gif"
    End If
End Sub
```

You first verify that this is the initial load of the page:

```
If Not IsPostBack Then
```

If that is the case, the Image control will display the first image. In that case, you set the text of the image to this value:

```
imgToView.AlternateText = "Image 1"
```

Note that this text will appear to visitors when they hover their mouse over the control.

The ImageURL property is set to the path of the image to be displayed through the Image control:

```
imgToView.ImageUrl = "./button3.gif"
```

Similarly, when visitors select one of the images in the DropDownList control, this code sets the Image control so that it displays the image visitors select:

```
Sub SubmitBtn_Click(Sender As Object, E As EventArgs)
    imgToView.AlternateText = ddlImages.SelectedItem.Text
        imgToView.ImageUrl = ddlImages.SelectedItem.Value
End Sub
```

▼ Creating a Basic ImageButton Control

An ImageButton control is a combination of a Button control and an Image control. As with a Button control, when clicked, the current page is submitted back to the server for processing. But as with an Image control, an image is displayed instead of the standard default button displayed with a Button control.

When you add an ImageButton control to your page, the compiler renders an HTML Input tag like this one:

```
<input
    type="image"
    name="imagebutOK"
    id="imagebutOK"
    src="path2image.gif"
    alt="Click to Submit"
    border="0"
/>
```

USE IT   The following ASP.NET page demonstrates the use of the ImageButton control. The page allows visitors to enter some information about themselves. When they click the ImageButton control, the information entered is echoed back to their browser.

The page has these controls defined:

```
<form runat="server">
<asp:label
    id="lblDataEntered"
    runat="server"
/>
<BR><BR>
Enter your Name:<BR>
<asp:textbox
    id="txtName"
    columns="25"
    maxlength="30"
    runat=server
/>
<BR><BR>
Enter your Email Address:<BR>
<asp:textbox
    id="txtEmail"
    columns="35"
    maxlength="50"
    runat=server
/>
<BR><BR>
Enter your Phone Number:<BR>
<asp:textbox
    id="txtPhone"
    columns="15"
    maxlength="15"
    runat=server
```

```
/>
<BR><BR>
<asp:imagebutton
    id="imagebutOK"
    alternatetext="Click to Submit"
    imageurl="./button.gif"
    onclick="SubmitBtn_Click"
    runat="server"
/>
</form>
```

Notice the definition of the ImageButton control. You specify the name through the ID property:

```
<asp:imagebutton
    id="imagebutOK"
```

Next, you can supply text that you want to appear when visitors hover their mouse over the ImageButton control:

```
alternatetext="Click to Submit"
```

This text would also appear if the image for the control could not be loaded.

You also need to specify the name of the image to display on the control:

```
imageurl="./button.gif"
```

as well as the name of the procedure to fire when the ImageButton control is clicked:

```
    onclick="SubmitBtn_Click"
    runat="server"
/>
```

That procedure needs to be defined like this:

```
Sub SubmitBtn_Click(Sender As Object, E As ImageClickEventArgs)
    lblDataEntered.Text = "You entered:<BR>" _
        & txtName.Text & "<BR>" _
        & txtEmail.Text & "<BR>" _
        & txtPhone.Text
End Sub
```

Notice that the name of the procedure needs to match the name that you supplied in the OnClick property. Also notice that the second parameter passed into the procedure needs to be of type ImageClickEventArgs instead of the standard EventArgs.

Determining the Coordinates Clicked on the Image of an ImageButton Control

If you had an image of a map or an image that you wanted to use to navigate to different pages based on the spot that was clicked on the image, you would want to know the exact position on the image that was clicked. That way you could write code that took action based on where the visitor clicked on an image.

The ImageButton control can supply that type of information.

USE IT This ASP.NET page shows you the technique you need to employ to retrieve the coordinates that the visitor clicks on an image. The page echoes back to the visitor the position that was clicked on an image control.

The page is defined with two controls:

```
<form runat="server">
<asp:label
    id="lblLocationClicked"
    runat="server"
/>
<BR><BR>
<asp:imagebutton
    id="imagebutOK"
    alternatetext="View Coordinates"
    imageurl="./button.gif"
    onclick="SubmitBtn_Click"
    runat="server"
/>
</form>
```

The Label control will display the position that the visitor clicked and the ImageButton control is used to submit the visitor's request.

When the visitor clicks on the ImageButton control, this code block fires:

```
Sub SubmitBtn_Click(Sender As Object, E As ImageClickEventArgs)
    Dim String1 as String
    Dim String2 as String
    If E.X < 18 then
        String1 = "Left"
    Else
        String1 = "Right"
    End If
    If E.Y < 18 then
        String2 = "Top"
    Else
```

```
        String2 = "Bottom"
    End If
    lblLocationClicked.Text = "You clicked in the " & String2 _
        & "-" & String1 & " portion of the image."
End Sub
```

Within this procedure we first test to see if the visitor clicked on the left half of the image, which in this example is approximately 36 pixels wide. You check this by querying the X property of the ImageClickEventArgs parameter, which contains the exact left-right coordinate on the image that was clicked:

```
If E.X < 18 then
```

If that is the case, Left is stored in a string:

```
String1 = "Left"
```

Otherwise, the text Right is stored:

```
String1 = "Right"
```

The same is done for the top-bottom position clicked by querying the Y property:

```
If E.Y < 18 then
    String2 = "Top"
Else
    String2 = "Bottom"
End If
```

The position clicked is then displayed back to the visitor through the Text property of the Label control:

```
lblLocationClicked.Text = "You clicked in the " & String2 _
    & "-" & String1 & " portion of the image."
```

Adding a Simple Button Control to an ASP.NET Page

If you create an ASP.NET that has more than one input field on it, you are very likely to want to include a Button control on that page. A Button control provides the mechanism for visitors to submit the data they entered back to your server so that it can be processed.

When you add a Button control to your ASP.NET page, the compiler renders a Submit Input tag like this one:

```
<input
    type="submit"
    name="butOK"
```

```
        value="  OK   "
        id="butOK"
/>
```

USE IT   The page presented in this tip shows you how to add a Button control to your ASP.NET page and how to create a code block that fires when visitors click the button. The page asks visitors to enter information about themselves. When visitors click the OK button, that information is displayed back to them through a Label control.

The page contains the following control definitions:

```
<form runat="server">
<asp:label
    id="lblDataEntered"
    runat="server"
/>
<BR><BR>
Enter your Name:<BR>
<asp:textbox
    id="txtName"
    columns="25"
    maxlength="30"
    runat=server
/>
<BR><BR>
Enter your Email Address:<BR>
<asp:textbox
    id="txtEmail"
    columns="35"
    maxlength="50"
    runat=server
/>
<BR><BR>
Enter your Phone Number:<BR>
<asp:textbox
    id="txtPhone"
    columns="15"
    maxlength="15"
    runat=server
/>
<BR><BR>
<asp:button
    id="butOK"
    text="  OK   "
    onclick="SubmitBtn_Click"
```

```
    runat="server"
/>
</form>
```

Take a look at the definition for the Button control. The name of the control is specified in the ID property:

```
<asp:button
    id="butOK"
```

The text that is displayed on the Button control is set through the Text property:

```
text="  OK  "
```

You also need to specify a value for the OnClick property. The name you put here is the name of the procedure that you want to run when the button is clicked:

```
    onclick="SubmitBtn_Click"
    runat="server"
/>
```

You then need to supply a procedure that has that name and has parameters like the ones in this definition:

```
Sub SubmitBtn_Click(Sender As Object, E As EventArgs)
    lblDataEntered.Text = "You entered:<BR>" _
        & txtName.Text & "<BR>" _
        & txtEmail.Text & "<BR>" _
        & txtPhone.Text
End Sub
```

Then, within that procedure, you would place your code that processed the fields on the page.

Using a Button Control as a Command Button

A Button control can be used in two ways. It can be used in the standard way, simply as a Submit button that sends the contents of the form to the server for processing. But the Button control can also be used as a Command button.

A Command button is useful on a page where you need a variety of buttons and you want to take different actions based on the button that vistors click. When used as a Command button, the Button control then calls a special procedure where the name and an additional argument related to the command clicked is passed on to the event procedure.

USE IT   The ASP.NET page that demonstrates this technique contains three buttons. Each button passes information on to the same procedure. The values that are passed into the procedure are displayed back to visitors through a Label control.

The page has the following controls defined:

```
<form runat="server">
<asp:label
    id="lblButtonPressed"
    runat="server"
/>
<BR><BR>
<asp:button
    id="butSortName"
    text="Sort By Name"
    oncommand="CommandButton_Click"
    commandname="Sort"
    commandargument="By Name"
    runat="server"
/>
<BR><BR>
<asp:button
    id="butSortPrice"
    text="Sort By Price"
    oncommand="CommandButton_Click"
    commandname="Sort"
    commandargument="By Price"
    runat="server"
/>
<BR><BR>
<asp:button
    id="lnkbutNewSearch"
    text="New Search"
    oncommand="CommandButton_Click"
    commandname="New Search"
    commandargument="None"
    runat="server"
/>
</form>
```

The Text property of a Button control serves the same purpose when the button is a Command button. It is the text that visitors see on the face of the button:

```
<asp:button
    id="butSortName"
    text="Sort By Name"
```

Then in the OnCommand property, you set the name of the procedure that is to be called when the button is clicked:

```
oncommand="CommandButton_Click"
```

You can also specify the name of the command:

```
commandname="Sort"
```

and any additional information through this property:

```
    commandargument="By Name"
    runat="server"
/>
```

These properties are available to the called procedure, as you can see here:

```
Sub CommandButton_Click(Sender As Object, E As CommandEventArgs)
    lblButtonPressed.Text = "You pressed: " _
        & E.CommandName & "<BR>With this argument: " _
        & E.CommandArgument & "<BR>"
End Sub
```

The CommandEventArgs parameter contains the information about the button that was clicked. You would then use that information to determine what action to take.

CHAPTER 4

List Web Controls

TIPS IN THIS CHAPTER

ASP.NET provides for you a variety of controls that you can use to display a list of information. Those lists come in two forms. One form is the type of data that has numerous fields to present visitors with a flowing list of the items and possibly allow them to add, edit, or delete from that list. ASP.NET provides controls like DataGrid, Repeater, and DataList for this type of functionality.

The other type of form that you may want to display is a list of text/value pairs. This type of data typically allows visitors to select an item or items in a list. ASP.NET provides controls like DropDownList, ListBox, RadioButtonList, and CheckBoxList for this functionality.

This chapter presents tips and techniques on using these controls. Many of these tips and techniques use an Access database to display and manipulate the data that they consume. Those databases can be found in the same zip file as the rest of the code that goes with this chapter.

Creating a Basic DropDownList Control

DropDownList controls are exceedingly helpful when you need to display a simple list of text to visitors for them to select from, or even when they don't need to select an item. For example, the control could be used to display a list of categories in your online catalog, a list of quick jump links to other pages at your site, or a list of questions in an online FAQ page.

When you add a DropDownList control to your ASP.NET page, the compiler renders the control to the visitors' browser as an HTML Select tag like this one:

```
<select name="ddl1" id="ddl1">
    <option value="Bu">Blue</option>
    <option selected="selected" value="Pu">Purple</option>
    <option value="Go">Gold</option>
</select>
```

Within the Select tag, each of the items that is to appear in the list is generated as an HTML Options tag.

USE IT This tip shows you how to define a basic DropDownList control with ListItem controls added within the DropDownList control. Just those controls are defined within the ASP.NET form on this page:

```
<asp:dropdownlist
    id="ddl1"
    runat="server"
>
    <asp:listitem value="Bu">Blue</asp:listitem>
    <asp:listitem value="Re">Red</asp:listitem>
    <asp:listitem value="Gr">Green</asp:listitem>
    <asp:listitem value="Pu" Selected>Purple</asp:listitem>
    <asp:listitem value="Ba">Black</asp:listitem>
    <asp:listitem value="Go" text="Gold"/>
</asp:dropdownlist>
```

The definition of the DropDownList begins with the name of the control being defined:

```
<asp:dropdownlist
```

This is followed by the name of the control that is to be run on the server:

```
id="ddl1"
runat="server"
```

Notice, though, that next you don't close the control's definition:

```
>
```

That is because you need to define controls within the DropDownList definition. Those controls are the ListItem controls. Each ListItem control is generated as an Option tag to the rendered page. Therefore, each of the items you want to appear in the list is added as a ListItem control. A ListItem control has two properties used to store the text of the item. Those are the Value and Text properties. The Text property, as is the case here, can be defined between the opening and closing tags of the control:

```
<asp:listitem value="Bu">Blue</asp:listitem>
```

The Text property contains the data that the visitor sees in the DropDownList control.

But you can optionally place a value in the Value property. This value is for your own internal use. It is typically set to the code that you want to store in the database. For example, if you had an ASP.NET page that allowed the addition of employee records, you may have a department field. That field would list the names of the departments. Therefore, you would set the Text property to the name of the department. But you would likely want to store the ID of the department in your database. Therefore, you would store the ID of the departments in the Value property:

```
<asp:listitem value="Re">Red</asp:listitem>
<asp:listitem value="Gr">Green</asp:listitem>
```

You can indicate the default selected item in the list by placing the Selected keyword in the tag of the list item:

```
<asp:listitem value="Pu" Selected>Purple</asp:listitem>
<asp:listitem value="Ba">Black</asp:listitem>
```

Notice the alternative definition of a ListItem control used here:

```
<asp:listitem value="Go" text="Gold"/>
```

In this case, you define the Value and Text properties explicitly so no closing tag is required.

After defining the ListItem controls, you need to close the DropDownList definition:

```
</asp:dropdownlist>
```

Working with the Appearance of a DropDownList Control

The DropDownList control contains properties that you can use to control the color and font displayed in the control. With effective use of these properties, you can render DropDownList controls that go well beyond the basic look seen on most ASP.NET pages.

The DropDownList controls defined in this technique show you how to use those properties.

 The following illustration displays the rendered DropDownList controls defined in this tip.

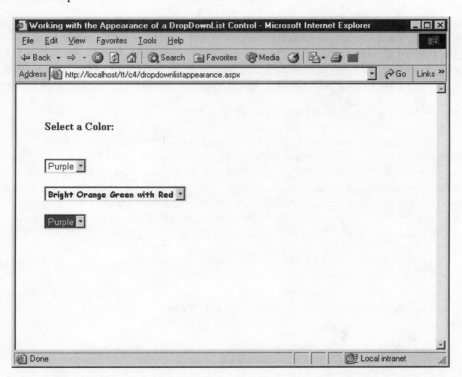

The ASP.NET defines three DropDownList controls that utilize the color and font properties of the control:

```
<form runat="server">
<BR><BR>
<B>Select a Color:</B><BR>
<BR><BR>
<asp:dropdownlist
```

```
    id="ddl1"
    accesskey="1"
    runat="server"
>
    <asp:listitem value="Bu">Blue</asp:listitem>
    <asp:listitem value="Re">Red</asp:listitem>
    <asp:listitem value="Gr">Green</asp:listitem>
    <asp:listitem value="Pu" Selected>Purple</asp:listitem>
    <asp:listitem value="Ba">Black</asp:listitem>
    <asp:listitem value="Go" text="Gold"/>
</asp:dropdownlist>
<BR><BR>
<asp:dropdownlist
    id="ddl2"
    font-name="Comic Sans MS"
    font-size="9pt"
    font-bold="True"
    backcolor="lightyellow"
    runat="server"
>
    <asp:listitem value="Bu">Blue</asp:listitem>
    <asp:listitem value="Re">Red</asp:listitem>
    <asp:listitem value="Gr">Green</asp:listitem>
    <asp:listitem value="SR" Selected>
        Bright Orange Green with Red</asp:listitem>
    <asp:listitem value="Ba">Black</asp:listitem>
    <asp:listitem value="Go" text="Gold"/>
</asp:dropdownlist>
<BR><BR>
<asp:dropdownlist
    id="ddl3"
    backcolor="darkred"
    forecolor="yellow"
    runat="server"
>
    <asp:listitem value="Bu">Blue</asp:listitem>
    <asp:listitem value="Re">Red</asp:listitem>
    <asp:listitem value="Gr">Green</asp:listitem>
    <asp:listitem value="Pu" Selected>Purple</asp:listitem>
    <asp:listitem value="Ba">Black</asp:listitem>
    <asp:listitem value="Go" text="Gold"/>
</asp:dropdownlist>
</form>
```

The first DropDownList control is defined as just a basic control. But notice the use of the AccessKey property:

```
<asp:dropdownlist
    id="ddl1"
    accesskey="1"
    runat="server"
>
```

This property is helpful when you have a page with numerous controls on it. The property allows visitors to press the ALT key in combination with the key set in the AccessKey property to instantly set the focus to that control.

QUICK TIP

Typically, you indicate the access key that visitors must enter by placing an underscore under the letter in the label that proceeds the control. For example, if you did have a color DropDownList control, you would likely have a Label with the text Color in it. You would want to format the word "color" as "Color" to inform visitors of the access key.

The second DropDownList control takes advantage of Font and background color properties:

```
<asp:dropdownlist
    id="ddl2"
```

Remember when you set the font name that you need to be careful about using exotic fonts that visitors may not have:

```
    font-name="Comic Sans MS"
    font-size="9pt"
    font-bold="True"
```

The background color of the control is set through the BackColor property:

```
    backcolor="lightyellow"
    runat="server"
>
```

The third DropDownList uses a dark background color with a light foreground color to offset it more from the other colors:

```
<asp:dropdownlist
    id="ddl3"
    backcolor="darkred"
    forecolor="yellow"
```

```
        runat="server"
>
```

Reading and Writing the Selected Item in a DropDownList Control

The DropDownList control contains a property that returns a ListItem control that represents the current selected item in the DropDownList control. That property, SelectedItem, is used to determine which item the visitor has selected.

The control also contains a property called SelectedIndex that you can use to set the item that is currently selected in the list based on its indexed position. The technique presented in this section shows you how to use those properties.

USE IT   The ASP.NET page presented here in code initially sets the selected item in a DropDownList control. When the page is submitted, the selection made by the visitor is echoed back to the visitor's browser through a Label control.

Three controls are defined on the page:

```
<form runat="server">
<BR><BR>
<asp:label
    id="lblDataSelected"
    runat="server"
/>
<BR><BR>
<asp:dropdownlist
    id="ddl1"
    accesskey="1"
    runat="server"
>
    <asp:listitem value="Bu">Blue</asp:listitem>
    <asp:listitem value="Re">Red</asp:listitem>
    <asp:listitem value="Gr">Green</asp:listitem>
    <asp:listitem value="Pu" >Purple</asp:listitem>
    <asp:listitem value="Ba">Black</asp:listitem>
</asp:dropdownlist>
<BR><BR>
<asp:button
    id="butOK"
    text="OK"
    type="Submit"
    onclick="SubmitBtn_Click"
```

```
        runat="server"
/>
</form>
```

The DropDownList control is defined as a basic DropDownList. The visitor clicks the Button control to submit the content of the page.

When the page first loads, the following code runs and uses the SelectedIndex property of the DropDownList control to select the third item in the list:

```
Sub Page_Load(ByVal Sender as Object, ByVal E as EventArgs)
    If Not IsPostBack Then
        ddl1.SelectedIndex = 2
    End If
End Sub
```

Note that the SelectedIndex property is zero-based. That is why the value of 2 in that property selects the third item in the list.

When the visitor clicks the Button control, the other code block on the page runs:

```
Sub SubmitBtn_Click(Sender As Object, E As EventArgs)
    lblDataSelected.Text = "Selected Text: " _
        & ddl1.SelectedItem.Text & "<BR>Selected Value: " _
        & ddl1.SelectedItem.Value & "<BR>Selected Index: " _
        & ddl1.SelectedIndex
End Sub
```

In code you use the Text property of the SelectedItem object to retrieve the text selected by the visitor and the Value property of the same object returns the value for the item selected.

As is done in this code block, you can use the SelectedIndex property to return the positional index of the item selected.

Writing Code That Fires When an Item Is Selected in a DropDownList Control

You may find yourself in need of code that runs automatically when the selected item in a DropDownList control changes. For example, if you had a list of page names and when one is selected you wanted the visitor to be taken to that page, you would need code that fires when the selected item changes.

The DropDownList control provides functionality to meet this need. This tip demonstrates how to use that functionality.

USE IT   This ASP.NET page contains a single DropDownList control. When the selected item in the DropDownList control changes, code fires changing the background color of the DropDownList control to match the color selected in the DropDownList control.

The DropDownList control has this definition:

```
<asp:dropdownlist
    id="ddl1"
    autopostback="True"
    onselectedindexchanged="ddl1_Changed"
    runat="server"
>
    <asp:listitem value="Bu">Blue</asp:listitem>
    <asp:listitem value="Re">Red</asp:listitem>
    <asp:listitem value="Gr">Green</asp:listitem>
    <asp:listitem value="Pu" >Purple</asp:listitem>
    <asp:listitem value="Ba">Black</asp:listitem>
</asp:dropdownlist>
```

First, notice that the AutoPostBack property is set to True:

```
autopostback="True"
```

This tells the compiler to post the page back to the server immediately when the selected item changes.

Then you need to specify through the OnSelectedIndexChanged property the name of the procedure that you want to run when the selected item changes:

```
onselectedindexchanged="ddl1_Changed"
```

And in code you need to define a procedure with that name like the one defined here:

```
Sub ddl1_Changed(Sender As Object, E As EventArgs)
    ddl1.BackColor = _
        System.Drawing.Color.FromName(ddl1.SelectedItem.Text)
End Sub
```

The procedure simply sets the background color of the DropDownList. Notice that you can't do this directly by placing the text color name into the BackColor property. Instead, you must create a Color object using the FromName method of that object and pass to that method the text color name selected in the DropDownList control.

Binding Database Data to a DropDownList Control

Frequently, you will want to use a DropDownList control by populating it from values in a database. The technique described in this section of the chapter shows you how to populate a DropDownList control from a table in an Access database.

 The ASP.NET page presented here retrieves department names and IDs from a table in an Access database and displays them to visitors in a DropDownList control. When the page is submitted, the visitors' selection is echoed back to them in a Label control.

At the top of the page, you need to include these two lines of code that import two namespaces:

```
<%@ Import Namespace="System.Data" %>
<%@ Import Namespace="System.Data.OLEDB" %>
```

The namespaces provide you with the objects you need to connect to and retrieve data from an Access database.

Within the ASP.NET Form defined on the page, the following controls are defined:

```
<form runat="server">
<BR><BR>
<asp:label
    id="lblDataSelected"
    runat="server"
/>
<BR><BR>
<asp:dropdownlist
    id="ddlDepartments"
    datatextfield="DeptName"
    datavaluefield="DeptID"
    runat="server"
/>
<BR><BR>
<asp:button
    id="butOK"
    text="OK"
    type="Submit"
    onclick="SubmitBtn_Click"
    runat="server"
/>
```

The Label control will display the visitor's selection and the Button control allows the page to be submitted.

But take a closer look at the DropDownList definition. The control is given the name ddlDepartments:

```
<asp:dropdownlist
    id="ddlDepartments"
```

Next, you supply the name of the database field that contains the value that you want displayed to the visitor in the DropDownList control through the DataTextField property:

```
datatextfield="DeptName"
```

You can also supply the name of the field that contains the hidden value for each item in the list that you will reference in code. That is typically the primary key field for the data being displayed:

```
    datavaluefield="DeptID"
    runat="server"
/>
```

When the page first loads, you need code like this to populate the DropDownList control:

```
Sub Page_Load(ByVal Sender as Object, ByVal E as EventArgs)
    If Not IsPostBack Then
        Dim DBConn as OleDbConnection
        Dim DBCommand As OleDbDataAdapter
        Dim DSPageData as New DataSet
        DBConn = New OleDbConnection( _
            "PROVIDER=Microsoft.Jet.OLEDB.4.0;" _
            & "DATA SOURCE=" _
            & Server.MapPath("/tt/C4/ddlDB.mdb;"))
        DBCommand = New OleDbDataAdapter _
            ("Select DeptID, DeptName " _
            & "From Departments " _
            & "Order By DeptName", DBConn)
        DBCommand.Fill(DSPageData, _
            "Departments")
        ddlDepartments.DataSource = _
            DSPageData.Tables("Departments").DefaultView
        ddlDepartments.DataBind()
    End If
End Sub
```

You only want this code to run when the page first loads, so you place the code in an If block like this:

```
If Not IsPostBack Then
```

If you didn't provide code like that, the list would be repopulated when the page was submitted.

Next, you need to define a connection object so that you can connect to the database:

```
Dim DBConn as OleDbConnection
```

You also need a DataAdapter object to retrieve data from the database:

```
Dim DBCommand As OleDbDataAdapter
```

And a DataSet object that will store the retrieved data:

```
Dim DSPageData as New DataSet
```

Next, you connect to the database. Notice the use of the MapPath method, which returns the physical path to the Web root:

```
DBConn = New OleDbConnection( _
    "PROVIDER=Microsoft.Jet.OLEDB.4.0;" _
    & "DATA SOURCE=" _
    & Server.MapPath("/tt/C4/ddlDB.mdb;"))
```

Next, you need to retrieve the name and ID of each department from the database:

```
DBCommand = New OleDbDataAdapter _
    ("Select DeptID, DeptName " _
    & "From Departments " _
    & "Order By DeptName", DBConn)
```

That data is placed into the DataSet object:

```
DBCommand.Fill(DSPageData, _
    "Departments")
```

You then indicate that the DropDownList control will use the data in the DataSet object:

```
ddlDepartments.DataSource = _
    DSPageData.Tables("Departments").DefaultView
```

And you bind the DropDownList control to that data, which populates the DropDownList control:

```
ddlDepartments.DataBind()
```

Using the SelectedItem object of the DropDownList control, you can retrieve the department name and ID that visitors selected when the page is submitted as is done here:

```
Sub SubmitBtn_Click(Sender As Object, E As EventArgs)
    lblDataSelected.Text = "Selected Text: " _
```

```
        & ddlDepartments.SelectedItem.Text _
        & "<BR>Selected Value: " _
        & ddlDepartments.SelectedItem.Value _
        & "<BR>Selected Index: " _
        & ddlDepartments.SelectedIndex
End Sub
```

Here, the visitors' selection is echoed back to them through a Label control.

Creating a DropDownList Control in Code

In addition to manually defining DropDownList controls on your page, you can also dynamically add those controls through code. You would typically do this in a situation where you didn't know ahead of time how many controls you needed.

For example, you may have a job application page where visitors must answer a series of multiple-choice questions such as the number of years of education, whether they have specific skills, or how long they have worked in a profession. You may want such a page to be dynamic enough so that a manger could add a new question to the database with its possible answers and you wouldn't have to change the definition of the ASP.NET page. Therefore, you would need to dynamically add an unknown number of DropDownList controls to your page.

USE IT The technique presented in this next page prompts visitors for a number. Then, based on that number, DropDownList controls are added to the page. And added to each DropDownList control are a series of ListItem controls.

Within the ASP.NET form defined on the page, these controls are initially defined:

```
<form
    id="frmMyPage"
    runat="server"
>
<B>Enter the number of DropDownList controls you want:</B><BR><BR>
<asp:TextBox
    id="txtNumber"
    runat=server
/>
<BR><BR>
<asp:button
    id="butOK"
    text="OK"
    onclick="SubmitBtn_Click"
    runat="server"
/>
```

The TextBox control retrieves from visitors the number of DropDownList controls to be added. The Button control is used to Submit the page for processing. Notice that the form is given a name. That is required in this situation so we can add controls to the form.

QUICK TIP

When you add controls directly to a form, those controls are appended to the end of the form. If you would like to locate controls in a specific place on the form, define a Panel control and then add controls to the Panel control.

When the OK button is clicked, the following code dynamically adds the DropDownList controls:

```
Sub SubmitBtn_Click(Sender As Object, E As EventArgs)
    Dim I as Integer
    Dim J as Integer
    For I = 1 to txtNumber.Text
        Dim MyDDL = New DropDownList
        MyDDL.ID = "ddlDynamic" & I
        For J = 1 to 3
            Dim MyLI as New ListItem
            MyLI.Text = "Control Number: " & I & "-" & J
            MyLI.Value = I & J
            MyDDL.Items.Add(MyLI)
        Next
        frmMyPage.Controls.Add(MyDDL)
        Dim MyLiteral = New LiteralControl
        MyLiteral.Text = "<BR><BR>"
        frmMyPage.Controls.Add(MyLiteral)
    Next
End Sub
```

For this page, two variables are needed for loops:

```
Dim I as Integer
Dim J as Integer
```

The other loop iterates through the number of DropDownList controls to add:

```
For I = 1 to txtNumber.Text
```

You then create a DropDownList control in code:

```
Dim MyDDL = New DropDownList
```

and give that control a name:

```
MyDDL.ID = "ddlDynamic" & I
```

Then the inner loop is defined. This is where the ListItem controls will be added to the DropDownList controls:

```
For J = 1 to 3
```

A ListItem control is defined:

```
Dim MyLI as New ListItem
```

and is given a value for its Text and Value properties:

```
MyLI.Text = "Control Number: " & I & "-" & J
MyLI.Value = I & J
```

The ListItem is added to the Items collection of the DropDownList control through the Add method:

```
MyDDL.Items.Add(MyLI)
```

After the inner loop adds all the ListItem controls:

```
Next
```

the DropDownList control is added to the form on the page:

```
frmMyPage.Controls.Add(MyDDL)
```

Next, a LiteralControl is defined. This control provides a way for us to place some formatting HTML text between each DropDownList control:

```
Dim MyLiteral = New LiteralControl
```

That formatting text is simply two line break tags:

```
MyLiteral.Text = "<BR><BR>"
```

That LiteralControl is added to the Controls collection of the Form:

```
frmMyPage.Controls.Add(MyLiteral)
```

The code then iterates back to the top of the procedure:

```
Next
```

The following illustration displays the output of this page.

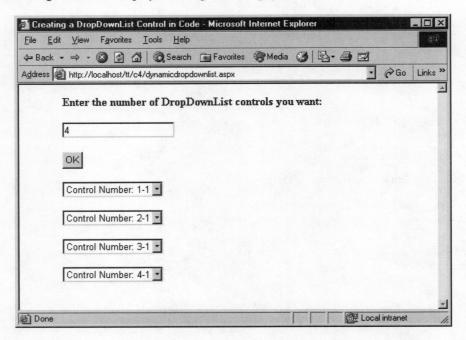

Notice the dynamically generated DropDownList controls. Also notice that the ListItem controls displayed in the DropDownList controls all contain a unique value as was created in the inner loop of the code.

Creating a Basic DataList Control

The DataList control provides a way for you to display repeating data in a table or free-flowing format. It differs from a Repeater control or a DataGrid control in that the data can be repeated across the same line of text on the rendered Web page. It also differs from those controls in that it does not have to be table-based.

The technique presented in this section shows you how to create a basic DataList control.

USE IT The following ASP.NET page displays the names and e-mail addresses for departments at a fictional company. The data comes from an Access database and is displayed through a DataList control.

Two controls are defined on this page:

```
<form runat="server">
<BR><BR>
<asp:Label
```

```
        id="lblMessage"
        Font-Size="12pt"
        Font-Bold="True"
        Font-Name="Lucida Console"
        text="Below is a list of all the departments with contact
            email address"
        runat="server"
/>
<BR><BR>
<asp:datalist
        id="dlDepts"
        runat="server"
        repeatcolumns=2
        repeatdirection="Horizontal"
        repeatlayout="table"
        gridlines="Both"
        backcolor="lightyellow"
        forecolor="darkred"
        borderwidth=3
        bordercolor="darkgreen"
>
        <itemtemplate>
            <%# "<B>Department:</B> " _
                & DataBinder.Eval(Container.DataItem, "DeptName") _
                & " - " _
                & DataBinder.Eval(Container.DataItem, "DeptEmail")
            %>
        </itemtemplate>
</asp:datalist>
</form>
```

The Label control simply displays an initial message to the visitor.

Take a close look at the DataList control's definition. You specify the name of the control through the ID property:

```
<asp:datalist
    id="dlDepts"
    runat="server"
```

The data displayed in the DataList control can be repeated with more than one record appearing on the same line. Use the RepeatColumns property to specify the number of records that should appear in a single row:

```
repeatcolumns=2
```

You use the RepeatDirection property to indicate whether the records are sequentially displayed horizontally or vertically. In this case, Horizontal is used:

```
repeatdirection="Horizontal"
```

That means that the second record will appear on the first line next to the first record. If you had used Vertical placement, the second record would be right below the first record.

The records displayed in the DataList control can be rendered within HTML Table tags or just as raw output using your own formatting. In this case, HTML Table tags will be used:

```
repeatlayout="table"
```

Use the value of Flow for this property if you want to completely supply your own formatting.

You specify whether you want gridlines to appear between records using the gridlines property:

```
gridlines="Both"
```

The property can also be set to None, Horizontal, or Vertical.

Additional basic formatting can be performed by setting the color, border, and font properties:

```
    backcolor="lightyellow"
    forecolor="darkred"
    borderwidth=3
    bordercolor="darkgreen"
>
```

Within the DataList control's definition, you need to, at a minimum, define the layout for the ItemTemplate. This template describes how each record should be displayed within the DataList control:

```
<itemtemplate>
```

Within that template, some heading text begins a record's format:

```
<%# "<B>Department:</B> " _
```

That is followed by the DeptName field from the bound database table:

```
& DataBinder.Eval(Container.DataItem, "DeptName") _
```

The fields are separated by some text:

```
& " - " _
```

Which is followed by the DeptEmail field:

```
    & DataBinder.Eval(Container.DataItem, "DeptEmail")
%>
```

The template definition can then be closed along with the DataList control's definition:

```
    </itemtemplate>
</asp:datalist>
```

When the page first loads, code that connects to the database and retrieves the data that is to be displayed needs to run:

```
Sub Page_Load(ByVal Sender as Object, ByVal E as EventArgs)
    If Not IsPostBack Then
        Dim DBConn as OleDbConnection
        Dim DBCommand As OleDbDataAdapter
        Dim DSPageData as New DataSet
        DBConn = New OleDbConnection( _
            "PROVIDER=Microsoft.Jet.OLEDB.4.0;" _
            & "DATA SOURCE=" _
            & Server.MapPath("/tt/C4/DepartmentDB.mdb;"))
        DBCommand = New OleDbDataAdapter _
            ("Select DeptName, DeptEmail " _
            & "From Departments " _
            & "Order By DeptName", DBConn)
        DBCommand.Fill(DSPageData, _
            "Departments")
        dlDepts.DataSource = _
            DSPageData.Tables("Departments").DefaultView
        dlDepts.DataBind()
    End If
End Sub
```

The code should only run the first time that the page is loaded:

```
If Not IsPostBack Then
```

If that is the case, you will need data objects to connect to the database and retrieve data:

```
Dim DBConn as OleDbConnection
Dim DBCommand As OleDbDataAdapter
Dim DSPageData as New DataSet
```

Next, you need to connect to your database, in this case an Access database located in the same folder as the ASP.NET page:

```
DBConn = New OleDbConnection( _
    "PROVIDER=Microsoft.Jet.OLEDB.4.0;" _
    & "DATA SOURCE=" _
    & Server.MapPath("/tt/C4/DepartmentDB.mdb;"))
```

Next, you need to retrieve the data from the database:

```
DBCommand = New OleDbDataAdapter _
    ("Select DeptName, DeptEmail " _
    & "From Departments " _
    & "Order By DeptName", DBConn)
```

That data is placed into a DataSet object:

```
DBCommand.Fill(DSPageData, _
    "Departments")
```

which is bound to the DataList control:

```
dlDepts.DataSource = _
    DSPageData.Tables("Departments").DefaultView
dlDepts.DataBind()
```

Using Templates with a DataList Control

The DataList control contains templates that you can use to format how the data is displayed. Take a look at this illustration.

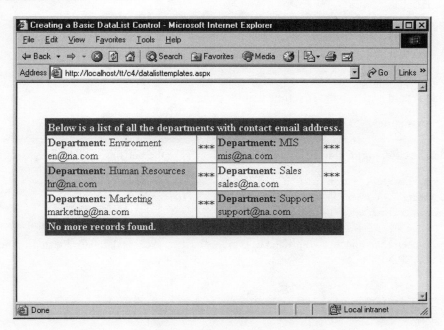

This screenshot shows the output of an ASP.NET page that uses a DataList control, which uses five different templates. The first row contains introductory information about the DataList. That is the HeaderTemplate. In the second row, the first record of data is displayed according to the format information in the ItemTemplate. The next record is displayed with different formatting, which is defined by the AlternatingItemTemplate.

Between each record you will note the use of "***" characters. This information is defined by the SeparatorTemplate. This template is where you would put any information that you wanted to appear between any records.

Then in the last row of the DataList is the FooterTemplate. Here you would place closing or summary information.

This technique shows you how to define these five templates.

USE IT   The ASP.NET page used in this example has a single control defined on its form, the DataList control:

```
<asp:datalist
    id="dlDepts"
    runat="server"
    repeatcolumns=2
    repeatdirection="Vertical"
    repeatlayout="table"
    gridlines="Both"
    backcolor="lightyellow"
    forecolor="darkred"
    borderwidth=3
    bordercolor="darkgreen"
>
    <headerstyle
        backcolor="darkred"
        forecolor="lightyellow"
        font-bold="true"
    />
    <headertemplate>
        Below is a list of all the <B>departments</B> with contact
        <B>email address</B>.
    </headertemplate>
    <itemtemplate>
        <%# "<B>Department:</B> " _
            & DataBinder.Eval(Container.DataItem, "DeptName") _
            & "<BR>" _
            & DataBinder.Eval(Container.DataItem, "DeptEmail")
        %>
    </itemtemplate>
    <alternatingitemstyle
```

```
            backcolor="lightgreen"
            forecolor="darkblue"
    />
    <alternatingitemtemplate>
        <%# "<B>Department:</B> " _
            & DataBinder.Eval(Container.DataItem, "DeptName") _
            & "<BR>" _
            & DataBinder.Eval(Container.DataItem, "DeptEmail")
        %>
    </alternatingitemtemplate>
    <separatortemplate>
        ***
    </separatortemplate>
    <footerstyle
        backcolor="darkred"
        forecolor="lightyellow"
        font-bold="true"
    />
    <footertemplate>
        No more records found.
    </footertemplate>
</asp:datalist>
```

When you specify templates for your DataList control, you can still specify the basic properties for the control as is done here:

```
<asp:datalist
    id="dlDepts"
    runat="server"
    repeatcolumns=2
    repeatdirection="Vertical"
    repeatlayout="table"
    gridlines="Both"
```

You can also specify the font, border, and color properties. These values become the default for all the template styles. So if you don't specify values for each template, the ones you define at the control level will be used:

```
    backcolor="lightyellow"
    forecolor="darkred"
    borderwidth=3
    bordercolor="darkgreen"
>
```

The sections can be defined in whatever order you prefer. Here, the header section is defined first. Within the HeaderStyle section you place any formatting that you want to use within this section:

```
<headerstyle
    backcolor="darkred"
    forecolor="lightyellow"
    font-bold="true"
/>
```

Then, between the tags of the HeaderTemplate, you place the HTML that you want to appear in the header row of the DataList control. Note that you can put whatever HTML you want there. You could place images or even form elements within that section:

```
<headertemplate>
    Below is a list of all the <B>departments</B> with contact
    <B>email address</B>.
</headertemplate>
```

Next, the item template is defined. This template is used for all records unless an AlternatingItemTemplate is defined. If that is the case, the template is used only for the odd numbered records:

```
<itemtemplate>
    <%# "<B>Department:</B> " _
        & DataBinder.Eval(Container.DataItem, "DeptName") _
        & "<BR>" _
        & DataBinder.Eval(Container.DataItem, "DeptEmail")
    %>
</itemtemplate>
```

Next, the style for the even numbered records is defined:

```
<alternatingitemstyle
    backcolor="lightgreen"
    forecolor="darkblue"
/>
```

as is the layout for that style:

```
<alternatingitemtemplate>
    <%# "<B>Department:</B> " _
        & DataBinder.Eval(Container.DataItem, "DeptName") _
        & "<BR>" _
        & DataBinder.Eval(Container.DataItem, "DeptEmail")
```

```
    %>
  </alternatingitemtemplate>
```

The SeparatorTemplate defines the HTML that you want to appear between each record of data:

```
  <separatortemplate>
      ***
  </separatortemplate>
```

Lastly, the footer section is defined. Here is the definition for the style to be used in that section:

```
  <footerstyle
      backcolor="darkred"
      forecolor="lightyellow"
      font-bold="true"
  />
```

That is followed by the HTML that you want placed into that section:

```
  <footertemplate>
      No more records found.
  </footertemplate>
</asp:datalist>
```

Removing Rows from a DataList Control

The DataList control can be used as a grid where visitors can add, update, and delete records right in the grid. The technique presented in this section shows you how to remove records from the DataList control.

USE IT This ASP.NET page displays a list of departments at a company in a DataList control. After the listing of each department, a link that says "Delete" appears. When visitors click that link, the selected record is removed from the database and the DataList control is updated.

The DataList control has this basic definition:

```
<asp:datalist
    id="dlDepts"
    runat="server"
    ondeletecommand="DataList_Delete"
    gridlines="Both"
    backcolor="lightyellow"
    forecolor="darkred"
>
```

Notice the OnDeleteCommand property. This value is the name of the procedure that you want to run when visitors select to delete a record.

Within the DataList control definition, the ItemTemplate has this definition:

```
<itemtemplate>
        <B>Department: </B>
        <asp:label
            id="lblID"
            runat="server"
            text='<%# DataBinder.Eval(Container.DataItem, "DeptID") %>'
            visible="False"
        />
        <%# DataBinder.Eval(Container.DataItem, "DeptName") _
            & " - " _
            & DataBinder.Eval(Container.DataItem, "DeptEmail")
        %>
        <asp:LinkButton
            id="butDelete"
            Text="Delete"
            CommandName="Delete"
            runat="server"
        />
    </itemtemplate>
```

Within that template, we first display the caption for the row:

```
<B>Department: </B>
```

That is followed by the definition of a Label control. Notice that it is set to invisible so visitors will not see the control. The Text property is set to the ID of the department record. This control will be referenced in code so that we can determine which record is to be deleted:

```
<asp:label
    id="lblID"
    runat="server"
    text='<%# DataBinder.Eval(Container.DataItem, "DeptID") %>'
    visible="False"
/>
```

That is followed by the other fields that are displayed to visitors for this record:

```
<%# DataBinder.Eval(Container.DataItem, "DeptName") _
    & " - " _
    & DataBinder.Eval(Container.DataItem, "DeptEmail")
%>
```

The data from the record is followed by a LinkButton control. This is the control that visitors click when they want to remove the record:

```
<asp:LinkButton
    id="butDelete"
    Text="Delete"
    CommandName="Delete"
    runat="server"
/>
```

In code, three procedures are defined. The first procedure is an internal procedure called by the other two procedures. That procedure merely connects to the database and populates the DataList control with the department records.

The second procedure fires the first time the page loads:

```
Sub Page_Load(ByVal Sender as Object, ByVal E as EventArgs)
    If Not IsPostBack Then
        BuildDataList
    End If
End Sub
```

The Page_Load procedure calls the internal procedure that populates the DataList control.

The third procedure on the page fires when a record in the DataList control is being deleted:

```
Sub DataList_Delete(sender As Object, e As DataListCommandEventArgs)
    Dim TheID as String
    TheID = CType(e.Item.FindControl("lblID"), Label).Text
    Dim DBConn as OleDbConnection
    Dim DBDelete As New OleDbCommand
    DBConn = New OleDbConnection( _
        "PROVIDER=Microsoft.Jet.OLEDB.4.0;" _
        & "DATA SOURCE=" _
        & Server.MapPath("/tt/C4/DepartmentDB.mdb;"))
    DBDelete.CommandText = "Delete From Departments Where " _
        & "DeptID = " & TheID
    DBDelete.Connection = DBConn
    DBDelete.Connection.Open
    DBDelete.ExecuteNonQuery()
    DBConn.Close
    BuildDataList
End Sub
```

First, you will need a variable to store the ID of the record to be deleted:

```
Dim TheID as String
```

We get the value for that ID by querying the value of the Label control that was used to store the ID in the DataList control:

```
TheID = CType(e.Item.FindControl("lblID"), Label).Text
```

Next, you need objects that allow you to connect to the Access database and delete a record:

```
Dim DBConn as OleDbConnection
Dim DBDelete As New OleDbCommand
```

First, you need to connect to the database:

```
DBConn = New OleDbConnection( _
    "PROVIDER=Microsoft.Jet.OLEDB.4.0;" _
    & "DATA SOURCE=" _
    & Server.MapPath("/tt/C4/DepartmentDB.mdb;"))
```

Then you need to place the SQL Delete query into a command object:

```
DBDelete.CommandText = "Delete From Departments Where " _
    & "DeptID = " & TheID
```

which is executed:

```
DBDelete.Connection = DBConn
DBDelete.Connection.Open
DBDelete.ExecuteNonQuery()
```

After deleting the record, you can close the database connection object:

```
DBConn.Close
```

and repopulate the DataGrid control:

```
BuildDataList
```

Editing Rows from a DataList Control

One of the nice features of the DataList Control is that it can be used to add, edit, and delete a record. In this section, you will see the technique required to edit a record. Editing a record is a two-step process. First, visitors select the record that they wish to update and it is placed in update mode. Then, they save the changes that they made to the record.

USE IT The basic definition for the DataList control when you want to allow for editing a record looks like this:

```
<asp:datalist
    id="dlDepts"
    runat="server"
    oneditcommand="DataList_Edit"
    onupdatecommand="DataList_Update"
    gridlines="Both"
    backcolor="lightyellow"
    forecolor="darkred"
>
```

Notice the two command properties. The first, OnEditCommand, is set to the name of the procedure that you want to run when visitors first go into Update mode:

```
oneditcommand="DataList_Edit"
```

The second property, OnUpdateCommand, is set to the name of the procedure that you want to run when visitors are done making changes to the record:

```
onupdatecommand="DataList_Update"
```

At a minimum, you will need to define two templates for the DataList control. The first is the ItemTemplate:

```
<itemtemplate>
        <B>Department: </B>
        <asp:label
            id="lblID"
            runat="server"
            text='<%# DataBinder.Eval(Container.DataItem, "DeptID") %>'
            visible="False"
        />
        <%# DataBinder.Eval(Container.DataItem, "DeptName") _
            & " - " _
            & DataBinder.Eval(Container.DataItem, "DeptEmail")
        %>
        <asp:LinkButton
            id="butEdit"
            Text="Edit"
            CommandName="Edit"
            runat="server"
        />
    </itemtemplate>
```

This is the basic template for all the records when they are not in edit mode. First, you place a description of the record:

```
<B>Department: </B>
```

That is followed by an invisible Label control, which stores the ID of the current record so that we can reference it in code:

```
<asp:label
    id="lblID"
    runat="server"
    text='<%# DataBinder.Eval(Container.DataItem, "DeptID") %>'
    visible="False"
/>
```

That is followed by the other fields in the record:

```
<%# DataBinder.Eval(Container.DataItem, "DeptName") _
    & " - " _
    & DataBinder.Eval(Container.DataItem, "DeptEmail")
%>
```

And lastly, you need to define a button that visitors can click to put themselves in Update mode:

```
<asp:LinkButton
    id="butEdit"
    Text="Edit"
    CommandName="Edit"
    runat="server"
/>
```

Once visitors are in Update mode, you need a way for them to make changes to the record. In other words, the fields that they can change need to be in TextBox controls. Therefore, you need to define a different template used only for the record that is being updated:

```
<edititemtemplate>
        <asp:label
            id="lblID"
            runat="server"
            text='<%# DataBinder.Eval(Container.DataItem, "DeptID") %>'
            visible="False"
        />
        Name:
        <asp:textbox
            id="txtName"
```

```
            text='<%# DataBinder.Eval(Container.DataItem, "DeptName") %>'
            runat="server"
        />
        <BR>
        Email:
        <asp:textbox
            id="txtEmail"
            text='<%# DataBinder.Eval(Container.DataItem, "DeptEmail") %>'
            runat="server"
        />
        <BR>
         <asp:LinkButton
             id="butUpdate"
              Text="Update"
              CommandName="Update"
              runat="server"
          />
    </edititemtemplate>
```

As with the ItemTemplate, you first define an invisible Label control that will store the ID of the record being edited:

```
<asp:label
    id="lblID"
    runat="server"
    text='<%# DataBinder.Eval(Container.DataItem, "DeptID") %>'
    visible="False"
/>
```

Next, you need to define a TextBox control that allows visitors to edit the name of the department:

```
<asp:textbox
    id="txtName"
    text='<%# DataBinder.Eval(Container.DataItem, "DeptName") %>'
    runat="server"
/>
```

The same is done for the department e-mail address:

```
<asp:textbox
    id="txtEmail"
    text='<%# DataBinder.Eval(Container.DataItem, "DeptEmail") %>'
    runat="server"
/>
```

You also need to define a button that visitors can click when they are ready to save their changes:

```
<asp:LinkButton
    id="butUpdate"
    Text="Update"
    CommandName="Update"
    runat="server"
/>
```

The code on the page is contained within four procedures. The first procedure is called by two of the other procedures and merely connects to the database and populates the DataList control.

The next procedure fires when the page first loads:

```
Sub Page_Load(ByVal Sender as Object, ByVal E as EventArgs)
    If Not IsPostBack Then
        BuildDataList
    End If
End Sub
```

It simply calls the internal procedure to populate the DataList control.

The third procedure fires when visitors select a record that they want to edit:

```
Sub DataList_Edit(sender As Object, e As DataListCommandEventArgs)
    dlDepts.EditItemIndex = CInt(e.Item.ItemIndex)
    BuildDataList
End Sub
```

This procedure marks that record as the current edit record so that it will appear through the EditItemTemplate.

The fourth procedure saves the changes made to the record:

```
Sub DataList_Update(sender As Object, e As DataListCommandEventArgs)
    Dim TheID as String
    Dim TheName as String
    Dim TheEmail as String
    TheID = CType(e.Item.FindControl("lblID"), Label).Text
    TheName = CType(e.Item.FindControl("txtName"), TextBox).Text
    TheEmail = CType(e.Item.FindControl("txtEmail"), TextBox).Text
    Dim DBConn as OleDbConnection
    Dim DBUpdate As New OleDbCommand
    DBConn = New OleDbConnection( _
        "PROVIDER=Microsoft.Jet.OLEDB.4.0;" _
        & "DATA SOURCE=" _
        & Server.MapPath("/tt/C4/DepartmentDB.mdb;"))
```

```
        DBUpdate.CommandText = "Update Departments set " _
            & "DeptName = '" & Replace(TheName, "'", "''") & "', " _
            & "DeptEmail = '" & Replace(TheEmail, "'", "''") & "' " _
            & "Where DeptID = " & TheID
        DBUpdate.Connection = DBConn
        DBUpdate.Connection.Open
        DBUpdate.ExecuteNonQuery()
        DBConn.Close
        dlDepts.EditItemIndex = -1
        BuildDataList
End Sub
```

First, you can store the values for the ID, name, and e-mail address for the edited record into local variables:

```
Dim TheID as String
Dim TheName as String
Dim TheEmail as String
TheID = CType(e.Item.FindControl("lblID"), Label).Text
TheName = CType(e.Item.FindControl("txtName"), TextBox).Text
TheEmail = CType(e.Item.FindControl("txtEmail"), TextBox).Text
```

Then, you need to define data objects:

```
Dim DBConn as OleDbConnection
Dim DBUpdate As New OleDbCommand
```

and connect to the database:

```
DBConn = New OleDbConnection( _
    "PROVIDER=Microsoft.Jet.OLEDB.4.0;" _
    & "DATA SOURCE=" _
    & Server.MapPath("/tt/C4/DepartmentDB.mdb;"))
```

Next, you need to supply the SQL syntax for updating the changed record:

```
DBUpdate.CommandText = "Update Departments set " _
    & "DeptName = '" & Replace(TheName, "'", "''") & "', " _
    & "DeptEmail = '" & Replace(TheEmail, "'", "''") & "' " _
    & "Where DeptID = " & TheID
```

That record is then saved in the database:

```
DBUpdate.Connection = DBConn
DBUpdate.Connection.Open
```

```
DBUpdate.ExecuteNonQuery()
DBConn.Close
```

Next, you need to place all the records in the DataList back in standard mode as defined by the ItemTemplate:

```
dlDepts.EditItemIndex = -1
```

and rebuild the DataList control:

```
BuildDataList
```

Adding Rows from a DataList Control

The DataList control allows you to directly edit and delete records that are in its list. But you can't use it directly to add records. Instead you need to externally add a record to the table and then place that new record in an Update mode. This technique shows you how to do that.

USE IT   This technique builds on the ASP.NET page presented in the previous tip. Please refer to that tip for an understanding of the update code. This page, though, adds one control and one procedure to that page:

```
<asp:inkbutton
    id="butAdd"
    text="Add"
    commandname="Add"
    oncommand="CommandAdd_Click"
    runat="server"
/>
```

The control is a LinkButton control that appears after the DataList control on the bottom of the page. The control displays the text "Add" and calls the following procedure to add a new record to the database and display it in the DataList control:

```
Sub CommandAdd_Click(Sender As Object, E As CommandEventArgs)
    Dim DBConn as OleDbConnection
    Dim DBAdd As New OleDbCommand
    DBConn = New OleDbConnection( _
        "PROVIDER=Microsoft.Jet.OLEDB.4.0;" _
        & "DATA SOURCE=" _
        & Server.MapPath("/tt/C4/DepartmentDB.mdb;"))
    DBAdd.CommandText = "Insert Into Departments (DeptName) " _
        & "values (' ')"
```

```
    DBAdd.Connection = DBConn
    DBAdd.Connection.Open
    DBAdd.ExecuteNonQuery()
    DBConn.Close
    dlDepts.EditItemIndex = 0
    BuildDataList
End Sub
```

First in this procedure, you need to add a record to the database. Therefore, you will need a connection and command object:

```
Dim DBConn as OleDbConnection
Dim DBAdd As New OleDbCommand
```

You then need to connect to the database:

```
DBConn = New OleDbConnection( _
    "PROVIDER=Microsoft.Jet.OLEDB.4.0;" _
    & "DATA SOURCE=" _
    & Server.MapPath("/tt/C4/DepartmentDB.mdb;"))
```

and insert a new blank record:

```
DBAdd.CommandText = "Insert Into Departments (DeptName) " _
    & "values (' ')"
DBAdd.Connection = DBConn
DBAdd.Connection.Open
DBAdd.ExecuteNonQuery()
```

After adding the new record you can close the database:

```
DBConn.Close
```

Since the records in the DataList control are sorted by the name of the department, this new record will appear first in the DataList control. Therefore, you need to place that first record of the DataList control in Update mode:

```
dlDepts.EditItemIndex = 0
```

and call the internal procedure to populate the DataList control:

```
BuildDataList
```

The effect of this code is that a new blank row is added to the database control. That blank row appears at the top of the DataList control and the record appears to visitors in Update mode so that they can enter their values.

Creating a Basic Repeater Control

The Repeater control is the most basic data listing control. Unlike the DataList or DataGrid controls, it does not have any style or formatting properties. If you wish to format the data displayed in a Repeater control you can use HTML tags defined within its templates.

This technique shows you how to create a basic Repeater control using just one template. The data displayed in the Repeater control comes from an Access database.

USE IT   This technique uses department records from an Access database. The ASP.NET form on this page contains just two controls as displayed here:

```
<form runat="server">
<BR><BR>
<asp:Label
    id="lblMessage"
    Font-Size="12pt"
    Font-Bold="True"
    Font-Name="Lucida Console"
    text="Below is a list of all the departments with contact
        email address"
    runat="server"
/>
<BR><BR>
<asp:repeater
    id="repDepts"
    runat="server"
>

    <itemtemplate>
        <%# "<B>Department:</B> " _
            & DataBinder.Eval(Container.DataItem, "DeptName") _
            & " - " _
            & DataBinder.Eval(Container.DataItem, "DeptEmail")
        %>
        <BR>
    </itemtemplate>
</asp:repeater>
</form>
```

The first is a Label control that describes the data displayed in the Repeater control.

After that, the Repeater control is defined. The name of the Repeater control is set through the ID property:

```
<asp:repeater
    id="repDepts"
```

```
        runat="server"
>
```

Within the Repeater control's definition you need to supply the format for the ItemTemplate. This template describes how the data should be displayed:

```
<itemtemplate>
```

First, some opening text is displayed:

```
<%# "<B>Department:</B> " _
```

Then fields from the database are displayed:

```
    & DataBinder.Eval(Container.DataItem, "DeptName") _
    & " - " _
    & DataBinder.Eval(Container.DataItem, "DeptEmail")
%>
```

Since the control does not supply any internal separation between records, here a line break is written to the browser:

```
        <BR>
    </itemtemplate>
</asp:repeater>
```

The code on the page is defined within a single procedure that fires when the page loads.

```
Sub Page_Load(ByVal Sender as Object, ByVal E as EventArgs)
    If Not IsPostBack Then
        Dim DBConn as OleDbConnection
        Dim DBCommand As OleDbDataAdapter
        Dim DSPageData as New DataSet
        DBConn = New OleDbConnection( _
            "PROVIDER=Microsoft.Jet.OLEDB.4.0;" _
            & "DATA SOURCE=" _
            & Server.MapPath("/tt/C4/DepartmentDB.mdb;"))
        DBCommand = New OleDbDataAdapter _
            ("Select DeptName, DeptEmail " _
            & "From Departments " _
            & "Order By DeptName", DBConn)
        DBCommand.Fill(DSPageData, _
            "Departments")
        repDepts.DataSource = _
            DSPageData.Tables("Departments").DefaultView
        repDepts.DataBind()
```

```
      End If
End Sub
```

The code should only run the first time the page loads:

```
If Not IsPostBack Then
```

If that is the case, you need to connect to the Access database:

```
Dim DBConn as OleDbConnection
Dim DBCommand As OleDbDataAdapter
Dim DSPageData as New DataSet
DBConn = New OleDbConnection( _
    "PROVIDER=Microsoft.Jet.OLEDB.4.0;" _
    & "DATA SOURCE=" _
    & Server.MapPath("/tt/C4/DepartmentDB.mdb;"))
And retrieve the department data:
DBCommand = New OleDbDataAdapter _
    ("Select DeptName, DeptEmail " _
    & "From Departments " _
    & "Order By DeptName", DBConn)
```

That data is placed into the DataSet object:

```
DBCommand.Fill(DSPageData, _
    "Departments")
```

which is bound to the Repeater control:

```
repDepts.DataSource = _
    DSPageData.Tables("Departments").DefaultView
repDepts.DataBind()
```

Using Templates with a Repeater Control

The Repeater control contains different templates that you can use to describe the appearance of different sections of the control. This technique shows you how to use five of those templates.

 This ASP.NET page displays department information records from an Access database through a Repeater control. That control is the single control defined on the page:

```
<asp:repeater
    id="repDepts"
    runat="server"
```

```
>
    <headertemplate>
        <I>Below is a list of all the <B>departments</B> with contact
        <B>email address</B>.</I><BR><BR>
    </headertemplate>
    <itemtemplate>
        <%# "<B>Department:</B> " _
            & DataBinder.Eval(Container.DataItem, "DeptName") _
            & " - " _
            & DataBinder.Eval(Container.DataItem, "DeptEmail")
        %>
        <BR>
    </itemtemplate>
    <alternatingitemtemplate>
        <I><%# "<B>Department:</B> " _
            & DataBinder.Eval(Container.DataItem, "DeptName") _
            & " - " _
            & DataBinder.Eval(Container.DataItem, "DeptEmail")
        %></I>
        <BR>
    </alternatingitemtemplate>
    <separatortemplate>
        <HR>
    </separatortemplate>
    <footertemplate>
        <BR><I>All records have been displayed.</I>
    </footertemplate>
</asp:repeater>
```

> ▶ **QUICK TIP**
>
> *You can define the templates in any order that you prefer, but you may find that your code is more readable if you define them in the order presented within this technique.*

The first template defined is the HeaderTemplate. This template appears before any of the data is presented. Here some opening text is displayed. Remember that the control does not generate any internal line breaks so you will need to include them yourself within the template's definitions:

```
<headertemplate>
    <I>Below is a list of all the <B>departments</B> with contact
    <B>email address</B>.</I><BR><BR>
</headertemplate>
```

The second template defined is the ItemTemplate. This template contains the formatting instructions for how the data is displayed within the Repeater control. If the AlternatingItemTemplate is not defined, this template is used for all records. Otherwise, this template is used for the odd numbered records:

```
<itemtemplate>
    <%# "<B>Department:</B> " _
        & DataBinder.Eval(Container.DataItem, "DeptName") _
        & " - " _
        & DataBinder.Eval(Container.DataItem, "DeptEmail")
    %>
    <BR>
</itemtemplate>
```

The third template defined is the AlternatingItemTemplate. This template contains formatting instructions for how the even numbered records are displayed. Supplying this template makes your data more readable to the visitor since every other record can have a slightly different appearance:

```
<alternatingitemtemplate>
    <I><%# "<B>Department:</B> " _
    & DataBinder.Eval(Container.DataItem, "DeptName") _
    & " - " _
    & DataBinder.Eval(Container.DataItem, "DeptEmail")
    %></I>
    <BR>
</alternatingitemtemplate>
```

The SeparatorTemplate defines what you want to appear between each record in the Repeater control. In this case, a horizontal line will be displayed:

```
<separatortemplate>
    <HR>
</separatortemplate>
```

The last template defined is the FooterTemplate. This templates contains the HTML that you want to appear after all the records in the DataList control have been presented:

```
<footertemplate>
    <BR><I>All records have been displayed.</I>
</footertemplate>
```

Creating a Basic DataGrid Control

If you need to display a list of records of data, probably the easiest control to use is the DataGrid control. The DataGrid control can be set up so that it automatically displays all the fields and records in a bound table without your having to specify any formatting information. The resulting rendered HTML output is a highly structured HTML table.

The technique presented in this section shows you how to define this type of basic DataGrid control.

USE IT   The following ASP.NET page displays employee data from an Access database. All the fields and all the records are displayed through a DataGrid control. That control and one other are the only controls defined on the ASP.NET page:

```
<form runat="server">
<BR><BR>
<asp:Label
    id="lblMessage"
    Font-Size="12pt"
    Font-Bold="True"
    Font-Name="Lucida Console"
    text="Employee List"
    runat="server"
/>
<BR><BR>
<asp:datagrid
    id="dgEmps"
    runat="server"
    autogeneratecolumns="True"
>
</asp:datagrid>
</form>
```

The first control is a Label control that displays descriptive text.

After that, the DataGrid control is defined. You supply the name of the control through the ID property:

```
<asp:datagrid
    id="dgEmps"
    runat="server"
```

Since you want the control to automatically generate all the columns in the table, the AutoGenerateColumns property needs to be set to True:

```
    autogeneratecolumns="True"
>
```

If the property is set to False, you would need to define the structure for each field to be displayed.

That is followed by the closing definition tag for the DataGrid control:

```
</asp:datagrid>
```

Only one procedure is defined on this ASP.NET page. That procedure runs when the page loads and it populates the DataGrid control:

```
Sub Page_Load(ByVal Sender as Object, ByVal E as EventArgs)
    If Not IsPostBack Then
        Dim DBConn as OleDbConnection
        Dim DBCommand As OleDbDataAdapter
        Dim DSPageData as New DataSet
        DBConn = New OleDbConnection( _
            "PROVIDER=Microsoft.Jet.OLEDB.4.0;" _
            & "DATA SOURCE=" _
            & Server.MapPath("/tt/C4/DGDB.mdb;"))
        DBCommand = New OleDbDataAdapter _
            ("Select * " _
            & "From Employees " _
            & "Order By LastName, FirstName", DBConn)
        DBCommand.Fill(DSPageData, _
            "Employees")
        dgEmps.DataSource = _
            DSPageData.Tables("Employees").DefaultView
        dgEmps.DataBind()
    End If
End Sub
```

You only want to run the code the first time that the page loads:

```
If Not IsPostBack Then
```

If that is the case, you will need data objects so that you can connect to the Access database and retrieve data:

```
Dim DBConn as OleDbConnection
Dim DBCommand As OleDbDataAdapter
Dim DSPageData as New DataSet
```

First, you need to connect to the database:

```
DBConn = New OleDbConnection( _
    "PROVIDER=Microsoft.Jet.OLEDB.4.0;" _
    & "DATA SOURCE=" _
    & Server.MapPath("/tt/C4/DGDB.mdb;"))
```

Next, you need to retrieve the records from the Employees table:

```
DBCommand = New OleDbDataAdapter _
    ("Select * " _
```

```
& "From Employees " _
& "Order By LastName, FirstName", DBConn)
```

> ### QUICK TIP
>
> *If you don't want to retrieve all the fields and all the records, just specify the field names you want in the Select statement and add a Where clause to limit the records returned.*

The data returned is placed into a DataSet object:

```
DBCommand.Fill(DSPageData, _
    "Employees")
```

That object is bound to the DataGrid control:

```
dgEmps.DataSource = _
    DSPageData.Tables("Employees").DefaultView
dgEmps.DataBind()
```

Creating BoundColumn Controls in a DataGrid Control

You can let a DataGrid control automatically display the columns in the bound records but you may find that you need to have more control over the format of the data. For example, when you let the DataGrid control automatically display the columns, the headers for the columns come from the names of the fields that they are displaying, and sometimes field names are not very readable to the end-user.

Another problem with letting the DataGrid define columns for you is that the DataGrid does not provide much formatting for dates and numbers. To solve both these problems, you need to define your own columns. The technique in this section shows you how to create BoundColumn controls within a DataGrid control.

USE IT   The ASP.NET page presented in this section displays employee records from an Access database. The records are displayed through BoundColumn controls in a DataGrid control. The following controls are defined within that ASP.NET page:

```
<form runat="server">
<BR><BR>
<asp:Label
    id="lblMessage"
    Font-Size="12pt"
    Font-Bold="True"
    Font-Name="Lucida Console"
    text="Employee List"
```

```
        runat="server"
/>
<BR><BR>
<asp:datagrid
    id="dgEmps"
    runat="server"
    autogeneratecolumns="false"
>
    <columns>
        <asp:boundcolumn
            HeaderText="Last Name"
            DataField="LastName"
        />
        <asp:boundcolumn
            HeaderText="First Name"
            DataField="FirstName"
        />
        <asp:boundcolumn
            HeaderText="Birth Date"
            DataField="BirthDate"
            DataFormatString="{0:d}"
        />
        <asp:boundcolumn
            HeaderText="Salary"
            DataField="Salary"
            DataFormatString="{0:c}"
        />
    </columns>
</asp:datagrid>
</form>
```

The first control is a Label control that displays some descriptive text.

After that, the DataGrid control is defined. Notice that the AutoGenerateColumns property is set to False. This means that you need to define your own controls:

```
<asp:datagrid
    id="dgEmps"
    runat="server"
    autogeneratecolumns="false"
>
```

The columns that you define are placed within a Columns tag:

```
<columns>
```

The first column is then defined:

```
<asp:boundcolumn
```

The HeaderText property is set to the text that you want to appear in the header for the column:

```
HeaderText="Last Name"
```

The DataField property is set to the name of the field that should be displayed in this column:

```
    DataField="LastName"
/>
```

The second BoundColumn control will display the FirstName field:

```
<asp:boundcolumn
    HeaderText="First Name"
    DataField="FirstName"
/>
```

The third column will display the BirthDate field:

```
<asp:boundcolumn
    HeaderText="Birth Date"
    DataField="BirthDate"
```

Notice the DataFormatString property. This value formats the field so that just the date portion is displayed:

```
    DataFormatString="{0:d}"
/>
```

The fourth column displays the Salary field:

```
<asp:boundcolumn
    HeaderText="Salary"
    DataField="Salary"
```

which is formatted as currency:

```
    DataFormatString="{0:c}"
/>
```

When the page loads, code that populates the records bound to the DataGrid control runs:

```
Sub Page_Load(ByVal Sender as Object, ByVal E as EventArgs)
    If Not IsPostBack Then
```

```
        Dim DBConn as OleDbConnection
        Dim DBCommand As OleDbDataAdapter
        Dim DSPageData as New DataSet
        DBConn = New OleDbConnection( _
            "PROVIDER=Microsoft.Jet.OLEDB.4.0;" _
            & "DATA SOURCE=" _
            & Server.MapPath("/tt/C4/DGDB.mdb;"))
        DBCommand = New OleDbDataAdapter _
            ("Select * " _
            & "From Employees " _
            & "Order By LastName, FirstName", DBConn)
        DBCommand.Fill(DSPageData, _
            "Employees")
        dgEmps.DataSource = _
            DSPageData.Tables("Employees").DefaultView
        dgEmps.DataBind()
    End If
End Sub
```

The code only runs when the page first loads:

```
If Not IsPostBack Then
```

If that is the case, you need data objects:

```
Dim DBConn as OleDbConnection
Dim DBCommand As OleDbDataAdapter
Dim DSPageData as New DataSet
```

You start by connecting to the database:

```
DBConn = New OleDbConnection( _
    "PROVIDER=Microsoft.Jet.OLEDB.4.0;" _
    & "DATA SOURCE=" _
    & Server.MapPath("/tt/C4/DGDB.mdb;"))
```

and you retrieve the employee data:

```
DBCommand = New OleDbDataAdapter _
    ("Select * " _
    & "From Employees " _
    & "Order By LastName, FirstName", DBConn)
DBCommand.Fill(DSPageData, _
    "Employees")
```

which is bound to the DataGrid control:

```
dgEmps.DataSource = _
    DSPageData.Tables("Employees").DefaultView
dgEmps.DataBind()
```

Using a HyperLinkColumn Control in a DataGrid Control

DataGrid controls provide an easy way that you can display table-type information. When you use a DataGrid control by generating your own column listings, the power and flexibility of the control increase. One of those types of columns is a HyperLinkColumn control. HyperLinkColumn controls provide a way for you to place data in a column that links to some other source.

For example, you may use a DataGrid to display links to other sites. You could use the HyperLinkColumn control in a DataGrid control to display the name of the site, and when visitors click on that name, they are taken to that site.

Or maybe you are displaying employee data and one of the fields being displayed is the employee's e-mail address. You could set that field up as a HyperLinkColumn control so that visitors could simply click on that address to open a new e-mail addressed to that employee.

The technique presented in this section of the chapter shows you how to do that.

USE IT   This ASP.NET connects to an Access database and displays an employee's name along with his or her e-mail address. The page uses BoundColumn and HyperLinkColumn controls of the DataGrid control.

Two top-level controls are defined on this page:

```
<form runat="server">
<BR><BR>
<asp:Label
    id="lblMessage"
    Font-Size="12pt"
    Font-Bold="True"
    Font-Name="Lucida Console"
    text="Employee List"
    runat="server"
/>
<BR><BR>
<asp:datagrid
    id="dgEmps"
    runat="server"
    autogeneratecolumns="false"
>
    <columns>
        <asp:boundcolumn
```

```
        HeaderText="Full Name"
        DataField="FullName"
    />
    <asp:HyperLinkColumn
        HeaderText="Email Address"
        DataNavigateUrlField="EmailAddress"
        DataNavigateUrlFormatString="mailto:{0}"
        DataTextField="EmailAddress"
    />
    </columns>
</asp:datagrid>
</form>
```

The first control is a Label control that defines the data being displayed. Then the DataGrid is defined. Notice that the AutoGenerateColumns property is set to False:

```
autogeneratecolumns="false"
```

This means that you need to provide controls for all the columns that you want to display. The first column defined is for the FullName field:

```
<asp:boundcolumn
    HeaderText="Full Name"
    DataField="FullName"
/>
```

The next column is defined through the HyperLinkColumn control:

```
<asp:HyperLinkColumn
```

The column will have this text in the header:

```
HeaderText="Email Address"
```

The EmailAddress field will be used in the HyperLink:

```
DataNavigateUrlField="EmailAddress"
```

The data in that field will replace the "{0}" text in the following property:

```
DataNavigateUrlFormatString="mailto:{0}"
```

The field that visitors will see is the EmailAddress field:

```
DataTextField="EmailAddress"
```

> ## QUICK TIP
>
> *You can specify two different fields for the data fields in the HyperLinkColumn control. For example, if you wanted to list the name of a Web site but link to the address of that Web site when clicked, you need to use two different fields. In that case, you would place the field name for the Web site in the DataTextField property and would place the field that stored the URL to the site in the DataNavigateUrlField.*

One procedure is defined on this page. That procedure populates the DataGrid control.

```
Sub Page_Load(ByVal Sender as Object, ByVal E as EventArgs)
    If Not IsPostBack Then
        Dim DBConn as OleDbConnection
        Dim DBCommand As OleDbDataAdapter
        Dim DSPageData as New DataSet
        DBConn = New OleDbConnection( _
            "PROVIDER=Microsoft.Jet.OLEDB.4.0;" _
            & "DATA SOURCE=" _
            & Server.MapPath("/tt/C4/DGDB.mdb;"))
        DBCommand = New OleDbDataAdapter _
            ("Select LastName + ', ' + FirstName " _
            & "as FullName, EmailAddress " _
            & "From Employees " _
            & "Order By LastName, FirstName", DBConn)
        DBCommand.Fill(DSPageData, _
            "Employees")
        dgEmps.DataSource = _
            DSPageData.Tables("Employees").DefaultView
        dgEmps.DataBind()
    End If
End Sub
```

The code should only run when the page loads:

```
If Not IsPostBack Then
```

If that is the case, you need data objects:

```
Dim DBConn as OleDbConnection
Dim DBCommand As OleDbDataAdapter
Dim DSPageData as New DataSet
```

And you need to connect to the Access database:

```
DBConn = New OleDbConnection( _
    "PROVIDER=Microsoft.Jet.OLEDB.4.0;" _
    & "DATA SOURCE=" _
    & Server.MapPath("/tt/C4/DGDB.mdb;"))
```

Then you need to retrieve the employee's name and e-mail address from the database. Note that the FullName field is derived by combining the first and last names of the employee:

```
DBCommand = New OleDbDataAdapter _
    ("Select LastName + ', ' + FirstName " _
    & "as FullName, EmailAddress " _
    & "From Employees " _
    & "Order By LastName, FirstName", DBConn)
```

Those records are placed into a DataSet object:

```
DBCommand.Fill(DSPageData, _
    "Employees")
```

which is bound to the DataGrid control:

```
dgEmps.DataSource = _
    DSPageData.Tables("Employees").DefaultView
dgEmps.DataBind()
```

> **QUICK TIP**
>
> *The HyperLinkColumn column control contains an additional property called Target. Setting the property to this value: Target="_blank" would cause a new browser window to open to display the link.*

Using a ButtonColumn Control in a DataGrid Control

One of the column types that you can place into a DataGrid control is a ButtonColumn control. The ButtonColumn control is rendered as a link or a button in each row of the DataGrid. You use the column to allow visitors to take some action against a specific record in a row. When the button is clicked, your procedure fires and the row of data for that button passes to it. This technique shows you how to define and use a ButtonColumn control.

USE IT   The ASP.NET page presented in this chapter displays the names of employees in a DataGrid control along with a button for each row of data. When the button is clicked, the rest of the data pertaining to the record clicked is displayed in a Label control.

The following controls are defined within the ASP.NET page:

```
<form runat="server">
<BR><BR>
<asp:Label
    id="lblMessage"
    runat="server"
/>
<BR><BR>
<asp:datagrid
    id="dgEmps"
    runat="server"
    autogeneratecolumns="false"
    onitemcommand="Click_Grid"
>
    <columns>
        <asp:boundcolumn
            HeaderText="Full Name"
            DataField="FullName"
        />
        <asp:boundcolumn
            DataField="OtherInfo"
            Visible=False
        />
        <asp:buttoncolumn
            HeaderText="Other Fields"
            ButtonType="PushButton"
            Text="Click to Display Other Fields"
        />
    </columns>
</asp:datagrid>
```

The Label control will display the additional information about the selected record.

Take a look at the DataGrid control's definition. The AutoGenerateColumns property is set to False so you need to define your own columns:

```
autogeneratecolumns="false"
```

Since the DataGrid will contain a ButtonColumn control, you need to define the name of the procedure that you want to run when the button is clicked. You do that through the OnItemCommand property:

```
onitemcommand="Click_Grid"
```

Three columns are defined in the DataGrid control. The first will display the full name of the employee:

```
<asp:boundcolumn
    HeaderText="Full Name"
    DataField="FullName"
/>
```

The second column is a hidden column; visitors will not see it. It contains all the other data for the record:

```
<asp:boundcolumn
    DataField="OtherInfo"
    Visible=False
/>
```

The data in that column will be displayed when the button is clicked.

The third column displays the button for each row of data:

```
<asp:buttoncolumn
```

This text will appear in the header for the column:

```
HeaderText="Other Fields"
```

And the button will be a standard push button:

```
ButtonType="PushButton"
```

You can also place the value LinkButton in this column to display a link instead of a button. But either way, the action is the same.

On the face of the button, this text will appear:

```
Text="Click to Display Other Fields"
```

Two procedures can be found on this page. The first one connects to Access and displays the data in the DataGrid.

The second procedure fires when one of the buttons in the DataGrid is clicked:

```
Sub Click_Grid(ByVal Sender as Object, ByVal E as DataGridCommandEventArgs)
    lblMessage.Text = E.Item.Cells(1).Text
End Sub
```

Passed into the procedure through the DataGridCommandEventArgs parameter is all the data for the row that was selected. Through the Cells collection we display to visitors the contents of the other fields stored in the OtherInfo column through the Label control's Text property:

```
lblMessage.Text = E.Item.Cells(1).Text
```

Using Templates with the DataGrid Control

The DataGrid control contains templates that you can use to control the output of the rows in the DataGrid control. Using these templates can effectively make your data more meaningful and easier to read. This technique shows you how to use four of the DataGrid control templates.

 The following ASP.NET page displays employee data in a DataGrid control. The control uses four templates to format the data and the DataGrid itself. Take a look at this illustration.

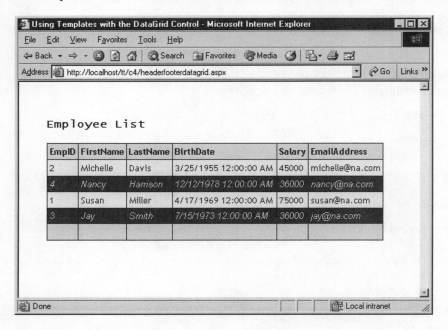

The first row of information contains the headers for the columns. The row can be formatted using the HeaderStyle property. The second row in the DataGrid contains the first row of data; that information can be formatted through the ItemStyle property. Each odd-numbered record uses that style.

The third row of the DataGrid control displays the second row of data. That row of data is formatted through the AlternatingItemStyle property. All the even-numbered records are formatted using this template. If you don't supply any style information for this template, the ItemStyle property is used.

The bottom row of the DataGrid control is formatted through the FooterStyle property. By default, this row is not displayed.

The following code shows the DataGrid control that was used to render this output.

```
<asp:datagrid
    id="dgEmps"
    runat="server"
```

```
        autogeneratecolumns="True"
        bordercolor="black"
        cellpadding=3
        cellspacing="0"
        font-name="Trebuchet MS"
        font-size="10pt"
        forecolor="Black"
        backcolor="Beige"
        showheader="True"
        showfooter="True"
        alternatingitemstyle-forecolor="Cornsilk"
        alternatingitemstyle-backcolor="DarkBlue"
        alternatingitemstyle-font-name="Arial"
        alternatingitemstyle-font-italic="True"
        headerstyle-backcolor="Burlywood"
        headerstyle-font-bold="True"
        footerstyle-backcolor="Burlywood"
        footerstyle-font-bold="True"
>
</asp:datagrid>
```

The name of the control is set through the ID property:

```
id="dgEmps"
With this grid the columns are being automatically generated:
autogeneratecolumns="True"
```

Through the base properties of the DataGrid control, you can set the border and spacing properties:

```
bordercolor="black"
cellpadding=3
cellspacing="0"
```

Next, font and color properties are set. These properties will be used unless they are overwritten with style properties for one of the templates. With this DataGrid control no style properties are set for the ItemStyle. Therefore, these default settings will be used for that template:

```
font-name="Trebuchet MS"
font-size="10pt"
forecolor="Black"
backcolor="Beige"
```

Next, you instruct the compiler to display both the header and footer sections:

```
showheader="True"
showfooter="True"
```

After that, the colors and font properties for the AlternatingItemStyle are set:

```
alternatingitemstyle-forecolor="Cornsilk"
alternatingitemstyle-backcolor="DarkBlue"
alternatingitemstyle-font-name="Arial"
alternatingitemstyle-font-italic="True"
```

That is followed by setting the style for the header:

```
headerstyle-backcolor="Burlywood"
headerstyle-font-bold="True"
```

and the footer template follows that:

```
footerstyle-backcolor="Burlywood"
footerstyle-font-bold="True"
```

Notice the use of the "-" character instead of "." to define the sub-properties of these templates. You can use this annotation to define the color and font properties of all the styles in the DataGrid control.

Sorting a DataGrid Control

In addition to how easy the DataGrid control makes displaying data, it also makes sorting data in the DataGrid relatively easy. Using the DataGrid control, the column headers can be turned into links that when clicked sort the data according to the column that was clicked. The technique presented in this section shows you how to use this functionality.

USE IT The ASP.NET page presented in this section displays employee records. The column headers display the names of the fields in each column as a link. When visitors click one of the links, the data is sorted by that field.

The DataGrid control on this page has the following definition:

```
<asp:datagrid
    id="dgEmps"
    allowsorting="True"
    onsortcommand="Sort_Grid"
    autogeneratecolumns="false"
    runat="server"
>
    <columns>
        <asp:boundcolumn
            headertext="Last Name"
            datafield="LastName"
            sortexpression="LastName"
```

```
            />
        <asp:boundcolumn
            headertext="First Name"
            datafield="FirstName"
            sortexpression="FirstName"
        />
        <asp:boundcolumn
            headertext="Birth Date"
            datafield="BirthDate"
            DataFormatString="{0:d}"
            sortexpression="BirthDate"
        />
        <asp:boundcolumn
            headertext="Salary"
            datafield="Salary"
            DataFormatString="{0:c}"
            sortexpression="Salary"
        />
    </columns>
</asp:datagrid>
```

Notice these two properties of the DataGrid control:

```
allowsorting="True"
onsortcommand="Sort_Grid"
```

The first tells the compiler that you want to allow the visitor to sort. Setting this property to True turns the column headers into links.

The second property stores the name of the procedure that you want to run when one of the column header links is selected.

Also notice the SortExpression property supplied in each of the column definitions:

```
sortexpression="LastName"
```

This property stores the name that you want passed into the sorting procedure. You will use this name to determine which field visitors want to sort by.

The code on the page is contained within two procedures. The first procedure is used to initially load the data grid with data when the page loads. The other procedure fires when the DataGrid control needs to be sorted:

```
Sub Sort_Grid(ByVal Sender as Object, _
    ByVal E as DataGridSortCommandEventArgs)
    Dim DBConn as OleDbConnection
    Dim DBCommand As OleDbDataAdapter
    Dim DSPageData as New DataSet
```

```
    DBConn = New OleDbConnection( _
        "PROVIDER=Microsoft.Jet.OLEDB.4.0;" _
        & "DATA SOURCE=" _
        & Server.MapPath("/tt/C4/DGDB.mdb;"))
    DBCommand = New OleDbDataAdapter _
        ("Select * " _
        & "From Employees Order By " _
        & E.SortExpression.ToString() , DBConn)
    DBCommand.Fill(DSPageData, _
        "Employees")
    dgEmps.DataSource = _
        DSPageData.Tables("Employees").DefaultView
    dgEmps.DataBind()
End Sub
```

Within this procedure you will need to connect to the Access database:

```
Dim DBConn as OleDbConnection
Dim DBCommand As OleDbDataAdapter
Dim DSPageData as New DataSet
DBConn = New OleDbConnection( _
    "PROVIDER=Microsoft.Jet.OLEDB.4.0;" _
    & "DATA SOURCE=" _
    & Server.MapPath("/tt/C4/DGDB.mdb;"))
```

and retrieve from that database the employee records. Notice the sorting used in that SQL statement. It is based on the SortExpression property of the DataGridSortCommandEventArgs parameter. This property is set to the value you supplied in the SortExpression property for the column that was clicked. Therefore, if you use the same name as the field name, you can place that value directly into the SQL statement:

```
DBCommand = New OleDbDataAdapter _
    ("Select * " _
    & "From Employees Order By " _
    & E.SortExpression.ToString() , DBConn)
DBCommand.Fill(DSPageData, _
    "Employees")
```

That data is then placed into the DataGrid control:

```
dgEmps.DataSource = _
    DSPageData.Tables("Employees").DefaultView
dgEmps.DataBind()
```

Displaying Pages of Data Through a DataGrid Control

If you have a DataGrid control that needs to display numerous records, you may find that it is impractical and difficult for visitors to view the data if it is all contained on the same DataGrid control. The DataGrid control contains page properties that provide an alternative to displaying all the records at the same time.

Using the paging mechanism you can set the number of records you want visitors to see on the DataGrid at one time. The DataGrid then generates arrows for visitors to click on that will take them to the next or previous pages of data. This technique shows you how to use that mechanism.

 USE IT This ASP.NET page contains a single control, a DataGrid control that allows visitors to view employee records from an Access database one page at a time. The control has this definition:

```
<asp:datagrid
    id="dgEmps"
    pagerstyle-backcolor="White"
    pagerstyle-forecolor="DarkGreen"
    pagerstyle-font-bold="True"
    allowpaging="True"
    pagesize=3
    onpageindexchanged="Page_Change"
    autogeneratecolumns="true"
    runat="server"
>
```

You use the PagerStyle properties to set the color and font properties for the row that will contain the arrows visitors will click to view the different pages of data:

```
pagerstyle-backcolor="White"
pagerstyle-forecolor="DarkGreen"
pagerstyle-font-bold="True"
```

For paging to be in effect, you need to turn it on:

```
allowpaging="True"
```

The PageSize property needs to be set to the number of records that you want visitors to see at one time on the DataGrid control:

```
pagesize=3
```

You also need to define the name of the procedure that is to run when visitors change the data page:

```
onpageindexchanged="Page_Change"
```

For this page, that procedure has this definition:

```
Sub Page_Change(sender As Object, e As DataGridPageChangedEventArgs)
    dgEmps.CurrentPageIndex = e.NewPageIndex
    Dim DSPageData As New DataSet
    Dim DBConn as OleDbConnection
    Dim DBCommand As OleDbDataAdapter
    DBConn = New OleDbConnection( _
        "PROVIDER=Microsoft.Jet.OLEDB.4.0;" _
        & "DATA SOURCE=" _
        & Server.MapPath("/tt/C4/DGDB.mdb;"))
    DBCommand = New OleDbDataAdapter _
        ("Select * " _
        & "From Employees " _
        & "Order By LastName, FirstName", DBConn)
    DBCommand.Fill(DSPageData, _
        "Employees")
    dgEmps.DataSource = _
        DSPageData.Tables("Employees").DefaultView
    dgEmps.DataBind()
End Sub
```

Most importantly is the first line of code:

```
dgEmps.CurrentPageIndex = e.NewPageIndex
```

That line of code sets the current page number that should be used for the DataGrid control. The rest of the code merely connects to the database to retrieve the desired data and binds it back to the DataGrid control.

Removing Rows from a DataGrid Control

You may find that you want to expand the functionality of the DataGrid controls that you define by allowing visitors to add, edit, and delete data from the DataGrid control as well as the underlying data source. This technique shows you how to remove a record from the DataGrid control and remove it from the underlying database table.

 The ASP.NET page presented in this section displays the names of employees from an Access database table. Also displayed is a button for each row of data, which when clicked deletes that record.

The DataGrid control has the following definition:

```
<asp:datagrid
    id="dgEmps"
```

```
    runat="server"
    autogeneratecolumns="false"
    onitemcommand="Click_Grid"
>
    <columns>
        <asp:boundcolumn
            HeaderText="Full Name"
            DataField="FullName"
        />
        <asp:boundcolumn
            DataField="EmpID"
            Visible=False
        />
        <asp:buttoncolumn
            HeaderText="Click to Delete"
            ButtonType="PushButton"
            Text="Delete Record"
        />
    </columns>
</asp:datagrid>
```

Notice this property in the DataGrid definition:

```
onitemcommand="Click_Grid"
```

This is the name of the procedure that you want to run when visitors click the Delete button. The first column in the DataGrid control displays the name of the employee:

```
<asp:boundcolumn
    HeaderText="Full Name"
    DataField="FullName"
/>
```

The second column is not displayed but contains the ID of the employee:

```
<asp:boundcolumn
    DataField="EmpID"
    Visible=False
/>
```

That column will be used to determine which record to delete.
   The third column displays a Delete button for each of the records:

```
<asp:buttoncolumn
    HeaderText="Click to Delete"
    ButtonType="PushButton"
```

```
        Text="Delete Record"
/>
```

When a Delete button is clicked, this code fires:

```
Sub Click_Grid(ByVal Sender as Object, ByVal E as DataGridCommandEventArgs)
    Dim TheID as String
    TheID = E.Item.Cells(1).Text
    Dim DBConn as OleDbConnection
    Dim DBDelete As New OleDbCommand
    DBConn = New OleDbConnection( _
        "PROVIDER=Microsoft.Jet.OLEDB.4.0;" _
        & "DATA SOURCE=" _
        & Server.MapPath("/tt/C4/DGDB.mdb;"))
    DBDelete.CommandText = "Delete From Employees Where " _
        & "EmpID = " & TheID
    DBDelete.Connection = DBConn
    DBDelete.Connection.Open
    DBDelete.ExecuteNonQuery()
    DBConn.Close
    BuildDataList
End Sub
```

Within the procedure, you need to declare a temporary variable:

```
Dim TheID as String
```

That variable is set to the ID of the record that is to be deleted. The Index of 1 in this reference refers to the second column in the DataGrid, which contains the ID of the record to be deleted:

```
TheID = E.Item.Cells(1).Text
```

You then need to declare data objects and connect to the database:

```
Dim DBConn as OleDbConnection
Dim DBDelete As New OleDbCommand
DBConn = New OleDbConnection( _
    "PROVIDER=Microsoft.Jet.OLEDB.4.0;" _
    & "DATA SOURCE=" _
    & Server.MapPath("/tt/C4/DGDB.mdb;"))
```

You then place a SQL delete statement into the command object. Note that the record being deleted is based on the ID of the record selected in the DataGrid control:

```
DBDelete.CommandText = "Delete From Employees Where " _
    & "EmpID = " & TheID
```

```
DBDelete.Connection = DBConn
DBDelete.Connection.Open
DBDelete.ExecuteNonQuery()
```

Then you need to close the connection object:

```
DBConn.Close
```

and call this internally defined procedure, which repopulates the DataGrid control:

```
    BuildDataList
```

Editing Rows from a DataGrid Control

In many situations you may want to allow visitors to directly add, edit, and delete records from a
DataGrid as well as the underlying data source. The DataGrid control has some built-in functionality
that makes editing records a little easier.

Using the DataGrid control, you can place a record in Update mode. When you do that, each field
in the row appears in a TextBox control allowing visitors to edit the record. When visitors then click
the Update button, your code saves that change.

The technique presented in this section shows you how to do this.

USE IT   This ASP.NET page displays a list of employee names. Visitors can enter any of the
employee names by clicking an Edit button in that row. They can then make their changes
through TextBox controls. When they click the Update button, their changes are saved to the database
and the grid is updated.

The DataGrid control on the page has this definition:

```
<asp:datagrid
    id="dgEmps"
    runat="server"
    autogeneratecolumns="false"
    oneditcommand="Edit_Grid"
    onupdatecommand="Update_Grid"
    >
    <columns>
        <asp:boundcolumn
            HeaderText="Last Name"
            DataField="LastName"
        />
        <asp:boundcolumn
            HeaderText="First Name"
            DataField="FirstName"
        />
```

```
        <asp:boundcolumn
            datafield="EmpID"
            visible=False
            readonly=true
        />
        <asp:editcommandcolumn
            edittext="Edit"
            updatetext="Update"
            itemstyle-wrap="false"
            headertext="Edit"
            headerStyle-wrap="false"
        />
    </columns>
</asp:datagrid>
```

You need to supply two procedure names through properties in the DataGrid definition:

```
oneditcommand="Edit_Grid"
onupdatecommand="Update_Grid"
```

The first is the name of the procedure that runs when visitors place themselves in Edit mode. The other is the name of the procedure that is to run when visitors save their changes.

After that, two columns are defined: One for the last name field and another for the first name field.

Followed by that is the definition of the EditCommandColumn. That column is where visitors will see the Edit or Update button:

```
<asp:editcommandcolumn
```

Within that definition you need to supply the text that visitors see on the Edit button:

```
edittext="Edit"
```

The same needs to be done for the Update button:

```
updatetext="Update"
itemstyle-wrap="false"
```

Then in code you need to supply procedures that match the names of the procedures defined for the Edit and Update buttons in the DataGrid definition. This code block runs when the Edit button is clicked:

```
Sub Edit_Grid(sender As Object, e As DataGridCommandEventArgs)
    dgEmps.EditItemIndex = e.Item.ItemIndex
    BuildDataList
End Sub
```

The first line of code highlights the record visitors select as the one that is to be placed into Edit mode. The second line of code calls an internal procedure that repopulates the DataGrid control with data from the Access database.

The next procedure runs when visitors click the Update button:

```
Sub Update_Grid(ByVal Sender as Object, ByVal E as DataGridCommandEventArgs)
    Dim TheID as String
    Dim LastName as String
    Dim FirstName as String
    TheID = E.Item.Cells(2).Text
    LastName = CType(e.Item.Cells(0).Controls(0), TextBox).Text
    FirstName = CType(e.Item.Cells(1).Controls(0), TextBox).Text
    Dim DBConn as OleDbConnection
    Dim DBUpdate As New OleDbCommand
    DBConn = New OleDbConnection( _
        "PROVIDER=Microsoft.Jet.OLEDB.4.0;" _
        & "DATA SOURCE=" _
        & Server.MapPath("/tt/C4/DGDB.mdb;"))
    DBUpdate.CommandText = "Update Employees " _
        & "Set LastName = '" & LastName &"', " _
        & "FirstName = '" & FirstName & "' " _
        & "Where EmpID = " & TheID
    DBUpdate.Connection = DBConn
    DBUpdate.Connection.Open
    DBUpdate.ExecuteNonQuery()
    DBConn.Close
    dgEmps.EditItemIndex = -1
    BuildDataList
End Sub
```

First, you need local variables to store the values of the edited record:

```
Dim TheID as String
Dim LastName as String
Dim FirstName as String
```

The ID field can be set directly to the value of the ID in the third cell of the DataGrid:

```
TheID = E.Item.Cells(2).Text
```

That cell is not visible to visitors.

Next, you store the text entered by visitors in the TextBox controls:

```
LastName = CType(e.Item.Cells(0).Controls(0), TextBox).Text
FirstName = CType(e.Item.Cells(1).Controls(0), TextBox).Text
```

Next, you need to define these data objects:

```
Dim DBConn as OleDbConnection
Dim DBUpdate As New OleDbCommand
```

and connect to the Access database:

```
DBConn = New OleDbConnection( _
    "PROVIDER=Microsoft.Jet.OLEDB.4.0;" _
    & "DATA SOURCE=" _
    & Server.MapPath("/tt/C4/DGDB.mdb;"))
```

You can then update the employee record visitors edited:

```
DBUpdate.CommandText = "Update Employees " _
    & "Set LastName = '" & LastName &"', " _
    & "FirstName = '" & FirstName & "' " _
    & "Where EmpID = " & TheID
DBUpdate.Connection = DBConn
DBUpdate.Connection.Open
DBUpdate.ExecuteNonQuery()
```

After closing the database connection:

```
DBConn.Close
```

you take the visitor out of Edit mode:

```
dgEmps.EditItemIndex = -1
```

and repopulate the DataGrid control:

```
BuildDataList
```

Adding Rows to a DataGrid Control

If you allow for the editing and deletion of records through a DataGrid control, you will probably want to provide a way for visitors to add a new record. The DataGrid control does not support this functionality directly, so you need to provide your own code. This technique shows you how to do that.

Note that the ASP.NET page presented in this section is based on "Editing Rows from a DataGrid Control," presented earlier in this chapter. Please refer to it for a description of the Update procedure.

USE IT   This page allows visitors to add an employee record to an Access database by clicking the Add button at the bottom of the page. When they do that, a new record is added and they are placed in Update mode for that new record.

The Add button has this definition:

```
<asp:LinkButton
    id="butAdd"
    text="Add"
    commandname="Add"
    oncommand="CommandAdd_Click"
    runat="server"
/>
```

When the LinkButton control is clicked, this procedure runs:

```
Sub CommandAdd_Click(Sender As Object, E As CommandEventArgs)
    Dim DBConn as OleDbConnection
    Dim DBAdd As New OleDbCommand
    DBConn = New OleDbConnection( _
        "PROVIDER=Microsoft.Jet.OLEDB.4.0;" _
        & "DATA SOURCE=" _
        & Server.MapPath("/tt/C4/DGDB.mdb;"))
    DBAdd.CommandText = "Insert Into Employees (LastName) " _
        & "values ('')"
    DBAdd.Connection = DBConn
    DBAdd.Connection.Open
    DBAdd.ExecuteNonQuery()
    DBConn.Close
    dgEmps.EditItemIndex = 0
    BuildDataList
End Sub
```

Within the procedure you will need data objects:

```
Dim DBConn as OleDbConnection
Dim DBAdd As New OleDbCommand
```

You start by connecting to the Access database:

```
DBConn = New OleDbConnection( _
    "PROVIDER=Microsoft.Jet.OLEDB.4.0;" _
    & "DATA SOURCE=" _
    & Server.MapPath("/tt/C4/DGDB.mdb;"))
```

and add a new blank record to the database:

```
DBAdd.CommandText = "Insert Into Employees (LastName) " _
    & "values ('')"
DBAdd.Connection = DBConn
DBAdd.Connection.Open
DBAdd.ExecuteNonQuery()
```

Then you need to close the database connection:

```
DBConn.Close
```

The records in the DataGrid control are sorted by LastName. Therefore, the new record just added will appear first in the list since the LastName field is blank. So you can place the first record of the DataGrid control in Update mode and visitors can enter data into the new record:

```
dgEmps.EditItemIndex = 0
```

Lastly, you need to call the internal procedure to re-populate the DataGrid control:

```
BuildDataList
```

Creating a Basic ListBox Control

The ListBox control provides a way for you to present a list of simple text/value data where visitors can select an item from the list. The ListBox differs from the DropDownList control in that there is no drop-down portion. The ListBox control instead displays the number of items you specify in the list at one time and the rest of the items can be scrolled to.

The technique presented in this section shows you how to create a basic ListBox control.

 The following ASP.NET page displays a list of colors to visitors through a ListBox control. That control has this definition:

```
<asp:listbox
    id="lb1"
    runat="server"
    rows=3
>
    <asp:listitem value="Bu">Blue</asp:listitem>
    <asp:listitem value="Re">Red</asp:listitem>
    <asp:listitem value="Gr">Green</asp:listitem>
    <asp:listitem value="Pu" Selected>Purple</asp:listitem>
    <asp:listitem value="Ba">Black</asp:listitem>
```

```
    <asp:listitem value="Go" text="Gold"/>
</asp:listbox>
```

The name for the control is supplied through the ID property:

```
<asp:listbox
    id="lb1"
    runat="server"
```

The Rows property is set to the number of items that appear at one time within the ListBox control:

```
    rows=3
>
```

Within the control's definition you can define the items that appear in the list. Each item is supplied with a value for the Text property. One way to do that is by placing the text between the control's definition:

```
<asp:listitem value="Re">Red</asp:listitem>
```

The other way is to explicitly set the value of the property:

```
<asp:listitem value="Go" text="Gold"/>
```

The Value property can also be set. This value is not seen by visitors but can be used by you to identify the item selected.

You can indicate the currently selected item by placing the keyword Selected within the item's definition:

```
<asp:listitem value="Pu" Selected>Purple</asp:listitem>
```

Checking the Value Selected in a ListBox Control

To effectively use a ListBox control, you need to be able to identify the item that visitors select in the ListBox. You can check that value through one of three properties. You can retrieve the text of the item selected, the value of the item selected, and the index of the item selected. This technique shows you how to do that.

USE IT   This ASP.Net page allows visitors to select a color from a ListBox control. The value of the item selected is displayed back to them through a Label control.

The page has this basic ListBox control defined:

```
<asp:listbox
    id="lb1"
```

```
    runat="server"
    rows=3
>
```

Also defined on the page is this Button control that allows visitors to submit the page for processing:

```
<asp:button
    id="butOK"
    text="OK"
    type="Submit"
    onclick="SubmitBtn_Click"
    runat="server"
/>
```

When that button is clicked, this procedure fires:

```
Sub SubmitBtn_Click(Sender As Object, E As EventArgs)
    lblDataSelected.Text = "Selected Text: " _
        & lb1.SelectedItem.Text & "<BR>Selected Value: " _
        & lb1.SelectedItem.Value & "<BR>Selected Index: " _
        & lb1.SelectedIndex
End Sub
```

The procedure echoes back to visitors the choice that they made in the list. That choice is determined by querying the properties of the SelectedItem object of the ListBox control. The Text property returns the text of the item selected, which is the value that visitors see.

The Value property is set to the internal value you assigned to the item selected, and the SelectedIndex property is set to the positional index of the item selected.

Allowing Multiple Selections in a ListBox Control

A major difference between the ListBox control and the DropDownList control is that the ListBox control allows visitors to select more than one item in the list. They do this by first selecting one item and then, while holding down the CTRL key, they can select another item.

This tip shows you how to allow for many items in a ListBox control to be selected.

USE IT   This ASP.NET page presents a list of colors to visitors. On this page, they can select more than one color.

The ListBox control has this definition:

```
<asp:listbox
    id="lb1"
    runat="server"
```

```
    selectionmode="multiple"
    rows=4
>
    <asp:listitem value="Bu">Blue</asp:listitem>
    <asp:listitem value="Re">Red</asp:listitem>
    <asp:listitem value="Gr">Green</asp:listitem>
    <asp:listitem value="Pu" Selected>Purple</asp:listitem>
    <asp:listitem value="Ba">Black</asp:listitem>
    <asp:listitem value="Go" text="Gold"/>
</asp:listbox>
```

The important property in this tip is the SelectionMode property. Setting it to Multiple allows visitors to select more than one item in the list. The default value of Single allows visitors to only select a single color from the list.

Writing Code That Fires When the Selection Changes in a ListBox Control

You may on occasion find that you need to have code run as soon as the item in a ListBox control changes. For example, maybe you have a list of employee names and when one of the employees is selected, you take visitors to another page that displays the full information for that employee. This technique shows you how to have code run when the item in a ListBox control changes.

USE IT The page presented in this section displays a list of colors in a ListBox control. When an item is selected in the list, the background color of the ListBox control changes to that of the color selected in the list.

The ListBox control has this definition:

```
id="lb1"
    runat="server"
    autopostback="True"
    onselectedindexchanged="lb1_Changed"
    rows=3
>
    <asp:listitem value="Bu">Blue</asp:listitem>
    <asp:listitem value="Re">Red</asp:listitem>
    <asp:listitem value="Gr">Green</asp:listitem>
    <asp:listitem value="Pu" >Purple</asp:listitem>
    <asp:listitem value="Ba">Black</asp:listitem>
</asp:listbox>
```

There are two important properties in this definition to note. First, notice the AutoPostBack property:

```
autopostback="True"
```

It must be set to True for the page to be submitted when the selected item changes. Also notice the OnSelectedIndexChanged property:

```
onselectedindexchanged="lb1_Changed"
```

This property is set to the name of the procedure that you want to run when the item in the list changes. That procedure has this definition:

```
Sub lb1_Changed(Sender As Object, E As EventArgs)
    lb1.BackColor = System.Drawing.Color.FromName(lb1.SelectedItem.Text)
End Sub
```

The procedure changes the background color of the ListBox control based on the color selected in the ListBox control.

Binding a ListBox Control to a Data Source

Instead of manually populating the controls in a ListBox control, you can populate the list from a data source such as a database table. This technique shows you how to bind a ListBox control to an Access database.

USE IT   This ASP.NET page displays a list of departments from an Access database table through a ListBox control. One field in the table is used to display the name of the department while another field is used to internally store the ID of the department. The ListBox control has this definition:

```
<asp:listbox
    id="lbDepartments"
    datatextfield="DeptName"
    datavaluefield="DeptID"
    rows=3
    runat="server"
/>
```

Two important properties to note here. First, the DataTextField property is set to the field that you want displayed in the ListBox control. The other important property, DataValueField, is set to the name of the field that contains the ID that you want passed with the selected item but is not displayed to visitors.

When the page first loads, the following code populates the ListBox control:

```
Sub Page_Load(ByVal Sender as Object, ByVal E as EventArgs)
    If Not IsPostBack Then
        Dim DBConn as OleDbConnection
        Dim DBCommand As OleDbDataAdapter
        Dim DSPageData as New DataSet
        DBConn = New OleDbConnection( _
            "PROVIDER=Microsoft.Jet.OLEDB.4.0;" _
            & "DATA SOURCE=" _
            & Server.MapPath("/tt/C4/ddlDB.mdb;"))
        DBCommand = New OleDbDataAdapter _
            ("Select DeptID, DeptName " _
            & "From Departments " _
            & "Order By DeptName", DBConn)
        DBCommand.Fill(DSPageData, _
            "Departments")
        lbDepartments.DataSource = _
            DSPageData.Tables("Departments").DefaultView
        lbDepartments.DataBind()
    End If
End Sub
```

The code only runs when the page first loads:

```
If Not IsPostBack Then
```

If that is the case, you need to define database objects:

```
Dim DBConn as OleDbConnection
Dim DBCommand As OleDbDataAdapter
Dim DSPageData as New DataSet
```

Then you need to connect to the Access database:

```
DBConn = New OleDbConnection( _
    "PROVIDER=Microsoft.Jet.OLEDB.4.0;" _
    & "DATA SOURCE=" _
    & Server.MapPath("/tt/C4/ddlDB.mdb;"))
And retrieve the department records:
DBCommand = New OleDbDataAdapter _
    ("Select DeptID, DeptName " _
    & "From Departments " _
    & "Order By DeptName", DBConn)
```

which are placed into a DataSet object:

```
DBCommand.Fill(DSPageData, _
    "Departments")
```

The ListBox control is bound to that DataSet object:

```
lbDepartments.DataSource = _
    DSPageData.Tables("Departments").DefaultView
lbDepartments.DataBind()
```

Creating a Basic RadioButtonList Control

ASP.NET provides numerous controls that you can use to present a list of information and allow visitors to select an item amongst that list. The RadioButtonList control is one of those controls. The control is rendered as a series of radio button controls, each containing the text and value for one of the items to be listed. This technique shows you how to create a basic RadioButtonList control and how to determine the value of the item selected.

USE IT   This ASP.NET page presents visitors with a list of colors through a RadioButtonList control. When the page is submitted by clicking the Button control on the page, the color visitors have selected is echoed back to them through a Label control.

The RadioButtonList control has this definition:

```
<asp:RadioButtonList
    id="rbl1"
    runat="server"
    cellpadding="5"
    cellspacing="5"
    repeatcolumns="3"
    repeatdirection="Vertical"
    repeatlayout="Table"
    textalign="Right"
>
    <asp:ListItem value="12">Blue</asp:ListItem>
    <asp:ListItem value="11">Red</asp:ListItem>
    <asp:ListItem value="2">Green</asp:ListItem>
    <asp:ListItem value="32">Purple</asp:ListItem>
    <asp:ListItem value="8">Black</asp:ListItem>
    <asp:ListItem value="15" Selected>Gold</asp:ListItem>
</asp:RadioButtonList>
```

The name of the control is supplied through the ID property:

```
<asp:RadioButtonList
    id="rbl1"
    runat="server"
```

The items in the RadioButtonList control are rendered through RadioButton controls. These controls are laid out on the resulting page through HTML Table tags. You can use these properties to set the spacing between cells in that HTML table:

```
cellpadding="5"
cellspacing="5"
```

The RepeatColumns property is set to the number of controls that you want to appear across the page before moving on to a new row in the rendered HTML table:

```
    repeatcolumns="3"
```

You have two options for the direction in which the items in the RadioButtonList are laid out: You can set them to have a vertical direction, which means that item number 2 will be beneath item number 1:

```
repeatdirection="Vertical"
```

or you can have item number 2 to the right of item number 1 by setting the property to Horizontal.

As mentioned previously, items in the RadioButtonList control can be laid out through an HTML table:

```
repeatlayout="Table"
```

But you can also set this property to Flow and the items will not be placed within HTML table elements.

A value of Right in the TextAlign property means that the text for each item appears to the right of the RadioButton control:

```
textalign="Right"
```

You can have the text appear before the radio button element by setting the TextAlign property to Left.

When the page is submitted for processing, the following code echoes the visitors' selection back to them through a Label control:

```
Sub SubmitBtn_Click(Sender As Object, E As EventArgs)
    lblMessage.Text = "Selected Text: " _
        & rbl1.SelectedItem.Text & "<BR>Selected Value: " _
        & rbl1.SelectedItem.Value & "<BR>Selected Index: " _
        & rbl1.SelectedIndex
End Sub
```

The code uses the SelectedItem object to return the text of the item selected through the Text property. The Value property returns the ID of the item selected and the SelectedIndex property returns the numeric position of the item in the list that was selected.

Writing Code That Fires When an Item Is Selected in a RadioButtonList Control

The RadioButtonList control provides an event that you can define code for that runs whenever the item selected in the RadioButtonList control changes. This technique shows you how to write code for this event.

USE IT This ASP.NET page allows visitors to select a color from a list of colors displayed through a RadioButtonList control. When visitors select a color, the page is automatically posted back to the server. During that event, client-side code is written back to the browser and visitors see the color they select in a JavaScript Alert box.

Here is the definition of the RadioButtonList control that is defined on that page:

```
<asp:RadioButtonList
    id="rbl1"
    runat="server"
    autopostback="True"
    onselectedindexchanged="rbl_Changed"
>

    <asp:ListItem value="12">Blue</asp:ListItem>
    <asp:ListItem value="11">Red</asp:ListItem>
    <asp:ListItem value="2">Green</asp:ListItem>
</asp:RadioButtonList>
```

Notice that the AutoPostBack property is set to True. Setting that property to that value sends the page to the server for processing as soon as an item in the list changes. Also notice the OnSelectedIndexChanged property. That property contains the name of the procedure that you want to run when the item does change. Here is the definition of that procedure:

```
Sub rbl_Changed(Sender As Object, E As EventArgs)
    Dim TheAlert as String
    TheAlert = "<SCRIPT LANGUAGE=""JavaScript"">" & Chr(13) _
        & "<!--" & Chr(13) & "alert(""You selected the color: " _
        & rbl1.SelectedItem.Text & """)" & Chr(13) _
        & "--><" & "/" & "SCRIPT>"
    Response.Write(TheAlert)
End Sub
```

First, a string variable is declared:

```
Dim TheAlert as String
```

That variable is set to JavaScript that will be sent back to the client's browser. The JavaScript will display the color selected by the visitor through an alert or message box:

```
TheAlert = "<SCRIPT LANGUAGE=""JavaScript"">" & Chr(13) _
    & "<!--" & Chr(13) & "alert(""You selected the color: " _
    & rbl1.SelectedItem.Text & """)" & Chr(13) _
    & "--><" & "/" & "SCRIPT>"
```

That string is written to the browser using the Write method of the Response object:

```
Response.Write(TheAlert)
```

Binding a RadioButtonList Control to a Data Source

You can manually define the items that appear in a RadioButtonList control by adding ListItem controls to the RadioButtonList control. But another way that you can populate the choices displayed in a RadioButtonList control is by binding it to a data source.

USE IT   The page presented in this section displays the name of departments and stores their IDs to the visitor through a RadioButtonList control. The data comes from an Access database table, which the RadioButtonList control is bound to.

The RadioButtonList control has this definition:

```
<asp:RadioButtonList
    id="rbl1"
    datatextfield="DeptName"
    datavaluefield="DeptID"
    runat="server"
/>
```

Notice the DataTextField property. That property is set to the name of the field that you want visitors to see in the RadioButtonList control. The DataValueField property is set to the name of the field that internally stores the ID of the department being displayed.

When the page first loads, the following code runs and populates the RadioButtonList control.

```
Sub Page_Load(ByVal Sender as Object, ByVal E as EventArgs)
    If Not IsPostBack Then
        Dim DBConn as OleDbConnection
        Dim DBCommand As OleDbDataAdapter
```

```
        Dim DSPageData as New DataSet
        DBConn = New OleDbConnection( _
            "PROVIDER=Microsoft.Jet.OLEDB.4.0;" _
            & "DATA SOURCE=" _
            & Server.MapPath("/tt/C4/ddlDB.mdb;"))
        DBCommand = New OleDbDataAdapter _
            ("Select DeptID, DeptName " _
            & "From Departments " _
            & "Order By DeptName", DBConn)
        DBCommand.Fill(DSPageData, _
            "Departments")
        rbl1.DataSource = _
            DSPageData.Tables("Departments").DefaultView
        rbl1.DataBind()
    End If
End Sub
```

The code only runs when the page first loads:

```
If Not IsPostBack Then
```

Within the procedure, you need data objects:

```
Dim DBConn as OleDbConnection
Dim DBCommand As OleDbDataAdapter
Dim DSPageData as New DataSet
```

and you need to connect to the Access database:

```
DBConn = New OleDbConnection( _
    "PROVIDER=Microsoft.Jet.OLEDB.4.0;" _
    & "DATA SOURCE=" _
    & Server.MapPath("/tt/C4/ddlDB.mdb;"))
```

Next, you need to retrieve the data from the database:

```
DBCommand = New OleDbDataAdapter _
    ("Select DeptID, DeptName " _
    & "From Departments " _
    & "Order By DeptName", DBConn)
DBCommand.Fill(DSPageData, _
    "Departments")
```

and bind the RadioButtonList control to that data:

```
rbl1.DataSource = _
    DSPageData.Tables("Departments").DefaultView
rbl1.DataBind()
```

Creating a Basic CheckBoxList Control

Another of the many controls that ASP.NET makes available to you for displaying a list of information is the CheckBoxList control. The CheckBoxList control renders a group of CheckBox controls. Each of the CheckBox controls within the CheckBoxList control is mutually exclusive from all other items in the list so visitors can select as many or as few of the CheckBox controls as they would like. The technique presented in this section shows you how to define this control and how to iterate through the CheckBox controls to determine which have been checked.

USE IT This ASP.NET page displays a list of colors through a CheckBoxList control. When the form on the page is submitted, the selections visitors have made are echoed back to them through a Label control. Here is the definition of the CheckBoxList control on this page:

```
<asp:checkboxlist
    id="cbl1"
    runat="server"
    cellpadding="5"
    cellspacing="5"
    repeatcolumns="3"
    repeatdirection="Horizontal"
    repeatlayout="Table"
    textalign="Right"
>
    <asp:ListItem value="12">Blue</asp:ListItem>
    <asp:ListItem value="11">Red</asp:ListItem>
    <asp:ListItem value="2">Green</asp:ListItem>
    <asp:ListItem value="32">Purple</asp:ListItem>
    <asp:ListItem value="8">Black</asp:ListItem>
    <asp:ListItem value="15" Selected>Gold</asp:ListItem>
</asp:checkboxlist>
```

The CheckBox controls displayed through the CheckBoxList control are rendered through an HTML table. Therefore, you can use the CellPadding and CellSpacing property to determine the distance between the items in the list. The RepeatColumns property is set to the number of CheckBox controls that you want to see across a single line in the rendered HTML table control.

But you don't have to have the output rendered through an HTML table. You can set the RepeatLayout property to Flow to have the controls rendered outside of a table structure.

When the page is submitted for processing this procedure fires:

```
Sub SubmitBtn_Click(Sender As Object, E As EventArgs)
    Dim MyItem as ListItem
    lblMessage.Text = ""
    For Each MyItem in cbl1.Items
        If MyItem.Selected = True Then
            lblMessage.Text = lblMessage.Text _
                & MyItem.Text & "<BR>"
        End If
    Next
End Sub
```

The procedure iterates through all the CheckBox items in the CheckBoxList control. Any of the items that are selected are written back to the browser through the Label control.

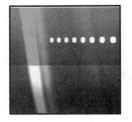

CHAPTER 5

Validation Web Controls

TIPS IN THIS CHAPTER

A SP.NET comes with a variety of validation controls that make it so much easier than ASP did in validating the text entered on a form by visitors. Best of all, most of the code is generated client-side so the page is not even submitted to your server for the validation checks to be performed. And most of the time, you don't have to write a single line of code for these rules to be checked. In this chapter, you will see tips and techniques that show you the power of these controls.

Using a RequiredFieldValidator Control

When you develop an ASP.NET form you will find that certain fields on that form must be entered by visitors. For example, you may have a form that requires visitors to enter a password or maybe you have a form where visitors need to enter a shipping address. Both of those fields would be required.

You require a field to have data in it on an ASP.NET page by using a RequiredFieldValidator control. That control requires visitors to enter something into the fields before submitting the form. This technique shows you how to use that control.

USE IT   This ASP.NET page asks visitors to enter their name and then press the OK button. If they leave the field blank, the form is not submitted to the server. Instead they see an error message letting them know that they must enter their name. Here are the controls defined on the page:

```
<form runat="server">
<BR><BR>
Enter Your Name:<BR>
<asp:textbox
    id="txtName"
    runat=server
/>
<asp:requiredfieldvalidator
    id="rfvName"
    controltovalidate="txtName"
```

```
        display="Dynamic"
        font-name="Verdana"
        font-size="10pt"
        fore-color="red"
        runat=server
>
You must enter your name!
</asp:requiredfieldvalidator>
<BR><BR>
<asp:button
        id="butOK"
        text="OK"
        type="Submit"
        onclick="SubmitBtn_Click"
        runat="server"
/>
</form>
```

The TextBox control is used by visitors to enter their name. The Button control is used to submit the page for processing.

But the page cannot be submitted for processing if the TextBox control is left blank because of the RequiredFieldValidator control. You use the ID property of that control to specify its name:

```
<asp:requiredfieldvalidator
        id="rfvName"
```

Next, place in the ControlToValidate property the name of the control that this control makes sure isn't left blank—in this case, the name TextBox control:

```
controltovalidate="txtName"
```

The Display property determines whether space on the page is reserved for the error message when the page is first displayed. If you set the property to Dynamic:

```
        display="Dynamic"
```

no space is reserved for the error message. If it needs to be displayed, space is allocated at that point. You can also set this property to Static to initially reserve the space for the error message.

Next you can set the formatting properties for the control:

```
        font-name="Verdana"
        font-size="10pt"
        fore-color="red"
        runat=server
>
```

▶ **QUICK TIP**

Use a string contrasting color with your RequiredFieldValidator controls. That way the visitor will be able to easily see the controls that failed validation.

Between the opening and closing tags of the control you place the text that you want to appear in the event that the visitor does not supply text into the control being validated:

```
You must enter your name!
```

The closing tag for the control follows that:

```
</asp:requiredfieldvalidator>
```

Checking Against an Initial Value with a RequiredFieldValidator Control

Sometimes in a TextBox control you may want to place some initial text and then make sure that the visitor changes that text. For example, if you had a field where the visitor was to enter a search term, you may initially place the text "Enter Search Term" into the TextBox control, which they would replace with their search term. You would want to make sure that they changed this text before performing the search. The RequiredFieldValidator control allows you to make this kind of validation check.

USE IT   The following ASP.NET page requires visitors to enter their name. Through the use of two RequiredFieldValidator controls, visitors must change the TextBox control from its initial value, but they must not leave it blank.

The page has this TextBox control defined:

```
<asp:textbox
    id="txtName"
    text="Enter Your Name"
    runat=server
/>
```

Notice the initial value placed in the TextBox control through the Text property. That value must be changed because of this RequiredFieldValidator control definition:

```
<asp:RequiredFieldValidator
    id="rfvName1"
    controltovalidate="txtName"
    initialvalue="Enter Your Name"
    display="Dynamic"
    font-name="Verdana"
```

```
    font-size="10pt"
    fore-color="red"
    runat=server
>
You must enter your name!
</asp:RequiredFieldValidator>
```

Notice that the ControlToValidate property is set to the TextBox control. Also notice the InitialValue property. It is set to the same value as the TextBox control's text property. This means that visitors cannot set or leave the TextBox control with this value before submitting the form.

A second RequiredFieldValidator control is also linked to the TextBox control through the ControlToValidate property. It makes sure visitors do not leave the TextBox control blank:

```
<asp:requiredfieldvalidator
    id="rfvName2"
    controltovalidate="txtName"
    display="Dynamic"
    font-name="Verdana"
    font-size="10pt"
    fore-color="red"
    runat=server
>
You must enter your name!
</asp:requiredfieldvalidator>
```

> ► **QUICK TIP**
>
> *You could use a RequiredFieldValidator with a value in the InitialValue property to prevent the visitor from entering a specific value that you do not allow. Just place that illegal value in the InitialValue property.*

Checking the Range of a Number Through the RangeValidator Control

The RangeValidator control allows a way for you to make sure that a number entered by the visitor falls in a specific range. For example, maybe you have a quantity field and visitors need to enter a number from 1 to 10. Or maybe you have a Number of Dependents field and visitors must enter a number from 0 to 12. The RangeValidator control can be used to enforce such rules.

USE IT The ASP.NET page presented in this technique shows you how to use the RangeValidator control to check and see if the value entered into a TextBox control is a number and that it is from 5 to 44 inclusive.

The TextBox control has this definition:

```
<asp:textbox
    id="txtNumber"
    runat=server
/>
```

The range entered into that field is checked through this RangeValidator control:

```
<asp:rangevalidator
    id="rngQuantity"
    controltovalidate="txtNumber"
    type="Integer"
    minimumvalue=5
    maximumvalue=44
    display="Dynamic"
    font-name="Verdana"
    font-bold="True"
    font-size="10pt"
    forecolor="blue"
    runat="server">
    The Quantity field must be from 5 to 44!
</asp:rangevalidator>
```

You set the name of the control through the ID property:

```
<asp:rangevalidator
    id="rngQuantity"
```

Then place into the ControlToValidate property the control that this control is validating:

```
controltovalidate="txtNumber"
```

You want to make sure that the value entered into the TextBox control is a number:

```
type="Integer"
```

and you set the range that the number can fall within through the MinimumValue property and the MaximumValue property:

```
minimumvalue=5
maximumvalue=44
```

Next, the Display property is set to "Dynamic," so the space for the error message is only allocated as needed:

```
display="Dynamic"
```

▶ | **QUICK TIP**

The RangeValidator control does not prevent the visitor from leaving the field blank. If you want to check a range and make sure the visitor enters a value, use a RangeValidator control and a RequiredFieldValidator control.

You can also format the font and color of the error message:

```
    font-name="Verdana"
    font-bold="True"
    font-size="10pt"
    forecolor="blue"
runat="server">
```

Between the opening and closing tags of the control you place the error message text:

```
    The Quantity field must be from 5 to 44!
</asp:rangevalidator>
```

Checking the Range of a Date Through the RangeValidator Control

On some of your ASP.NET forms you may have fields in which visitors must enter a date and that date must fall within a specified range. For example, a birth date field would have a range that the date should fall between, as would a date on an invoice. You can use the RangeValidator control to make sure the data entered by a visitor is a date within a specific range. This tip shows you how to do that.

 This page presents visitors with a TextBox where they must enter a date that is any date in the 1990s. The TextBox control on the page has this definition:

```
<asp:textbox
    id="txtDate"
    runat=server
/>
```

When visitors leave that field or when they try to submit the page, this RangeValidator control checks their entry:

```
<asp:RangeValidator
    id="rngDate"
    controltovalidate="txtDate"
    type="Date"
```

```
        minimumvalue="1/1/1990"
        maximumvalue="12/31/1999"
        display="Dynamic"
        runat="server">
        The Date field must be from 1/1/1990 to 12/31/1999!
</asp:RangeValidator>
```

Notice that the ControlToValidate property is set to the TextBox control. Also notice that the Type property is set to Date, therefore a Date check is performed. You set the minimum date, as well as the maximum date, that the field can fall in through the MinimumValue property and the MaximumValue property. Then, between the opening and closing tags of the control, you enter the error message that is displayed if the data entered in the TextBox control violates the rule.

Validating User Input Against a Value Through the CompareValidator Control

The CompareValidator control allows you to check the entry made by the visitor against some other control or code. This tip shows you how to make sure that the value entered by visitors matches a specific value that you supply in the control's definition. This would be helpful in a situation where you needed visitors to answer a question to match exactly the answer that you supply.

USE IT   This ASP.NET page asks visitors a question. If visitors do not answer the question exactly, the form on the page cannot be submitted. This question as well as a TextBox control for entering the answer are defined at the top of the page:

```
What is the next generation of ASP called?<BR>
<asp:textbox
    id="txtAnswer"
    runat=server
/>
```

When visitors leave the field, the value entered is checked against the correct answer through the use of this CompareValidator control:

```
<asp:CompareValidator
    id="cvCheckAnswer"
    controltovalidate="txtAnswer"
    valuetocompare="ASP.NET"
    runat=server>
    Incorrect Answer!
</asp:comparevalidator>
```

The ControlToValidate property is set to the TextBox control. The ValueToCompare property is set to the exact value that the visitor must enter into the TextBox control for validation to pass. If visitors do not answer the question in that way, they will see the error message "Incorrect Answer!" supplied between the opening and closing tags of the control's definition.

QUICK TIP

The CompareValidator control does not check to see if visitors leave the control blank. To check the value entered by visitors into a TextBox control, and to make sure that visitors do not leave the control blank, use the CompareValidator control along with a RequiredFieldValidator control.

Validating User Input Against the Value in Another Control Using the CompareValidator Control

If you have a page where you allow visitors to create a login, you typically ask them for a user name and password. When they enter their password, you typically ask them to enter it twice to make sure that they enter the correct password. On such a page you would want to make sure that visitors entered the same value in both TextBox controls. The CompareValidator control provides for this functionality.

USE IT The ASP.NET page reviewed in this technique asks visitors to enter the same value in two separate TextBox controls. A CompareValidator control makes sure that the value entered by visitors is the same in both controls.

On that page, these two TextBox controls are defined:

```
<asp:textbox
    id="txtSame1"
    runat=server
/>
<BR>
<asp:textbox
    id="txtSame2"
    runat=server
/>
```

The values entered are compared through this CompareValidator control:

```
<asp:comparevalidator
    id="cvCheckValues"
    controltovalidate="txtSame1"
    controltocompare="txtSame2"
```

```
    runat=server
>
    <BR>Please enter the same value in both boxes.
</asp:comparevalidator>
```

The name of one of the controls that you wish to test is placed into the ControlToValidate property. Then in the ControlToCompare property you place the name of the control for which the value must match the first.

If the two values do not match, the page is not submitted and the visitor sees the text specified between the tags of the CompareValidator control. Notice the use of an HTML tag within that text. You can place whatever HTML tags you want within this property.

Comparing a Field to a Date Data Type Using the CompareValidator Control

One of the ways that you can use the CompareValidator control is to make sure that visitors enter a date into a control. This technique shows you how to do that.

USE IT The following ASP.NET page asks visitors to enter a date into a TextBox control. If visitors do not enter a date, they see an error message and they are not allowed to submit the page for processing.

Within the body of the page, this TextBox control is defined, allowing visitors to enter a date:

```
<asp:textbox
    id="txtDate"
    runat=server
/>
```

That value entered into that TextBox control is validated through this CompareValidator control:

```
<asp:comparevalidator
    id="cvCheckDate"
    controltovalidate="txtDate"
    operator="DataTypeCheck"
    type="Date"
    runat="server"
>
    You must enter a date!
</asp:CompareValidator>
```

First, notice the ControlToValidate property. It is set to the name of the TextBox control, which is the control that the CompareValidator control is validating.

Next, notice the value in the Operator property. This property needs to be set to the special value "DataTypeCheck." This value in this property indicates that you are not using a comparison against another value, but instead want to perform a comparison on a data type.

You specify the data type that the value must match through the Type property. Here it is set to "Date," so the value entered must be a date. Then, between the opening and closing tags of the control's definition, you place the text that is displayed if the value entered violates the validation rule.

Comparing a Field to a Numeric Data Type Using the CompareValidator Control

You may frequently have fields on forms that require visitors to place a number into that field. You can use the CompareValidator control to make sure that visitors enter a number. This technique shows you how to use the CompareValidator control for that purpose.

USE IT The ASP.NET page presented in this tip asks visitors to enter a whole number. If they do not, they will see an error message. The TextBox control that visitors are to enter the number into has this definition:

```
<asp:textbox
    id="txtNumber"
    runat=server
/>
```

Validating that input is this CompareValidator control:

```
<asp:comparevalidator
    id="cvCheckNumber"
    controltovalidate="txtNumber"
    operator="DataTypeCheck"
    type="Integer"
    runat="server"
>
    You must enter a whole number!
</asp:CompareValidator><BR><BR>
```

Notice that the ControlToValidate property is set to the name of the TextBox control. The Operator control is set to the value "DataTypeCheck," which means that the test being performed is just to make sure that the value entered is of a certain type.

The Type property is set to "Integer." This means visitors must enter a whole number only. If you wish to validate a number with a fractional amount, enter Double in this property. You can also set this property to Currency to test for a monetary entry.

If visitors do not enter a whole number, they will see the error message declared within the opening and closing tags of the CompareValidator control's definition.

Using a Comparison Operator with the CompareValidator Control

The CompareValidator control can be used to test to see if a value entered is not equal to some other value, or is greater than or less than some other value. This technique shows you how to use the CompareValidator control with a comparison operator.

USE IT This ASP.NET page prompts visitors to enter a whole number that is more than five in value. If visitors do not do that, they will see an error message.

The TextBox control has this definition:

```
<asp:textbox
    id="txtNumber"
    runat=server
/>
```

Then, to validate the entry into the TextBox control, you will find the CompareValidator control.

```
<asp:comparevalidator
    id="cvCheckNumber"
    controltovalidate="txtNumber"
    valuetocompare=5
    operator="GreaterThan"
    type="Integer"
    runat="server"
>
    You must enter a whole number that is more than 5!
</asp:CompareValidator>
```

Notice that the ControlToValidate property is set to the name of the TextBox control. The ValueToCompare property is set to 5, which is the number that the value entered must be greater than.

The Operator property is set to the type of comparison you wish to perform. Here it is set to GreaterThan, so visitors must enter a number that is greater than the value in the ValueToCompare property. You can also set this property to GreaterThanEqual, LessThan, LessThanEqual, Equal, or NotEqual.

Using a RegularExpressionValidator Control to Test a ZIP Code

If you ask visitors for their address you likely will be asking them for their ZIP code. You can use the RegularExpressionValidator control to make sure that visitors enter a five-digit number to help validate their input and to reduce visitor-entry error. This tip shows you how to use the RegularExpressionValidator to perform that task.

USE IT This ASP.NET page prompts visitors for their ZIP code. If visitors enter something other than a five-digit number, they are asked to reenter their ZIP code.

Three controls are defined on this ASP.NET page. The first is the TextBox control that visitors use to enter their ZIP code:

```
<asp:textbox
    id="txtZipCode"
    runat=server
/>
```

The third control is a Command button control that visitors would press to submit the page for processing. Between those two controls is this RegularExpressionValidator control that makes sure visitors enter a five-digit number:

```
<asp:regularexpressionvalidator
    id="regZipCode"
    controltovalidate="txtZipCode"
    validationexpression="^\d{5}$"
    display="Dynamic"
    font-name="Arial"
    font-size="11"
    runat=server
>
    ZIP code must be a number in the form of 12345.
</asp:regularexpressionvalidator>
```

The ID field is set to the name of the RegularExpressionValidator:

```
<asp:regularexpressionvalidator
    id="regZipCode"
```

Then, in the ControlToValidate property you place the name of the control that this control tests:

```
controltovalidate="txtZipCode"
```

The ValidationExpression property contains the regular expression that tests the entry. In this case, you are checking to see if five numbers have been entered:

```
validationexpression="^\d{5}$"
```

With the Display property set to "Dynamic," the space for the error message is only used when the error message is displayed:

```
display="Dynamic"
```

Next, you can set some formatting properties for the control:

```
font-name="Arial"
font-size="11"
runat=server
>
```

Then, between the opening and closing tags of the RegularExpressionValidator control, you place the text of the error message that is displayed if visitors violate the rule.

```
ZIP code must be a number in the form of 12345.
</asp:regularexpressionvalidator>
```

Using a RegularExpressionValidator Control to Prevent the Entry of a Special Character

You may find that you want to prevent visitors from entering a specific special character into a TextBox control. For example, you may need to prevent them from using some character reserved by the database server or some other character that you use for some internal meaning.

You can use the RegularExpressionValidator control to perform this test. This technique shows you how to do that.

USE IT The ASP.NET page presented in this section asks visitors to enter any value into a TextBox control. If the text entered by visitors contains the "'" character, they are prompted to change their entry.

Within the ASP.NET form, this TextBox control is defined for visitors' input:

```
<asp:textbox
    id="txtValue"
    runat=server
/>
```

Then a RegularExpressionValidator control that makes sure visitors do not enter a "'" character is defined:

```
<asp:regularexpressionvalidator
    id="regZipCode"
    controltovalidate="txtValue"
    validationexpression="[^']*"
    display="Dynamic"
    font-name="Arial"
    font-size="11"
    runat=server
>
    You must not use the ' character.
</asp:regularexpressionvalidator>
```

First, notice that the ControlToValidate property is set to the name of the TextBox control. Then notice the string in the ValidationExpression property. The regular expression character "*" states that visitors can enter any number of characters, but that none may be the "'" character. That's the "^'", which means "not an apostrophe."

Between the opening and closing tags for the control, you specify the error message that you want displayed if the rule is violated.

Validating a Phone Number with a RegularExpressionValidator Control

Frequently, you will have a form that asks visitors for their phone number. To make sure that they put in a valid phone number, you can at least make sure that the number entered matches your expected pattern for phone numbers. This technique shows you how to use the RegularExpressionValidator control to perform that task.

 The following ASP.NET page asks visitors to enter their phone number in the form of (999) 999-9999. If they do not, they are prompted to reenter their phone number.

Within the form on the page, a TextBox control that allows visitors to enter their phone number is defined:

```
<asp:textbox
    id=" txtPhoneNumber "
    runat=server
/>
```

After that, a RegularExpressionValidator control is defined that makes sure visitors enter a phone number:

```
<asp:regularexpressionvalidator
    id="regPhoneNumber"
    controltovalidate="txtPhoneNumber"
    validationexpression="\(\d{3}\) \d{3}\-\d{4}"
    display="Dynamic"
    font-name="Arial"
    font-size="11"
    runat=server
>
    You must enter a phone number in the form of (999) 999-9999.
</asp:regularexpressionvalidator>
```

Note that the ControlToValidate property is set to the TextBox control. Take a close look at the pattern in the ValidationExpression property. First, visitors must enter a "(":

```
\ (
```

That needs to be followed by three digits:

```
\d{3}
```

which needs to be followed by the text ")":

```
\ )
```

After that visitors need to enter three more digits:

```
\d{3}
```

followed by a "-":

```
\ -
```

and then four more digits:

```
\d{4}
```

If visitors do not enter text that matches this pattern, they would see the error message defined between the tags of the RegularExpressionValidator control.

Validating an E-mail Address with a RegularExpressionValidator Control

The RegularExpressionValidator control is a powerful control that allows you to test the text entered by visitors in a variety of formats. For example, you may want to test to see if an e-mail address follows an expected pattern. The technique shows you how to use the RegularExpressionValidator control to make such a test.

USE IT   The following code from an ASP.NET page prompts visitors for their e-mail address. The e-mail address must contain one or more characters, followed by the "@", followed by two or more characters, followed by a "." character, followed by a domain grouping like com, edu, or gov. If the text entered does not match the pattern, visitors are asked to reenter their e-mail address.

Visitors enter their email address through a TextBox control:

```
<asp:textbox
    id="txtEmail"
    runat=server
/>
```

That is followed by the RegularExpressionValidator control, which makes sure the text entered matches the e-mail address pattern:

```
<asp:regularexpressionvalidator
    id="regEmail"
    controltovalidate="txtEmail"
    validationexpression="\w+\w*\@\w+\w+\w*\.(com|edu|org|gov)"
    display="Dynamic"
    font-name="Arial"
    font-size="11"
    runat=server
>
    You must enter an email address in the form of me@na.com.
</asp:regularexpressionvalidator>
```

Take a close look at the ValidationExpression. First, visitors must enter a single standard character:

```
\w+
```

That can be followed by any number of standard characters:

```
\w*
```

Next, visitors must enter the "@" character:

```
\@
```

That must be followed by at least two standard characters:

```
\w+\w+
```

which can be followed by additional characters:

```
\w*
```

After that visitors must enter a "." character:

```
\.
```

and one of these character groupings must end the e-mail address:

```
(com|edu|org|gov)
```

Validating Against a Range of Possible Values Using the CustomValidator Control

You may find that the built-in functionality of the validation controls does not give you the data checking that you need. In that case, you can use the CustomValidator control and write your own code that validates the text entered into a control. One of those times may be when you want to check the value entered into a control against a range of values. This tip shows you how to do that.

 The ASP.NET page presented with this tip asks visitors to enter an answer to a question. Then a CustomValidator control with an event procedure checks to see if the answer is correct.

At the top of the form on the ASP.NET page, you will find the question and the control definition for the TextBox:

```
What languages can you use with ASP.NET?<BR>
<asp:textbox
    id="txtAnswer"
    runat=server
/>
```

That is followed by the CustomValidator control definition:

```
<asp:customvalidator
    id="cvRange"
    controltovalidate="txtAnswer"
    onservervalidate="Answer_ServerValidation"
    display="Dynamic"
    font-name="Verdana"
    font-bold="True"
    font-size="10pt"
    runat="server">
    <BR>Incorrect answer please try again!
</asp:CustomValidator>
```

Notice that the ControlToValidate property is set to the name of the TextBox control. Also notice the OnServerValidate property. This property is set to the name of the procedure that performs the custom validation for this control.

Other properties for this control set the style of the error message. The text of that message is displayed between the opening and closing tags of the CustomValidator control.

The procedure that runs to perform the validation has this code:

```
Sub Answer_ServerValidation(source As object, E As ServerValidateEventArgs)
    If E.Value = "VB" or E.Value = "VB.NET" or E.Value = "C#" _
        or E.Value = "C#.NET" or E.Value = "A bunch of others." Then
        E.IsValid = True
```

```
    Else
        E.IsValid = False
    End If
End Sub
```

The code must be defined with these parameters:

```
Sub Answer_ServerValidation(source As object, E As ServerValidateEventArgs)
```

You use the Value property of the ServerValidateEventArgs parameter to determine the value entered into the control that you are testing. In this case that value is the Text property of the txtAnswer TextBox control. Here you check the value entered to see if it matches one of the expected values:

```
If E.Value = "VB" or E.Value = "VB.NET" or E.Value = "C#" _
    or E.Value = "C#.NET" or E.Value = "A bunch of others." Then
```

If it does, the control is valid and the form can be processed:

```
E.IsValid = True
```

Otherwise, the control is not valid:

```
E.IsValid = False
```

Validating Against a Positive, Even, Whole Number Using the CustomValidator Control

Using the CustomValidator control, you can perform a large variety of validation tests. This next technique shows you how you can use the CustomValidator control to check to see if a number is positive, greater than zero, and an even number.

 The ASP.NET page presented with this technique asks visitors to enter a number. If it matches the mentioned pattern, the page can be submitted for processing; otherwise, it cannot.

Visitors enter their number through this TextBox control:

```
<asp:textbox
    id="txtAnswer"
    runat=server
/>
```

This CustomValidator control links to that TextBox control through the ControlToValidate property:

```
<asp:customvalidator
    id="custom9"
```

```
    controltovalidate="txtAnswer"
    onservervalidate="Answer_ServerValidation"
    display="Dynamic"
    font-name="Verdana"
    font-bold="True"
    font-size="10pt"
    runat="server">
    <BR>Incorrect answer please try again!
</asp:CustomValidator>
```

The procedure specified in the OnServerValidate property runs to test the validation. That procedure has the following code.

```
Sub Answer_ServerValidation(source As object, E As ServerValidateEventArgs)
    If  E.Value = CLng(E.Value) Then
        If E.Value Mod 2 = 0 Then
            If E.Value > 0 Then
                E.IsValid = True
            Else
                E.IsValid = False
            End If
        Else
            E.IsValid = False
        End If
    Else
        E.IsValid = False
    End If
End Sub
```

First, in code you check to see if the number is a whole number:

```
If  E.Value = CLng(E.Value) Then
```

Then, if it is, you check to see if the number is even by seeing if it is evenly divisible by two:

```
If E.Value Mod 2 = 0 Then
```

If it is, you perform one more check to see if the number entered is greater than zero:

```
If E.Value > 0 Then
```

If that is the case, the data entered into the control is valid. If any of the checks fail, the control is not valid.

Validating a Percentage Using the CustomValidator Control

One of the ways that you can use the CustomValidator control is to check to see if the value entered into a TextBox control is a percentage. This next tip shows you how to use the CustomValidator control for that purpose.

USE IT   The following ASP.NET code asks visitors to enter a percentage between 0 and 100. If they do, the page can be processed. If visitors do not enter a correct percentage, they are asked to reenter the value.

Visitors enter their percentage through this TextBox control:

```
<asp:textbox
    id="txtAnswer"
    runat=server
/>
```

Then this CustomValidator control validates their input by calling the code specified in the OnServerValidate property:

```
<asp:customvalidator
    id="cvPercent"
    controltovalidate="txtAnswer"
    onservervalidate="Answer_ServerValidation"
    display="Dynamic"
    font-name="Verdana"
    font-bold="True"
    font-size="10pt"
    runat="server">
    <BR>Incorrect answer please try again!
</asp:CustomValidator>
```

That procedure has this definition:

```
Sub Answer_ServerValidation(source As object, E As ServerValidateEventArgs)
    Dim TheNumber as Single
    If Right(E.Value, 1) = "%" Then
        TheNumber = Left(E.Value, Len(E.Value) - 1)
        If TheNumber > 100 or TheNumber < 0 Then
            E.IsValid = False
        Else
            E.IsValid = True
        End If
    Else
```

```
        E.IsValid = False
    End If
End Sub
```

The code performs two checks. First, it checks to see if the text entered into the TextBox control ends with a "%" character:

```
If Right(E.Value, 1) = "%" Then
```

If it doesn't, the text entered into the TextBox control is invalid.

Otherwise, it checks to see if the number portion entered falls within the restricted range:

```
If TheNumber > 100 or TheNumber < 0 Then
```

If it doesn't, the control is not valid. Otherwise, the control is valid.

Validating for a Date in the Current Year Using the CustomValidator Control

You may find that some of the fields you ask visitors to enter on your ASP.NET pages need to be dates. You may also find that those dates need to fall in a range that changes based on the current date. For example, maybe you need visitors to enter a date that falls within the current year. This technique shows you how to do that using the CustomValidator control.

USE IT The ASP.NET page presented in this section asks visitors to enter a date in the current year. If they do, the form can be processed. If they don't enter a date in the current year or don't enter a date at all, the page cannot be processed.

Visitors enter the date through this TextBox control:

```
<asp:textbox
    id="txtDate"
    runat=server
/>
```

The text entered into that control is validated through this CustomValidator control:

```
<asp:customvalidator
    id="customDate"
    controltovalidate="txtDate"
    onservervalidate="Date_ServerValidation"
    display="Dynamic"
    font-name="Verdana"
    font-bold="True"
```

```
     font-size="10pt"
     runat="server">
     You must enter a date in the current year!
</asp:CustomValidator>
```

This CustomValidator control validates the input by calling the procedure specified in the OnServerValidate property. That procedure contains this code:

```
Sub Date_ServerValidation(source As object, E As ServerValidateEventArgs)
    If  IsDate(E.Value) Then
        If  Year(E.Value) = Year(Today) Then
            E.IsValid = True
        Else
            E.IsValid = False
        End If
    Else
        E.IsValid = False
    End If
End Sub
```

The procedure performs two checks on the text being validated. First, it checks that the text entered is a date:

```
If  IsDate(E.Value) Then
```

Next, it checks to see if the year entered in that date matches the current year:

```
If  Year(E.Value) = Year(Today) Then
```

If both of those checks pass, the text entered in the TextBox control is valid. Otherwise, the text entered is not valid.

Creating a Basic ValidationSummary Control

When you have many fields on an ASP.NET page that you are checking through validation controls, you may want to summarize your error messages in one location instead of listing them next to each control that violates one of your rules. The ValidationSummary control provides this functionality. If any of the rules you establish on your page through validation controls do not pass, the summary control displays the text you specify for each of the rules violated at the location you indicate. This tip shows you how to create a basic ValidationSummary control.

USE IT   The ASP.NET page presented in this tip asks visitors to enter their name and a date in two separate TextBox controls. Validation controls make sure that the data entered in the first TextBox control is present and that a date is found in the second TextBox control.

If the rules are violated, visitors see the erring text through a ValidationSummary control. They also see a "*" character next to any field that violates a rule.

Within the form, these two TextBox controls allow the visitors' input:

```
<asp:textbox
    id="txtName"
    runat=server
/>
<asp:textbox
    id="txtDate"
    runat=server
/>
```

The first control is required through the use of this RequiredFieldValidator control:

```
<asp:requiredfieldvalidator
    id="rfvName"
    controltovalidate="txtName"
    errormessage="The name field is required!"
    runat=server
>
*
</asp:requiredfieldvalidator>
```

Notice the ErrorMessage property. This property is set to the text that you want displayed in the ValidationSummary control. Then between the tags, a "*" character is used and will appear next to the TextBox control if the rule is violated.

The second TextBox control must be a date because of this CompareValidator control:

```
<asp:comparevalidator
    id="cvCheckDate"
    controltovalidate="txtDate"
    operator="DataTypeCheck"
    type="Date"
    errormessage="The date field must be a date!"
    runat="server"
>
*
</asp:CompareValidator>
```

Again, notice the use of the ErrorMessage property, which is set to the text that is displayed through the ValidationSummary control. However, the "*" character will appear next to the control if the rule is violated.

At the top of the form, you will find the ValidationSummary control's definition:

```
<asp:validationsummary
    id="vsAllErrors"
```

```
    showsummary="True"
    runat="server"
    headertext="For these reasons, your data could not be processed:"
    displaymode="list"
    font-name="Comic Sans MS"
    font-size="12"
/>
```

The name of the control is set through the ID property:

```
<asp:validationsummary
    id="vsAllErrors"
```

You place the value True in the ShowSummary property to display a list of error messages at the spot where this control is defined:

```
showsummary="True"
runat="server"
```

The HeaderText property is set to the text that you want to appear before the error message:

```
headertext="For these reasons, your data could not be processed:"
```

The error messages will appear in the form of a list:

```
displaymode="list"
```

You can also set font and color properties for the control:

```
    font-name="Comic Sans MS"
    font-size="12"
/>
```

Creating an Error List Using the ValidationSummary Control

The ValidationSummary control is a great control to display error messages. It can be used in a variety of forms. One of those forms is to display the error messages as a bullet list at the top of the page. This technique shows you how to use the ValidationSummary control in that way.

USE IT   Take a look at the screenshot rendered from this technique.

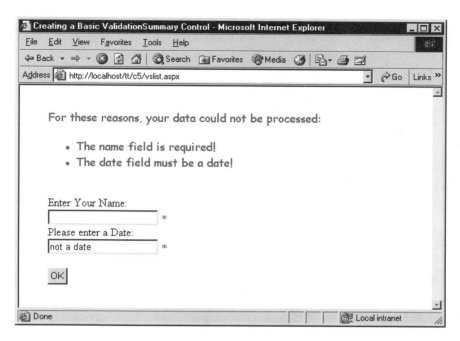

This page requires that visitors enter their name and a date. The name field is required and the date field must be a date. Notice the text that displays the bulleted error messages at the top of the page. Those error messages are displayed through a ValidationSummary control. Also notice the "*" characters next to the TextBox controls. Those messages are placed using the standard validation controls. So using these controls together should make it easy for your visitors to identify controls that they need to reenter data through.

The two TextBox controls on the page have these definitions:

```
<asp:textbox
    id="txtName"
    runat=server
/>
<asp:textbox
    id="txtDate"
    runat=server
/>
```

The name field is required through this RequiredFieldValidator control:

```
<asp:requiredfieldvalidator
    id="rfvName"
    controltovalidate="txtName"
    errormessage="The name field is required!"
    runat=server
```

```
>
*
</asp:requiredfieldvalidator>
```

And the date field must be a date because of the CompareValidator control:

```
<asp:comparevalidator
    id="cvCheckDate"
    controltovalidate="txtDate"
    operator="DataTypeCheck"
    type="Date"
    errormessage="The date field must be a date!"
    runat="server"
>
*
</asp:comparevalidator>
```

At the top of the page, this ValidationSummary control is defined:

```
<asp:validationsummary
    id="vsAllErrors"
    showsummary="True"
    runat="server"
    headertext="For these reasons, your data could not be processed:"
    displaymode="bulletlist"
    font-name="Comic Sans MS"
    font-size="12"
/>
```

Notice the ShowSummary property. Since it is set to True, a list of error messages is displayed within the control. Notice that the DisplayMode property is set to "BulletList." This means that the error messages appear as bulleted items.

Displaying Error Messages in a Message Box Using the ValidationSummary Control

Another great feature of the ValidationSummary control is that you can display the list of validation error messages generated by the data entered by visitors through a message box. So when visitors try to submit the page for processing, they see a message box, or an alert box, with the error messages in it. The technique presented in this section shows you how to do that.

USE IT   This ASP.NET page prompts visitors for their name and a date. The name field is required and the date field must be a date. If these rules are not met, visitors see a message box informing them of their data errors and the page is not processed.

On the page, two TextBox controls and two validation controls are defined:

```
<asp:textbox
    id="txtName"
    runat=server
/>
<asp:requiredfieldvalidator
    id="rfvName"
    controltovalidate="txtName"
    errormessage="The name field is required!"
    runat=server
>
*
</asp:requiredfieldvalidator>
<asp:textbox
    id="txtDate"
    runat=server
/>
<asp:comparevalidator
    id="cvCheckDate"
    controltovalidate="txtDate"
    operator="DataTypeCheck"
    type="Date"
    errormessage="The date field must be a date!"
    runat="server"
>
*
</asp:CompareValidator>
```

The first TextBox control is for the name, and the RequiredFieldValidator control makes sure they enter a value. The second TextBox control is for the date, and the CompareValidator control makes sure that it is a date.

Also defined on the page is this ValidationSummary control:

```
<asp:validationsummary
    id="vsAllErrors"
    showsummary="False"
    showmessagebox="True"
    runat="server"
    headertext="For these reasons, your data could not be processed:"
/>
```

Notice that the ShowSummary property is set to False. This means a list of error messages on the page will not be present. Also notice the ShowMessageBox property. Setting this property to True is what generates the message box when the visitor violates a rule and submits the page for processing.

CHAPTER 6
Other Web Controls

TIPS IN THIS CHAPTER

A SP.NET comes with a variety of controls that make developing an ASP.NET page much simpler to do. In this chapter, tips and techniques are presented using four of those controls. First, tips and techniques using the Calendar control will be presented. Then the tips and techniques for the AdRotator control will be presented. That will be followed by tips and techniques for the Panel control. And finally, tips and techniques for the Table control will be presented.

▼ Creating a Basic Calendar Control

The Calendar control combines some of the best aspects of ASP.NET to produce a control that is very flexible and easy to use. The control renders itself in the visitor's browser as a well-defined HTML table that displays dates in a month. With client-side JavaScript generated by the control, no code is required on your part to allow visitors to change months or years, or to select a date. If you have ever tried to generate your own Calendar interface, you know how much code such a control requires and you should find yourself pleased that the control is part of the basic ASP.NET libraries.

The technique presented in this section shows you how to define a basic Calendar control.

The ASP.NET page presented in this chapter displays to visitors a basic Calendar and asks them to select a date. The Calendar controls definition on this page is shown here:

```
<asp:Calendar
    id="Mycal"
    runat="server"
    cellpadding="3"
    cellspacing="3"
    daynameformat="Short"
    firstdayofweek="Monday"
    nextprevformat="FullMonth"
    titleformat="MonthYear"
    font-name="Tahoma"
    font-size="12"
    backcolor="ivory"
/>
```

You set the name of the control through the ID property:

```
<asp:Calendar
    id="Mycal"
    runat="server"
```

Since the control is rendered through an HTML table, you can set the amount of space that appears between dates in the Calendar control through the CellPadding and CellSpacing properties:

```
cellpadding="3"
cellspacing="3"
```

You can set the format for the names displayed for the days of the week through the DayNameFormat property. Here it is set to Short, which means the days will be displayed as an abbreviation:

```
daynameformat="Short"
```

You can also set this property to FirstLetter, FirstTwoLetters, or Full.

The FirstDayOfWeek property is set to the day of the week that should be displayed first in the Calendar control. In addition to setting this property to the weekday that you wish the calendar to start at, you can also set this value to Default. Using Default displays the weekdays in the default style stored on the server:

```
firstdayofweek="Monday"
```

Displayed at the top of the Calendar control are links that allow visitors to change months. You set the text that is displayed in those links through the NextPrevFormat property. Here it is set to the full name of the next and previous months:

```
nextprevformat="FullMonth"
```

You can also set the property to ShortMonth to see an abbreviation of the month.

Also displayed at the top of the Calendar control is a title. You can set the format of that title with the TitleFormat property. Here the current month and year being viewed are displayed:

```
titleformat="MonthYear"
```

You can also set this property to Month, which displays only the month in the title.

The look of the control can be defined by setting the font and color properties:

```
    font-name="Tahoma"
    font-size="12"
    backcolor="ivory"
/>
```

Here's the screenshot displayed when running this page.

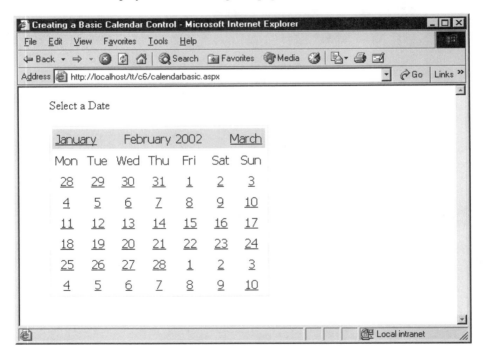

Notice the top row of the Calendar control. Visitors would select a different month by selecting the Previous or Next Month links. Also notice in that row that the current month and year are displayed as were set in the properties for this control. Finally, notice that the first day of the week is set to Monday and was also set through the properties of the control.

Formatting the Header Styles in a Calendar Control

The flexible Calendar control provides different styles you can set to control the look and feel of different sections of the control. In this tip, you will see how you can use the DayHeaderStyle, TitleStyle, and NextPrevStyle properties to control the look of the Calendar control.

 The ASP.NET page presented in this section displays a Calendar control that uses Header styles to control its format. Take a look at the screenshot from this page.

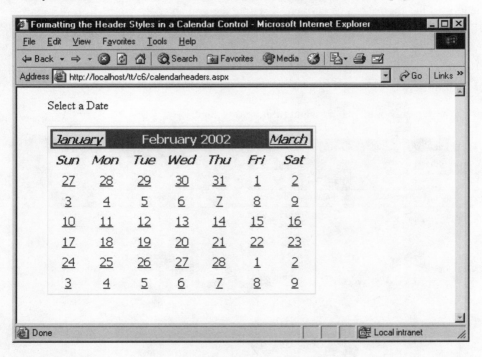

Notice in this screenshot the font and color settings in the first two rows of the Calendar control. The definition of the Calendar control that produces this output is displayed here:

```
<asp:Calendar
    id="Mycal"
    runat="server"
    cellpadding="3"
    cellspacing="3"
    daynameformat="Short"
    firstdayofweek="Default"
    nextprevformat="FullMonth"
```

```
      titleformat="MonthYear"
      font-name="Tahoma"
      font-size="12"
      backcolor="ivory"
      dayheaderstyle-font-bold="True"
      dayheaderstyle-font-italic="True"
      dayheaderstyle-forecolor="DarkBlue"
      titlestyle-backcolor="#3366ff"
      titlestyle-forecolor="white"
      titlestyle-font-bold="True"
      nextprevstyle-font-italic="True"
      nextprevstyle-backcolor="Yellow"
/>
```

Three different style settings are used in this definition. The first is the DayHeaderStyle:

```
dayheaderstyle-font-bold="True"
dayheaderstyle-font-italic="True"
dayheaderstyle-forecolor="DarkBlue"
```

This style defines the look and feel of the row that contains the weekdays.

Another style that is set in this Calendar control is the TitleStyle:

```
titlestyle-backcolor="#3366ff"
titlestyle-forecolor="white"
titlestyle-font-bold="True"
```

The settings placed in this style set the defaults used in the full first row of the Calendar control. This is the area where the title of the calendar appears, as well as the area where the next and previous months appear. But you can also set the NextPrevStyle properties:

```
nextprevstyle-font-italic="True"
nextprevstyle-backcolor="Yellow"
```

These are used to determine the look of the next and previous month links. So if you don't set these properties, the TitleStyle will be used.

▶ | **QUICK TIP**

If you don't use the different style properties, they typically default to the style used in the definition of the underlying control. So if you don't use the DayHeaderStyle but do set the BackColor property of the control to red, the DayHeaderStyle will inherit that value for its BackColor property.

Formatting Date Sections in a Calendar Control

In addition to controlling the look of the header styles in the Calendar control, you can also control the appearance of different dates within the dates section of the Calendar control. The tip presented in this section shows you how to use four of those styles.

 This ASP.NET page uses the TodayDayStyle, SelectedDayStyle, WeekendDayStyle, and the OtherMonthDayStyle properties to control the layout of the date portion of the Calendar control. This screenshot shows the output of this page.

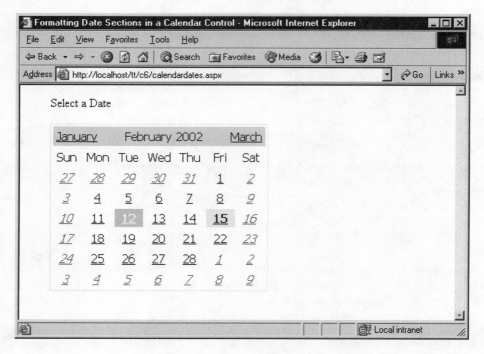

Notice the numbers 27 through 31 in the first row of the dates. These dates are from January. You can set the look of these dates using style properties. The style of the current date, the 15, and the selected date are also set to appear in a different style. Additionally, the weekend days appear in a different style.

Here's the definition for the Calendar control used on this page:

```
<asp:Calendar
    id="Mycal"
    runat="server"
```

```
        cellpadding="3"
        cellspacing="3"
        daynameformat="Short"
        firstdayofweek="Default"
        nextprevformat="FullMonth"
        titleformat="MonthYear"
        font-name="Tahoma"
        font-size="12"
        backcolor="ivory"
        todaydaystyle-Font-Bold="True"
        todaydaystyle-backcolor="Yellow"
        selecteddayStyle-backcolor="#ffcc66"
        selecteddayStyle-font-bold="True"
        weekenddaystyle-font-italic="True"
        weekenddaystyle-forecolor="Red"
        othermonthdaystyle-font-italic="True"
        othermonthdaystyle-backcolor="white"
        othermonthdaystyle-forecolor="gray"
/>
```

The TodayDayStyle is used to control the font and color properties for the current system date:

```
todaydaystyle-Font-Bold="True"
todaydaystyle-backcolor="Yellow"
```

The SelectedDayStyle determines the appearance of the date that is clicked on in the Calendar control by visitors:

```
selecteddayStyle-backcolor="#ffcc66"
selecteddayStyle-font-bold="True"
```

You set the font and color properties of the weekend dates through the WeekendDayStyle properties:

```
weekenddaystyle-font-italic="True"
weekenddaystyle-forecolor="Red"
```

The days that appear before the current month or after the current month can have their appearance set through the OtherMonthDayStyle properties:

```
othermonthdaystyle-font-italic="True"
othermonthdaystyle-backcolor="white"
othermonthdaystyle-forecolor="gray"
```

Showing and Hiding Sections in a Calendar Control

You may find that you want to provide your own custom title in a Calendar control. Or you may decide that you don't wish to have the weekdays appearing in the Calendar control. The Calendar control provides properties for showing and hiding different sections of a Calendar control.

USE IT The page presented in this section generates a Calendar control that displays nothing except the dates in a month. It does this using the Show properties of the Calendar control.

Take a look at the definition for this control:

```
<asp:Calendar
    id="Mycal"
    runat="server"
    cellpadding="3"
    cellspacing="3"
    showgridlines="true"
    showdayheader="False"
    shownextprevmonth="False"
    showtitle="false"
/>
```

The ShowGridLines property is used to affect whether the HTML table cell lines between the dates in the Calendar control appear. If you set the property to True, you will see them. If you set the property to False, the control does not display grid lines.

If the ShowDayHeader property is set to True, you will see the days of the week in the Calendar control. If it is set to False, you will not.

The ShowNextPrevMonth property is used to determine whether the links to the next and previous months are displayed. If that property is set to True, they are. And if the property is set to False, they are not displayed in the Calendar control.

Setting the ShowTitle property to True will display the month or the month/year text in the first row of the control. If you set it to False, this text is not displayed.

Setting Custom Previous and
Next Month Text in the Calendar Control

You may find that the default link that visitors click in the Calendar control to view the next or the previous month is not what you want displayed in your Calendar control. Typically, the name of that next or previous month is displayed. But if you find that is not descriptive enough or if you feel that you need some other custom text to appear in that space in the Calendar control, you can supply your own link text.

USE IT The Calendar control presented in this tip shows you how to use three properties to supply your own custom text in the previous and next month links. Here is the definition for that control:

```
<asp:Calendar
    id="Mycal"
    runat="server"
    cellpadding="3"
    cellspacing="3"
    nextprevformat="CustomText"
    nextmonthtext="Next"
    prevmonthtext="Prev"
/>
```

First, you need to set the NextPrevFormat property to CustomText:

```
nextprevformat="CustomText"
```

Then, in the NextMonthText property you place whatever text you want to appear in the link spot for the next month in the Calendar control:

```
nextmonthtext="Next"
```

In the PrevMonthText property you place the text that should appear as a link in the Calendar control that takes visitors to the previous month:

```
prevmonthtext="Prev"
```

Writing Code That Fires When a Date Is Selected in a Calendar Control

When you use a Calendar control it is likely that you will want to take some action when visitors select a date or at least do something with the date selected. For example, you may have visitors select a date that they will arrive at your hotel. When they select the date in a Calendar control, you may want to place that date in a TextBox control. This technique shows you how to write a procedure that runs when the date in a Calendar control changes and how to determine the date selected by visitors.

USE IT This page displays a Calendar control to visitors. When they select a date in the Calendar control, the date they selected is displayed back to them in a Label control.

The Label control on the page has this definition:

```
<asp:Label
    id="lblMessage"
    runat="server"
    Font-Bold="True"
/>
```

And the Calendar control has this definition:

```
<asp:Calendar
    id="Mycal"
    runat="server"
    cellpadding="3"
    cellspacing="3"
    onselectionchanged="calSelectChange"
/>
```

Notice the OnSelectionChanged property. This property is set to the name of the procedure that you want to run when visitors select a date in the Calendar control. That procedure has this definition:

```
Sub calSelectChange(ByVal Sender as Object, ByVal E as EventArgs)
    lblMessage.Text = "You selected " _
        & MyCal.SelectedDate
End Sub
```

You determine the date selected in the Calendar control through the SelectedDate property. That value is placed into the Text property of the Label control.

Displaying a Date in the Calendar Control

When you first display a Calendar control, you may want to nominate an initial date as the selected date. For example, you may have some date from a database that you want to display. Or maybe visitors typically select a date that is one month from today. Therefore, you would want the control to default to a date one month from the current date. The technique presented in this section shows you how to set the initial date selected in the Calendar control.

USE IT This ASP.NET page displays a Calendar control. The initial selected date in that Calendar control is set to one month in the future of the system date on the server. The Calendar control on that page has this definition:

```
<asp:Calendar
    id="Mycal"
    runat="server"
    cellpadding="3"
    cellspacing="3"
/>
```

When the page first loads, the following code runs:

```
Sub Page_Load(ByVal Sender as Object, ByVal E as EventArgs)
    If Not IsPostBack Then
```

```
    MyCal.SelectedDate = DateAdd( _
        Microsoft.VisualBasic.DateInterval.Month, 2, Today())
    MyCal.VisibleDate = DateAdd( _
        Microsoft.VisualBasic.DateInterval.Month, 2, Today())
  End If
End Sub
```

The code only runs when the page first loads. The SelectedDate property of the Calendar control is set to one month in the future by using the DateAdd function.

If that is all you do, the currently selected date will be set to that value, but the month displayed in the Calendar control will be the current month. However, if you also set the VisibleDate property to the date you want selected, the month for that date will be displayed in the Calendar control.

Allowing the Selection of Multiple Dates in a Calendar Control

By default, the Calendar control allows visitors to select a single date as the selected date. But you can also allow visitors to select a date range through the Calendar control in the form of a week or a month. The technique presented in this section of the chapter shows you how to do that.

 The ASP.NET page presented in this section provides links in the Calendar control for the selection of an entire week or month. Take a look at the screenshot derived from this page:

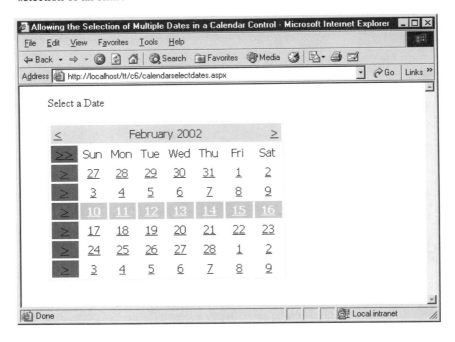

Notice the new column that appears before Sunday in the Calendar control. That column allows for the selection of multiple dates. If visitors select the ">>" link, the entire month is selected. If visitors click on any of the ">" links beneath that one, that week is selected. Also, visitors can still select a single date by clicking it.

The code that produces this Calendar control is displayed here:

```
<asp:calendar
    id="Mycal"
    runat="server"
    cellpadding="3"
    cellspacing="3"
    selectionmode="DayWeekMonth"
    selectorstyle-font-bold="True"
    selectorStyle-backcolor="#3366ff"
    font-name="Tahoma"
    font-size="12"
    backcolor="ivory"
    selecteddaystyle-backcolor="#ffcc66"
    selecteddaystyle-font-bold="True"
/>
```

The property that controls what type of date selection can be made is the SelectionMode property:

```
selectionmode="DayWeekMonth"
```

Here it is set to DayWeekMonth, which means visitors can select a day, a full week, or the entire month. You can also set this value to Day and DayWeek.

If you set the SelectionMode property to DayWeek or DayWeekMonth, you can control the appearance of the selection column through the SelectorStyle properties:

> ▶ **QUICK TIP**
>
> *If you do not want visitors to be able to select a date at all, set the SelectionMode property to None.*

```
selectorstyle-font-bold="True"
selectorStyle-backcolor="#3366ff"
```

Reading Selected Dates in a Date Range Through the Calendar Control

If you allow visitors to select a range of dates, whether a week or a month, you will likely want to read the dates they select. When a single date is selected, all you need to do is query the SelectedDate property. But when a range of dates is selected, you need to use the SelectedDates collection. This technique shows you how to do that.

USE IT   The ASP.NET page presented in this technique allows visitors to select a single date, a week of dates, or an entire month. Once a selection is made, visitors see the list of dates selected back through a Label control.

The Calendar control has this definition:

```
<asp:calendar
    id="Mycal"
    runat="server"
    cellpadding="3"
    cellspacing="3"
    selectionmode="DayWeekMonth"
    selectorstyle-font-bold="True"
    selectorStyle-backcolor="#3366ff"
    font-name="Tahoma"
    font-size="12"
    backcolor="ivory"
    selecteddaystyle-backcolor="#ffcc66"
    selecteddaystyle-font-bold="True"
    onselectionchanged="calSelectChange"
/>
```

Notice that the SelectionMode property is set to DayWeekMonth, allowing visitors to select a range of dates. Also notice that the OnSelectionChanged property is set. That means that when a date is selected the procedure calSelectChange fires. That procedure has this definition:

```
Sub calSelectChange(ByVal Sender as Object, ByVal E as EventArgs)
    Dim i as Integer
    lblMessage.Text = "You selected:"
    For i = 0 to MyCal.SelectedDates.Count - 1
        lblMessage.Text = lblMessage.Text & "<BR>" _
            & MyCal.SelectedDates(i).ToShortDateString()
    Next
End Sub
```

In this procedure, you iterate through all the selected dates in the Calendar control:

```
For i = 0 to MyCal.SelectedDates.Count - 1
```

The value of each selected date is appended to the text in the Label control:

```
lblMessage.Text = lblMessage.Text & "<BR>" _
    & MyCal.SelectedDates(i).ToShortDateString()
```

Displaying a Selected Range of Dates in the Calendar Control

You may find in a Calendar control that you need to not just select a single date in code but you need to select a series of dates. For example, maybe when visitors select a single date, you want to mark all the weekdays that go with that date. Or maybe you want to display the start date and the end date of a report you will be showing. This technique shows you how to have a range of dates highlighted in the Calendar control.

 The following ASP.NET page marks the current date as well as the next four days as selected in a Calendar control when the page first loads. The Calendar control has this definition:

```
<asp:calendar
    id="Mycal"
    runat="server"
    cellpadding="3"
    cellspacing="3"
    selectionmode="DayWeekMonth"
    selectorstyle-font-bold="True"
    selectorStyle-backcolor="#3366ff"
    font-name="Tahoma"
    font-size="12"
    backcolor="ivory"
    selecteddaystyle-backcolor="#ffcc66"
    selecteddaystyle-font-bold="True"
/>
```

Notice that the SelectionMode property is set to DayWeekMonth. Therefore, visitors would be able to select a range of dates. But a range of dates is automatically selected when the page first loads through this code:

```
Sub Page_Load(ByVal Sender as Object, ByVal E as EventArgs)
    If Not IsPostBack Then
        Dim I as Integer
        For i = 0 to 4
            MyCal.SelectedDates.Add(DateAdd( _
                Microsoft.VisualBasic.DateInterval.Day, _
                i, Today()))
        Next
    End If
End Sub
```

Since the PostBack property is checked, the code only runs when the page first loads. Within the code block a loop is established that will run five times. And within that loop a date is added to the

SelectedDates collection using the Add method of that collection. The date that is added is based on the current date and the offset of the looping variable. Each of the five dates added through the iterations of this loop will appear as selected dates in the Calendar control.

Writing Code That Fires When the Month Changes in a Calendar Control

When the month that is displayed within a Calendar control changes because visitors select the previous month or next month links, an event fires that you can code for. This technique shows you how to do that.

USE IT   This ASP.NET page presents visitors with a Calendar control. When visitors change to a new month, the old month and the new month are echoed to them through a Label control. That Label control has this definition:

```
<asp:Label
    id="lblMessage"
    runat="server"
    Font-Bold="True"
/>
```

The Calendar control on that page has this definition:

```
<asp:Calendar
    id="Mycal"
    runat="server"
    cellpadding="3"
    cellspacing="3"
    onvisiblemonthchanged="calMonthChange"
/>
```

Notice the OnVisibleMonthChanged property. When you place a value in this property the procedure that matches that value runs whenever the month displayed in the Calendar control changes.

That procedure has this definition:

```
Sub calMonthChange(ByVal source As Object, _
    ByVal e As MonthChangedEventArgs)
    lblMessage.Text = "<BR>You changed from month " _
        & e.PreviousDate.Month & " and year " _
        & e.PreviousDate.Year & " to month " _
        & e.NewDate.Month & " and year " _
        & e.NewDate.Year
End Sub
```

Notice the second parameter of the procedure, MonthChangedEventArgs. That parameter returns to you the PreviousDate and the NewDate properties. Those properties contain the month and year of the previous month displayed and the new month displayed, respectively. Using those properties, visitors see the month and the year for the current month as well as the month they were looking at prior to the change.

Controlling the Appearance of Individual Cells of Dates in the Calendar Control

The Calendar control has an event that you can write code for that fires every time a cell is created in the Calendar control. Passed into that procedure is the date that is being displayed. Therefore, you can have code that modifies the appearance of an individual cell based on the date being displayed. This technique shows you how to do that.

USE IT   The ASP.NET page presented in this section displays a Calendar control. In code, the DayRender event is used to change the appearance of the cells that display certain holidays. The Calendar control has this definition:

```
<asp:Calendar
    id="Mycal"
    runat="server"
    cellpadding="3"
    cellspacing="3"
    ondayrender="DateDisplayed"
/>
```

Notice the OnDayRender property. If you place a value in that property, the name of a procedure that matches that value runs whenever a date is created in the Calendar control. That procedure has this definition:

```
Sub DateDisplayed(source As Object, e As DayRenderEventArgs)
    If e.Day.Date.Month = "2" and e.Day.Date.Day = "14" Then
        e.Cell.BackColor = System.Drawing.Color.Red
        e.Cell.ForeColor = System.Drawing.Color.Yellow
    ElseIf e.Day.Date.Month = "12" and e.Day.Date.Day = "25" Then
        e.Cell.BackColor = System.Drawing.Color.Green
        e.Cell.ForeColor = System.Drawing.Color.Red
    ElseIf e.Day.Date.Month = "10" and e.Day.Date.Day = "31" Then
        e.Cell.BackColor = System.Drawing.Color.Orange
        e.Cell.ForeColor = System.Drawing.Color.Black
    End If
End Sub
```

Notice the second parameter of the procedure, DayRenderEventArgs. This parameter allows you to see the date that is being displayed through the Day property. If that date matches one of the holiday dates that the code catches, the Cell property of the DayRenderEventArgs parameter is used to change the appearance of that cell.

Creating an Ad File for an AdRotator Control

To be able to use an AdRotator control, you will want to create an AdRotator file that determines what ads are displayed and in what proportion those ads are displayed. This technique shows you how to do that.

USE IT An Ad file for an AdRotator control must follow a very specific structure. First, you need to save the file with a .xml extension. Then note the name of the file as you will use it in code when you create an Ad file.

The basic structure of an Ad file looks like this:

```
<Advertisements>
   <Ad>
      <ImageUrl>./SampleBanner.gif</ImageUrl>
      <NavigateUrl>http://www.google.com</NavigateUrl>
      <AlternateText>Click me now!</AlternateText>
      <Impressions>71</Impressions>
   </Ad>
   <Ad>
      <ImageUrl>./AnotherSample.gif</ImageUrl>
      <NavigateUrl>http://www.microsoft.com</NavigateUrl>
      <AlternateText>Go to Microsoft Site</AlternateText>
      <Impressions>70</Impressions>
   </Ad>
</Advertisements>
```

The contents of the files are placed within opening and closing Advertisements tags:

```
<Advertisements>
```

Within those tags, each ad is defined with opening and closing Ad tags:

```
<Ad>
```

Then within each of those tags you define the ad. First, you place the path to the picture to be displayed with the ad through the ImageURL tag:

```
<ImageUrl>./AnotherSample.gif</ImageUrl>
```

Then within the NavigateURL tag you place the site that visitors should go to if they click on the ad:

```
<NavigateUrl>http://www.microsoft.com</NavigateUrl>
```

Within the AlternateText tag you place the text visitors see if they hover their mouse over the image of the ad:

```
<AlternateText>Go to Microsoft Site</AlternateText>
```

And within the Impressions tag you place the proportion that this ad should be displayed at when compared with all the other ads in the Ad file:

```
<Impressions>70</Impressions>
```

So if you make this number the same for all the ads in the Ad file, each ad would have an equal likelihood of being displayed. If you gave one ad a number twice as large as the rest of the ads, that ad would be twice as likely to be displayed.

QUICK TIP

To determine the percentage of time a single ad will be displayed, add up all the impression values. Divide that by the number of impressions set to the ad in question. Then multiply that value by 100 and you will have the percentage.

Using a Basic AdRotator Control

Once you have defined an Ad file you will likely want to use that file with an AdRotator control in code. The AdRotator control uses the value in an Ad file to determine what ad image to display. The control is rendered as an HTML anchor tag with an embedded HTML image tag. This tip shows you how to use a basic AdRotator control.

 The ASP.NET page defined for this tip contains a single control. That control is the AdRotator control. It has the following definition:

```
<asp:adrotator
    advertisementfile="AdRotatorBasic.xml"
    target="_blank"
    bordercolor="blue"
    borderwidth=3
    runat="server"
/>
```

First, in the AdvertisementFile property you set the name of the Ad file:

```
advertisementfile="AdRotatorBasic.xml"
```

Often when visitors click on a banner ad, you want the destination site to open in a new window. You can do that using the Target property and setting it to the value "_blank":

```
target="_blank"
```

You can also set the color of the border displayed around the ad image:

```
bordercolor="blue"
```

And the width of that border:

```
borderwidth=3
```

Creating an Ad File for an AdRotator Control That Uses the Keyword Tag

Sometimes when you have banner ads on your ASP.NET pages you want to display certain ads on one page but not on other pages. For example, maybe you have a site that displays restaurants in different cities. Based on the city being viewed, you may want to display banner ads just for that city.

The Ad file and the AdRotator control support this functionality. This technique shows you how to create an Ad file that allows for the filtering of ads.

 The Ad file presented with this technique uses the Keyword attribute to allow for the filtering of ads through an AdRotator control. That Ad file has this definition:

```
<Advertisements>
    <Ad>
        <ImageUrl>./SampleBanner.gif</ImageUrl>
        <NavigateUrl>http://www.google.com</NavigateUrl>
        <AlternateText>Click me now!</AlternateText>
        <Keyword>ShowMe</Keyword>
        <Impressions>71</Impressions>
    </Ad>
    <Ad>
        <ImageUrl>./AnotherSample.gif</ImageUrl>
        <NavigateUrl>http://www.microsoft.com</NavigateUrl>
        <AlternateText>Go to Microsoft Site</AlternateText>
        <Keyword>ShowMe</Keyword>
```

```
    <Impressions>70</Impressions>
  </Ad>
  <Ad>
    <ImageUrl>./DoesNotExist.gif</ImageUrl>
    <NavigateUrl>http://www.microsoft.com</NavigateUrl>
    <AlternateText>Won't see me</AlternateText>
    <Keyword>DoNotShowMe</Keyword>
    <Impressions>2000</Impressions>
  </Ad>
</Advertisements>
```

Notice the Keyword tag. The first two ads have this keyword:

```
<Keyword>ShowMe</Keyword>
```

and the third ad has this keyword:

```
<Keyword>DoNotShowMe</Keyword>
```

When you define an AdRotator control, if you were to filter on the first keyword, then only the first two ads would be displayed. If you filtered by the keyword used in the third ad, then only that ad would be displayed. If you were to use no filtering with your AdRotator control, all the ads could be viewed.

Using a Keyword AdRotator Control

If you create an AdRotator control on an ASP.NET page that needs to filter the ads displayed and only display a subset of those ads, you need to use the Keyword property for the AdRotator control. This tip shows you how to use that property.

 The AdRotator control defined on this page will only display two of the three ads defined in an Ad file because it filters those ads. That control has the following definition:

```
<asp:adrotator
    advertisementfile="AdRotatorKeyword.xml"
    keywordfilter="ShowMe"
    target="_blank"
    bordercolor="blue"
    borderwidth=3
    runat="server"
/>
```

Notice the KeywordFilter property. Since it is present, only ads that have the value "ShowMe" in their Keyword tag within the Ad file will be displayed. An ad with any other value will not be displayed on this page.

Writing Code That Fires When an Ad Is Created Using an AdRotator Control

You may find yourself in need of having code that runs whenever an ad is created through the AdRotator control. For example, you may want to store in a database the fact that a specific ad was displayed and information on that impression. The AdRotator control provides an event called AdCreated that you can write code for to run when an ad is created. This technique shows you how to do that.

USE IT   The ASP.NET page presented in this section displays an ad through the Ad Rotator control. It also displays information about the ad being displayed using the AdCreated event through the Text property of a Label control. That Label control has this definition:

```
<asp:Label
    id="lblMessage"
    runat="server"
/>
```

The AdRotator control has this definition:

```
<asp:adrotator
    id="ad1"
    onadcreated="AdCreated_Event"
    advertisementfile="AdRotatorCustom.xml"
    target="_blank"
    bordercolor="blue"
    borderwidth=3
    runat="server"
/>
```

Notice the use of the OnAdCreated property. The value you place in that property is used to determine the name of the procedure to run when an ad is created through the AdRotator control. That procedure has this definition:

```
Sub AdCreated_Event(ByVal Sender as Object, _
    ByVal E as AdCreatedEventArgs)
    lblMessage.Text = "Here is information on the ad " _
        & "currently being displayed:<BR>" _
        & "<BR>Alternate Text: " & E.AlternateText _
        & "<BR>Image URL: " & E.ImageURL _
        & "<BR>Navigate URL: " & E.NavigateURL
End Sub
```

Notice the second parameter in this procedure, AdCreatedEventArgs. That parameter returns to you the information about the ad being displayed. So it is used here to display back to visitors the basic information about the ad being displayed.

Creating an Ad File for an AdRotator Control That Uses a Custom Tag

In addition to the basic tags that you can place within an Ad file, you can also insert your own custom tags. These tags could simply be comments that you add to each ad to help you note something about the ad. Or they could be values that you want to use in code when an ad is created through the AdRotator control. For example, you may want to store the name of the company that the ad is being displayed for. That way, when the ad is displayed you will know who to charge the ad's impression to. This tip shows you how to create an Ad file that contains a custom tag.

 The Ad file created for this tip has the following definition:

```
<Advertisements>
    <Ad>
        <ImageUrl>./SampleBanner.gif</ImageUrl>
        <NavigateUrl>http://www.google.com</NavigateUrl>
        <AlternateText>Click me now!</AlternateText>
        <Impressions>71</Impressions>
        <AccountName>BLR</AccountName>
    </Ad>
    <Ad>
        <ImageUrl>./AnotherSample.gif</ImageUrl>
        <NavigateUrl>http://www.microsoft.com</NavigateUrl>
        <AlternateText>Go to Microsoft Site</AlternateText>
        <Impressions>70</Impressions>
        <AccountName>TVB</AccountName>
    </Ad>
</Advertisements>
```

Notice the use of the custom tag AccountName:

```
<AccountName>TVB</AccountName>
```

This tag can now be referenced in code when an ad is created through the AdRotator control. Notice the structure of the custom tag. It contains opening and closing tags that have the exact same name. You can use this technique to create a large variety of your own custom tags.

Using a Custom Tag in an AdRotator Control

If you place a Custom tag in an Ad file, you may want to reference the value of that Custom tag in code when an ad is created through an AdRotator control. This tip shows you how to do that.

USE IT The following ASP.NET page displays a banner ad to visitors through the AdRotator control. When an ad is created, the value in the Custom tag AccountName is displayed to visitors through the Text property of a Label control. That Label control has this definition:

```
<asp:Label
    id="lblMessage"
    runat="server"
/>
```

The AdRotator control has this definition:

```
<asp:adrotator
    id="ad1"
    onadcreated="AdCreated_Event"
    advertisementfile="AdRotatorCustom.xml"
    target="_blank"
    bordercolor="blue"
    borderwidth=3
    runat="server"
/>
```

Notice that the OnAdCreated property is being used. That means that this procedure will run whenever an ad is created:

```
Sub AdCreated_Event(ByVal Sender as Object, _
    ByVal E as AdCreatedEventArgs)
    lblMessage.Text = "Here is the account name for the ad: " _
        & E.AdProperties("AccountName").ToString()
End Sub
```

The procedure uses the AdProperties collection of the AdCreatedEventArgs parameter to determine the value of the AccountName Custom property. The value of that property is displayed through a Label control.

Creating a Basic Panel Control

The Panel control is used to group together other controls into some logical structure to help with the programming of an ASP.NET page. The control itself does not have any visible output that visitors see in their browser. Instead, you place other controls and HTML elements within the definition of the Panel control. This technique shows you how to create a basic Panel control.

USE IT The ASP.NET page created for this technique defines a Panel control with HTML elements and TextBox controls contained within it. The Panel control has this definition:

```
<asp:panel
    id="Panel1"
    runat="server"
    height="80%"
    width="90%">
    Enter your name:<BR>
    <asp:textbox
    id="txtName"
    runat=server
    />
    <BR>
    Enter your password:<BR>
    <asp:textbox
    id="txtPassword"
    runat=server
    />
    <BR>
</asp:Panel>
```

First, the Panel control is defined and given a name through the ID property:

```
<asp:panel
    id="Panel1"
    runat="server"
```

You can set the width and height that the controls defined within the Panel control can consume on the browser through the Width and Height properties:

```
height="80%"
width="90%">
```

Then, within the Panel control definition, you can place standard HTML elements:

```
Enter your name:<BR>
```

as well as ASP.NET controls like this TextBox control:

```
<asp:textbox
    id="txtName"
    runat=server
/>
```

Using Panel Controls to Control Code Flow

One of the best uses of the Panel control is to group controls onto different Panel controls and then display those Panel controls one at a time, allowing visitors to enter a few fields at a time as with a wizard. For example, if you needed visitors to enter their basic information, billing address, shipping address, and credit card information, you could ask them to supply that information through one large ASP.NET page. Or you could ask them for information on four separate pages. But you could combine the two and ask visitors for each group of information on its own Panel control. Then when they finished entering, say, their billing address, you would hide that panel and show them the shipping panel.

Using this method you would have all the fields on a single page, but visitors would see only a few fields at a time. This technique shows you how to create a page that uses Panel controls in this way.

USE IT   This ASP.NET page prompts visitors for their name, e-mail address, phone number, and fax number. The values they enter into these fields are echoed back to the visitor through a Label control. The page uses three Panel controls to control the flow of the data entry.

The first Panel control has this definition:

```
<asp:panel
    id="PanelNameEmail"
    runat="server"
    visible="True"
>
    Enter your name:<BR>
    <asp:textbox
        id="txtName"
        runat=server
    />
    <BR>
    Enter your email address:<BR>
    <asp:textbox
        id="txtEmail"
        runat=server
    />
    <BR>
    <asp:button
    id="butNameEmail"
    text="OK"
    onclick="PanelNameEmail_Click"
```

```
    runat="server"
    />
</asp:Panel>
```

Notice that the Panel control has its Visible property initially set to True. That means the controls on this Panel control will be displayed when the page first loads.

Also notice the Button control on this page. It will call the procedure PanelNameEmail_Click when it is clicked.

The second Panel control is called PanelPhoneNumbers. It prompts visitors for their phone and fax numbers. That Panel control has this definition:

```
<asp:panel
    id="PanelPhoneNumbers"
    runat="server"
    visible="False"
>
    Enter your Phone Number:<BR>
    <asp:textbox
        id="txtPhoneNumber"
        runat=server
    />
    <BR>
    Enter your Fax Number:<BR>
    <asp:textbox
        id="txtFaxNumber"
        runat=server
    />
    <BR>
    <asp:button
    id="butPhoneNumbers"
    text="OK"
    onclick="PanelPhoneNumbers_Click"
    runat="server"
    />
</asp:Panel>
```

Notice that the Visible property for this Panel control is set to False. Therefore, when the page first loads the controls, this Panel control will not be displayed. This Panel control also has a Button control defined on it. It calls a different procedure than the first when the button is clicked.

The third Panel control displays the values entered by visitors through a Label control. That Panel control has this definition:

```
<asp:panel
    id="PanelSummary"
    runat="server"
    visible="False"
```

```
>
    <asp:label
        id="lblSummary"
        runat=server
    />
    <BR>
    <asp:button
    id="butSummary"
    text="Change Values"
    onclick="PanelSummary_Click"
    runat="server"
    />
</asp:Panel>
```

This Panel control is also invisible when the page first loads. It, too, has a Button control that calls the procedure named PanelSummary_Click when it is clicked.

When the first Button control is pressed, this code runs:

```
Sub PanelNameEmail_Click(Sender As Object, E As EventArgs)
    PanelNameEmail.Visible = False
    PanelPhoneNumbers.Visible = True
End Sub
```

The code simply hides the first Panel control and displays the second Panel control.

This code runs when the button on the second Panel control is pressed:

```
Sub PanelPhoneNumbers_Click(Sender As Object, E As EventArgs)
    lblSummary.Text = "Name: " & txtName.Text & "<BR>" _
        & "Email: " & txtEmail.Text & "<BR>" _
        & "Phone Number: " & txtPhoneNumber.Text & "<BR>" _
        & "Fax Number: " & txtFaxNumber.Text & "<BR>"
    PanelPhoneNumbers.Visible = False
    PanelSummary.Visible = True
End Sub
```

This procedure displays the values entered on the first two Panel controls through a Label control. It then hides the second Panel control and displays the third Panel control.

The other procedure on this page fires when the button on the third Panel control is pressed:

```
Sub PanelSummary_Click(Sender As Object, E As EventArgs)
    PanelSummary.Visible = False
    PanelNameEmail.Visible = True
End Sub
```

This procedure cycles visitors back to the first Panel control by hiding the third one and displaying the first one.

Setting the Style of a Panel Control

Another good use of the Panel control is to control the look and feel of the controls that are displayed within it. For example, if you had a series of Label controls and TextBox controls that you wanted to all have a particular font and color scheme, you could place values in each of the controls on that page. But you could also place those values once in a Panel control. Then if you define the page controls within a Panel control, they will inherit the base property values of the Panel control. This tip shows you how to create a Panel control that does this.

 USE IT The ASP.NET page presented in this section defines a single Panel control with subordinate controls and HTML elements. Those subordinate controls use the style properties of the Panel control.

The Panel control has this definition:

```
<asp:panel
    id="Panel1"
    runat="server"
    font-name="Arial"
    font-bold="True"
    forecolor="yellow"
    backcolor="red"
    borderstyle=3
    bordercolor="green"
    borderwidth=4
    horizontalalign="Center"
>

    Enter your name:<BR>
    <asp:textbox
    id="txtName"
    runat=server
    />
    <BR>
    Enter your password:<BR>
    <asp:textbox
    id="txtPassword"
    runat=server
    />
</asp:Panel>
```

> **QUICK TIP**
>
> *The Panel control also contains a property called BackImageURL. You can set this property to the location of an image that you would like to have displayed as the background of the Panel control.*

The controls defined within the Panel control will use these base font and style properties:

```
font-name="Arial"
font-bold="True"
forecolor="yellow"
backcolor="red"
```

You can also set the border properties for the Panel control to help offset the controls within the Panel control from other controls on the page:

```
borderstyle=3
bordercolor="green"
borderwidth=4
```

The HorizontalAlign property is used to determine how the controls are laid out within the surface of the Panel control. Here all the subordinate elements and controls are centered:

```
horizontalalign="Center"
```

You can also set this property to Left, Right or Justify.

Creating an HTML Table Using the Table Control

The ASP.NET Table control provides a way for you to create an HTML table that is defined like other ASP.NET controls. This technique shows you how to define a basic Table control.

USE IT   The ASP.NET page presented in this section has a single control defined—a Table control. That control has this definition:

```
<asp:table
    id="table1"
    runat="server"
    cellpadding=5
    cellspacing=1
    gridlines="Both"
>
    <asp:tablerow>
        <asp:tablecell>
        <B>Product</B>
        </asp:tablecell>
        <asp:tablecell>
        <B>Quantity</B>
        </asp:tablecell>
    </asp:tablerow>
    <asp:tablerow>
        <asp:tablecell>
        Socks
        </asp:tablecell>
        <asp:tablecell>
        5
        </asp:tablecell>
```

```
    </asp:tablerow>
    <asp:tablerow>
        <asp:tablecell>
        Shirts
        </asp:tablecell>
        <asp:tablecell>
        52
        </asp:tablecell>
    </asp:tablerow>
 </asp:table>
```

First, the properties for the Table control are set. Use the ID property to set the name of the control:

```
<asp:table
    id="table1"
    runat="server"
```

Since the control is rendered as an HTML table, you can set the basic HTML table elements through these properties:

```
cellpadding=5
cellspacing=1
gridlines="Both"
```

Then within the Table control you define HTML rows by inserting TableRow controls:

```
<asp:tablerow>
```

Within each TableRow control, you define each cell in the row through a TableCell control:

```
<asp:tablecell>
    Socks
</asp:tablecell>
```

Creating a Table Control in Code

You may find that you need to write out to visitors' browsers a basic HTML table. But that table cannot be predefined. It may depend on some visitor input or it may depend on the values in a database table. This technique shows you how to create a Table control in code and display that control on the rendered page.

USE IT The ASP.NET page defined for this technique creates a Table control when the page is first loaded. The table displays the coordinates of each cell through the rendered HTML table.

No controls are defined on the page, but the Form is given a name so that the Table control can be added to it in code:

```
<form id="frmMyPage" runat="server">
</form>
```

When the page loads, this procedure runs:

```
Sub Page_Load(ByVal Sender as Object, ByVal E as EventArgs)
    Dim MyTable = New Table
    Dim NumRows as Integer
    Dim NumColumns as Integer
    For NumRows = 1 to 3
        Dim TheRow = New TableRow
        For NumColumns = 1 to 4
            Dim TheCell = New TableCell
            TheCell.Text = NumRows & "," & NumColumns
            TheRow.Cells.Add(TheCell)
        Next
        MyTable.Rows.Add(TheRow)
    Next
    frmMyPage.Controls.Add(MyTable)
End Sub
```

First, you define a Table control:

```
Dim MyTable = New Table
```

Then you define a variable that will be used in a loop to determine the number of rows to display:

```
Dim NumRows as Integer
```

Another is defined for the number of cells in each row:

```
Dim NumColumns as Integer
```

The outer loop will iterate through the rows of the table. Three will be created:

```
For NumRows = 1 to 3
```

Then a TableRow control is defined:

```
Dim TheRow = New TableRow
```

Next, the inner loop is defined for the number of cells in the row, which will have four:

```
For NumColumns = 1 to 4
```

You then define a TableCell control:

```
Dim TheCell = New TableCell
```

Next, text is placed into the TableCell control:

```
TheCell.Text = NumRows & "," & NumColumns
```

That TableCell is added to the TableRow:

```
TheRow.Cells.Add(TheCell)
```

After the inner loop the TableRow is added to the table:

```
MyTable.Rows.Add(TheRow)
```

And the table is added to the page:

```
frmMyPage.Controls.Add(MyTable)
```

Adding a Row to a Table Control in Code

If you use a Table control you may find that you want the visitor to be able to add a row to the Table control. Or you may find that you need to append rows to the Table control in code. This tip shows you how to do that.

USE IT This page defines a Table control that displays product names and quantities. Visitors are allowed to add a row to the Table control by entering their own product and quantity through TextBox controls.

The Table control has this definition:

```
<asp:table
    id="table1"
    runat="server"
>
    <asp:tablerow>
        <asp:tablecell>
        <B>Product</B>
```

```
        </asp:tablecell>
        <asp:tablecell>
        <B>Quantity</B>
        </asp:tablecell>
    </asp:tablerow>
</asp:table>
```

The Table control is defined with a single TableRow. That row displays column headers for the rendered HTML table.

Also defined on this page are two TextBox controls:

```
<asp:textbox
    id="txtProduct"
    runat=server
/>
<asp:textbox
    id="txtQuantity"
    runat=server
/>
```

And a Button control:

```
<asp:button
id="butSubmit"
text="OK"
onclick="SubmitBtn_Click"
runat="server"
/>
```

When that Button control is pressed, this code block fires:

```
Sub SubmitBtn_Click(Sender As Object, E As EventArgs)
    Dim TheRow = New TableRow
    Dim TheProduct = New TableCell
    Dim TheQuantity = New TableCell
    TheProduct.Text = txtProduct.Text
    TheQuantity.Text = txtQuantity.Text
    TheRow.Cells.Add(TheProduct)
    TheRow.Cells.Add(TheQuantity)
    Table1.Rows.Add(TheRow)
End Sub
```

The code block defines a TableRow and two TableCell controls. The values entered by visitors into the TextBox controls are placed into the TableCell control. Those controls are added to the TableRow control, and that control is appended to the Table control defined on the page.

CHAPTER 7

Internet Explorer Web Controls

TIPS IN THIS CHAPTER

A really helpful feature of ASP.NET is its expandability. Developers around the world can create their own controls that you can easily define within your own applications. One set of controls that was created by Microsoft but is outside of the standard ASP.NET controls is the Internet Explorer Web Controls.

The main controls included with the Internet Explorer Web Controls are the MultiPage control, the TabStrip control, the Toolbar control, and the TreeView control. These controls also define their own numerous controls that can be defined within their space. The tips and techniques discussed in this chapter are all based on the Internet Explorer Web Controls.

The Internet Explorer Web Controls namespace does not come with ASP.NET. You need to download it from Microsoft. At the time of writing, this free library can be downloaded by going to **http://www.asp.net**. From there select the link to the Control Library. You will find on that page numerous controls, including the Internet Explorer Web Controls, that you can download and install on your server.

Creating a Basic MultiPage Control

The MultiPage control with the PageView control is a container in which to place other controls. You can use the controls as a wizard or as a formatting container for subordinate controls. To be able to use the MultiPage control on your ASP.NET page, you need to import its Namespace. This tip shows you how to do that and how to define a basic MultiPage control.

 When you want to include a MultiPage control on your ASP.NET page, you need to first import the namespace that the control is located in with syntax like this:

```
<%@ Import Namespace="Microsoft.Web.UI.WebControls" %>
```

That line of code needs to be placed with your other directives at the top of the page.

Then you can register a TagPrefix for the library. Note that the name you place in the TagPrefix property is the same name that you will use when you define a MultiPage control or any other control in this namespace:

```
<%@ Register TagPrefix="IEControls"
    Namespace="Microsoft.Web.UI.WebControls"
    Assembly ="Microsoft.Web.UI.WebControls"
%>
```

Now within the form on the ASP.NET page you can define a MultiPage control:

```
<IEControls:multipage
    id="MyMultiPage"
    runat="server"
    borderstyle=9
    borderwidth=3
    bordercolor="DarkBlue"
    width="90%"
    height="50%"
    >
</IEControls:multipage>
```

Notice that the TagPrefix, IEControls, is the same as was defined in the register tag. That prefix and the name of the control are used in the first line of the control's definition:

```
<IEControls:multipage
```

The name of the control is placed into the ID property:

```
id="MyMultiPage"
runat="server"
```

The MultiPage control has border properties that you can use to offset the control from other content on the ASP.NET page:

```
borderstyle=9
borderwidth=3
bordercolor="DarkBlue"
```

You can also set the width and the height that the control can occupy on the page:

```
    width="90%"
    height="50%"
>
```

Then the control's definition ends using the TagPrefix followed by the name of the control:

```
</IEControls:multipage>
```

Adding a PageView Control to a MultiPage Control

Once you define a MultiPage control you likely will want to add basic controls like TextBox and Label controls to the MultiPage control. You do that through a PageView control. A MultiPage control contains PageView controls. Each PageView control can contain numerous other controls and HTML elements. This technique shows you how to add a PageView control to your MultiPage control.

USE IT The ASP.NET page created for this technique defines a MultiPage control with a single PageView control. On that control, two TextBox controls are defined, allowing visitors to enter their name and password.

At the top of the page, you need to import the namespace that includes the MultiPage control and the PageView control:

```
<%@ Import Namespace="Microsoft.Web.UI.WebControls" %>
```

You also can include a TagPrefix for the controls:

```
<%@ Register TagPrefix="IEControls"
    Namespace="Microsoft.Web.UI.WebControls"
    Assembly ="Microsoft.Web.UI.WebControls"
%>
```

Within the form on the ASP.NET page, these controls are defined:

```
<IEControls:multipage
    id="MyMultiPage"
    runat="server"
    borderstyle=9
    borderwidth=3
    bordercolor="DarkBlue"
    width="90%"
    height="50%"
    >
    <IEControls:PageView
        id="pv1"
        runat=server
        font-name="Arial"
        font-bold=True
        forecolor="yellow"
        backcolor="darkred"
    >
        Enter your name:<BR>
        <asp:textbox
        id="txtName"
        runat=server
        />
        <BR>
        Enter your password:<BR>
        <asp:textbox
        id="txtPassword"
        runat=server
        />
        <BR>
    </IEControls:PageView>
</IEControls:multipage>
```

Notice that you first define the MultiPage control. Then within that definition, the PageView control is defined:

```
<IEControls:PageView
```

You can give the PageView control a name through the ID property:

```
id="pv1"
runat=server
```

You can then set font and color properties for the PageView control. These values will be used by the subordinate controls as their default font and color values:

```
font-name="Arial"
font-bold=True
forecolor="yellow"
backcolor="darkred"
```

Then, within the PageView control definition, you can place other controls. On this page, two TextBox controls are added, as well as HTML elements.

Using the MultiPage Control as an Interface for a Wizard

The MultiPage control provides a way for you to define pages of information displayed at different times but all contained on the same page. Such functionality allows you to create a wizard interface for gathering basic information about visitors and then taking some action with that information.

For example, say that you wanted to allow visitors to create an account on your system. You may want them to enter basic information, followed by their preferences, and follow that with them letting you know the features they want to subscribe to. After filling in each field, the visitors' account would be created. This technique shows you how to create a MultiPage control with PageView controls that visitors can navigate through.

 USE IT   This ASP.NET page asks visitors for their name, e-mail address, and password through TextBox controls. Each TextBox control is placed on a separate PageView control. On each PageView control visitors can navigate through other PageView controls using a Previous or Next button.

The MultiPage control has this basic definition:

```
<IEControls:multipage
    id="MyMultiPage"
    runat="server"
    selectedindex=0
    >
```

Notice the use of the SelectedIndex property. This property is set to the ordinal number of the PageView control that you want displayed by default when the page is first loaded. The property is 0-based. Therefore, a value of 0 would display the first page.

Within the MultiPage control three PageView controls are defined. Each is similar to this one:

```
<IEControls:PageView
        id="pv1"
        runat=server
        font-name="Arial"
        font-bold=True
        forecolor="yellow"
```

```
      backcolor="darkred"
    >
```

Each PageView control is defined with different colors to make them stand out more as a separate page. With the PageView control definition, a TextBox control is defined allowing visitors to enter the text requested on that page:

```
<asp:textbox
    id="txtName"
    runat=server
/>
```

After that, a button that allows visitors to navigate to the previous page in the MultiPage control is defined:

```
<asp:button
    id="butPrev1"
    text="Previous"
    onclick="Prev1_Click"
    runat="server"
/>
```

as is a Button control allowing visitors to navigate to the next page in the MultiPage control:

```
<asp:button
    id="butNext1"
    text="Next"
    onclick="Next1_Click"
    runat="server"
/>
```

When visitors click one of the Previous buttons, code like this fires:

```
Sub Prev1_Click(Sender As Object, E As EventArgs)
    MyMultiPage.SelectedIndex = 2
End Sub
```

Here, the visitor has clicked on the Previous button on the first page. Therefore, he or she needs to be taken to the third page in the MultiPage control. You do that through the SelectedIndex property of the MultiPage control.

When one of the Next buttons is clicked, code like this fires:

```
Sub Next1_Click(Sender As Object, E As EventArgs)
    MyMultiPage.SelectedIndex = 1
End Sub
```

The visitor is navigating from the first page to the second page. Therefore the SelectedIndex property is set to 1.

Providing Navigation in a MultiPage Control Using a DropDownList

If you have a MultiPage control that contains many PageView controls, you may find that you need to allow visitors to jump from any page to any other page in the MultiPage control. A DropDownList control provides a good navigational aide in such a situation.

USE IT The ASP.NET page in this technique prompts visitors for their name, e-mail address, and password. Each of these values is entered through a TextBox control that is placed on its own PageView control. A DropDownList control that is defined outside of the MultiPage control allows the visitor to navigate to any of the pages in the MultiPage control.

The MultiPage control has this basic definition:

```
<IEControls:multipage
    id="MyMultiPage"
    runat="server"
    selectedindex=0
    >
```

Since the SelectedIndex property is set to 0, the first page in the MultiPage control will be displayed when the page first loads.

Within the MultiPage control, three PageView controls like this one are defined:

```
<IEControls:PageView
    id="pv1"
    runat=server
    font-name="Arial"
    font-bold=True
    forecolor="yellow"
    backcolor="darkred"
>
```

Then within each of the PageView controls, a TextBox control is defined:

```
<asp:textbox
    id="txtName"
    runat=server
/>
```

Also defined on this page is a DropDownList control:

```
<asp:dropdownlist
    id="ddl1"
    autopostback="True"
    onselectedindexchanged="ddl1_Changed"
    runat="server"
>
    <asp:listitem value="0">Name</asp:listitem>
    <asp:listitem value="1">Email</asp:listitem>
    <asp:listitem value="2">Password</asp:listitem>
</asp:dropdownlist>
```

The DropDownList control displays three items. Each is the name of one of the fields on the different PageView controls. The value for each ListItem control corresponds to the ordinal number of the corresponding PageView control.

Notice that the DropDownList control has AutoPostBack set to True and a value in the OnSelectedIndexChanged property. That means that when visitors change the selection in the DropDownList control, that page is posted back to the server and this procedure runs:

```
Sub ddl1_Changed(Sender As Object, E As EventArgs)
    MyMultiPage.SelectedIndex = ddl1.SelectedItem.Value
End Sub
```

The procedure uses the SelectedIndex property to display the page selected in the DropDownList control by the visitor.

Adding Controls to a PageView Control in Code

A PageView control is a container for other controls. Being that, the PageView control is a good control to use in situations where you need to dynamically add controls to a page through code. This technique shows you how to do that.

USE IT   The ASP.NET page presented with this technique asks visitors for a number on one PageView control. Then on a second page view control the number they entered is used to create that many TextBox controls.

The PageView controls are defined within this MultiPage control:

```
<IEControls:multipage
    id="MyMultiPage"
    runat="server"
    >
```

The first PageView has this definition:

```
<IEControls:PageView
    id="pv1"
    runat=server
>
```

It contains a TextBox control for entering a number:

```
<asp:textbox
    id="txtNumber"
    runat=server
/>
```

and a Button control that visitors use to submit their entry:

```
<asp:button
    id="butOK"
    text="  OK  "
    onclick="OK_Click"
    runat="server"
/>
```

The second PageView control does not contain any controls:

```
<IEControls:PageView
    id="pv2"
    runat=server
>
</IEControls:PageView>
```

When visitors click the OK button, this procedure fires:

```
Sub OK_Click(Sender As Object, E As EventArgs)
    Dim I as Integer
    For I = 1 to txtNumber.Text
        Dim MyTextBox = New TextBox
        MyTextBox.ID = "txtDynamic" & I
        MyTextBox.Text = "Control Number: " & I
        pv2.Controls.Add(MyTextBox)
    Next
    MyMultiPage.SelectedIndex = 1
End Sub
```

The procedure adds TextBox controls to the second PageView control. The number of controls added is based on the number entered into the TextBox control.

Creating a Basic TabStrip Control

The TabStrip control provides a way for you to display a series of button-like elements that take some action when one of the buttons is selected. Often the action taken is to take visitors to some other page within the current functionality.

This technique shows you how to define a basic TabStrip control on your ASP.NET page.

 To define a TabStrip control on your ASP.NET page, you first need to import the namespace that contains the control:

```
<%@ Import Namespace="Microsoft.Web.UI.WebControls" %>
```

Then, you need to register the namespace:

```
<%@ Register TagPrefix="IEControls"
    Namespace="Microsoft.Web.UI.WebControls"
    Assembly ="Microsoft.Web.UI.WebControls"
%>
```

Notice the use of the TagPrefix parameter. That name will be used in the control's definition.

The TabStrip control has this basic definition:

```
<IEControls:TabStrip
    id="MyTabStrip"
    runat="server"
    forecolor="DarkBlue"
    backcolor="DarkBlue"
    width="20%"
    >
</IEControls:TabStrip>
```

You set the name of the control through the ID property. The ForeColor property is used as the default color for the text on any Tab controls added to the TabStrip control. The BackColor property is set to the background color of the control where there are no Tab controls defined. You can use the width property to limit how wide the control can appear within the rendered page.

Setting the Orientation of a TabStrip Control

The TabStrip control can be displayed with the buttons next to each other or one on top of each other. This tip shows you how to change the TabStrip control's orientation.

 The TabStrip control on this ASP.NET page has this definition:

```
<IEControls:TabStrip
    id="MyTabStrip"
    runat="server"
    orientation="Horizontal"
    >
</IEControls:TabStrip>
```

The position of the Tab controls in a TabStrip control is set through the Orientation property. Here the property is set to Horizontal, so the buttons will appear next to each other. You can also set the property to Vertical to have the buttons appear one on top of each other.

▶ | **QUICK TIP**
_____

You can set whether the TabStrip control appears at the top of the page or the bottom of a page based on where you define it. Just make it the first control on the page to have it be on the top or make it the last control defined to have it rendered on the bottom.

Working with Tabs in a TabStrip Control

A TabStrip control does not produce any rendered output to the visitors' browser without Tab controls defined on it. Within the definition of the TabStrip control, you place the definition of a Tab control. Then, based on the Tab control that visitors select, you would take some action. This technique shows you how to define Tab controls within a TabStrip control and how to have code automatically fire when visitors click one of the Tab controls in the TabStrip control.

USE IT   The ASP.NET page presented for this technique displays three Tab controls though a TabStrip control. When visitors click on one of the Tab controls, they see the ordinal position of the Tab control selected.

The TabStrip control has this definition:

```
<IEControls:tabstrip
    id="MyTabStrip"
    runat="server"
    forecolor="DarkBlue"
    backcolor="DarkBlue"
    onselectedindexchange="TabStrip_Clicked"
    autopostback="True"
    >
```

Notice the use of the OnSelectedIndexChange property. You set this property to the name of the procedure that you want to run when one of the Tab controls is selected. Since the AutoPostBack property is set to True, this procedure will run immediately when a Tab control is clicked.

► **QUICK TIP**

With regards to the OnSelectedIndexChange property, the TabStrip control does not follow the convention used by other ASP.NET controls. For other controls the property is called OnSelectedIndexChanged. Be careful, because if you use that name with the TabStrip control, no action is taken.

Then within the TabStrip control, three Tab controls like this one are defined:

```
<IEControls:tab
        id="Tab1"
        runat="server"
        text=" The first button "
        tooltip="Click Me!!!"
    />
```

The name for a Tab control can be set through the ID property. The Text property is set to the text you want to appear on the face of the tab. Notice that you can place HTML elements within the Text property. You can also use the ToolTip property and set it to the text that you want to appear to visitors in a little box when they hover their mouse over the Tab control.

Also declared on this page is a Label control that displays the Tab control's ordinal reference:

```
<asp:label
    id="lblMessage"
    runat=server
/>
```

The following procedure runs when visitors select one of the Tab controls:

```
Sub TabStrip_Clicked(Sender As Object, E As EventArgs)
    lblMessage.Text = "You clicked tab number " _
        & MyTabStrip.SelectedIndex & "."
End Sub
```

The procedure uses the SelectedIndex property of the TabStrip control to display back to the visitor the number for the Tab control that was clicked.

Using TabSeparator Controls with a TabStrip Control

A second type of control that you can place within a TabStrip control is a TabSeparator control. The TabSeparator control provides space between Tab controls within a TabStrip control. The TabSeparator control does not provide any link for visitors as the Tab controls do. This tip shows you how to define a TabSeparator control.

USE IT   This ASP.NET page defines a TabStrip control with three Tab controls. Between
the definition of the Tab controls a TabSeparator control is defined.
The TabStrip control has this definition:

```
<IEControls:tabstrip
    id="MyTabStrip"
    runat="server"
    forecolor="DarkBlue"
    backcolor="DarkBlue"
    >
```

The ForeColor property will be inherited by the Tab controls with the text displayed, and the
BackColor property is the color that the TabSeparator controls will use.
The Tab controls have a definition like this one:

```
<IEControls:tab
    id="Tab1"
    runat="server"
    text=" The first button "
/>
```

Then between the definition of each of the Tab controls a TabSeparator control is defined:

```
<IEControls:TabSeparator />
```

Since you won't be referencing the control in code, you don't need to give the control a name
or supply any other properties.

Setting Styles Within a TabStrip Control

The TabStrip control contains six styles that you can set to determine the appearance of the Tab controls
and the TabSeparator controls defined within a TabStrip control. Three of those styles are for the Tab
controls and the other three are for the TabSeparator control. This tip shows you how to define those
six styles.

USE IT   The ASP.NET page created for this tip defines three Tab controls with a TabSeparator
control between each tab. In the TabStrip definition, the six style properties are set. The
TabStrip control has this definition:

```
<IEControls:tabstrip
    id="MyTabStrip"
    runat="server"
```

```
tabdefaultstyle="color:darkblue;background-color:gray;
    font-family:Arial"
tabselectedstyle="color:darkred;background-color:yellow;
    font-family:Comic Sans MS;font-weight:bold"
tabhoverstyle="color:red;background-color:green;
    font-weight:Bold"
sepdefaultstyle="background-color:darkblue"
sepselectedstyle="background-color:purple"
sephoverstyle="background-color:gold"
>
```

First, notice the structure of the six style properties. They are different from the way you set font and color properties in standard ASP.NET controls. Instead of using syntax like this:

```
StyleName-Font-Name = "Arial"
```

you use Cascading Style Sheet value pairs. To create a pair, you combine the name of the item with its value, separated by a colon. Then you separate each value pair with a semicolon.

The TabDefaultStyle is the style used for all tabs that are currently not the selected tab. The TabSelectedStyle is the style used for the currently selected tab. And the value in the TabHoverStyle is used to set the appearance of a Tab control when visitors hover their mouse over the control.

Similarly, the SepDefaultStyle is the style used by default for the TabSeparator controls. The SepSelectedStyle is the style for a TabSeparator control that sits next to the selected Tab control. And the SepHoverStyle is the style used on a TabSeparator control that surrounds a Tab control that visitors hover their mouse over.

Using Images on Tab Controls in a TabStrip Control

The Tab controls defined within a TabStrip control can have three different images associated with their appearance. These images are displayed just to the left of the text defined on the Tab control. This technique shows you the properties you need to use to display images on Tab controls.

USE IT This page defines a TabStrip control with three Tab controls. Each of the Tab controls uses three image properties to display a different icon based on whether the Tab has been selected, not selected, or in hover-mode.

The TabStrip control has this basic definition:

```
<IEControls:tabstrip
    id="MyTabStrip"
    runat="server"
    >
```

Within the TabStrip control, three Tab controls like this one are defined:

```
<IEControls:tab
    id="Tab1"
    runat="server"
    text=" The first button "
    defaultimageurl="./3.ico"
    selectedimageurl="./smile.ico"
    hoverimageurl="./4.ico"
/>
```

The DefaultImageURL property is set to the path to the image that you want displayed next to the text in the Tab control when the Tab control is not currently selected. The SelectedImageURL property is set to the path to the image that you want displayed when the Tab control has been selected. And the HoverImageURL property is set to the path to the image that you want displayed when visitors hover their mouse over the Tab control.

Using a TabStrip Control with a MultiPage Control

Two of the main Internet Explorer controls that work very well with each other are the TabStrip control and the MultiPage control. The TabStrip control contains a property that allows you to link the TabStrip control with the MultiPage control. In doing so, you define a Tab control for each PageView control in your MultiPage control. Then when visitors select a Tab control they are taken to the corresponding PageView control. This technique shows you how to use this functionality.

USE IT   The page presented for this technique includes a TabStrip control that allows visitors to navigate to one of the three PageView controls included in the MultiPage control. The page prompts visitors for their name, e-mail address, and password through TextBox controls, each defined on its own PageView control.

The TabStrip control has this definition:

```
<IEControls:tabstrip
    id="MyTabStrip"
    runat="server"
    targetid="MyMultiPage"
>
```

Notice the TargetID property. This property is set to the name of the MultiPage control that you are linking this TabStrip to.

The first Tab control has this definition:

```
<IEControls:tab
    id="Tab1"
    runat="server"
```

```
      text=" Name "
/>
```

When visitors click on this Tab control they are taken to the content on the first PageView control.
The second Tab control has this definition:

```
<IEControls:tab
       id="Tab2"
       runat="server"
       Text=" Email Address "
    />
```

This Tab control will link visitors to the Email Address PageView control.
The third Tab control links visitors to the third PageView control:

```
<IEControls:tab
    id="Tab3"
    runat="server"
    Text=" Password "
/>
```

The MultiPage control has this definition:

```
<IEControls:multipage
    id="MyMultiPage"
    runat="server"
>
```

Notice that the ID property matches the value in the TargetID property of the TabStrip control.
Three PageView controls are defined within the MultiPage control that correspond to one of the
Tab controls like this one:

```
<IEControls:PageView
    id="pv1"
    runat=server
    font-name="Arial"
    font-bold=True
    forecolor="yellow"
    backcolor="darkred"
>
```

Then within each of the PageView controls a TextBox control is defined for the visitors' entry:

```
<asp:textbox
    id="txtName"
```

```
    runat=server
/>
```

Creating a Basic Toolbar Control

At the top of many applications such as Word or Internet Explorer you see a toolbar. A toolbar provides a way for the user to quickly utilize some functionality of the application. ASP.NET developers can use the Toolbar control to create something similar to the toolbar you see in standard applications. Through the specialized controls that you place onto a Toolbar control you can allow visitors to enter a value for a setting, take some action, navigate to a page, or perform some other task. This technique shows you what you need to do to be able to define a basic Toolbar control on your ASP.NET page.

USE IT The Toolbar control is part of the Internet Explorer Web Controls namespace. Therefore, you need to import that namespace into your ASP.NET page:

```
<%@ Import Namespace="Microsoft.Web.UI.WebControls" %>
```

You also need to register the namespace and give it a TagPrefix:

```
<%@ Register TagPrefix="IEControls"
    Namespace="Microsoft.Web.UI.WebControls"
    Assembly ="Microsoft.Web.UI.WebControls"
%>
```

When you define a Toolbar control you use that tag prefix along with the type of control you are doing, as you can see here in this page's Toolbar control definition:

```
IEControls:toolbar
    id="MyTB"
    runat="server"
    defaultstyle="color:darkblue;font-family:Arial"
    orientation="Horizontal"
    >
</IEControls:toolbar>
```

The name of the control is set through the ID property. You can use the DefaultStyle property to determine the default font and color properties for all the controls declared within the Toolbar control. The Orientation property determines whether the controls defined on the Toolbar control appear next to or on top of each other. If you set this property to Horizontal, the controls are placed next to each other. If you set this property to Vertical, the controls are placed one on top of the other.

Adding a ToolbarButton Control to a Toolbar Control

One of the controls that you will likely want to add to a Toolbar control is the ToolbarButton control. This control is similar to a Button control in that visitors click it to take some action. When defined, the ToolbarButton control is defined within the space of the Toolbar control and can appear with just text or with an image followed by text. This technique shows you how to define a ToolbarButton control on a Toolbar control.

USE IT This page presents visitors with a Toolbar that contains two buttons for them to click to take some action. When visitors click one of the buttons, the name of the button is echoed back to them through a Label control.

The Toolbar control has this definition:

```
<IEControls:toolbar
    id="MyTB"
    runat="server"
    defaultstyle="color:darkblue;font-family:Arial"
    orientation="Horizontal"
    autopostback="true"
    onbuttonclick="ToolBarClick"
    >
```

Notice that the AutoPostBack property is set to True. That means when visitors take an action on the Toolbar, such as clicking a button, the page is returned to the server for processing. The procedure that will run in that condition is the procedure specified in the OnButtonClick property.

Within the Toolbar control, this ToolbarButton control is defined:

```
<IEControls:ToolBarButton
    id="Filter"
    runat="server"
    tooltip="Filter Records"
    imageurl="filter.ico"
    text="  Filter "
/>
```

Notice the name of the control is placed into the ID property. The control can have a picture associated with it. Here it is set through the ImageURL property. The Text property is set to the text that you want to appear on the Button control. The special HTML character for a space, " ," is used to properly situate the text on the surface of the button.

The second ToolbarButton control has this definition:

```
<IEControls:ToolBarButton
    id="Print"
    runat="server"
```

```
    Tooltip="Print Record"
    ImageUrl="printer.ico"
    Text="  Print "
/>
```

The ImageURL property is set to a different image. Also defined on the page is a Label control that will display the name of the button clicked:

```
<asp:Label
    id="lblMessage"
    runat="server"
    Font-Bold="True"
/>
```

When either of the buttons is clicked, the following code fires:

```
Sub ToolBarClick(ByVal Sender as Object, ByVal E as EventArgs)
    lblMessage.Text = "You clicked the button named: " _
        & Sender.ToString()
End Sub
```

By using the name of the Sender object, you can determine the name of the button that was clicked, firing this event.

Take a look at the screenshot for this page:

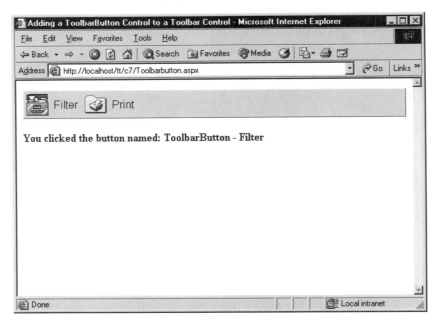

Notice the text displayed through the Label control. The type of control is displayed along with the name of the control that was clicked by the visitor.

Adding a ToolbarCheckButton Control to a Toolbar Control

One of the controls that you can define on a Toolbar control is the ToolbarCheckButton control. This control renders itself within the space of a Toolbar button control. It behaves like a push button control in the sense that it has on and off positions. When visitors click it on, the button appears to stay pushed in and when visitors click the button again, it appears off and released. This technique shows you how to define a ToolbarCheckButton control within a Toolbar control.

USE IT The ASP.NET page presented in this section of the chapter displays a ToolbarCheckButton control defined within a Toolbar control. When visitors click the ToolbarCheckButton control the orientation of the Toolbar control toggles between horizontal and vertical.

The Toolbar control has this definition:

```
<IEControls:toolbar
    id="MyTB"
    runat="server"
    defaultstyle="color:darkblue;font-family:Arial"
    orientation="Vertical"
    autopostback="true"
    onbuttonclick="ToolBarClick"
>
```

You can set the style of the font and colors that the controls within the Toolbar control use through the DefaultStyle property. Since AutoPostBack is set to True and a value is supplied in the OnButtonClick property, code will fire when one of the ToolbarCheckButton controls is clicked.

The ToolbarCheckButton control has this definition:

```
<IEControls:toolbarcheckbutton
    id="OrientationMode"
    runat="server"
    tooltip="Toggle Toolbar Orientation"
    text=" Orientation"
/>
```

The ID property for this control can be set to the name of the control. The Text property is set to the text that you want to appear on the surface of the ToolbarCheckButton control.

When the ToolbarCheckButton control is clicked, this code runs:

```
Sub ToolBarClick(ByVal Sender as Object, ByVal E as EventArgs)
    If MyTB.Orientation = 1 Then
        MyTB.Orientation = 0
    Else
        MyTB.Orientation = 1
    End If
End Sub
```

The code simply toggles the Orientation property between horizontal (1) and vertical (0).

Adding a ToolbarCheckGroup Control to a Toolbar Control

A ToolbarCheckGroup control provides a way for you to group ToolbarCheckButton controls together so that visitors can only select one of the buttons in a group. You can also force visitors to have one item in the group selected. When used together, these controls add to the functionality of the Toolbar control. This technique shows you how to define a ToolbarCheckGroup control.

USE IT This ASP.NET page displays a ToolbarCheckGroup control with three ToolbarCheckButton controls all defined within a Toolbar control. When clicked, the button's name is displayed through a Label control.

The Toolbar control has this definition:

```
<IEControls:toolbar
    id="MyTB"
    runat="server"
    defaultstyle="color:darkblue;font-family:Arial"
    autopostback="true"
    onbuttonclick="ToolBarClick"
>
```

Notice that the AutoPostBack property is set to True. That means the page will be submitted for processing when visitors click one of the buttons. The procedure that will run in that case is the one named in the OnButtonClick property.

Within the Toolbar control, this ToolbarCheckGroup control is defined:

```
<IEControls:ToolBarCheckGroup
        id="Group1"
        runat="server"
```

```
        forceselection="True"
    >
```

You supply the name for the group through the ID property. Since the ForceSelection property is set to True, visitors cannot deselect a selected ToolbarCheckButton control. Instead, they must select a different choice. If the ForceSelection property is set to False, visitors can deselect one of the buttons, leaving none selected.

Three ToolbarCheckButton controls are defined within the ToolbarCheckGroup control. Each one has a definition like this one:

```
<IEControls:toolbarcheckbutton
    id="TBCB1"
    runat="server"
    text="Button 1"
/>
```

Also defined on the page is a Label control that displays the name of the button selected:

```
<asp:label
    id="lblMessage"
    runat="server"
    font-bold="True"
/>
```

When one of the ToolbarCheckButton controls is selected, this code runs:

```
Sub ToolBarClick(ByVal Sender as Object, ByVal E as EventArgs)
    lblMessage.Text = "You clicked button: " _
        & Group1.SelectedCheckButton.ID
End Sub
```

The SelectedCheckButton property of the ToolbarCheckGroup control returns the ToolbarCheckButton in the group that has been selected by the visitor. So, here the ID of that control is displayed in the Label control.

Adding a ToolbarDropDownList Control to a Toolbar Control

One of the controls that can be placed on the Toolbar control renders itself very similarly to a DropDownList control. That control is the ToolbarDropDownList. Not only does the control render itself like a DropDownList control but it is programmatically very similar to the DropDownList control. This technique shows you how to create and work with a ToolbarDropDownList control.

USE IT   The ASP.NET page presented in this section displays to visitors a list of page names in a ToolbarDropDownList control. When visitors select the name of the page, that page name is displayed through a Label control. You could use such a device to redirect visitors to the page that they select.

The ToolbarDropDownList control is defined within this Toolbar control:

```
<IEControls:toolbar
    id="MyTB"
    runat="server"
    defaultstyle="color:darkblue;font-family:Arial"
    autopostback="true"
>
```

Notice that AutoPostBack is set to True. That means the page will be returned to the server for processing. But no procedure is mentioned to fire. That is because the procedure that fires when an item is selected in the list is specified in the definition of the ToolbarDropDownList control:

```
<IEControls:toolbardropdownlist
    id="ddlSiteSection"
    runat="server"
    onselectedindexchanged="ddl1_Changed"
>
    <asp:listitem>Home</asp:listitem >
    <asp:listitem >News</asp:listitem >
    <asp:listitem >Employees</asp:listitem >
    <asp:listitem >Contact Information</asp:listitem >
</IEControls: toolbardropdownlist >
```

The name of the ToolbarDropDownList control is set through the ID property. Notice that a value is placed in the OnSelectedIndexChanged property. That procedure will run when the visitor selects an item in the ToolbarDropDownList control.

Notice also the use of ListItem controls within the ToolbarDropDownList. These are the same controls that you define within a DropDownList control.

Also defined on the page is a Label control:

```
<asp:Label
    id="lblMessage"
    runat="server"
    font-bold="True"
/>
```

The value for the Text property in that control is set when this procedure fires:

```
Sub ddl1_Changed(ByVal Sender as Object, ByVal E as EventArgs)
    lblMessage.Text = "You selected item: " _
```

```
        & ddlSiteSection.SelectedItem.Text
End Sub
```

The procedure fires when the item selected in the ToolbarDropDownList control changes. It merely places the name of the item selected into the Text property of the Label control.

Adding a ToolbarLabel Control to a Toolbar Control

Frequently, on a Toolbar control you will want to just display some text that is not in the form of a button. In other words, you want to display text that doesn't have any action taken against it. For example, you may want to display the visitor's name or maybe you want to display the current database that the visitor is working with. The ToolbarLabel control provides this functionality.

USE IT The ASP.NET page presented for this technique shows you how to use a ToolbarLabel control. On this page, visitors see the current date and time on a Toolbar control through the ToolbarLabel control.

The Toolbar control has this definition:

```
<IEControls:toolbar
    id="MyTB"
    runat="server"
    defaultstyle="color:darkblue;font-family:Arial"
>
```

Within that control, this ToolbarLabel control is defined:

```
<IEControls:toolbarlabel
        id="tblDate"
        runat="server"
        tooltip="Current Date"
        imageurl="clock1.ico"
    />
```

The ID of a ToolbarLabel control contains the name of the control. The text placed in the ToolTip property appears to visitors if they hover their mouse over the control. The ImageURL property is optionally set to the name of an image that you would like to appear to the left of the control.

The other ToolbarLabel control has this definition:

```
<IEControls:toolbarlabel
    id="tblTime"
    runat="server"
    tooltip="Current Time"
    imageurl="clock2.ico"
/>
```

Notice that it uses a different image in the ImageURL property.

QUICK TIP

In this example the ImageURL property is set to the location of an image that is in the same folder as the ASP.NET page. But you can specify the full address of the image through this property if the image is in a different location.

When the page loads, this code runs:

```
Sub Page_Load(ByVal Sender as Object, ByVal E as EventArgs)
    tblDate.Text = Today()
    tblTime.Text = TimeOfDay()
End Sub
```

The Text property of the first ToolbarLabel control is set to today's date, and the Text property of the second ToolbarLabel control is set to the current time on the server.

Adding a ToolbarTextBox Control to a Toolbar Control

The Toolbar control provides controls that you can define that are similar to some of the standard ASP.NET controls. One of those controls is the ToolbarTextBox control. That control is very similar to the TextBox control in how it appears and behaves. This technique shows you how to define a ToolbarTextBox control.

USE IT This page displays a ToolbarTextBox control within a Toolbar control. The control prompts visitors for search text. Once they leave the ToolbarTextBox field the page is submitted for processing and they see the text they entered in a Label control.

The Toolbar control has this definition:

```
<IEControls:toolbar
    id="MyTB"
    runat="server"
    defaultstyle="color:darkblue;font-family:Arial"
    autopostback="True"
>
```

Notice that AutoPostBack is set to True. Therefore, the page will be submitted for processing when an item changes in the Toolbar control. Defined within that control is this ToolbarTextBox control:

```
<IEControls:toolbartextbox
    id="txtSearchTerm"
    runat="server"
```

```
    text="Enter Search Term"
    columns=20
    maxlength="30"
    textmode="SingleLine"
    ontextchanged="Search_Changed"
/>
```

The ID property is set to the name of the control. The Text property is set to an initial value but since this is similar to a TextBox control, the visitor can change the value. The Columns property is set to the width of the control within the Toolbar control. The MaxLength property is set to the number of characters that visitors can type into the control.

The TextMode property is different from the TextBox control. In the ToolbarTextBox control, this property can be set to SingleLine for a standard TextBox appearance or it can be set to Password. In that case, it behaves like a password-type TextBox control.

The OnTextChanged property is set to the name of the procedure that you want to run when visitors complete changing the text in the control.

Also defined on the page is this Label control:

```
<asp:Label
    id="lblMessage"
    runat="server"
    font-bold="True"
/>
```

This code block fires when visitors change and leave the ToolbarTextBox control:

```
Sub Search_Changed(Sender As Object, E As EventArgs)
    lblMessage.Text = "Searching for: " & txtSearchTerm.Text
End Sub
```

The procedure echoes the text visitors entered into the ToolbarTextBox control back to them through the Label control.

Adding a ToolbarSeparator Control to a Toolbar Control

On standard Toolbar controls that you see used in applications, the items in the Toolbar are frequently grouped together. You see this logical group because of an engraved vertical line between items in the Toolbar. The Toolbar control also has a device for visually grouping items within it together. This is done through the ToolbarSeparator control.

The ToolbarSeparator is a very simple device that renders itself as a small vertical line between two other Toolbar controls. This tip shows you how to define a ToolbarSeparator control.

USE IT   This ASP.NET page demonstrates the use of the ToolbarSeparator control. It contains
a Toolbar control with two ToolbarTextBox controls. The ToolbarTextBox controls are
separated by a ToolbarSeparator control.

The Toolbar control has this definition:

```
<IEControls:toolbar
    id="MyTB"
    runat="server"
    defaultstyle="color:darkblue;font-family:Arial"
>
```

And within that Toolbar control two ToolbarTextBox controls like this one are defined:

```
<IEControls:toolbartextbox
    id="txtSearchTerm"
    runat="server"
/>
```

Visually the two ToolbarTextBox controls are separated by a vertical line generated through this
ToolbarSeparator control:

```
<IEControls:ToolBarSeparator
    id="Sep1"
    runat="server"
/>
```

You can give the ToolbarSeparator control a name through the ID property. You can also define
two of these controls next to each other to display a double vertical line, adding more visual separation.

Using Style Properties of the Toolbar Control

The Toolbar control contains three sets of styles that you can use to determine the look of the controls that
are defined within a Toolbar control. These style properties allow you to set the look of the control
based on whether it is currently selected, whether the visitor's mouse is hovering over it, or whether
no action is being taken with it. This technique shows you how to use these three style properties.

USE IT   The ASP.NET page presented for this technique displays three ToolbarCheckButton
controls within a Toolbar control. The Toolbar control contains style properties so that
the ToolbarCheckButton controls have a different appearance based on their current state.

The Toolbar control has this definition:

```
<IEControls:toolbar
    id="MyTB"
    runat="server"
```

```
defaultstyle="color:darkblue;background-color:gray;
    font-family:Arial"
selectedstyle="color:darkred;background-color:chalk;
    font-family:Arial"
hoverstyle="color:green;background-color:yellow;font-family:
    Comic Sans MS"
>
```

The style properties are set through three settings. The first is the DefaultStyle property. The style placed in that property is used by any control that is neither selected, nor has the visitor's mouse hovering over the control.

The next style defined is the SelectedStyle. That style is used for items that are currently selected, such as a ToolbarCheckButton that is depressed.

The third style is the HoverStyle. The value placed in that style is used when the visitor's mouse is hovering over one of the controls in the Toolbar control.

Notice that these style properties differ from how you set font and color properties in standard ASP.NET controls. Here you use Cascading Style Sheet syntax. That syntax is based on name/value pairs, where the name and value are separated by a colon and each pair is separated by a semi-colon.

Also defined on the page are three ToolbarCheckButton controls like this one:

```
<IEControls:toolbarcheckbutton
    id="TBCB1"
    runat="server"
    text="Button 1"
/>
```

These controls are defined within a ToolbarCheckGroup control.

Adding Controls to a Toolbar Control Through Code

You may find that you need to add controls to a Toolbar control dynamically. In other words, you may not know ahead of time whether you need to display a ToolbarLabel control or you may need to add an unknown number of ToolbarLabel controls to a Toolbar control. In that case, you would need to add controls dynamically to your Toolbar control. This technique shows you how to do that.

USE IT The ASP.NET page presented for this technique dynamically adds a ToolbarLabel control to a Toolbar control based on the day of the week. If today is a Monday, the control is added. Otherwise, it is not.

The Toolbar control has this basic definition:

```
<IEControls:toolbar
    id="MyTB"
    runat="server"
    defaultstyle="color:darkblue;font-family:Arial"
```

```
        >
</IEControls:toolbar>
```

Notice that no controls are initially defined within it.

When the page loads, this code block runs:

```
Sub Page_Load(ByVal Sender as Object, ByVal E as EventArgs)
    If (WeekDay(Today())) = 2 Then
        Dim MyTBL = New ToolBarLabel
        MyTBL.Text = "2:00 PM Meeting Today!"
        MyTBL.ToolTip = "The weekly meeting is on for today."
        MyTB.Items.Add(MyTBL)
    End If
End Sub
```

First, you check to see if the current day of the week is Monday by seeing if the WeekDay function returns a 2:

```
If (WeekDay(Today())) = 2 Then
```

If that is the case, you define a ToolbarLabel control:

```
Dim MyTBL = New ToolBarLabel
```

You then place text reminding visitors that a meeting will be held today into the Text and ToolTip properties of the ToolbarLabel control:

```
MyTBL.Text = "2:00 PM Meeting Today!"
MyTBL.ToolTip = "The weekly meeting is on for today."
```

That control is then added to the Toolbar control:

```
MyTB.Items.Add(MyTBL)
```

Notice that the Toolbar control does not have a Controls collection like you see in other container controls defined in ASP.NET. Instead, you add a control through the Items collection of the Toolbar control.

Creating a Basic TreeView Control

The TreeView control provides a way for you to hierarchically display information. A TreeView control contains a list of items called *nodes*. Each node can have its own collection nodes, giving you a deep level of data definition. Each of the nodes can be expanded or collapsed allowing visitors looking at a TreeView control to only see the level of the data that they are interested in. Files and folders are an example of data that is organized through a TreeView type of control. But on your ASP.NET pages you may want to use a TreeView control to display departments in a store, records in a CD collection, or players on different sports teams.

This technique shows you what you need to do to be able to define a TreeView control on an ASP.NET page.

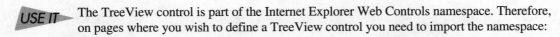 The TreeView control is part of the Internet Explorer Web Controls namespace. Therefore, on pages where you wish to define a TreeView control you need to import the namespace:

```
<%@ Import Namespace="Microsoft.Web.UI.WebControls" %>
```

You also need to register the namespace and give it a TagPrefix to make the controls in that library easier to define:

```
<%@ Register TagPrefix="IEControls"
    Namespace="Microsoft.Web.UI.WebControls"
    Assembly ="Microsoft.Web.UI.WebControls"
%>
```

Once you have set these page directives, you can define a TreeView control like this one:

```
<IEControls:treeview
    id="tvBasic"
    autoselect="False"
    showplus="True"
    showlines="True"
    expandlevel=2
    runat="server">
</IEControls:treeview>
```

Notice that the TagPrefix property is used in the definition of the control:

```
<IEControls:treeview
```

The ID property is set to the name that you wish to give the control:

```
id="tvBasic"
```

When visitors navigate through the nodes in the TreeView control they can use the arrows on their keyboard for that navigation. When the AutoSelect property of the TreeView control is set to True, scrolling through the TreeView control using the keyboard selects an item. If the property is set to False, it does not:

```
autoselect="False"
```

When two nodes meet up in a TreeView control you can have a plus sign display so visitors know that they can expand the node. You control whether that plus sign is there through the ShowPlus property. If the property is set to True, the plus signs are used. Otherwise, they are not:

```
showplus="True"
```

Between the nodes in a TreeView control you can have lines appear. You control whether the lines appear through the ShowLines property:

```
showlines="True"
```

The ExpandLevel property of the TreeView control determines by default the number of levels down the hierarchy of the TreeView control that are expanded:

```
expandlevel=2
```

Between the opening and closing tags of the TreeView control is where TreeNode controls are defined:

```
    runat="server">
</IEControls:treeview>
```

Working with TreeNode Controls in a TreeView Control

If you create a TreeView control you will need to add TreeNode controls to it to display any information. TreeNode controls display an item in the TreeView control's hierarchy. The TreeNode control can contain child TreeView controls or it can stand on its own. This technique shows you how to define TreeNode controls within a TreeView control.

 This page displays the names of departments at a store. Each department can stand on its own or have its other departments under it.

The TreeView control has this definition:

```
<IEControls:treeview
    id="tvBasic"
    autoselect="False"
    showplus="True"
    showlines="True"
    expandlevel=2
    runat="server">
```

Within the opening and closing tags of the TreeView control these TreeNode controls are defined:

```
<IEControls:treenode text="Clothing">
    <IEControls:treenode text="Men's"/>
    <IEControls:treenode text="Women's"/>
    <IEControls:treenode text="Children's">
        <IEControls:treenode text="Socks"/>
        <IEControls:treenode text="Shirts"/>
        <IEControls:treenode text="Pants"/>
    </IEControls:treenode>
</IEControls:treenode>
<IEControls:treenode text="Electronics">
    <IEControls:treenode text="TV/VCR"/>
    <IEControls:treenode text="Audio"/>
    <IEControls:treenode text="Car"/>
    <IEControls:treenode text="Computer"/>
</IEControls:treenode>
```

Notice that there are two top-level nodes. Those are the Clothing and Electronics department. Each has other departments defined within it.

Notice, too, the difference between a TreeNode control that contains others and one that stands on its own. When a TreeNode control contains TreeNode controls, those child controls are defined within the opening and closing tags of the parent control:

```
<IEControls:treenode text="Electronics">
</IEControls:treenode>
```

But with a TreeNode control that stands on its own, the opening and closing tags are self-contained:

```
<IEControls:treenode text="TV/VCR"/>
```

Take a look at the screenshot from this page:

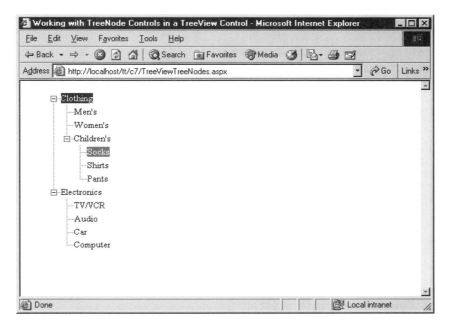

When the page was first loaded, this is how it was expanded. Since the ExpandLevel property is set to 2, all levels are displayed. Notice also that the lines and the node junction boxes appear due to the ShowLines property and the ShowPlus property both being set to True.

The Clothing item is the currently selected item. The visitor pressed the ENTER key or clicked on it with his or her mouse. Then the visitor used the arrow keys to navigate down the hierarchy, stopping at the Socks item, which is colored differently but is not selected.

Adding TreeNode CheckBox Controls to a TreeView Control

In addition to adding text TreeNode controls to a TreeView control, you can also add CheckBox type TreeNode controls to a TreeView control. Those controls are rendered as a CheckBox followed by text. You could use such a control to provide a way for visitors to select from a long list of options that were grouped together hierarchically. For example, maybe you want to display a list of different categories that visitors may want to search. You could list those categories as one long list. But if you use a TreeView control, it will be easier for visitors to find the categories that they want to search.

USE IT   The ASP.NET page presented in this technique shows you how to define TreeNode controls that are rendered as CheckBox controls. The TreeView control on the page has this basic definition:

```
<IEControls:treeview
    id="tvBasic"
    autoselect="True"
runat="server">
```

Within the opening and closing tags of the TreeView control, these TreeNode controls are defined:

```
<IEControls:treenode text="Electronics">
    <IEControls:treenode
        text="TV/VCR"
        checkbox="True"/>
    <IEControls:treenode
        text="Audio"
        checkbox="True"/>
    <IEControls:treenode
        Checked
        text="Car"
        checkbox="True"/>
    <IEControls:treenode
        text="Computer"
        checkbox="True"/>
</IEControls:treenode>
```

The top-level node is the Electronics node. It is not a CheckBox node, but it can be. Within that node, four TreeView controls are defined as CheckBox nodes. This is done by setting the CheckBox property to True for the TreeView control.

You can also have any of the items checked by default by using the Checked keyword in the control's definition as is done with the Car item.

Using TreeNode Controls as Links Within a TreeView Control

Another way that TreeNode controls can be used is as links. When visitors select a TreeNode, they are directed to a site associated with the node. This would be useful to direct an individual to a location in your site from a page such as a Site Map page. This technique shows you how to use the TreeNode control in that way.

USE IT   The ASP.NET page for this technique displays a list of site names in the form of a TreeView control. When visitors select one of the items, they are taken to the site that goes along with that item.

The TreeView control on that page has this definition:

```
<IEControls:treeview
    id="tvBasic"
    autoselect="False"
    showplus="True"
    showlines="True"
    expandlevel=2
runat="server">
```

Then within the TreeView control, these TreeNode controls are defined:

```
<IEControls:treenode Text="Search Engines">
    <IEControls:treenode
        text="Google"
        target="_blank"
        navigateurl="http://www.google.com"
    />
    <IEControls:treenode
        text="Yahoo"
        target="_blank"
        navigateurl="http://www.yahoo.com"
    />
    <IEControls:treenode
        text="Excite"
        target="_blank"
        navigateurl="http://www.excite.com"
    />
</IEControls:treenode>
```

Notice the structure of the TreeNode link items. You set the text displayed for the link through the Text property. The NavigateURL property is set to the location of the site that the visitor is to be redirected to. And you can use the Target property to specify that you want the link to appear in a new Window when it is selected.

Using Images with TreeNode Controls in a TreeView Control

When you display a TreeNode control through a TreeView control to the visitor, the TreeNode control can have an image displayed with it. In fact, based on its state it can have one of three images associated with it displayed. This technique shows you how to define the association between the TreeNode and its images.

USE IT In this technique, a TreeView control is used to display department names at a store within a hierarchical format. The TreeNode controls that display the department names also display different images based on the state of the TreeNode.

The TreeView control has this definition:

```
<IEControls:treeview
    id="tvBasic"
    runat="server"
    imageurl="3.ico"
    expandedimageurl="Smile.ico"
    selectedimageurl="4.ico"
>
```

The ImageURL property is set to the base image to use when the item is not selected, nor is it expanded. The ExpandedImageURL property is set to the page of the image that you want displayed when a node has been expanded. And when the node has been selected, the path stored in the SelectedImageURL property is used to determine the image to display.

Within the TreeView control, TreeNode controls are defined in the basic format like this one:

```
IEControls:treenode Text="Men's"/>
```

Take a look at the screenshot generated from running this ASP.NET page:

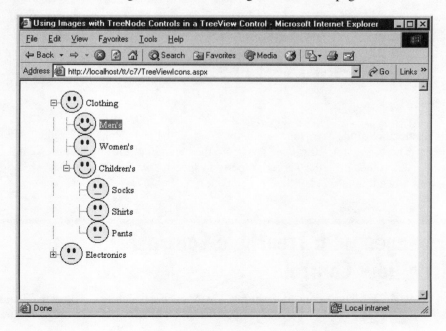

Notice how the three different images are used. Expanded nodes use a special image but the collapsed ones use the default. And also notice that the selected item uses a different image than the non-selected items.

Setting Styles in a TreeView Control

The TreeView control contains style elements that you can use to define the appearance of the TreeNode controls that it contains. These different styles are used in three different circumstances. This technique shows you how to define the appearance of the TreeNode controls through these style properties.

USE IT The ASP.NET page that goes with this technique displays a list of store departments through a TreeView control. The appearance of the TreeNode controls is defined through the style properties of the TreeView control.

The TreeView control has this definition:

```
<IEControls:treeview
    id="tvBasic"
    defaultstyle="color:darkblue;background-color:pink;
        font-family:Arial"
    selectedstyle="color:red;background-color:purple;
        font-family:Arial"
    hoverstyle="color:green;background-color:yellow;font-family:
        Comic Sans MS"
    runat="server">
```

The first style set is through the DefaultStyle property. The Cascading Style Sheet value placed here is used for all non-selected TreeNode controls regardless of whether they are collapsed or expanded.

The next style defined is through the SelectedStyle property. This style is used by the TreeNode control that is currently the selected item in the TreeView control.

The third style is set through the HoverStyle property. The style defined in this property is displayed to visitors when they pass their mouse over any of the TreeNode controls except the currently selected item.

QUICK TIP

The TreeNode control also has DefaultStyle, SelectedStyle, and HoverStyle properties. Therefore, you can override the values placed into the TreeView properties with those in a TreeNode control so that a single node will have its own unique appearance.

Writing Code That Fires When a TreeNode Control in a TreeView Control Is Selected

If you add a TreeView control to your ASP.NET page, you are likely to want to have code that fires when an item in the TreeView control has been selected. The TreeView control provides an event that you can code for. The event provides for you the node that has been selected, as well as the node that the visitor was on prior to that. This technique shows you how to do that.

USE IT This ASP.NET page displays a list of departments in a hierarchy through a TreeView control. When visitors select a node, they see the ID of the node, as well as the ID of the node they were at prior to selecting the current node, echoed back to them through the Text property of a Label control.

The TreeView control has this definition:

```
<IEControls:treeview
    id="tvBasic"
    onselectedindexchange="Node_Selected"
    autopostback="True"
    runat="server">
```

Notice that the AutoPostBack property is set to True. That means the page will be submitted back to the server for processing when a TreeNode control has been selected. The procedure that will run when a node change is specified through the OnSelectedIndexChange property.

> ### QUICK TIP
>
> *Note that this property name does not follow the standard name for this event with other ASP.NET controls as does a DropDownList control. This is also a new name for this event compared with previous versions of this control.*

Within the TreeView control, TreeNode controls such as this one are defined:

```
<IEControls:treenode Text="Men's"/>
```

This procedure fires when the selected node changes:

```
Sub Node_Selected(ByVal Sender as Object, _
    ByVal E as TreeViewSelectEventArgs)
    lblMessage.Text = "You selected node " & E.NewNode.ToString() _
        & " and moved from node " & E.OldNode.ToString() & "."
End Sub
```

Notice the special TreeViewSelectEventArgs parameter defined in this procedure. You use the NewNode and the OldNode properties of that parameter to determine the positional ID of the node that was selected.

Writing Code That Fires When a TreeNode Expands

You may find that you need to have code run when visitors expand a node in a TreeView control. For example, maybe you have your page defined around the space used by a TreeView control. So the size of that control would change when a TreeNode expanded. In that case, you would need code to run when this occurred so that you could resize the rest of the page. This tip shows you how to write code that fires when a node in a TreeView control expands.

USE IT When visitors select a TreeNode control that has subordinate controls, that control is expanded. On this page, visitors see a message every time they expand one of the TreeNode controls.

The TreeView control on that page has this definition:

```
<IEControls:treeview
    id="tvBasic"
    onexpand="Node_Expand"
    autopostback="True"
    runat="server">
```

Notice the use of the OnExpand property. The procedure specified in this property will fire when a node expands. And since the AutoPostBack property is set to True, the event will fire immediately when a node expands.

Defined within the TreeView control are TreeNode controls like this one:

```
<IEControls:treenode Text="Clothing">
```

When one of those TreeNode controls expands, this code block fires:

```
Sub Node_Expand(ByVal Sender as Object, _
    ByVal E as TreeViewClickEventArgs)
    lblMessage.Text = "You expanded node " _
        & E.Node.ToString() & "."
End Sub
```

Notice that the procedure has a TreeViewClickEventArgs parameter passed into it. That parameter is used to supply the positional ID of the TreeNode that was expanded.

Writing Code That Fires When a TreeNode Collapses

Once a node in a TreeView control has been expanded by selecting it, visitors can collapse the node by selecting it again. If you need code to fire when a TreeNode control collapses, you can use the OnCollapse event of the TreeView control. This tip shows you how to write code for this event.

USE IT The page based on this tip displays a list of department names through a TreeView control. When visitors collapse an expanded node, they see the positional ID of the node that was collapsed.

The TreeView control in this example has this definition:

```
<IEControls:treeview
    id="tvBasic"
    oncollapse="Node_Collapse"
    autopostback="True"
    runat="server">
```

Notice the use of the OnCollapse property. This property is set to the name of the procedure that you want to run when a TreeNode control collapses. That procedure has this definition:

```
Sub Node_Collapse(ByVal Sender as Object, _
    ByVal E as TreeViewClickEventArgs)
    lblMessage.Text = "You expanded node " _
        & E.Node.ToString() & "."
End Sub
```

Passed into the procedure is a parameter of type TreeViewClickEventArgs. You can use that parameter to determine the position of the item that was collapsed through the Node property. That value is placed with some fixed text into the Text property of a Label control.

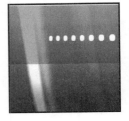

CHAPTER 8

Creating Your Own Controls

TIPS IN THIS CHAPTER

One of the extra features offered with ASP.NET is the ability to create your own controls. Typically, when you create your own control, you start by encapsulating other controls and then building on that to provide yourself with a solution to a common but complex problem.

For example, say that you had numerous ASP.NET pages where you ask the visitor to select a ZIP code. Then, based on that ZIP code, you display the city and state that it goes with. Such functionality would likely be made up of a DropDownList control that contained ZIP codes or a TextBox control for entering ZIP codes. Either way, once the visitor selected or made their entry, you would place the city and state in Label controls.

A great way to implement this kind of functionality would be through a User control. You could create a User control that contained these base controls. You would then expose properties that allowed the developer using the control to retrieve the ZIP code, city, and state values.

The tips and techniques presented in this chapter show you how to create and use a User control.

Implementing a User Control on an ASP.NET Page

Creating ASP.NET controls provides you with a variety of programmatic improvements. But you can't take advantage of those improvements without using your controls on an ASP.NET page. This tip shows you what you need to do to be able to define one of your own controls on your ASP.NET pages.

USE IT   The ASP.NET page presented in this section of the chapter registers a simple user control on the page and then defines one of those controls both in code and within the form of the ASP.NET page. At the top of the ASP.NET page, you need to register the control:

```
<%@ Register
    TagPrefix="My"
    TagName="SimpleControl"
    Src=".\TheControls.ascx"
%>
```

The TagPrefix can be set to whatever name that you want to use to define your control in code along with the TagName property to indicate that you are creating this type of control. The Src property is set to the path where the user control file is defined.

Once you make this definition, you can define your control in code like this:

```
<My:SimpleControl
    id="MSC1"
    runat="server"
/>
```

Notice that the "My:SimpleControl" tag name is a combination of the TagPrefix and TagName properties set in the register tag. You then supply the user control with a name and indicate that it should run on the server. If the control has any write-able properties, you can set them within the control's definition. For example, if the control had a NumLines property you could set it like this:

```
<My:SimpleControl
    id="MSC1"
    runat="server"
    NumLines=5
/>
```

Or in code you could set the property like this:

```
MSC1.NumLines = 5
```

Instantiating a user control and adding it to the page dynamically in code is a little different from a standard control's instantiation. Here's how you do that:

```
Dim MyControl as UserControl = _
    LoadControl(".\TheControls.ascx")
MyForm.Controls.Add(MyControl)
```

You dimension the variable as a UserControl data type. And in that same line you use the LoadControl method, passing to it the path to your control. Once done, you have an instantiated variable of your control. You can then add it to the page like any other control.

If the control has methods, you use them in your ASP.NET page just like any other control. For example, if the control had a method called Clear that didn't return a value, you would call it like this:

```
MyControl.Clear()
```

and if the method returned a value, you would call it like this:

```
X = MyControl.Clear()
```

Adding Controls to a User Control

One of the most basic uses of a User control is to create a control that simply displays a group of other controls on other pages. For example, say that you always had the same footer on a series of ASP.NET pages. Or say that you had a navigation bar that was the same across your site. You could write the same code on several ASP.NET pages. But instead, you could encapsulate the footer or the navigation bar into a User control. Then on each of the pages that needed the item you would simply define one of your controls. This technique shows you how to create a User control that contains other controls.

USE IT The ASP.NET page presented for this technique creates a User control. That control renders itself as two TextBox controls and two Label controls defined neatly within an HTML table.

Since the controls are defined within a User control, the file is saved with the extension .ascx. This is the entire content of that User control file:

```
<Table style="font: 10pt verdana;border-width:1;
    border-style:solid;border-color:black;"
    cellspacing="15">
<TR>
<TD>
<asp:Label
    id="lbl1"
    runat="server"
    Font-Bold="True"
    Text="User Name: "
/>
</TD>
<TD>
<asp:TextBox
    id="txtUserName"
    runat=server
/>
</TD>
</TR>
<TR>
<TD>
<asp:Label
    id="lbl2"
    runat="server"
    Font-Bold="True"
    Text="Password: "
/>
</TD>
<TD>
<asp:TextBox
    id="txtPassword"
    runat=server
    TextMode="Password"
/>
</TD>
</TR>
</Table>
```

First, notice that there are no code blocks. You are not required to include code blocks in a User control and since this control simply displays other controls, that is not necessary.

Next, notice that the controls on the page are not defined within an ASP.NET form. That is because this file, saved as a User control, will have its contents placed on an ASP.NET page within a form.

In other words, when you define this control on your ASP.NET page it is as if you are inserting this code at that spot within the form on that page.

The page instead is placed within an HTML table to provide the desired font and color of the control.

Once you define this page, you can register the control on your ASP.NET page:

```
<%@ Register
    TagPrefix="My"
    TagName="SimpleControl"
    Src=".\UserControlControls.ascx"
%>
```

And define it like this:

```
<My:SimpleControl
    id="MSC1"
    runat="server"
/>
```

The output of this control on that page is shown here:

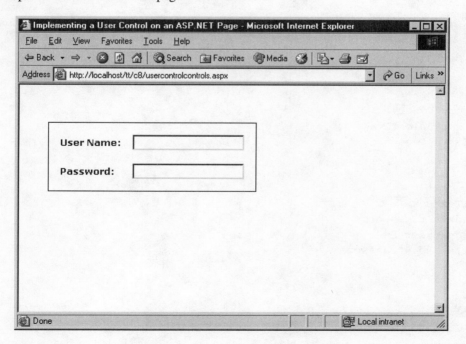

Notice that the control is rendered within an HTML table as was defined in the control's definition. Also notice that two Label controls and two TextBox controls are defined within the control's space.

Creating Read-Only Properties in a User Control

When you create a User control you will likely want to add properties to it. This gives the developers who use your control the capability to customize it or to retrieve values from your control. One type of property that you can create is a Read-Only property. This type of property can only be *retrieved* by the developer who uses your control; they cannot *set* this type of property. Returning the current system date through a property is a good use of a read-only property. Or if you had a property that returned the current version of a control, that would best be left as a read-only property. This technique shows you how to create read-only properties.

USE IT When defined on an ASP.NET page, the User control presented in this technique displays controls allowing the visitor to enter his or her name and password. The control exposes three read-only properties that return the data entered into TextBox controls as well as the version of the control.

Within the User control file, two TextBox controls are defined. The first allows the entry of the visitor's name:

```
<asp:TextBox
    id="txtUserName"
    runat=server
/>
```

A second allows the visitor to enter his or her password:

```
<asp:TextBox
    id="txtPassword"
    runat=server
    TextMode="Password"
/>
```

When the page that the control is placed on first loads, this code runs since it is placed in the Load event of the User control:

```
Sub Page_Load(ByVal Sender as Object, ByVal E as EventArgs)
    If Not IsPostBack Then
        txtUserName.Text = "Your Name Here"
    End If
End Sub
```

The code simply places default text into the first TextBox control. Notice that this code could only run from the User control file. That is because the ASP.NET page that defines your User control does not have direct access to the underlying controls. Instead, you provide the access to the underlying controls through your own properties.

This control exposes three properties. All of them are read-only. The first property is called UserName and returns a string:

```
Public ReadOnly Property UserName() As String
    Get
        UserName = txtUserName.Text
    End Get
End Property
```

That property returns the text entered into the first TextBox control.

The next read-only property returns the password entered into the txtPassword TextBox control:

```
Public ReadOnly Property Password() As String
    Get
        Password = txtPassword.Text
    End Get
End Property
```

The third property is called Version and returns the version number of this control:

```
Public ReadOnly Property Version() As String
    Get
        Version = "2.3.145"
    End Get
End Property
```

Once saved, you can define the User control on an ASP.NET page:

```
<My:SimpleControl
    id="MSC1"
    runat="server"
/>
```

This page not only displays the user control, it also defines a Button control:

```
<asp:button
    id="butOK"
    text="  OK  "
    onclick="SubmitBtn_Click"
    runat="server"
/>
```

and a Label control:

```
<asp:label
    id="lblMessage"
    runat="server"
/>
```

When the Button control is pressed, the following code runs:

```
Sub SubmitBtn_Click(Sender As Object, E As EventArgs)
    lblMessage.Text = "You entered: " & MSC1.UserName _
        & " " & MSC1.Password & "<BR>Control Version: " _
        & MSC1.Version
    'MSC1.UserName = "Bob"
End Sub
```

The code references the exposed, read-only properties of the User control. The values in those properties are placed into the Label control.

Notice the line of code that is commented out. This line of code is trying to set a value to the property. This is not allowed since the property is read-only. If the code were to run it would generate an error.

Creating Write-Only Properties in a User Control

When you create User controls you can supply properties in that control that developers can use that are write-only. That means the developers who use your control can set the value of a property but they cannot retrieve the value. This technique shows you how to create write-only properties.

USE IT   The ASP.NET User control presented in this section exposes a control that displays TextBox controls that visitors can enter their name and password into. The control also exposes to the developer two read-only properties that control font characteristics of the Label controls that are defined within the User control.

Within the definition of the User control, these two TextBox controls are defined:

```
<asp:TextBox
    id="txtUserName"
    runat=server
/>
<asp:TextBox
    id="txtPassword"
    runat=server
    TextMode="Password"
/>
```

Also defined within the control are two Label controls similar to this one:

```
<asp:Label
    id="lbl1"
    runat="server"
    Font-Bold="True"
    Text="User Name: "
/>
```

The User control exposes two write-only properties. The first is called FontName:

```
Public WriteOnly Property FontName() As String
    Set
        lbl1.Font.Name = value
        lbl2.Font.Name = value
    End Set
End Property
```

This property takes the value passed in and assigns it to the Font.Name properties of the two Label controls. Notice in the Property definition that the keyword WriteOnly is used. Also notice that within the property definition only a Set structure is used.

The other property is called FontBold:

```
Public WriteOnly Property FontBold() As Boolean
    Set
        lbl1.Font.Bold = value
        lbl2.Font.Bold = value
    End Set
End Property
```

It is used to indicate whether the text in the Label controls has a Bold weight. Notice that the value passed into the property is passed in through the keyword Value.

Once you have saved this control, you can instantiate it on an ASP.NET page:

```
<My:SimpleControl
    id="MSC1"
    runat="server"
    fontname="Comic Sans MS"
    fontbold="False"
/>
```

Notice that the write-only properties can be set in the control's definition. But they can also be set in code:

```
MSC1.FontName = "Arial"
MSC1.FontBold = "True"
```

Creating Read/Write Properties in a User Control

When you create your own controls, you will likely want to expose read/write properties to the developer that is using your control. These properties can have their values set and the developer can check their value. For example, most of the values entered into controls by the visitor would be well defined if they were read/write. This tip shows you how to create properties that are read/write.

USE IT   The User control created for this tip renders itself as two TextBox controls and two Label controls that are intended to be used for visitors' names and passwords. The User control exposes two read/write properties that allow the developer to check and overwrite the text displayed in the two Label controls.

Within the User control, these two Label controls are defined:

```
<asp:Label
    id="lbl1"
    runat="server"
    Font-Bold="True"
    Text="User Name: "
/>
<asp:Label
    id="lbl2"
    runat="server"
    Font-Bold="True"
    Text="Password: "
/>
```

The first read/write property defined is called UserNameLabel:

```
Public Property UserNameLabel() As String
    Get
        UserNameLabel = lbl1.Text
    End Get
    Set
        lbl1.Text = value
    End Set
End Property
```

In the Get structure, the text in the first Label control is returned. In the Set structure, the value passed into the procedure is used as the text in the first Label control.

The second read/write property performs the same functionality for the Password TextBox Label:

```
Public Property PasswordLabel() As String
    Get
        PasswordLabel = lbl2.Text
    End Get
```

```
Set
    lbl2.Text = value
End Set
End Property
```

Once this control is defined, it can be registered on the ASP.NET pages you wish to use it on. Then you can define the control:

```
<My:SimpleControl
    id="MSC1"
    runat="server"
    fontname="Comic Sans MS"
    fontbold="False"
/>
```

And here or in code you can read or write these two read/write properties:

```
Sub Page_Load(ByVal Sender as Object, ByVal E as EventArgs)
    If MSC1.UserNameLabel = "User Name: " Then
        MSC1.UserNameLabel = "Your Name: "
    End If
    MSC1.PasswordLabel = UCase(MSC1.PasswordLabel)
End Sub
```

Here, if the text for the UserNameLabel matches a certain value, then it is set to a different value. The PasswordLabel property is set to its text converted to uppercase.

Adding Subs to a User Control

You can add two types of methods to a User control—either Subs or Functions. Subs return a value and Functions do not. This technique shows you how to create a Sub-type method in your User control and then call that method from an ASP.NET page.

USE IT This User control allows visitors to supply their user name and password. The User control exposes a single method that can be used by the developer that uses the control. The method clears both or either of the TextBox controls defined within the User control.

The User control has two TextBox controls defined like this one:

```
<asp:TextBox
    id="txtUserName"
    runat=server
/>
```

In code, a single method that does not return a value is exposed. That method is called ClearText:

```
Public Sub ClearText (TextToClear as String)
    If TextToClear = "All" Then
        txtUserName.Text = ""
        txtPassword.Text = ""
    ElseIf TextToClear = "UserName" Then
        txtUserName.Text = ""
    ElseIf TextToClear = "Password" Then
        txtPassword.Text = ""
    Else
        Err.Raise(vbObjectError + 513, _
            "User Control Error!", _
            "TextToClear parameter must be set to " _
            & "All, UserName or Password!")
    End If
End Sub
```

First, notice that the method is declared as Public. That means it is exposed to pages that include this control. Then notice it is defined as a Sub, which means it does not have a return value. Also, in the definition notice that a parameter is passed into the method. That parameter is called TextToClear.

If the parameter is set to All, both TextBox controls are cleared. If the parameter is set to UserName, then just the UserName TextBox control has its Text property cleared. If the developer passes Password into the method through the parameter, just the Password TextBox control is cleared.

But if this parameter does not contain one of those three values, notice what happens. The Raise method of the Err object is called and an error is returned back to the developer. The error message explains what the valid values of the parameter are. Note that if the developer does not handle the error, the error message will be displayed in the visitor's browser like any other error.

Once the control has been saved it can be registered and defined on an ASP.NET page like this:

```
<My:SimpleControl
    id="MSC1"
    runat="server"
/>
```

Then in code the method can be called:

```
Sub Clear_Click(Sender As Object, E As EventArgs)
    MSC1.ClearText("All")
    'MSC1.ClearText("None")
End Sub
```

Here it is called when a Button control is clicked. Notice that passed into the method is the parameter value "All." Therefore, both TextBox controls will be cleared.

Notice the commented line of code. That line of code would produce an error since it passes an invalid value into the method.

Adding Functions to a User Control

One type of method that you can add to your User control is a method that returns a value, a Function. Like Subs, you can pass values into Function-type methods through parameters. In this technique, you will see how you can add a Function to your User control.

USE IT The User control created for this technique could be used on an ASP.NET page where visitors need to enter their user name and password. The control encapsulates TextBox and Label controls that allow visitors to enter their name and password. The User control also includes a Function-type method that validates visitors' entries.

Defined within the user control are two TextBox controls like this one:

```
<asp:TextBox
    id="txtUserName"
    runat=server
/>
```

Also defined on this control is a method called ValidateLogin:

```
Public Function ValidateLogin (TestUserName as String, _
    TestPassword as String) as Boolean
  If txtUserName.Text = TestUserName and _
      txtPassword.Text = TestPassword Then
      ValidateLogin = True
  Else
      ValidateLogin = False
  End If
End Function
```

This method is declared as a Function since it has a return value. The return value is of a Boolean data type. Passed into the method are two parameters. One is for the correct user name and the other is for the correct password. If the values passed in match the values entered in the control's TextBox controls, the method returns True. Otherwise, the method returns False.

Once you create this User control, you can add it to an ASP.NET page like this one:

```
<My:SimpleControl
    id="MSC1"
    runat="server"
/>
```

Then in code you can call the ValidateLogin method. Here it is used to validate the entry into the page:

```
Sub SubmitBtn_Click(Sender As Object, E As EventArgs)
    If MSC1.ValidateLogin("Bob", "aspx") Then
        lblMessage.Text = "Entry allowed!"
    Else
        lblMessage.Text = "Entry denied!"
    End If
End Sub
```

Based on whether the entry is valid, the visitor sees one of two messages through a Label control.

Using Events in User Controls

You may find that you want to include events that you wish to run when some action occurs within your control. You can code those events just like a control's event in an ASP.NET page. Then, when a developer adds your control to their page, your events will fire as if they were part of that page. This technique shows you how to do that.

USE IT   This User control contains two TextBox controls that allow visitors to enter their name and password. When visitors leave the user name field, the text they entered is converted to uppercase.

Within the User control's definition, this TextBox control is defined for the visitor's name:

```
<asp:TextBox
    id="txtUserName"
    runat=server
    autopostback="True"
    ontextchanged="UserName_Changed"
/>
```

Notice that AutoPostBack is set to True. Even though this control is part of a User control, when that User control is placed on an ASP.NET page, the page will be posted back to the server for processing when the visitor changes and leaves that TextBox control. When they do that, the procedure named in the OnTextChanged property will fire.

That procedure has this definition:

```
Sub UserName_Changed(Sender As Object, E As EventArgs)
    txtUserName.Text = UCase(txtUserName.Text)
End Sub
```

The procedure modifies the user name entered by the visitor so that it appears in uppercase.

Creating an Interfaceless User Control

Another way that you can use a User control is as a library for your functions that do not have any visible interface. In other words, you can create a User control that does not have any HTML interface in it. The User control would just be used in code to return values. This technique shows you how to use a User control in this way.

USE IT The User control presented for this technique exposes one property and three methods that return mathematical results to the calling ASP.NET page. The User control has this definition:

```
<%@ Control className="UserControlNoInterface" %>
<script language="VB" runat="server">
Public ReadOnly Property ReturnPI() As Double
    Get
        ReturnPI = Math.PI
    End Get
End Property
Public Function RoundPI(DecimalPlaces as Integer)
    RoundPI = Math.Round(Math.PI, DecimalPlaces)
End Function
Public Function CircleCircumference(TheRadius as Double) _
    as Double
    CircleCircumference = 2 * TheRadius * Math.PI
End Function
</script>
```

First, notice the Control tag at the top of the page:

```
<%@ Control className="UserControlNoInterface" %>
```

This tag allows you to instantiate the control directly in code so that you can call its methods and properties.

The first code block is a read-only property. This property returns the value of PI:

```
Public ReadOnly Property ReturnPI() As Double
    Get
        ReturnPI = Math.PI
    End Get
End Property
```

Next, a method is defined. The method returns PI rounded to the number of digits indicated by the parameter passed into the method:

```
Public Function RoundPI(DecimalPlaces as Integer)
    RoundPI = Math.Round(Math.PI, DecimalPlaces)
End Function
```

One other method, CircleCircumference, is defined. This method returns the circumference of a circle based on the radius of the circle passed into the method:

```
Public Function CircleCircumference(TheRadius as Double) _
    as Double
    CircleCircumference = 2 * TheRadius * Math.PI
End Function
```

With the control defined in this way, you can use its property and methods in the code of an ASP.NET page such as this one:

```
Sub Page_Load(ByVal Sender as Object, ByVal E as EventArgs)
    Dim MyControl as UserControl = _
        LoadControl("UserControlNoInterface.ascx")
    lblMessage.Text = "PI: " & _
        CType(MyControl, UserControlNoInterface).ReturnPI _
        & "<BR>PI Rounded: " _
        & CType(MyControl, _
    UserControlNoInterface).RoundPI(3) _
        & "<BR>Circle Circumference: " _
        & CType(MyControl, UserControlNoInterface). _
            CircleCircumference(2)
End Sub
```

First, the control is instantiated. Then you can refer to the property and methods of the control by using the CType function.

CHAPTER 9
E-mail

TIPS IN THIS CHAPTER

Y ou will find that the complexities of your ASP.NET applications do not have to get very deep before you need to include e-mail capabilities within them. For example, if you have an e-commerce application you may want to send visitors a receipt when they place an order. If you have a news site, you may want to send visitors daily news briefings via e-mail. And if you have an auction site you may want to let visitors know the status of their bids when new bids are placed.

ASP.NET developers can easily solve these problems using the System.Web.Mail namespace. That namespace contains two primary objects. The first is the SmtpMail object. This object allows you to connect to an e-mail server and to send an e-mail message.

The other object is the MailMessage object. That object allows you to set numerous properties with regards to the e-mail message. The tips and techniques presented in this chapter will show you how to use these objects.

Sending a Simple E-mail Message in Code

You may have many different ASP.NET pages that need to send out a simple e-mail. For example, when visitors place an order within your Web site, you may want to send them a receipt. Or you may have a page where visitors ask for additional information about some topic. You could automate that process by sending the information to the visitors via e-mail. This technique shows you how to send a simple e-mail message.

USE IT The ASP.NET page presented with this technique displays TextBox controls to visitors where they can enter their e-mail address and a destination e-mail address, as well as the subject and text of an e-mail message. When visitors click the Button control, an e-mail message is sent based on the information they placed into the TextBox controls.

Since the page sends an e-mail, you need to import the namespace that contains the objects necessary to send an e-mail:

```
<%@ Import Namespace="System.Web.Mail" %>
```

Within the form on the ASP.NET page, TextBox controls like this one are defined for the "from" and "to" e-mail addresses as well as the subject of the message:

```
<asp:textbox
    id="txtFromEmail"
    runat="server"
/>
```

A MultiLine TextBox control is defined for the text of the message:

```
<asp:textbox
    id="txtMessage"
    runat="server"
```

```
    textmode="MultiLine"
    rows="5"
/>
```

as is a Button control for submitting the request:

```
<asp:button
    id="butOK"
    text="Send"
    Type="Submit"
    OnClick="SubmitBtn_Click"
    runat="server"
/>
```

When the button is clicked, the following code block fires:

```
Sub SubmitBtn_Click(Sender As Object, E As EventArgs)
    Dim TheMailMessage as New MailMessage
    Dim TheMailConnection as SmtpMail
    TheMailMessage.From = txtFromEmail.Text
    TheMailMessage.To = txtToEmail.Text
    TheMailMessage.Subject = txtSubject.Text
    TheMailMessage.Body = txtMessage.Text
    TheMailConnection.Send(TheMailMessage)
End Sub
```

To send an e-mail message, you need to define a MailMessage object that contains the message:

```
Dim TheMailMessage as New MailMessage
```

and a SmtpMail object that provides a connection to the mail server so the e-mail message can be sent:

```
Dim TheMailConnection as SmtpMail
```

▶ **QUICK TIP**

By default, an SmtpMail object connects to the local server to send an e-mail message. But you can override that default by setting the SmtpServer property of the SmtpMail object to the name of the server that you wish to send the e-mail through.

You set the send of the e-mail message through the From property of the MailMessage object:

```
TheMailMessage.From = txtFromEmail.Text
```

The To property contains the e-mail address of the recipient of the e-mail:

```
TheMailMessage.To = txtToEmail.Text
```

The subject of the e-mail message is set through the Subject property:

```
TheMailMessage.Subject = txtSubject.Text
```

And the text of the message is set through the Body property of the MailMessage object:

```
TheMailMessage.Body = txtMessage.Text
```

To send the e-mail message, the Send method of the SmtpMail object is used. Passed to that method is the MailMessage object:

```
TheMailConnection.Send(TheMailMessage)
```

Using the Send Method Directly

In addition to sending an e-mail by passing a MailMessage object to the Send method of the SmtpMail object, you can just directly send an e-mail through the Send method. This tip shows you how to do that.

USE IT   The Send method of the SmtpMail object has two forms. In one form, you pass to it a MailMessage object. In the other form you pass to it four strings representing the sender of the message, the addressee of the message, the subject of the message, and the Text of the message. The ASP.NET page presented with this tip uses the second form of the Send method.

The page contains TextBox controls like this one for entering the message properties:

```
<asp:textbox
    id="txtFromEmail"
    runat="server"
/>
```

Also a Button control is defined:

```
<asp:button
    id="butOK"
    text="Send"
    Type="Submit"
    OnClick="SubmitBtn_Click"
    runat="server"
/>
```

That Button control fires this code when it is clicked:

```
Sub SubmitBtn_Click(Sender As Object, E As EventArgs)
    Dim TheMailConnection as SmtpMail
    TheMailConnection.Send(txtFromEmail.Text, _
        txtToEmail.Text, _
        txtSubject.Text, txtMessage.Text)
End Sub
```

The procedure simply calls the Send method of the SmtpMail object, passing to it the values entered by the visitor on the ASP.NET page.

Setting the Priority of an E-mail Message

When you send an e-mail through your own e-mail program you can signal the importance of the message by giving it a higher or lower priority. When you send an e-mail through code using ASP.NET, you can also indicate the importance of a message through the Priority property and the enumerated values that it can be set to. This tip shows you how to use this property.

USE IT This ASP.NET page allows visitors to send e-mail messages by entering the basic e-mail information. But visitors can also select the importance of the e-mail message being sent. The page uses TextBox controls like this one for the basic e-mail properties:

```
<asp:textbox
    id="txtToEmail"
    runat="server"
/>
```

It also defines a DropDownList control for the selection of the importance of the e-mail message:

```
<asp:dropdownlist
    id="ddlPriority"
    runat="server"
>
    <asp:listitem>High</asp:listitem>
    <asp:listitem>Normal</asp:listitem>
    <asp:listitem>Low</asp:listitem>
</asp:dropdownlist>
```

and a Button control is defined for submitting the page for processing:

```
<asp:button
    id="butOK"
    text="Send"
```

```
            Type="Submit"
            OnClick="SubmitBtn_Click"
            runat="server"
    />
```

The following code runs when the Button control is clicked:

```
Sub SubmitBtn_Click(Sender As Object, E As EventArgs)
    Dim TheMailMessage as New MailMessage
    Dim TheMailConnection as SmtpMail
    TheMailMessage.From = txtFromEmail.Text
    TheMailMessage.To = txtToEmail.Text
    TheMailMessage.Subject = txtSubject.Text
    TheMailMessage.Body = txtMessage.Text
    If ddlPriority.SelectedItem.Text = "High" Then
        TheMailMessage.Priority = MailPriority.High
    ElseIf ddlPriority.SelectedItem.Text = "Normal" Then
        TheMailMessage.Priority = MailPriority.Normal
    Else
        TheMailMessage.Priority = MailPriority.Low
    End If
    TheMailConnection.Send(TheMailMessage)
End Sub
```

The Priority property is used to indicate the importance of the e-mail message. That property is set to a value based on the item selected in the DropDownList that corresponds to an enumeration in MailPriority.

Sending an E-mail to Other Recipients

Beyond sending an e-mail to a recipient through the To property, you can also send e-mail to Carbon Copy recipients and Blind Carbon Copy recipients through the CC and BCC properties. This technique shows you how to use those properties.

USE IT   The ASP.NET page presented for this technique allows visitors to enter in basic e-mail information. In addition, they can enter recipients of the e-mail through the CC and BCC properties.

The page contains standard TextBox controls for retrieving whom the message is to and from as well as the subject of the message similar to this one:

```
<asp:textbox
    id="txtToEmail"
    runat="server"
/>
```

Basic TextBox controls are also used to retrieve recipients of the e-mail that will be copied through a TextBox control like this one:

```
<asp:textbox
    id="txtCCEmail"
    runat="server"
/>
```

An additional TextBox control allows visitors to enter the text of the message:

```
<asp:textbox
    id="txtMessage"
    runat="server"
    textmode="MultiLine"
    rows="5"
/>
```

and a Button control submits the page for processing:

```
<asp:button
    id="butOK"
    text="Send"
    Type="Submit"
    OnClick="SubmitBtn_Click"
    runat="server"
/>
```

When the Button control is clicked, this code fires:

```
Sub SubmitBtn_Click(Sender As Object, E As EventArgs)
    Dim TheMailMessage as New MailMessage
    Dim TheMailConnection as SmtpMail
    TheMailMessage.From = txtFromEmail.Text
    TheMailMessage.To = txtToEmail.Text
    TheMailMessage.CC = txtCCEmail.Text
    TheMailMessage.BCC = txtBCCEmail.Text
    TheMailMessage.Subject = txtSubject.Text
    TheMailMessage.Body = txtMessage.Text
    TheMailConnection.Send(TheMailMessage)
End Sub
```

Notice the use of the CC property, which sends the e-mail message to Carbon Copy recipients. And notice the BCC property, which sends the e-mail to Blind Carbon Copy recipients.

> **QUICK TIP**
>
> *You can assign the To, CC, or BCC properties to more than one recipient without sending the message twice. Just separate each e-mail address in those properties with a semi-colon to indicate that more than one recipient is listed.*

Attaching a File to an E-mail Message

You may find that when you send an e-mail message in code you want to send a file attachment with that e-mail. For example, maybe you have a page that lists information about products that you have. You may have advanced technical information about the product that you do not wish to display on the page. You could provide a link for visitors to have that technical information sent to them.

Or maybe you allow visitors to run a report that will take time to process. When the report is complete, you save the report as a file that they will need to retrieve.

Both of these problems could be solved by sending visitors an e-mail with a file attachment. This technique shows you how to send e-mail attachments through code on your ASP.NET pages.

USE IT   The ASP.NET page presented with this technique prompts visitors for their e-mail address. Once they enter it and click the Button control on the page, they are sent a product catalog as an attachment to an e-mail message.

Defined within the page is this TextBox control for entering their e-mail address:

```
<asp:textbox
    id="txtToEmail"
    runat="server"
/>
```

Also defined on the page is a Button control for processing the visitors' requests:

```
<asp:button
    id="butOK"
    text="Send"
    Type="Submit"
    OnClick="SubmitBtn_Click"
    runat="server"
/>
```

When that control is clicked, this code block fires:

```
Sub SubmitBtn_Click(Sender As Object, E As EventArgs)
    Dim TheMailMessage as New MailMessage
```

```
    Dim TheMailConnection as SmtpMail
    Dim TheAttachment as MailAttachment
    TheMailMessage.From = "me@mycompany.com"
    TheMailMessage.To = txtToEmail.Text
    TheMailMessage.Subject = "Product Catalog"
    TheMailMessage.Body = "Attached is the information " _
        & "you requested."
    TheAttachment = New MailAttachment( _
        Server.MapPath("/TT/C9/Catalog.txt"))
    TheMailMessage.Attachments.Add(TheAttachment)
    TheMailConnection.Send(TheMailMessage)
End Sub
```

Notice that a MailAttachment object is defined in this procedure:

```
Dim TheAttachment as MailAttachment
```

This object will contain the contents of the file to be sent.

You supply the name of the file that you wish to attach to the e-mail message by instantiating the MailAttachment object and passing into that declaration the path to the file to be attached:

```
TheAttachment = New MailAttachment( _
    Server.MapPath("/TT/C9/Catalog.txt"))
```

Next, the MailAttachment object is added to the Attachments collection of the MailMessage object using the Add method:

```
TheMailMessage.Attachments.Add(TheAttachment)
```

That attachment then becomes part of the e-mail so that when the Send method is called the file is sent as an attachment to the e-mail.

Sending Multiple Files in an E-mail Message

You may have an ASP.NET page at your site that lists files that can be e-mailed to the visitor. These files could be a list of help documents, job openings, product specifications, and so on. To make it easier for visitors, you would likely want to allow them to select more than one file to be sent to them within a single request. This technique shows you how to do that.

USE IT   The ASP.NET page presented with this technique displays to visitors through a ListBox control files that can be downloaded. The ListBox control allows visitors to select multiple items. When they submit their selection, they are sent an e-mail with all the files selected attached.

Defined on this ASP.NET page is a TextBox control that allows visitors to enter their e-mail address:

```
<asp:textbox
    id="txtToEmail"
    runat="server"
/>
```

Also defined on the page is this ListBox control that visitors use to select the files that they want sent to them:

```
<asp:listbox
    id="lbFiles"
    runat="server"
    selectionmode="multiple"
    rows=3
>
    <asp:listitem value="catalog.txt">
        Catalog</asp:listitem>
    <asp:listitem value="locations.txt">
        Locations</asp:listitem>
    <asp:listitem value="privacy.txt">
        Privacy</asp:listitem>
    <asp:listitem value="jobs.txt">
        Jobs</asp:listitem>
</asp:listbox>
```

Notice that the SelectionMode property of this control is set to Multiple. This allows visitors to select more than one file in the list at a time by holding down the CTRL key.

Also notice that stored in the Value property for each ListItem is the name of the corresponding file.

One other control is defined on this page. A Button control allows visitors to submit their request:

```
<asp:button
    id="butOK"
    text="Send"
    Type="Submit"
    OnClick="SubmitBtn_Click"
    runat="server"
/>
```

When visitors click this button, the following code block runs:

```
Sub SubmitBtn_Click(Sender As Object, E As EventArgs)
    Dim TheMailMessage as New MailMessage
    Dim TheMailConnection as SmtpMail
```

```
    Dim TheAttachment as MailAttachment
    Dim TheItem as ListItem
    TheMailMessage.From = "me@mycompany.com"
    TheMailMessage.To = txtToEmail.Text
    TheMailMessage.Subject = "File Request"
    TheMailMessage.Body = "Attached is the information " _
        & "you requested."
    For Each TheItem in lbFiles.Items
        If TheItem.Selected = True Then
            TheAttachment = New MailAttachment( _
                Server.MapPath("/TT/C9/" & TheItem.Value))
            TheMailMessage.Attachments.Add(TheAttachment)
        End If
    Next
    TheMailConnection.Send(TheMailMessage)
End Sub
```

The procedure defines a ListItem object:

```
Dim TheItem as ListItem
```

Then a loop is defined so that each of the ListItem controls in the ListBox control can be iterated through:

```
For Each TheItem in lbFiles.Items
```

For each of the items in the list, you check to see if they were selected:

```
If TheItem.Selected = True Then
```

If the item was selected, the corresponding file is attached to the e-mail message:

```
TheAttachment = New MailAttachment( _
    Server.MapPath("/TT/C9/" & TheItem.Value))
TheMailMessage.Attachments.Add(TheAttachment)
```

Notice the use of the MapPath method. This method returns the path to the Web root. You would need to substitute the path after that which contained the location of the files being attached.

Sending an HTML E-mail Message

When you send out an e-mail message through your e-mail program, you may find that just basic text isn't enough. Most e-mail programs support a way for you to change fonts and colors and even embed graphics into the body of an e-mail message. This is typically done by sending the e-mail message as HTML.

The MailMessage object also supports sending HTML e-mail messages. With this functionality, you can send e-mail messages that are much better formatted and more dynamic than a standard text message. This technique shows you how to send out HTML e-mail messages.

USE IT The ASP.NET page presented in this section would be used to send visitors information about a product. But instead of just sending the product information as raw text, HTML elements are used to format the message.

Within the form on the page, a TextBox control is defined for entering visitors' e-mail address:

```
<asp:textbox
    id="txtToEmail"
    runat="server"
/>
```

and a Button control allows the page to be submitted:

```
<asp:button
    id="butOK"
    text="Send HTML Email"
    Type="Submit"
    OnClick="SubmitBtn_Click"
    runat="server"
/>
```

When the Button control is clicked, this code block fires:

```
Sub SubmitBtn_Click(Sender As Object, E As EventArgs)
    Dim TheMailMessage as New MailMessage
    Dim TheMailConnection as SmtpMail
    Dim TheMessage as String
    TheMessage = "<HTML><BODY>" _
        & "<B>Product Name: </B>Shoes<BR>" _
        & "<B>Description: </B>These shoes " _
        & "are very nice!<BR>" _
        & "<B>Price: </B>$48.96<BR><BR>" _
        & "</BODY></HTML>"
    TheMailMessage.From = "me@mycomapny.com"
    TheMailMessage.To = txtToEmail.Text
    TheMailMessage.Subject = "HTML Email"
    TheMailMessage.Body = TheMessage
    TheMailMessage.BodyFormat = MailFormat.Html
    TheMailConnection.Send(TheMailMessage)
End Sub
```

First notice the text of the message. Notice that it is really the contents of a Web page. You can place just about any HTML elements inside the message.

Next, notice the use of the BodyFormat property. You must set this property to the MailFormat.Html enumeration for the message to be sent as HTML. If you don't, the message is simply sent as raw text.

Once the BodyFormat property has this value, you can send the message, and if the visitor's e-mail client can display HTML messages, the visitor will see the message with all of its formatting.

Embedding Graphics in an E-mail Message

In addition to formatting as HTML the text of the e-mail message that you send through code, you can also include links to images on these HTML e-mails. These images are not sent with the e-mail message. Instead you link to their location through the HTML in the e-mail. This technique shows you how to embed images in your HTML e-mail messages.

USE IT The ASP.NET page presented with this technique allows visitors to enter their e-mail address so that they can receive information about a product. Included with the e-mail sent about the product is a picture of the product, as well as an image used in the background of the e-mail message.

Defined within the ASP.NET page is this TextBox control used to enter the visitor's e-mail address:

```
<asp:textbox
    id="txtToEmail"
    runat="server"
/>
```

The other control defined on the page is this Button control. It submits the visitor's request:

```
<asp:button
    id="butOK"
    text="Send HTML Email"
    Type="Submit"
    OnClick="SubmitBtn_Click"
    runat="server"
/>
```

When that button is clicked, this code runs:

```
Sub SubmitBtn_Click(Sender As Object, E As EventArgs)
    Dim TheMailMessage as New MailMessage
    Dim TheMailConnection as SmtpMail
    Dim TheMessage as String
    TheMessage = "<HTML><BODY BACKGROUND=""bg.gif"" " _
        & "TEXT=""DarkRed"">" _
```

```
          & "<B>Product Name: </B>Pants<BR>" _
          & "<B>Description: </B>" _
          & "These pants will last!<BR>" _
          & "<B>Price: </B>$12.77<BR><BR>" _
          & "<img src=""pants.gif"" border=2>" _
          & "</BODY></HTML>"
      TheMailMessage.From = "me@mycomapny.com"
      TheMailMessage.To = txtToEmail.Text
      TheMailMessage.Subject = "HTML Email"
      TheMailMessage.Body = TheMessage
      TheMailMessage.BodyFormat = MailFormat.Html
      TheMailMessage.URLContentLocation = _
          "http://LocalHost/tt/C9/"
      TheMailConnection.Send(TheMailMessage)
End Sub
```

Notice that the text of the message includes links to graphics. Also notice that the BodyFormat property has been set to HTML. Doing that causes the message to be sent as HTML instead of raw text.

Additionally, notice the URLContentLocation property. This property needs to be set to the base directory where the images that go with this e-mail message are located. Therefore, this path is combined with the image filenames to form the full path to the embedded graphic.

Take a look at the screenshot produced from the e-mail sent by this ASP.NET page.

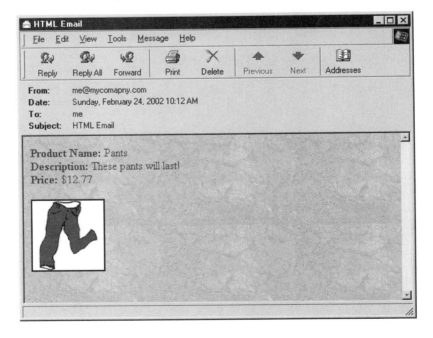

The e-mail message contains not just the text set in the Body property but also graphics. Those graphics include the image of the product as well as a background image.

Adding a Form to an E-mail Message

You can use the e-mail objects in code to send a raw text message. You can use e-mail objects in code to send HTML e-mails. But you can also use e-mail objects in code to send forms to the recipient of the e-mail message. This allows recipients to respond to a request right in the e-mail and send their request back to the server for processing, again through the e-mail message.

You could use this mechanism to poll employees at your company. An e-mail sent to employees would ask them a question. Right in the e-mail they would enter their response and submit it to the server for processing.

Or you could put a form in an HTML e-mail message that would allow a customer to order a product right from the e-mail message. This tip shows you how to send and process such a request.

USE IT   To accomplish the functionality of this tip, two ASP.NET pages are required, as is an HTML e-mail message. Visitors enter their e-mail address on one ASP.NET page. They are then sent an HMTL e-mail message with a form. When they respond to that e-mail message by clicking a Submit button on the e-mail, another ASP.NET page processes their request.

On the first ASP.NET page a TextBox control is defined for visitors to enter their e-mail message:

```
<asp:textbox
    id="txtToEmail"
    runat="server"
/>
```

A Button control is also defined on that page for processing visitors requests:

```
<asp:button
    id="butOK"
    text="Send HTML Email"
    Type="Submit"
    OnClick="SubmitBtn_Click"
    runat="server"
/>
```

When the button is clicked, this code runs:

```
Sub SubmitBtn_Click(Sender As Object, E As EventArgs)
    Dim TheMailMessage as New MailMessage
    Dim TheMailConnection as SmtpMail
    Dim TheMessage as String
    TheMessage = "<HTML><BODY>" _
```

```
        & "<FORM method=""post"" action=""" _
        & "http://LocalHost/tt/C9/processrequest.aspx"">" _
        & "<B>Product Name: </B>Shoes<BR>" _
        & "<B>Description: </B>" _
        & "These shoes are very nice!<BR>" _
        & "<B>Price: </B>$48.96<BR>" _
        & "<B>Quantity: </B><input name=""txtQuantity"" " _
        & "type=""text""/><BR>" _
        & "<input type=""submit"" value=""Order""/>" _
        & "<BR></FORM></BODY></HTML>"
    TheMailMessage.From = "me@mycomapny.com"
    TheMailMessage.To = txtToEmail.Text
    TheMailMessage.Subject = "HTML Email"
    TheMailMessage.Body = TheMessage
    TheMailMessage.BodyFormat = MailFormat.Html
    TheMailConnection.Send(TheMailMessage)
End Sub
```

The code block sends an HTML e-mail to the e-mail address entered into the TextBox control. Notice the content of the e-mail message. It contains a standard HTML form. The form defines a Text input element for entering the quantity of the product that the recipients of the e-mail want to order.

The recipients submit the quantity to order by clicking the Submit HTML element on the page. When they do that, the value entered into the Input element is submitted to the ASP.NET page indicated by the value in the Action parameter of the Form tag.

The code on that page would process the visitors' orders. In this case, it echoes the quantity entered into the e-mail message back to the visitors when the page loads:

```
Sub Page_Load(ByVal Sender as Object, ByVal E as EventArgs)
    Response.Write("The quantity you ordered is: " _
        & Request.Form("txtQuantity"))
End Sub
```

Sending an E-mail Blast

You may find that you have a database table containing customers that want to receive e-mail from you regarding some aspect of your company. Or maybe you need to send a message to all the employees at your company to inform them of a meeting. In those cases, an e-mail blast page may be helpful. An e-mail blast page sends e-mails one at a time out to a group of people based on records in a database table. This technique shows you how to do that.

USE IT   With this ASP.NET page visitors enter their e-mail message. When they submit the message the code connects to an Access database and sends the e-mail message out to all the employees listed in a database table.

Within the form on the ASP.NET page, TextBox controls similar to this one allow visitors to enter the content of their e-mail message:

```
<asp:textbox
    id="txtFromEmail"
    runat="server"
/>
```

A Button control also is defined on the page so that visitors can submit the e-mail blast request:

```
<asp:button
    id="butOK"
    text="Send"
    Type="Submit"
    OnClick="SubmitBtn_Click"
    runat="server"
/>
```

When they click that Button, this code block fires:

```
Sub SubmitBtn_Click(Sender As Object, E As EventArgs)
    Dim TheMailMessage as New MailMessage
    Dim TheMailConnection as SmtpMail
    Dim DBConn as OleDbConnection
    Dim DBCommand As OleDbDataAdapter
    Dim DSPageData as New DataSet
    Dim I as Long
    TheMailMessage.From = txtFromEmail.Text
    TheMailMessage.Subject = txtSubject.Text
    TheMailMessage.Body = txtMessage.Text
    DBConn = New OleDbConnection( _
        "PROVIDER=Microsoft.Jet.OLEDB.4.0;" _
        & "DATA SOURCE=" _
        & Server.MapPath("/tt/C9/EmailDB.mdb;"))
    DBCommand = New OleDbDataAdapter _
        ("Select EmailAddress " _
        & "From Employees", DBConn)
    DBCommand.Fill(DSPageData, _
        "EmailAddress")
    For I = 0 to DSPageData.Tables("EmailAddress"). _
        Rows.Count - 1
        TheMailMessage.To = _
            DSPageData.Tables("EmailAddress"). _
            Rows(I).Item("EmailAddress")
        TheMailConnection.Send(TheMailMessage)
```

```
    Next
End Sub
```

The code first sets some initial properties of the e-mail message that won't change. Those values come from the text entered by the visitors into the TextBox controls.

Then a connection is made to the Access database and all the e-mail addresses for the employee records are retrieved. Next, the code starts a loop so that each record can be processed. Within that loop each employee is sent his or her own e-mail message.

CHAPTER 10

Application Issues

TIPS IN THIS CHAPTER

A s your ASP.NET pages become more complex and you find that they need to be grouped together, you'll need to create an ASP.NET application. Once you create an ASP.NET application you can configure that application using a Global.asax file and a Web.Config file. The Global.asax file provides a way for you to define code that runs when an application starts and stops or when a session starts or stops. The Web.Config file is an XML file that you can use to store application settings. The tips and technique presented in this chapter show you how to use these files and how to work with Session and Application objects.

Also presented in this chapter are tips and techniques you would use in an ASP.NET application when you needed to determine information about the visitor's operating system and browser.

Creating a Global.asax Configuration File

Often, you need to logically group together your ASP.NET pages. For example, if you have an e-commerce site, you want to group your pages together in such a way that visitors can browse through your catalog, add items to their shopping cart, remove items, and check out while you maintain information about their activity. You need to group pages together so that the visitors' state is maintained from page to page.

You do this by creating an ASP.NET application. In an ASP.NET application, your individual ASP.NET pages are treated as part of a collective project, instead of as stand-alone files.

Once you create an ASP.NET application, you can add a file called a Global.asax configuration file to that application. This technique shows you how to create an ASP.NET application and add the Global.asax file.

USE IT   You create an ASP.NET application though IIS. Therefore, you need to open IIS and browse to the folder that you wish to place the Global.asax file in. Right-click on that folder and select Properties. From the Directory tab in the Properties dialog, press the Create button. Apply your changes and your folder as an ASP.NET application.

A Global.asax configuration file provides a way for you to run code when visitors enter the first page of your application, as well as providing ways to code other events. The procedures that you define within a Global.asax configuration file are procedures that do not fall within the activity of a single page. The code is code that belongs to the entire ASP.NET application.

A Global.asax configuration file is created as a standard text file. You must call the file Global.asax. You place the file either in the root of your ASP.NET application or in the Web root. If you place the file in a folder that is not an ASP.NET application and a Global.asax file is defined above that folder's location, the Global.asax configuration file will not be used.

This is the basic structure of a Global.asax configuration file:

```
<SCRIPT LANGUAGE="VB" RUNAT="Server">
Sub Application_OnStart()

End Sub
Sub Application_OnEnd()

End Sub
Sub Session_OnStart()

End Sub
Sub Session_OnEnd()

End Sub
</SCRIPT>
```

At the top of the file, you include an opening Script tag:

```
<SCRIPT LANGUAGE="VB" RUNAT="Server">
```

The tag indicates the programming language of the code in this file and that it will run on the server.

After that, you start to define the procedures that can be included. Each procedure is defined as a Sub and includes a closing Sub line. The use of each of these procedures will be discussed in following tips.

The first procedure is called Application_OnStart and fires when the ASP.NET application first loads:

```
Sub Application_OnStart()

End Sub
```

The second procedure is called Application_OnEnd and fires when the application closes:

```
Sub Application_OnEnd()

End Sub
```

The third procedure is called Session_OnStart. This procedure fires whenever a new user enters any page within your ASP.NET application:

```
Sub Session_OnStart()

End Sub
```

And when visitors leave your application because you close it or because their activity becomes idle, this procedure fires:

```
Sub Session_OnEnd()

End Sub
```

At the end of the Global.asax configuration file, you need to include a closing Script tag:

```
</SCRIPT>
```

Coding the Application_OnStart Event

When your Web site or ASP.NET application first starts, the code you supply in the Application_ OnStart event of the Global.asax configuration file runs. The application starts when the first page is requested in your ASP.NET application or Web site that has been requested since the Web service began. This technique shows you how to write code for this event.

USE IT   An ASP.NET page and a Global.asax file were defined for this technique. The code in the Global.asax file places values in configuration variables, which are then used by the ASP.NET page.

This code can be found in the Application_OnStart event of the Global.asax file:

```
Sub Application_OnStart()
    Application("ApplicationName") = "My Site"
```

```
    Application("FontColor") = "Red"
    Application("ShippingCharge") = .03
End Sub
```

The first line of code in the event sets the name of the site. The second line of code sets the color that will be used as the font for the application. And the third line of code sets the percent for the shipping charge within this ASP.NET application.

The ASP.NET page that uses the Global.asax file contains these two Label controls:

```
<asp:label
    id="lblAppName"
    font-size="14"
    runat="server"
/>
<BR><BR>
<asp:label
    id="lblMessage"
    runat="server"
    text="Enter your order total to
        see the shipping charge"
/>
```

Also included is a TextBox control in which visitors can enter their order total:

```
<asp:textbox
    id="txtOrderTotal"
    columns="25"
    maxlength="30"
    runat=server
/>
```

and a Button control so that they can submit their order total:

```
<asp:button
    id="butOK"
    text="  OK  "
    onclick="SubmitBtn_Click"
    runat="server"
/>
```

When the page loads, the following code runs:

```
Sub Page_Load(ByVal Sender as Object, ByVal E as EventArgs)
    lblAppName.Text = Application("ApplicationName")
    lblAppName.ForeColor = System.Drawing.Color.FromName _
        (Application("FontColor"))
```

```
        lblMessage.ForeColor = System.Drawing.Color.FromName _
            (Application("FontColor"))
End Sub
```

The code uses the application variables defined in the Global.asax file. The first line of code places the name of the application into a Label control. The other lines of code use the color specified in the application variable as the color for the text in the Label controls.

The other procedure fires when the Button control is clicked:

```
Sub SubmitBtn_Click(Sender As Object, E As EventArgs)
    lblMessage.Text = FormatCurrency(txtOrderTotal.Text * _
        Application("ShippingCharge"))
End Sub
```

The procedure uses the ShippingCharge application variable to determine the amount of shipping on the order total entered by the visitor.

Coding the Application_OnEnd Event

You may find that you would like to have code run when your ASP.NET application ends. For example, maybe you want to write the date and time that your application ends. This technique shows you how to do that. Note, though, that the Application_OnEnd event will not fire when the system fails. In other words, if your server reboots because of a power outage, the Application_OnEnd event will not fire.

USE IT   The Global.asax file created for this technique writes the date and time that the application ended to the System Application Log. To do that, the code uses an EventLog class, which requires you to import this namespace:

```
<%@ Import Namespace="System.Diagnostics" %>
```

The Application_OnEnd event has this definition:

```
Sub Application_OnEnd()
    Dim MyLog as New EventLog
    MyLog.Log = "Application"
    MyLog.Source = "My Test ASP.NET application"
    MyLog.WriteEntry("The application ended at " _
        & Now() & ".")
End Sub
```

The procedure declares an EventLog object. That object will write an entry to the Application Log as is specified in the Log property. The name of this application is placed into the Source property. And the WriteEntry method of the EventLog class writes the current date and time to the Application log.

When that code runs, an Application Log entry like the one displayed in this screenshot is created:

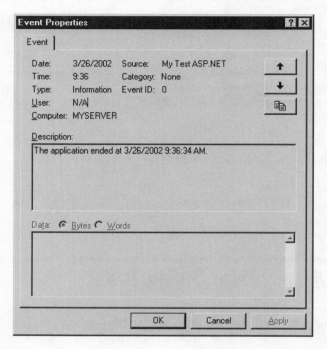

Notice that the name of the application appears in the Source entry, and the text we passed through the WriteEntry event appears in the Description box.

Coding the Session_OnStart Event

Frequently, you will want code that runs whenever new visitors enter your ASP.NET application. Typically, you want that code to run, regardless of the page through which visitors enter your site. For example, maybe you only want visitors to enter your site through a single page. This tip shows you how to do that.

USE IT The code placed into the Global.asax file for this tip requires visitors to go to the Welcome page regardless of the page that they enter your site through. In other words, if visitors bookmark your Contact Us page and select that bookmark, they will be taken to the Welcome page instead.

Here is the code in the Global.asax file that does that:

```
Sub Session_OnStart()
    If Len(Session("WhenEntered")) = 0 Then
```

```
        Response.Redirect("./welcome.aspx")
        Session("WhenEntered") = Now()
    End If
End Sub
```

The procedure checks to see if a Session variable has been set. If it hasn't that means that the visitors have just entered your site. In that case, they are sent to the Welcome page and the time that they entered the site is placed into a Session variable.

Coding the Session_OnEnd Event

The Session_OnEnd event fires when the visitors' session becomes inactive. The visitors' session becomes inactive when you explicitly end their session by calling the Abandon method of the Session object or because visitors have not requested a page at your site over a period of time that exceeds the number of minutes in the Timeout property of the Session object.

You would want to place clean-up code in this type of event. For example, if you had any Session-level objects you would want to close them. Or if you were tracking a visitor through your site, you would want to indicate that the visitor had left your site. This technique shows you how to do that.

USE IT   The code written for this technique adds to the code in the Global.asax file by writing an entry to the Application Log whenever visitors end their session. Here is that code:

```
Sub Session_OnEnd()
    Dim MyLog as New EventLog
    MyLog.Log = "Application"
    MyLog.Source = "A session that started on " _
        & Session("WhenEntered") & " ended at " _
        & Now()
End Sub
```

The procedure creates an EventLog object. That object is used to write the time visitors entered the site and exited the site to the Application Log.

Using an Error Handler in a Global.asax File

In addition to the standard four events that you can add to your Global.asax file, you can also define a procedure that fires when an un-handled error occurs on one of your ASP.NET pages. This technique shows you how to do that.

If an error does occur on one of your ASP.NET pages, you may not want visitors to see the raw error message. You may want them to be sent to a different error page. This code, added to the Global.asax file, does that:

```
Sub Application_Error(Sender as Object, e as EventArgs)
    Response.Redirect("./ErrorsHappen.aspx")
End Sub
```

The name of the procedure must be Application_Error. Now, when an error does occur and it is not handled on the page that produced the error, visitors will be sent to the page specified in this procedure.

Working with Session Variables

Whether you are using a Global.asax file or not, you will find that you need Session variables. Session variables provide a way for you to pass values between pages in your ASP.NET application. For example, when visitors log into your site, you would want to pass on the users' ID from page to page. Or if you allow visitors to configure the look of your site, you would want to store the configuration that they entered into Session variables.

Session variables are a collection of key-value items that you add to the Session Items collection. This technique shows you how to create, refer to, and remove items from the Session Items collection.

 The page created for this technique prompts visitors for their name, which is then placed into a Session variable. Visitors enter their name into this TextBox control:

```
<asp:textbox
    id="txtUserName"
    columns="25"
    maxlength="50"
    runat=server
/>
```

They then submit their entry by clicking the Button control:

```
<asp:button
    id="butOK"
    text="  OK  "
    onclick="SubmitBtn_Click"
    runat="server"
/>
```

Also defined on the page is a Label control that displays information about Session variables back to visitors:

```
<asp:label
    id="lblStuff"
    font-size="12pt"
    font-name="Tahoma"
    runat="server"
/>
```

When the page first loads, the following code block fires:

```
Sub Page_Load(ByVal Sender as Object, ByVal E as EventArgs)
    If Not IsPostBack Then
        Session("WhenEntered") = Now()
    End If
End Sub
```

Notice that the code will only run the first time the page is loaded. When that happens, a Session variable called WhenEntered is created and added to the Session Items collection. That variable is set to the current system date and time.

The other procedure on the ASP.NET page fires when the Button control is clicked:

```
Sub SubmitBtn_Click(Sender As Object, E As EventArgs)
    Session("UserName") = txtUserName.Text
    lblStuff.Text = "You entered the site on: " _
        & Session("WhenEntered") & "<BR>Your name is: " _
        & Session("UserName") & "<BR><BR>Total items in " _
        & "collection: " & Session.Count & "<BR><BR>"
    Session.RemoveAll
    lblStuff.Text = lblStuff.Text & "After removing all " _
        & "session varaibles the count is: " _
        & Session.Count
End Sub
```

First, a new item is added to the Session Items collection called UserName:

```
Session("UserName") = txtUserName.Text
```

That item is set to the value entered by visitors into the TextBox control.

Then the values of the items in the Session Items collection are echoed back to the visitors:

```
lblStuff.Text = "You entered the site on: " _
    & Session("WhenEntered") & "<BR>Your name is: " _
    & Session("UserName") & "<BR><BR>Total items in " _
    & "collection: " & Session.Count & "<BR><BR>"
```

Notice that the visitor will see the total number of items in that collection. In this case, that value is two.

The Session Items collection has a method called RemoveAll. The method clears all the items from the Session Items collection:

```
Session.RemoveAll
```

Therefore, when you now display the total number of items in the collection:

```
lblStuff.Text = lblStuff.Text & "After removing all " _
    & "session varaibles the count is: " _
    & Session.Count
```

the visitor will see that the count is zero.

Setting and Retrieving Session Properties

A session, in ASP.NET terminology, is a single visitor traversing your site. You can set properties and retrieve information about visitors' sessions through the Session object. This tip shows you how to do that.

USE IT The page created for this technique displays information about visitors' sessions back to the visitors through a Label control. That Label control has this definition:

```
<asp:label
    id="lblMessage"
    font-size="12pt"
    font-name="Tahoma"
    runat="server"
/>
```

The only code on the page runs when the page is loaded:

```
Sub Page_Load(ByVal Sender as Object, ByVal E as EventArgs)
```

A session is kept active as long as visitors make a request to a page before a specified period of time elapses. That period of time is determined through the TimeOut property:

```
Session.TimeOut = 2
```

The TimeOut property is set to the number of minutes that can pass between page calls without the visitors' session ending. In this case, the property is set to two minutes.

Next, the value in this property is displayed to visitors through the Label control:

```
lblMessage.Text = "Without activity, your session " _
    & "will expire in " & Session.TimeOut _
    & " minutes.<BR>"
```

The IsCookieLess property of the Session object is a Boolean property. If the property is True, cookies are not in use and session state is maintained through an ID in the link to each page. If the property is set to False, the Session state is maintained through a Cookie object.

Here, we check this property and display text to visitors based on whether cookies are in use:

```
If Session.IsCookieless Then
    lblMessage.Text = lblMessage.Text & "Cookies " _
        & "are not being used to store " _
        & "session data.<BR>"
Else
    lblMessage.Text = lblMessage.Text & "Cookies " _
        & "are being used to store " _
        & "session data.<BR>"
End if
```

When visitors first enter your site, they are making a page request. During that first request the IsNewSession is set to True. During all other requests, the property is set to False. Text, based on the value of that property, is displayed to visitors:

```
If Session.IsNewSession Then
    lblMessage.Text = lblMessage.Text _
        & "The request made to this page spawned a " _
        & "new session.<BR>"
Else
    lblMessage.Text = lblMessage.Text _
        & "The request made to this page did not " _
        & "spawn a new session.<BR>"
End if
```

Visitors also see the value of the Mode property:

```
lblMessage.Text = lblMessage.Text _
    & "Current Session State mode: " _
    & Session.Mode
```

The Mode property of the Session object is set to the location where session data is stored. If the property is set to InProc, the session data is stored within the Web server. If the property is set to SQLServer, the data is stored out of process within SQL Server. The property can also be set to StateServer, which means that it is stored on the server outside of IIS.

Working with Application Variables

If you have data that you need to share across all the visitors to your ASP.NET application, you need to create Application variables. For example, if you needed to calculate the shipping charge on a visitor's order as a direct percentage of the order, you could store that in an Application variable. Or if you needed to store information like the name of your application or the footer text that should appear on all the pages of the site, you could store that information in Application variables. This technique shows you how to create Application variables and how to retrieve their values.

USE IT The ASP.NET code written for this technique creates Application variables in a Global.asax file and then writes the values of those variables on an ASP.NET page. Here is the code in the Global.asax file that creates the Application variables:

```
Sub Application_OnStart()
    Application("ApplicationName") = "My Site"
    Application("FontColor") = "Red"
    Application("ShippingCharge") = .03
End Sub
```

In this case, the variables are set when the application first loads. But you can set and create them anywhere that you want. Three Application variables are created. Notice that two of the Application variables are strings and that one is a number. You can create an Application variable of any basic data type.

Once you have created Application variables, you can refer to them in code. Take a look at this code that references the Application variables:

```
Sub Page_Load(ByVal Sender as Object, ByVal E as EventArgs)
    Dim I as Integer
    lblMessage.Text = "All Application variables:<BR>"
    For I = 0 to Application.Count - 1
        lblMessage.Text = lblMessage.Text _
            & Application.GetKey(I) & ": " _
            & Application(I) & "<BR>"
    Next
End Sub
```

Application variables are placed into the Items collection of the Application object. The Items collection stores the variables in key/value format. In this procedure, you iterate through the collection and display the name of the Application variable followed by its value. Note that the name of the variable is retrieved through the GetKey method.

Locking and Releasing Application Variables

Since Application variables are used across all the sessions of your ASP.NET application, any of those sessions can change the values of the Application variables. Therefore, there is a danger that one session may be changing the value of an Application variable while another is attempting to do the same thing. To prevent this problem from occurring, you use the Lock and Unlock methods of the Application object. This tip shows you how to do that.

USE IT   This tip creates an Application variable that stores the total number of visitors that enter your site. As a new session is created, the variable is incremented. As the variable is incremented, it is protected through the Lock and Unlock methods. Here is the code that does that:

```
Sub Session_OnStart()
    Application.Lock
    Application("TotalUsers") = Application("TotalUsers") _
        + 1
    Application.Unlock
End Sub
```

The Lock method locks the Application variables so that no other session can access them. The other sessions have to wait for them to be released. Therefore, immediately after changing the values of the Application variables, you need to release them using the Unlock method.

Creating Application Objects in a Global.asax File

You may find that you want to create an object that you wish to use across your ASP.NET application. For example, maybe you need to have an array that you wish to access across many different pages or maybe you wish to share a database connection object with different sessions on different pages. This tip shows you how to do that.

USE IT   The code written for this technique creates an application-level database connection object. Once created, any of the pages in any of the sessions can use the database connection. The following code initializes the connection object:

```
Sub Application_OnStart()
    Application("appConn") = New OleDbConnection( _
        "PROVIDER=Microsoft.Jet.OLEDB.4.0;" _
        & "DATA SOURCE=" & Server.MapPath _
        ("/tt/C16/EmpOfTheMonth/EmpDB.mdb;"))
End Sub
```

To create an Application object, you simply define it and set its type. In this case, the object is created when the application starts. Therefore, until the application ends, an object will persist in memory that connects to the Access database specified in the connection string.

Creating Session Objects in a Global.asax File

You may find that you need to create an object that can persist within an individual session that can be accessed from page to page. For example, maybe you need to create a Mail object and use it over and over again. Or maybe you want to create an EventLog object that you wish to initially set the properties for and use over and over again. You can do this through a Session object. This tip shows you how to do that.

USE IT In this example, an EventLog object is created with Session scope. Once it's created, any page within the session can reference the object. This code creates that object:

```
Sub Session_OnStart()
    Session("TheEventLog") = New EventLog
    Session("TheEventLog").Log = "Application"
End Sub
```

You create the Session object by assigning it to the object type you wish it to be. In this case, it is created when the session first starts. After that, you can set its properties and use it here or on other pages to write entries to the Application log.

Using a Web.Config File

One way that you can set the configuration of your ASP.NET application is through a Global.asax file. When you create a Global.asax file, you use a single file that is located in the root of the application. Another way that you can create a configuration file for an ASP.NET application is through a Web.Config file. This technique shows you how to create a Web.config file.

USE IT A Web.config file differs from the Global.asax file in that it doesn't have to be located in the root of the ASP.NET application. You can place a Web.config file in any folder you like. The settings placed in the file are then used by all the files in the folder and any subordinate folders. If you create an additional Web.config file in a subordinate folder, it will be used by all the files in that subordinate folder and its child folders, instead of the Web.config file in that parent folder.

Additionally, if you don't include a configuration value in your child-level configuration file that is included in the parent configuration file, the value in the parent configuration file will be used. For example, if you placed a Web.config file in the root of your ASP.NET application and included a tag for the Timeout property of the Session object but didn't include the tag in a child folder, the value in the parent folder would be used. But if you did include a value in the child Web.config file, it would override the value in the parent file.

> **QUICK TIP**
>
> Camel-case *means that the first word is not capitalized but subsequent words are. For example, these are camel-case variable names: myObject, empName, empFirstName, employee.*

Since it is a text file, a Web.config file can be created using any text editor. It is stored as an XML file. Therefore, it must contain balanced tags that include opening and closing tags. Since it is an XML file, case is sensitive, and Microsoft has chosen to use the camel-case naming convention for many of the tags. Therefore, be careful with case as you work with this file.

The most basic Web.config file contains these opening and closing tags:

```
<configuration>

</configuration>
```

Between these tags, you place all the configuration settings for this Web.config file.

Using the Errors Section of a Web.Config File

A benefit of using a Web.Config file is that it makes it easy for you to transport the configuration of your ASP.NET application from one server to another server. Since you can place configuration settings right in this file instead of in a registry entry, you just need to copy the file to the destination server.

A very helpful section that you can define in the Web.Config file is the Errors section. This section allows you to define redirection actions that you want to take when an error occurs. This technique shows you how to do that.

USE IT The Web.Config file created for this technique defines the name of the page that visitors should be taken to if an error occurs. It also defines pages that visitors should be taken to if server errors are thrown.

The case-sensitive Web.Config file has this definition:

```
<configuration>
    <system.web>
        <customErrors
            defaultRedirect="ErrorsHappen.html"
            mode="On"
        >
            <error
                statusCode="404"
                redirect="MyPageNotFound.html"
            />
            <error
                statusCode="500"
                redirect="MyInternalError.html"
            />
        </customErrors>
    </system.web>
</configuration>
```

You start with the opening Configuration tag:

```
<configuration>
```

Then you define the opening System.Web tag, where many other web-related configuration tags are placed:

```
<system.web>
```

Next, you define the CustomErrors tag. The DefaultRedirect tag is the page that visitors are taken to for all errors except those redefined within this tag:

```
<customErrors
    defaultRedirect="ErrorsHappen.html"
    mode="On"
>
```

Notice that the Mode property is set to On. This means that you want to use your custom error tags. If you set the property to Off, these tags would be ignored. You can also set the property to RemoteOnly. When you do that, you will not see the error pages when you connect to your site through the server. But all other computers will see the error pages.

Within the CustomErrors tag, you can define Error tags:

```
<error
    statusCode="404"
    redirect="MyPageNotFound.html"
/>
```

Each Error tag defines the action you want to take when a specific error occurs. The StatusCode property is set to the error number and the Redirect property is set to the name of the page that visitors should be taken to when the error occurs. In this last tag, visitors will be taken to the page specified when they attempt to go to a page that was not found.

In this tag, visitors are taken to the page specified in the Redirect property when the elusive error 500 is thrown:

```
<error
    statusCode="500"
    redirect="MyInternalError.html"
/>
```

After defining your Error tags, you need to close the CustomErrors section:

```
</customErrors>
```

as well as the two top-level sections:

```
    </system.web>
</configuration>
```

Adding Application Settings to a Web.Config File

One of the main purposes of a Web.Config file is to make it easier for you to install your ASP.NET application on another server. When you do have an ASP.NET application that is installed on many different servers, you frequently want to allow for some customization to the application. For example, maybe you want to allow each installation to have its own title or color scheme. Or maybe certain pages of your application are only visible on some of the installations of your application.

You can store these types of settings through the AppSettings section of a Web.Config file. This technique shows you how to define those tags within a Web.Config file.

 The Web.Config file defined for this technique includes three AppSettings tags. That file has this definition:

```
<configuration>
    <appSettings>
        <add key="AppTitle" value="My Application" />
        <add key="ShowFooter" value="True" />
        <add key="FooterText"
            value="This is the text of the footer" />
    </appSettings>
</configuration>
```

You start with the outer Configuration tag:

```
<configuration>
```

Next, you supply the opening AppSettings tag:

```
<appSettings>
```

Then, you can start adding your application settings. You supply the name of the setting through the Key property and the value for the setting through the Value property. This first setting stores the name of the ASP.NET application:

```
<add key="AppTitle" value="My Application" />
```

The second setting stores a Boolean value that indicates whether the footer section should be displayed:

```
<add key="ShowFooter" value="True" />
```

And if the footer section will be displayed, the text for that section is set through the FooterText application setting:

```
<add key="FooterText"
    value="This is the text of the footer" />
```

You then close the application setting section:

```
</appSettings>
```

and the configuration section:

```
</configuration>
```

Retrieving Web.Config Application Settings in Code

Once you add application settings to your Web.Config file, you will want to refer to their values within your ASP.NET page. This technique shows you how to retrieve those values.

 The page created for this technique refers to a Web.Config file that defines three application settings. Those values are used to determine the text that is displayed on the page.

The text is displayed through one of these two Label controls defined within the body of the page:

```
<asp:label
    id="lblMessage"
    font-size="12pt"
    font-name="Tahoma"
    runat="server"
/>
<asp:label
    id="lblFooter"
    font-size="12pt"
    font-name="Tahoma"
    runat="server"
/>
```

The code that populates the text in these controls fires when the page loads:

```
Sub Page_Load(ByVal Sender as Object, ByVal E as EventArgs)
```

The title of the application is placed into the first Label control. That text comes from one of the application settings defined in the Web.Config file:

```
lblMessage.Text = _
    ConfigurationSettings.AppSettings("AppTitle")
```

The value is retrieved through the ConfigurationSettings object. That object contains an object called AppSettings, which contains a collection of items. You retrieve the value for the item by specifying the name of the item in the collection.

Next, you check to see if a Boolean AppSetting item is set to True:

```
If ConfigurationSettings.AppSettings("ShowFooter") Then
```

If it is, the text of the second Label control is set to the text contained in a different AppSetting item:

```
lblFooter.Text = _
    ConfigurationSettings.AppSettings("FooterText")
```

As you can see, using application settings provide an easy way for you to customize the behavior of your ASP.NET application.

Setting Session Properties Through a Web.Config File

In addition to using a Web.Config file to store custom errors and application settings, you can use the Web.Config file to set initial values for some of the Session properties. This tip shows you how to do that.

USE IT The Web.Config file created for this technique has this definition:

```
<configuration>
    <system.web>
        <sessionState
            cookieless="true"
            timeout="60"
        />
    </system.web>
</configuration>
```

The definition begins with the opening Configuration tag:

```
<configuration>
```

That is followed by the System.Web tag:

```
<system.web>
```

You then define the SessionState tag, which is where the Session properties can be set:

```
<sessionState
```

In this case, the application will not use cookies to store session data:

```
cookieless="true"
```

and the Timeout property is set to 60 minutes:

```
timeout="60"
```

After that, you need to close the SessionState section:

```
/>
```

and the other two sections:

```
    </system.web>
</configuration>
```

Determining the Visitors' Browser Type Using the HttpBrowserCapabilities Class

If you have a site that includes advanced layout or code functionality, you may find that you need to determine the browser in use by visitors so that you can determine whether they can use the functionality on the page. You can determine the browser type by using the HttpBrowserCapabilities class. This technique shows you how to do that.

 The page created for this technique uses the HttpBrowserCapabilities class to display the name of the visitors' browser through a Label control. The Label control has this definition:

```
<asp:label
    id="lblMessage"
    font-size="12pt"
    font-name="Tahoma"
    runat="server"
/>
```

The Text property of that Label control is populated when the page loads:

```
Sub Page_Load(ByVal Sender as Object, ByVal E as EventArgs)
```

You need to declare an instance of the HttpBrowserCapabilities class:

```
Dim BCaps As HttpBrowserCapabilities
```

That class is set to the Browser object returned through the Request object:

```
BCaps = Request.Browser
```

The name of the browser is then retrieved through the Browser property:

```
lblMessage.Text = "Browser Name: " _
    & BCaps.Browser & "<BR>" _
```

Also displayed is the version of the visitors' browser:

```
& "Browser Major Version: " & BCaps.MajorVersion & "<BR>" _
& "Browser Minor Version: " & BCaps.MinorVersion & "<BR>"
```

Using the HttpBrowserCapabilities Class to Determine the Visitors' Operating System

You may find that you want to determine the operating system being used by visitors. This may be to determine the level of client-side code that they can run, to determine the security that they support, or merely for statistical reasons. You can determine the visitors' operating system by using the HttpBrowserCapabilities class. This tip shows you how to do that.

 The ASP.NET page created for this technique displays a visitors' operating system back to them through the Text property of a Label control. The Label control has this definition:

```
<asp:label
    id="lblMessage"
    font-size="12pt"
    font-name="Tahoma"
    runat="server"
/>
```

When the page loads, the following code block sets the text in that Label control:

```
Sub Page_Load(ByVal Sender as Object, ByVal E as EventArgs)
```

You will need an HttpBrowserCapabilities object:

```
Dim BCaps As HttpBrowserCapabilities
```

which points to the visitors' browser capabilities:

```
BCaps = Request.Browser
```

You then use the Platform property of that object to display the visitors' operating system:

```
lblMessage.Text = "Operating System: " _
    & BCaps.Platform & "<BR>" _
```

You also display whether the visitors' operating system is a Windows 16-bit system, Windows 32-bit system, or neither:

```
& "Is OS Windows 16-bit based: " _
& BCaps.Win16 & "<BR>" _
& "Is OS Windows 32-bit based: " _
& BCaps.Win32 & "<BR>"
```

Checking for Script and Code Capabilities in the Visitors' Browser Using the HttpBrowserCapabilities Class

As your Web sites become more complex, you may find that you want to include code that runs through the visitors' browser on their end. Such code is referred to as *client-side code*. If you do decide to include client-side code, you will want to make sure that the visitors' browser supports your code language. If it doesn't, you may want to redirect visitors to a page that shows them how to download a browser that does work for your site.

USE IT This tip shows you how to use the HttpBrowserCapabilities to determine the script and code capabilities supported by the visitors' browser.

Those capabilities are displayed through this label control:

```
<asp:label
    id="lblMessage"
    font-size="12pt"
    font-name="Tahoma"
    runat="server"
/>
```

The text in that Label control is set when the page loads:

```
Sub Page_Load(ByVal Sender as Object, ByVal E as EventArgs)
```

You will need to declare an instance of the HttpBrowserCapabilities class:

```
Dim BCaps As HttpBrowserCapabilities
```

which points to the visitors' Browser object:

```
BCaps = Request.Browser
```

Then that object is used to display the code languages supported by the visitors' browser:

```
lblMessage.Text = "Supports ActiveX Controls: " _
    & BCaps.ActiveXControls & "<BR>" _
```

```
       & "Supports Java Applets: " _
       & BCaps.JavaApplets & "<BR>" _
       & "Supports JavaScript: " _
       & BCaps.JavaScript & "<BR>" _
       & "Supports VBScript: " _
       & BCaps.VBScript & "<BR>"
```

The ActiveXControls property returns a True/False value, indicating whether ActiveX controls can be displayed on the visitors' browser. The JavaApplets property returns a True/False value, indicating whether the visitors' browser can have Java Applets embedded into a page.

You check to see if the visitors' browser supports client-side JavaScript by querying the True/False JavaScript property. The VBScript property returns a True/False value, indicating whether the visitors' browser supports client-side VBScript.

Testing Whether Visitors Are Using a Beta Browser

As new versions of browsers become available, they typically are released first in a beta form. While they are in that form, some of the functionality of your site may not work correctly. Therefore, you may want to determine whether visitors are viewing your site through a beta browser. This tip shows you how to check that.

USE IT The ASP.NET page created for this technique displays back to visitors text stating whether they are using a beta browser or not. The Label that displays that text has this definition:

```
<asp:label
    id="lblMessage"
    font-size="12pt"
    font-name="Tahoma"
    runat="server"
/>
```

The text for that Label control is set when the page loads:

```
Sub Page_Load(ByVal Sender as Object, ByVal E as EventArgs)
    Dim BCaps As HttpBrowserCapabilities
    BCaps = Request.Browser
    If BCaps.Beta Then
        lblMessage.Text = "You are using a Beta browser!"
    Else
        lblMessage.Text = "You are not using a " _
            & "Beta browser!"
    End If
End Sub
```

Here, the Beta property of the HttpBrowserCapabilities class is used to determine whether or not the visitors' browser is a beta browser. Based on that True/False value, different text is displayed.

Determining if the Visitors' Browser Supports Cookies Using the HttpBrowserCapabilities Class

Cookies provide a way for you to store data on the visitors' computer that can persist between visits to your site. They are often used to store visitors' log in information or configuration options. But before you start writing cookies on the visitors' computer, you need to make sure that their browser supports cookies. This tip shows you how to do that.

 The ASP.NET page created for this tip displays back to visitors information on whether their browser supports cookies. That text is placed into this Label control:

```
<asp:label
    id="lblMessage"
    font-size="12pt"
    font-name="Tahoma"
    runat="server"
/>
```

When the page loads, the following code populates the Text property in that Label control:

```
Sub Page_Load(ByVal Sender as Object, ByVal E as EventArgs)
```

An instance of the HttpBrowserCapabilities class needs to be declared:

```
Dim BCaps As HttpBrowserCapabilities
```

That instance points to the Browser object of the Request object:

```
BCaps = Request.Browser
```

You then check to see if the Cookies property returns True:

```
If BCaps.Cookies Then
```

If it does, visitors will see this text:

```
lblMessage.Text = "Your browser supports cookies!"
```

Otherwise, visitors see this text:

```
Else
    lblMessage.Text = "You browser does not " _
        & "support cookies!"
End If
```

Redirecting Visitors to a Page Based on Their Browser Type

The tip presented in this section shows you how to write code that directs visitors to a page based on their browser type. You do this when your site becomes so specialized that you need to have separate versions of your site for the different major browser brands.

USE IT The ASP.NET page created for this tip has no visible interface. It simply redirects visitors to another page based on the type of browser they are using. You would likely name a page like this Index.aspx and let it be the default page displayed when visitors enter your site. The page would then redirect visitors to another page based on the browser they were using.

The code that does this fires when the page loads:

```
Sub Page_Load(ByVal Sender as Object, ByVal E as EventArgs)
    Dim BCaps As HttpBrowserCapabilities
    BCaps = Request.Browser
    If BCaps.Browser = "IE" Then
        Response.Redirect("./IEHome.html")
    ElseIf BCaps.Browser = "Netscape" Then
        Response.Redirect("./NetscapeHome.html")
    Else
        Response.Redirect("./OtherHome.html")
    End If
End Sub
```

An "If" statement is used to query the value in the Browser property of the HttpBrowserCapabilities class. Based on that value, visitors are taken to one of three pages. If they are using an Internet Explorer browser, the Browser property returns "IE". If they are using a Netscape browser, the property returns "Netscape". If the property has any other value, visitors are sent to the third page.

Determining Visitors' IP Address and Host Name

When visitors connect to your site, they connect to you through an IP address. For many visitors, that IP address changes each time they connect to you. That is because they connect through a modem and share IP addresses with other members who connect through the same Internet Service Provider. But even though their IP address does change, you may want to store it along with the host name registered to that IP address. This helps you determine the type of people who are connecting to you. For example, are your visitors connecting to you through AOL or some other major ISP? You can use the Request object to determine this information about your visitors. This technique shows you how to do that.

USE IT The ASP.NET page created for this technique displays back to visitors their IP address and host name. That information is placed into this Label control:

```
<asp:label
    id="lblMessage"
    font-size="12pt"
    font-name="Tahoma"
    runat="server"
/>
```

When the page loads, this code block fires:

```
Sub Page_Load(ByVal Sender as Object, ByVal E as EventArgs)
    lblMessage.Text = "Your IP Address: " _
        & Request.UserHostAddress & "<BR>" _
        & "Your Host Name: " _
        & Request.UserHostName & "<BR>"
End Sub
```

The UserHostAddress property of the Request object returns the IP address that visitors are connecting through. The UserHostName field returns the host name for that IP address.

Checking to See Where Visitors Came From

When you try to understand the traffic that comes to your site, you quickly want to answer the question, where did the visitors come from? Did they come from a search engine or are they entering the site through another site that has your link? Such information is called *referrer data*. Using the URLReferrer object of the Request object, you can determine the page that visitors clicked on to come to your site. This technique shows you how to do that.

USE IT Two pages were created for this technique. One is simply an HTML page that has a link to the other ASP.NET page. That page displays to visitors the page they clicked on to get to it. That information is displayed through this Label control:

```
<asp:label
    id="lblMessage"
    font-size="12pt"
    font-name="Tahoma"
```

```
        runat="server"
/>
```

When the page loads, the following code retrieves the referral information:

```
Sub Page_Load(ByVal Sender as Object, ByVal E as EventArgs)
    Dim TheRef As Uri
    TheRef = Request.UrlReferrer
    lblMessage.Text = "You connected to this page " _
        & "from this page: " & TheRef.AbsolutePath _
        & "<BR>Using this protocol: " _
        & TheRef.Scheme
End Sub
```

A URI object is defined and is set to the URLReferrer object of the Request object. Then, the AbsolutePath property is retrieved, which returns the address of the page the visitors were on before clicking on a link to this page. The Scheme property is set to the name of the protocol, such as HTTP, that they connected through.

Retrieving Visitor and Server Information Through the ServerVariables Collection

Another way that you can retrieve information about visitors or about the page and server that the code is running on is through the ServerVariables collection. This collection contains information like the encoding type supported, the accepted language, the type of connection, the name of the page that the code is running on, the name of the server, and the name of the Web server software. The items returned in this collection differ from machine to machine but are often helpful when you want to learn more about visitors or the server that the page is running on. This technique shows you how to do that.

USE IT   The page created for this technique iterates through the entire collection of ServerVariables. Each variable is written to a Label control. That Label control has this definition:

```
<asp:Label
    id="lblMessage"
    runat="Server"
/>
```

The code that is contained on the page runs when the page loads:

```
Sub Page_Load(ByVal Sender as Object, ByVal E as EventArgs)
```

In this procedure, you need a string array:

```
Dim NameArray() As String
```

and a NameValueCollection object:

```
Dim VisitorSV As NameValueCollection
```

as well as a number for a For loop:

```
Dim I as Integer
```

All the values for the ServerVariables are placed into the NameValueCollection object:

```
VisitorSV = Request.ServerVariables
```

and the names for the values, the keys, are placed in the string array:

```
NameArray = VisitorSV.AllKeys
```

You then start a loop so that you can process each item in the array:

```
For I = 0 To UBound(NameArray)
```

Within the loop, you display the name of the key along with its value through the Label control:

```
    lblMessage.Text = lblMessage.Text _
        & NameArray(I) & ": " _
        & VisitorSV.Item(I) & "<BR>"
Next
```

The result of this code is that visitors see a name/value list of all the ServerVariables. You could then use this list to determine which items you would like to use on your site.

CHAPTER 11
Code-Behind Files

TIPS IN THIS CHAPTER

A s your development becomes more complex you may find that you are working with a team of other professionals. You may be developing ASP.NET pages but your company may have someone else who designs the page. This other person may know nothing about code but may have great skill in layout and design.

In the days of ASP, when you were presented with such a group of professionals, typically the page would simply be passed from one person to another. If the layout person needed to make a change you then had to go back in to make sure that your code wasn't affected by the change. And if you needed to change the code, the designer would have to make sure you didn't disrupt the layout.

With ASP.NET, developers and designers can each have their own separate file to work on through code-behind files. Code-behind files split an ASP.NET page into two parts. One part, the ASP.NET page, contains the design elements. This file would be used by the designer to add controls to a page and to determine the layout of the page.

The developer would use a code-behind file. A code-behind file links to an ASP.NET page. The code-behind file can gain access to any or all of the controls and events on the ASP.NET page that it links to. This allows the developer to have his or her own file for coding the page without having to worry about affecting the design of the page.

In this chapter, tips and techniques are presented to show you how to create and use a code-behind file. Also presented are tips and techniques that you can use to link to a code library file called an Include file.

Creating and Linking to a Code-Behind File

If you decide that you want to use code-behind files with your ASP.NET pages, you need to become familiar with the structure of those pages. When you create a code-behind file it must contain certain tags and definitions. And the ASP.NET page that uses the code-behind file must also contain special tags and structure. This tip shows you what you need to do to be able to use code-behind files.

USE IT First, you need to give your code-behind file a name. The name is important because it will be used on the ASP.NET page that uses the code-behind file. If the code in the code-behind file is written in VB.NET, the name of the file needs to have the extension .vb. So if you had a code-behind file that was for a page called About Us, you may want to name the code-behind file something like this:

```
about_us.vb
```

> **QUICK TIP**
>
> *If you are creating a code-behind file in C#, you need to end the code-behind file name with the extension .cs.*

At the top of the code-behind file you need to place the name of any namespaces that the code-behind file needs to reference in a form like this:

```
Imports System.Data
Imports System.Data.OLEDB
```

The Imports keyword is followed by the name of the namespace that you are importing.

Next, you need to define a class within the code-behind file:

```
Public Class clsTest
```

This class is what the ASP.NET page will import and use for its code. The name you give the class is important because you will use that name to signify the connection between the code-behind file and the ASP.NET page on the ASP.NET page.

Then, right after the opening class definition, you need to place this line of code:

```
Inherits System.Web.UI.Page
```

This indicates that the code-behind file is based on the structure of an ASP.NET page. If you leave this line of code out, you will get an error.

After that you can define controls, procedures, and events that the code-behind file will use. Once you have completed the coding of your code-behind file, you need to close the class definition:

```
End Class
```

Now that you have defined your code-behind file, you need to link the ASP.NET page that will use it to the code-behind file. You do that using the Page directive:

```
<%@ Page
    language=VB
    debug=true
    src="MyCodeBehind.vb"
    Inherits="clsTest"
%>
```

The important properties in the Page directive definition are the Src property and the Inherits property. The Src property needs to be set to the name of the code-behind file. The Inherits property needs to be set to the name of the class that you defined within the code-behind file that this ASP.NET page will use.

Once you have done this, the two files are linked together and behave as a single unit of functionality.

Creating Procedures in a Code-Behind File

One of the ways that you can use a code-behind file is as a code repository for other pages. This repository could contain complex procedures or procedures that are often included on your ASP.NET pages. Once they are in a code-behind file, you could link to the code-behind file from your ASP.NET page without having to rewrite the code in that file.

For example, say that you had some complex data processing code that provides access to your SQL Server database. And say that you have some new developers at your company who know how to create an ASP.NET page but know nothing about database access. You could place all the database code in a code-behind file that the developers link to. Then you would provide them with simple calls to accomplish the complex database activity.

This technique shows you how to create and use a code-behind file as a code repository.

USE IT   This technique defines a code-behind file with three procedures. Those procedures are called by an ASP.NET page that links to it.

The code-behind file has this definition:

```
Imports System
Public Class clsProcsInCodeBehind
    Inherits System.Web.UI.Page
    Public Function RoundPI(DecimalPlaces as Integer)
        RoundPI = Math.Round(Math.PI, DecimalPlaces)
    End Function
    Public Function CircleCircumference _
        (TheRadius as Double) as Double
        CircleCircumference = 2 * _
            TheRadius * Math.PI
    End Function
    Public Function SystemInfo()
        SystemInfo ="Machine Name: " & Server.MachineName _
            & "<BR>Current Script Timeout: " _
            & Server.ScriptTimeOut _
            & " seconds<BR>Path to Page: " _
            & Server.MapPath("") _
            & "<BR>System Date/Time: " _
            & Date.Now()
    End Function
End Class
```

The code-behind file includes a procedure that uses the Math class. Therefore, the file needs to import the System class:

```
Imports System
```

Next, a class is defined within the code-behind file:

```
Public Class clsProcsInCodeBehind
```

As with all classes used by ASP.NET pages defined in a code-behind file, the class needs to include this inheritance:

```
Inherits System.Web.UI.Page
```

Following that is the definition of the first procedure in the class. This procedure returns the value of PI rounded to the number of digits passed into the procedure:

```
Public Function RoundPI(DecimalPlaces as Integer)
    RoundPI = Math.Round(Math.PI, DecimalPlaces)
End Function
```

The next procedure returns the circumference of a circle based on the radius passed into it:

```
Public Function CircleCircumference(TheRadius as Double) _
    as Double
    CircleCircumference = 2 * TheRadius * Math.PI
End Function
```

The third procedure returns information about the system through the Server object, as well as the current date and time through the Now method of the Date object:

```
Public Function SystemInfo()
    SystemInfo = "Machine Name: " & Server.MachineName _
    & "<BR>Current Script Timeout: " _
    & Server.ScriptTimeOut & " seconds<BR>Path to Page: " _
    & Server.MapPath("") & "<BR>System Date/Time: " _
    & Date.Now()
End Function
```

The last line in the code-behind file closes the class definition:

```
End Class
```

The ASP.NET page that links to this code-behind file includes this Page directive:

```
<%@ Page
    language=VB
    debug=true
    src="ProcsInCodeBehind.vb"
    Inherits="clsProcsInCodeBehind"
%>
```

The directive indicates that the page links to the one class defined within the code-behind file.
On the body of the ASP.NET page, three Label controls like this one are defined:

```
<asp:label
    id="lblMessage1"
    runat="Server"
/>
```

When the page loads, the following code runs:

```
Sub Page_Load(ByVal Sender as Object, ByVal E as EventArgs)
    lblMessage1.Text = "Pi to three digits: " & RoundPI(3)
    lblMessage2.Text = "Circumference of a " _
        & "4cm Radius Circle: " _
        & CircleCircumference(4)
    lblMessage3.Text = SystemInfo()
End Sub
```

Notice that the code directly calls the three procedures defined in the code-behind file. It places the return values from those procedures into the Text properties of the Label controls.

Inheriting Controls in a Code-Behind File

Frequently, code-behind files have been used in situations where there is one designer who creates the design of the page and one developer who writes the code for the page. The designer decides on the layout of the page and places controls on the page. The developer writes the code that gives the page its functionality. The designer works with the ASP.NET page and the developer works in the code-behind file.

But the developer needs to gain access to the controls that the designer defined on the ASP.NET page. The developer needs to read and write values to the controls and determine their state. This technique shows you how to access controls defined on an ASP.NET page through a code-behind file.

USE IT This technique defines an ASP.NET page with three Label controls and a TextBox control. A code-behind file sets some of the properties of those controls to determine the values that they display and other parameters of those controls.

At the top of the ASP.NET page, the code-behind file links with this Page directive:

```
<%@ Page
    language=VB
    debug=true
    src="ControlsInCodeBehind.vb"
    Inherits="clsControlsInCodeBehind"
%>
```

The ASP.NET page defines three Label controls like this one:

```
<asp:label
    id="lblMessage1"
    runat="Server"
/>
```

and it defines this TextBox control:

```
<asp:textbox
    id="txtSample1"
    runat="Server"
/>
```

The code-behind file defines this class:

```
Public Class clsControlsInCodeBehind
```

which, like all classes defined for ASP.NET pages, must include this inheritance:

```
Inherits System.Web.UI.Page
```

Next, you need to state the name and type of each control on the ASP.NET page that you wish to programmatically control from the code-behind file:

```
Protected WithEvents txtSample1 As _
    System.Web.UI.WebControls.TextBox
Protected WithEvents lblMessage1 As _
    System.Web.UI.WebControls.Label
Protected WithEvents lblMessage2 As _
    System.Web.UI.WebControls.Label
Protected WithEvents lblMessage3 As _
    System.Web.UI.WebControls.Label
```

Notice that each definition contains the exact name of the control on the ASP.NET page along with the control's type.

Now that you have defined these controls you can control them from the code within the code-behind file. Here, properties for these controls are set through the Page_Init event, which fires the first time the page loads:

```
Private Sub Page_Init(ByVal sender As System.Object, _
    ByVal e As System.EventArgs)
    lblMessage1.Text = "Won't see this."
    lblMessage1.Visible = False
    lblMessage2.Text = Date.Now
    lblMessage3.Text = "Server Name: " _
        & Server.MachineName
    txtSample1.MaxLength = 30
    txtSample1.Text = "Enter some text!"
End Sub
```

Notice that the first Label control will not be seen since its Visible property is set to False.

Inheriting Events in a Code-Behind File

Once you have controls defined on an ASP.NET page that you are accessing in your code-behind file, you will want to control the events of those underlying controls. For example, if the ASP.NET page contained a Button control, you would want to have code in the code-behind file that ran when the button was pressed. This technique shows you how to do that.

USE IT This technique defines an ASP.NET page that contains TextBox and Label controls, as well as a Button control. When text is entered into one of the TextBox controls, it is changed to uppercase through code in the code-behind file. When numbers are entered into two of the other TextBox controls and the Button control is pressed, other code in the code-behind file adds the numbers.

The ASP.NET page contains these two Label controls that will have the current system time placed in them at different intervals:

```
<asp:label
    id="lblMessage1"
    runat="Server"
/>
<asp:label
    id="lblMessage2"
    runat="Server"
/>
```

The page also defines this TextBox control that visitors will use to enter text that they want converted to uppercase:

```
<asp:textbox
    id="txtUCase"
    runat="Server"
/>
```

Two other TextBox controls are defined for numeric input:

```
<asp:textbox
    id="txtNumber1"
    runat="Server"
/>
<asp:textbox
    id="txtNumber2"
    runat="Server"
/>
```

and a Button control will add those numbers:

```
<asp:button
    id="butAdd"
    text="Add"
    runat="server"
/>
```

Notice that no procedure name is mentioned in the Button control's definition. The procedure that fires is instead defined in the code-behind file.

At the top of the ASP.NET page, the code-behind file links through the Page directive:

```
<%@ Page
    language=VB
    debug=true
    src="EventsInCodeBehind.vb"
    Inherits="clsEventsInCodeBehind"
%>
```

The code-behind file defines this one class:

```
Public Class clsEventsInCodeBehind
```

which is based on the Page class:

```
Inherits System.Web.UI.Page
```

After that statement, all the controls on the ASP.NET page are defined here so that they can be programmatically controlled from the code-behind file:

```
Protected WithEvents txtUCase As _
System.Web.UI.WebControls.TextBox
Protected WithEvents txtNumber1 As _
    System.Web.UI.WebControls.TextBox
Protected WithEvents txtNumber2 As _
    System.Web.UI.WebControls.TextBox
Protected WithEvents lblMessage1 As _
    System.Web.UI.WebControls.Label
Protected WithEvents lblMessage2 As _
    System.Web.UI.WebControls.Label
Protected WithEvents butAdd As _
    System.Web.UI.WebControls.Button
```

Four events are defined within the code-behind file. The first event fires when the class is initially defined, which means when the page first loads. In this case, one of the Label controls is set to the current system date and time and the AutoPostBack property of one of the TextBox controls is set to True:

```
Private Sub Page_Init(ByVal sender As System.Object, _
    ByVal e As System.EventArgs)
    lblMessage1.Text = Date.Now
    txtUcase.AutoPostBack = True
End Sub
```

Since this code only fires when the page first loads, that means that the text in the lblMessage1 control will not change if the page is submitted for processing.

This event, however, runs each time the page loads:

```
Private Sub Page_Load(ByVal sender As System.Object, _
    ByVal e As System.EventArgs)
    lblMessage2.Text = Date.Now
End Sub
```

That means that the time will change in the Text property of the lblMessage2 control when the page first loads and when the page is posted for processing.

Since the AutoPostBack property of the first TextBox control was set to True, we can include code that runs immediately when the text in that control changes. That event is defined here:

```
Sub txtUCase_Change(Sender As System.Object, _
    E As System.EventArgs) Handles txtUCase.TextChanged
    Dim TempString as String
    TempString = txtUCase.Text
    txtUCase.Text = TempString.ToUpper()
End Sub
```

You can give the event whatever name you like. But notice the Handles clause in the event's definition. That tells the compiler to run this procedure whenever the text in the txtUCase changes. That procedure converts the text entered in the TextBox control to uppercase.

The other event fires when the Button control is pressed:

```
Sub butAdd_Click(Sender As System.Object, _
    E As System.EventArgs) Handles butAdd.Click
    butAdd.Text = CSng(txtNumber1.Text) _
        + CSng(txtNumber2.Text)
End Sub
```

Notice that the Handles clause indicates that this procedure should run when the button called butAdd is pressed. The procedure adds the two numbers in the two other TextBox controls and places the result into the Text property of the Button control.

Creating Code-Behind Files Used by Many ASP.NET Pages

Depending on the complexity of your site, you may find that it is easier to maintain one or just a few code-behind files that are used by numerous ASP.NET pages. To do this, you must define more than one class within your code-behind file. This technique shows you how to do that.

USE IT To demonstrate this technique, two ASP.NET pages are defined, but only a single code-behind file is defined. Each of the ASP.NET pages contains a single Label control defined like this one is:

```
<asp:label
    id="lblMessage1"
    runat="Server"
/>
```

The first ASP.NET page links to the code-behind file with this Page directive:

```
<%@ Page
    language=VB
    debug=true
    src="ManyCodeBehind.vb"
    Inherits="clsMany1CodeBehind"
%>
```

The other links to the code-behind file with this Page directive:

```
<%@ Page
    language=VB
    debug=true
    src="ManyCodeBehind.vb"
    Inherits="clsMany2CodeBehind"
%>
```

Notice that both directives use the same code-behind file as is set through the Src property. But they each refer to a different class through the Inherits property.

The code-behind file contains this definition:

```
Imports System
Public Class clsMany1CodeBehind
    Inherits System.Web.UI.Page
    Protected WithEvents lblMessage1 As _
        System.Web.UI.WebControls.Label
    Private Sub Page_Init(ByVal sender As System.Object, _
```

```
        ByVal e As System.EventArgs)
        lblMessage1.Text = "In page 1 through " _
            & "clsMany1CodeBehind."
    End Sub
End Class
Public Class clsMany2CodeBehind
    Inherits System.Web.UI.Page
    Protected WithEvents lblMessage1 As _
        System.Web.UI.WebControls.Label
    Private Sub Page_Init(ByVal sender As System.Object, _
        ByVal e As System.EventArgs)
        lblMessage1.Text = "In page 2 through " _
            & "clsMany2CodeBehind."
    End Sub
End Class
```

Notice that the code-behind file contains two distinct class definitions. One definition is used by one of the ASP.NET pages and the other class definition is used by the other ASP.NET page. These classes do not relate to each other. Once defined, you can link to either class from your ASP.NET pages.

► ## QUICK TIP

You may find that you want to use the same class in a code-behind file for more than one ASP.NET page. For example, you may host numerous sites and offer to host a Chat page for the sites. The code for the Chat page would be the same across the different sites you host. But you would want to let each customer design the layout of the page as long as it contained required elements. Then you could have all the Chat pages refer to your one class in your one code-behind file. The customers would simply link to the class that you created.

▼ Creating an Include Code Library

You may find that you have procedures that you need to use in many different pages. These procedures would likely be utility procedures that you frequently find yourself copying and pasting from page to page. The problem with just copying and pasting procedures is that when you need to change one of the procedures, you have to change it in numerous places.

Instead of going that route, you could create an Include file and place your procedures in it. Then from your ASP.NET pages you would reference your Include file. This tip shows you how to create an Include file.

USE IT ► An Include file is typically made up of procedures. The entire contents of an Include file are inserted by the compiler into an ASP.NET page that refers to it.

Here are the contents of an Include file:

```
<script runat=server>
Function MakeLength(StringToSize as String, _
    PadCharacter as String, SizeToLength as Integer)
    If Len(StringToSize) >= SizeToLength Then
        MakeLength = Left(StringToSize, SizeToLength)
    Else
        MakeLength = StringToSize
        Do Until Len(MakeLength) = SizeToLength
            MakeLength = MakeLength & PadCharacter
        Loop
    End If
End Function
Public Function SystemInfo()
    SystemInfo = "Machine Name: " & Server.MachineName _
        & "<BR>Current Script Timeout: " _
        & Server.ScriptTimeOut _
        & " seconds<BR>Path to Page: " _
        & Server.MapPath("") & "<BR>System Date/Time: " _
        & Date.Now()
End Function
</script>
```

Notice that the procedures are defined within opening and closing script tags. The first procedure takes a string and sizes it to the length passed into it. The second procedure uses the Server object to return system information.

Once saved, the Include file can be referenced by any ASP.NET page.

Linking to an Include Code Library

Once you have created a code library in an Include file, you will want to link to it from your ASP.NET pages. This tip shows you how to do that.

 USE IT This ASP.NET page uses an Include code library that contains two Label controls defined like this one:

```
<asp:label
    id="lblMessage1"
    runat="Server"
/>
```

Outside of any code block, the ASP.NET page contains this special Include tag:

```
<!-- #include file="CodeLibrary.inc" -->
```

The tag tells the compiler to place the contents of the file named in the File property at the exact location where this tag is found.

Once this line has been added, you can refer to any of the procedures in the Include file as if they were part of the page. Here, two of the procedures of the Include file are called when the page loads:

```
Sub Page_Load(ByVal Sender as Object, ByVal E as EventArgs)
    lblMessage1.Text = MakeLength("Bob", "X", 12)
    lblMessage2.Text = SystemInfo()
End Sub
```

The procedures of the Include file are used to populate the contents of the Label controls.

CHAPTER 12

Working with IIS

TIPS IN THIS CHAPTER

The Internet Information Services (IIS) is the tool that you use to host your Web pages and Web sites on your server. IIS comes with later versions of Windows NT and comes automatically with Windows 2000 Server. The tool provides the mechanism for you to enable visitors to request different types of Web pages.

Using IIS you can add Web sites, manage properties of your Web sites, create ASP.NET applications, and much more. The tips and techniques presented in this chapter show you how to use some of the functionality of IIS.

Setting Application Protection

If you use one computer as your development and production server or if you have a variety of developers using your server, you may want to protect your IIS server against failure due to one of the Web sites or ASP.NET applications it hosts causing an error. This tip shows you how you can do that.

 USE IT Web sites and ASP.NET applications contain a setting called Application Protection. To use this setting, open IIS and browse to the site or ASP.NET application that you wish to work with. Then, right-click on the item and select properties.

If you are modifying a Web site, switch to the Home Directory tab. If you are viewing an ASP.NET application, change to the Directory tab. You should see a property page like the one displayed in this screenshot.

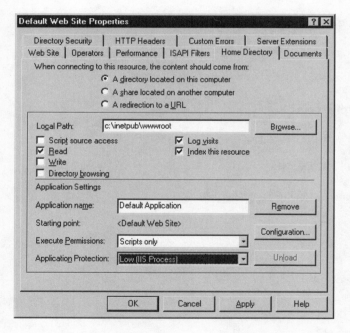

Notice the Application Protection property at the bottom of this dialog. This property provides a way for you to isolate Web sites and ASP.NET applications from other sites and applications as well as from IIS itself.

The property allows you to establish what should happen if the site or application has a catastrophic failure. If this property is set to Low, the site or ASP.NET application runs in the same memory space as IIS. Therefore, if the site or application fails it will bring down IIS with it.

The second setting for this property is Medium. If you set your ASP.NET applications or Web sites to this value, they will not bring down IIS if they fail. With this setting, all applications and sites are pooled together in a single processor space. Therefore, they will bring down other ASP.NET applications or Web sites if one fails.

The highest level of protection is offered by setting the property to High. In that case, the Web site or ASP.NET application runs in its own processor space. Therefore, it should not affect IIS or other applications if it fails.

> ### QUICK TIP
>
> *Setting the Application Protection property to High does offer the best protection to other ASP.NET applications and Web sites. But you encounter a significant performance hit by doing this. Therefore, it is best to use this value only for sites or applications that have a high risk associated with them.*

Creating a Web Site

Within IIS, you can host numerous Web sites. Adding a Web site can be a simple process since a wizard walks you through the creation. This technique shows you how to use the wizard.

USE IT   To add a new Web site to your server, open IIS. Then, right-click on your server and select New | Web site. The first screen welcomes you to the wizard. Click the Next button.

The second dialog in the wizard asks you for the name or description of the Web site. This text is just for you and helps you identify the Web site. It will appear as the name of the site within IIS. Enter a name and click the Next button.

The third dialog is displayed in this screenshot.

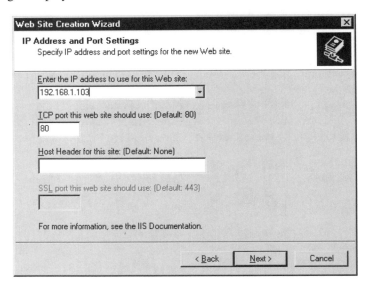

In the first text box of this dialog, you need to enter the IP address that this Web site will be accessed through. If you only have a single IP address or you wish the Web site to be used across all your IP addresses, select All Assigned. Otherwise, select the IP address that you wish to use.

In the second field, you enter the port number. Typically, the port number of 80 will be used. That is the default for browsers. You can enter a different number but you need to make sure it doesn't conflict with another protocol. If you do enter a different port number, visitors will have to enter the port number in their browser when they address your Web site.

For example, if you were to use port number 442, the address to the site would need to include that port number in a form like this:

```
http://192.168.1.103:442
```

If you are hosting more than one site on this computer, you can enter the domain name of the site in the Host Header text box. After entering these values click the Next button to continue.

Next, you need to enter the location of this site on your server. Browse to that location and click the Next button.

On the fifth dialog, you can select what type of activity visitors can do through this site. Click the Next button and the Finish button to complete the addition of your new Web Site. You will now see it listed within IIS.

Sharing an IP Address Across Web Sites

If you host more than one Web site on your server and have a single IP address to work with, you will need to share the IP address across the Web sites. By sharing an IP address, both or all of the sites can be directed to your server but within your server visitors will be directed to the correct Web site. This technique shows you how to do that.

 IIS provides a mechanism whereby when visitors enter your site, the Web site that they are looking for is passed in, along with the IP address of the Web site. Using that information, IIS directs visitors to the correct Web site when more than one Web site is shared on the same computer.

To do that, you need to tell IIS the domain name or names that should be used with each Web site. To do that, open IIS and browse to one of your Web sites. Right-click on the site and select Properties. On the Web Site tab, click the Advanced button. You should see the following screenshot.

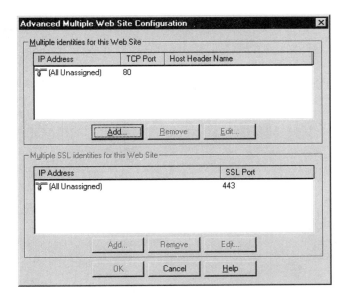

Click the Add button and you will be prompted for the IP address to use, the Port Number, and the Host Header name. If you have a single IP address just use All Assigned and the default port of 80. Most importantly, you need to set the Host Header Name. This is the domain name that visitors enter to get to your site. Therefore, if your site was called Google, you would enter this value in the Host Header Name field:

```
www.google.com
```

You would then perform this same task for the other sites that you host. After doing that, visitors will be directed to the appropriate site based on the address that they enter.

Limiting Web Site Connections

You may find that you wish to limit the total number of connections that you offer through a Web site. You may do this as a way to control the amount of activity one of your developers can get through your site or you might do it to protect your computer from getting overwhelmed by Web site requests. This technique shows you how you can limit connections to a Web site.

USE IT ▶ To limit the number of connections allowed to a Web site, open IIS and browse to the Web site that you wish to limit. Then, right-click on the site and select Properties. Select the Web Site tab and you should see a dialog like the one displayed in this screenshot.

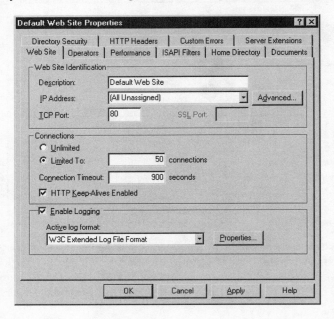

Notice the Connections section on this tab. This is where you limit the number of simultaneous connections. Click the Limit To radio button and then enter the maximum number of connections. Once you do that, the Web site will not be allowed to exceed the number of connections you entered.

Logging Page Activity

IIS provides a way for you to keep track of basic information related to visitors to your site. You do this by enabling logging. This tip shows you how to do that.

USE IT ▶ Using the logging options provided within IIS, you can create text files that contain information about who visited your site, what they requested, and the status of the request.

To enable logging of your Web site, open IIS and browse to the Web site that you wish to work with. Next, right-click on the Web site and select Properties. Then, switch to the Web Site tab.

At the bottom of the tab you will see the Enable Logging section. If you check the Enable Logging box, all activity to this Web site will be logged. You can save the log information in one of four formats. One of those formats is W3C Extended Log File Format. If you wish to log your files to a text file, this format provides the most flexibility.

Select that type and click the Properties button. You should see a dialog like the one displayed in this screenshot.

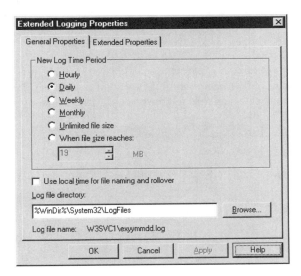

From this dialog you can set how often a new log file is created. At the bottom of this dialog, you can also enter the location that the log files should be saved to. Browse to that location if you wish to change it. Notice the Use Local Time check box. By default, new files are created and dated using Greenwich Mean Time. If you wish to use your local time instead, check this box.

Next, switch to the Extended Properties tab. From here you can select which of the fields you wish to include in the log. Once you are done, apply your changes and your Web site will now have its activity logged.

Logging Page Activity into a Database

One of the ways that you can log activity that occurs at your Web site is to log it into a database. If you do that, it makes it easier for you to query and manage the activity of your site. This technique shows you how to log page activity to a database.

 Before you can start logging Web site data to a database, you need to create the database. Therefore, go into SQL Server and create a new database.

Next, the database must contain a table that contains very specific fields with certain names and types in it. The easiest way to do this is to run the SQL script that comes with IIS. That script is called logtemp.sql and is typically found in this path:

```
C:\winnt\system32\inetsrv\
```

If you do not find the file in that location, you may not have installed IIS in the default location. Just search your hard drive for it. Once you find the file, run it in the SQL Server Query Analyzer against the SQL Server database that you created. The SQL file will add the needed table to your database.

Next, you need to create a DSN that points to the database that you just created. Once you do all this preliminary work, you need to start IIS. Then browse to the Web site that will use database logging. Right-click on that database and select Properties.

On the Web Site tab, check the Enable Logging box and select ODBC Logging as the Active Log Format. Then click the Properties button to see the dialog displayed in this screenshot.

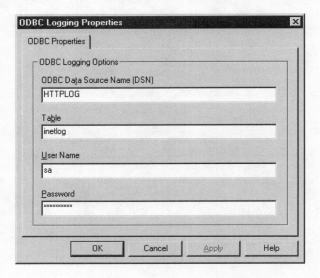

In this dialog, you need to enter the exact names that you used to create and connect to your SQL Server database. First, you must enter the exact name of the DSN you created that points to the SQL Server database. Next, you need to enter the name of the table that you created where the log entries will go. If you used the script to create the table, it is probably called "inetlog," but check it just in case, since this script could change. Also, you need to enter the user name and password required to gain access to this database.

If you do all this correctly, you should now be able to browse to a page of your site and have the hit information recorded in your SQL Server database.

Excluding Files from Logging

If you are logging the activity to your web site, you may find that you have pages that you do not wish to log the activity from. For example, maybe you have created a maintenance page that you frequently go to to perform a task, and the activity to that page is cluttering your log. You can remove that page from logging. This tip will show you how to do that.

USE IT   To exclude a file from being logged, open IIS. Then browse to the file that you wish to exclude. Right-click on the file and select Properties. When the Properties dialog opens, switch to the File tab. On that tab you should see a Log Visits check box. To exclude the file from logging, uncheck this box.

Limiting Web Site Resource Use

If your server hosts many different Web sites, you may find that you want to limit the maximum amount of bandwidth or processing power that a Web site on your server can consume. Doing so can reduce the risk of a site bringing down the entire server. This technique shows you how to put these limitations into effect.

 USE IT   To limit the amount of bandwidth or processor usage a Web site consumes, open IIS. Then browse to the Web site, right-click on it, and select Properties. If you switch to the Performance tab, you should see what is displayed in this screenshot.

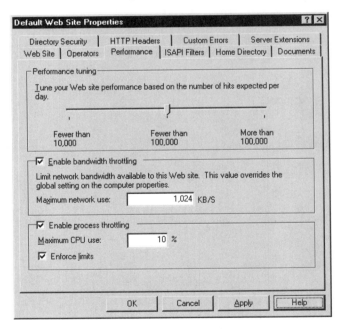

To limit the amount of bandwidth that a Web site can use, check the Enable Bandwidth Throttling check box. Then, enter a value in the Maximum Network Use text box. The value you enter into that box stands for the maximum number of kilobytes per second that the Web site can use before the site's use is restricted.

Also on this tab you can limit the amount of processing power that the Web site can use. Check the Enable Process Throttling check box to use this limitation. In the text box, enter the maximum amount of processing the site can use as a percentage of all processing capacity.

Notice the Enforce Limits check box. If the box is checked, the site cannot exceed the processor limit imposed. If the box is not checked, the site can exceed the limitation. If it does exceed the limitation, an entry is made in the system log.

Setting the Location of Your Web Site

Typically, the files that make up your Web site are located on the server within the Web root. But they do not have to be located there. You can set up your Web site so that the files are located on the server outside of the Web root, on a different server, or as a redirection to another site. This technique shows you how to do that.

USE IT   To change the location of a Web site, you need to open IIS. Then, browse to the Web site you wish to change. Right-click on it and select Properties. After that, change to the Home Directory tab. You should see this dialog:

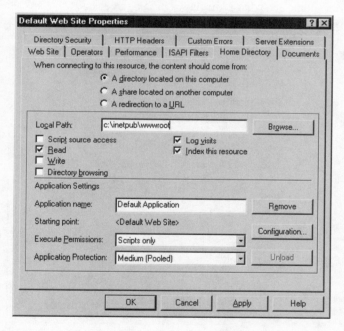

Notice at the top of this dialog that you have three ways that you can indicate the location of the Web site. First, you can choose a directory on this computer. If you do that, you can click the Browse button to select the folder that contains the top-level of this site.

Your second option is to set the site so that it points to a network share. When you do that, you enter the path of the share in the text box. You will be presented with a Connect As button that you can click to indicate the name and password that should be used for the connection to that site.

Your third option is to indicate that you want visitors to be redirected to another site when they come to your site. When you do that, you are presented with a text box for entering the site that visitors should be redirected to. This is often helpful when you want to temporarily take your site down. You could redirect visitors to some other site that tells them when your site will be back up.

Allowing Directory Browsing

By default, when visitors enter a directory in your Web site that does not include a default file, they see an error message that says directory browsing is not allowed. Typically, this is how you want it. You don't want visitors seeing the raw list of files in a folder. But on occasion, you may want visitors to be able to see all the files in a folder.

For example, maybe you have a folder that contains images that visitors can browse through. You may want visitors just to see the file list and select from it the image they wish to see. To do that, you need to turn on Directory Browsing. This technique shows you how to do that.

USE IT   To allow visitors to browse the contents of a folder, you need to open IIS and browse to the folder that you wish to allow browsing in. Right-click on that folder and select Properties. In the Directory tab, you will see a Directory Browsing check box. Check that box.

Now, when visitors browse directly to that folder and it does not contain a default page like default.html, they will see a page like the one displayed here:

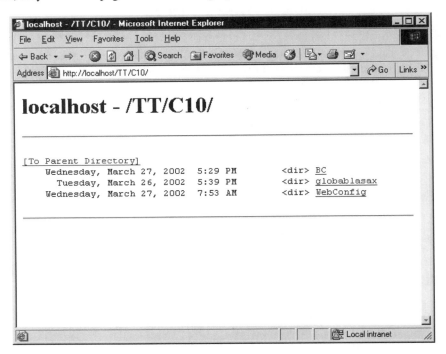

Notice that visitors see all the files in this folder, including other folders. They can then select the item they wish to see since each file is listed as a link.

Allowing File Uploads

If you have an ASP.NET page that allows visitors to upload files, you need to make sure that the folder visitors are uploading to allows that functionality. This tip shows you how to do that.

USE IT To allow visitors to upload files to a folder on your system, you need to configure the folder so that it allows file writing. To do that, open IIS and browse to the folder where the files should be placed. Then right-click on the folder and select Properties. Change to the Directory tab.

On that tab you should see a Write check box. Check that box and visitors can write files to this folder. But be careful: This option does not restrict the size of the file being uploaded or the number of files. Therefore, you would need to monitor this folder to make sure visitors are not using up too much of your resources with file uploads.

Setting Execute Permissions

When visitors come to your ASP.NET application and request a page, they are actually executing and running a script on your server. Typically, you want to allow visitors to do this. If you have a folder that just contains HTML files, visitors do not need this kind of access. This technique shows you how to change the executable permission on a folder.

USE IT You can modify the execute permissions on a Web site, an ASP.NET application, or a folder. To do this, you need to open IIS and browse to the site, application, or folder that you wish to modify. Then, right-click on the item and select Properties. Change to the Directory tab and you should see something like this dialog:

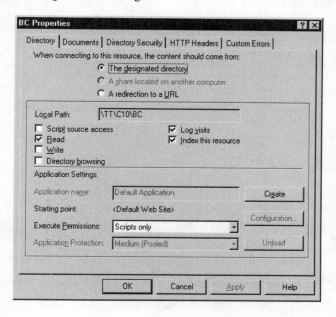

Notice the Execute Permissions drop-down list. You have three options in this drop-down list. Usually, it is set to Scripts Only, which allows visitors to run ASP and ASP.NET pages as well as other script-based pages.

You can also set this property to Scripts and Executables, which would allow visitors to not only run your scripts but also launch any .exe files located in the folder. The third option is None. If you set the folder to this option, visitors cannot run any scripts or executables in that folder.

Setting Default Documents

When visitors enter the address of your Web site in a form like this:

```
http://www.google.com/
```

they are not actually requesting a page. They are indicating a path to a folder. When visitors do this, you can direct them to the default page that should be viewed. This technique shows you how to do that.

 To modify the default documents that are searched for when visitors enter a Web site without entering a specific page name, open IIS and browse to the site you wish to modify. Then, right-click on the site and select Properties. Select the Documents tab to see the following dialog:

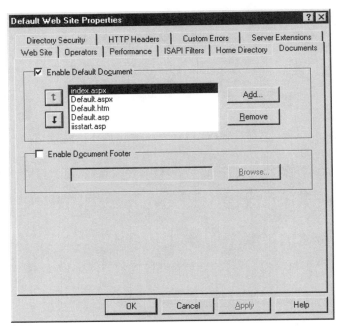

First, notice the Enable Default Document check box. If this is checked, visitors can browse to the site without entering a specific page name. Otherwise, visitors must enter the exact page they wish to view.

Next, notice the list box. Displayed in this list box are the names of the files that IIS will search for when the visitor enters the site. In this case, it will first look for a file named Index.aspx. If it finds that file, that is the page visitors will be taken to. Otherwise, IIS will go down the list and look for each of the pages until it finds a matching page. If none of the pages match, visitors will see an error message.

Notice the up and down arrows to the left of the list. This is how you bump up or down the priority of one default file over another default file.

Also notice the Add button. You click this button to add a new default file to the list. If you click the Remove button, the selected file name will be removed from the list.

Using Document Footers

You may find that you wish to append information to the bottom of every page that is requested of your Web site or folder. For example, maybe you want to display copyright information or maybe you want to supply a link to a page with legal information at the bottom of all your pages. You could place that information at the bottom of each page manually. But you could also use document footers. This technique shows you how to do that.

USE IT To use document footers, you need to open IIS and browse to the folder or Web site that will display the footer. Then right-click on that item and select Properties. Select the Documents tab to see this dialog:

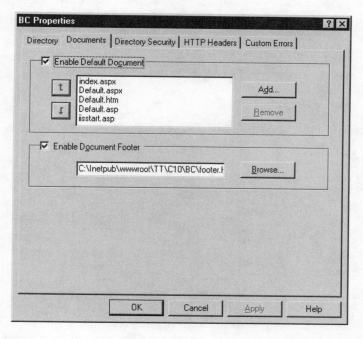

To use a document folder, you need to check the box titled Enable Document Footer. Then click the browse button and browse to the page that should be used as the footer.

When you create the footer page, note that it will be appended to any requested page from the site. Therefore, the footer page should not include outer HTML tags like the Header and Body tags.

Restricting Web Access by IP Address

You may find that you need to exclude certain IP addresses from entering your Web site. Or maybe you only want to allow certain IP addresses to gain access to your site. IIS provides a mechanism that you can use to restrict access to your Web site based on the IP address of the visitor. This technique shows you how to do that.

 USE IT   To restrict access to a Web site based on an IP address, you need to open IIS. Then, browse to the Web site that you want to configure, right-click on it, and select Properties. Next, switch to the Directory Security tab.

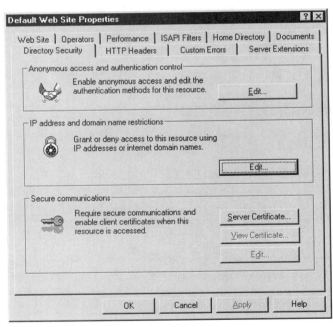

Notice the IP Address and Domain Name Restrictions section of this dialog. This is where you will set your restrictions. Click the Edit button.

You are then taken to another dialog. From there you can select one option where all IP addresses are allowed access except the ones you list in a list box. Another option allows you to grant access only to those IP addresses listed in the list box. Buttons on the dialog allow you to add and remove IP addresses from the list.

Removing Anonymous Access to a Site

You may find that you have a site or a page that you do not wish to have the anonymous Web user gain access to. For example, maybe you have a page that is intended just for existing customers. This tip shows you how to remove access from the anonymous Web user to your site.

USE IT   You can remove the capability of the anonymous Web visitor to view a page, folder, or site. You do that by opening IIS and browsing to the item you wish to secure. Then right-click on the item and select Properties. Next, switch to the Directory Security or Folder Security tab. You should see the following dialog:

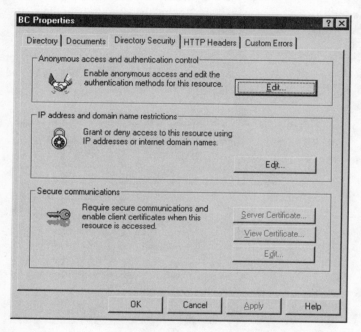

Notice the top section of the dialog. This is where you control anonymous access to the item. Click the Edit button in the top part of the page. You are then taken to a different dialog. At the top of that dialog you will see a check box that says Anonymous Access. Uncheck that box to prohibit the anonymous visitor from being able to access your site, folder, or page. Visitors will then have to enter a user name and password to gain access to the item.

Creating Custom Headers

When visitors request a page from your site, they are sent the contents of the Web page. Also sent to the browser are HTTP headers. These headers are additional name/value items that the browser may or may not use as special instructions for setting up and displaying the page. In addition to the default headers sent by IIS, you can create your own headers that are sent with a page when it is requested. This technique shows you how to do that.

USE IT You can add custom headers that are sent with every page in a site, with every page in a folder, or with only a single page. To add a custom header, open IIS and browse to the item that you wish to add the custom header to. Right-click on the item and select Properties. Next, change to the HTTP Headers tab to see the following dialog:

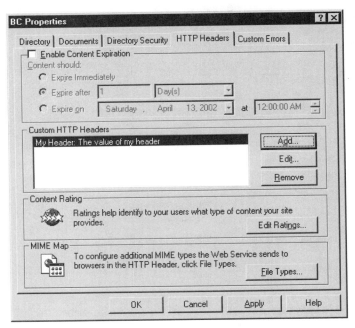

Notice the Custom HTTP Headers section in the middle of the dialog. To add a new custom header, click the Add button. You then are presented with a second dialog where you supply the name of your header and its value. You can also click the Edit button to modify an existing custom header or the Remove button to delete the custom header.

Editing Error Pages

When visitors come to your site and request a page that does not exist, they are taken to a page that informs them of that problem. Within IIS, you can modify the name of the page that visitors are taken to when a particular error occurs. This tip shows you how to do that.

 USE IT You can modify error pages associated with a specific error number at the site, folder, or page level. To perform the modification, you need to start IIS. Then browse to the site, folder, or page that you wish to modify the error pages for. Right-click on that item and select Properties. Change to the Custom Errors tab to see this dialog:

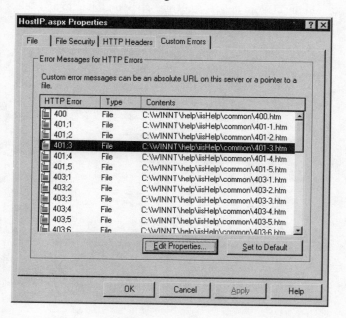

The dialog lists the number for a variety of error messages and shows you the action that is taken when that error occurs. To modify one of the items in the list, select it and click the Edit Properties button. You are then taken to a dialog where you can enter the path to the page you want displayed when the error occurs. Once you make your change, your page will be displayed when that error occurs.

Using Basic Text Error Messages

When an error occurs because of a request visitors make, they are typically redirected to the HTML error page that matches the error number that was thrown. But you can also supply a simple text file to display when an error occurs. This tip shows you how to do that.

USE IT You can make this modification to a single page, a folder, or an entire Web site. First, you need to open IIS and browse to the item you wish to modify. Then right-click on the item and select Properties. When the dialog opens, change to the Custom Errors tab. Find the error number in the list you wish to modify, select it, and click the Edit Properties button to display the Error Mapping Properties dialog:

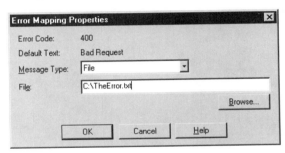

Notice that the Message Type is set to File. Once it is set to that value, you can browse to the text file that you wish to display when the error occurs.

Inheriting Properties to New Sites and Folders

You may find that every time you create a new site on your server you need to modify certain properties to suit the way you like your sites set up. For example, maybe you change the default coding language or you change the default timeout property. Instead of making this modification to each new site, you can change the default specification so that a new site will contain your changes. This technique shows you how to do that.

USE IT When a new site or ASP.NET application is created, it inherits its properties from the item above it. That means an ASP.NET application inherits its properties from the Web site and the Web site inherits its properties from the default server properties.

To modify those default server properties, you need to open IIS, right-click on the server, and select Properties. You should then see the following dialog:

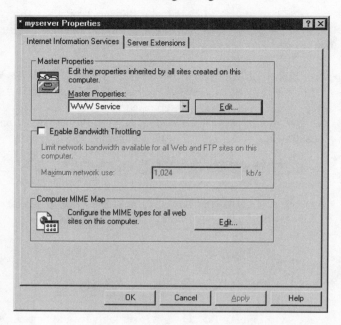

Notice the Master Properties section at the top of this dialog. Make sure the drop-down list is set to WWW Service and click the Edit button. You are then taken to the master property settings for all Web sites on this server. Make the desired modifications to this dialog. Now when you create a new site, the values you have entered here will be used as the default properties for the new site.

Compressing Web Site Files

When visitors request a page from your site, the content of the page is sent in its raw form. If the page is a large text file, it is sent as uncompressed raw text. Some browsers support the reception of compressed files. This allows a smaller file to be transmitted, which reduces the bandwidth use on both the client and server ends. IIS supports the transmission of compressed files when a request is made. This technique shows you how to turn on file compression.

USE IT   Compression can only be set at the server level. To turn on compression, you need to start IIS, right-click on the server item, and select Properties. Then select the WWW Service Master Properties and click the Edit button. Change to the Service tab.

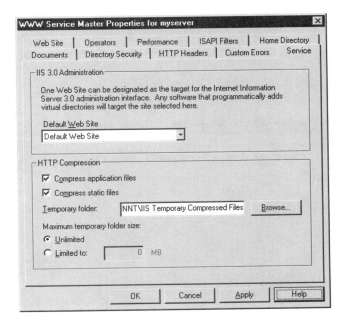

If you wish to compress static files like HTML files, check the Compress Static Files box. But the page is not actually compressed until the first request for the page is made. Once it is compressed, it is stored compressed in the location indicated in the Temporary Folder text box. All subsequent requests will be sent the previously compressed version of the static file.

You can also choose to compress the output of your ASP.NET pages by checking the Compress Application Files check box. Since your ASP.NET pages are dynamic, they are compressed each time that they are requested.

Creating a Virtual Directory

You may find that you want to include a folder within a Web site that is not part of the actual directory structure of the site. For example, you may have a portion of your site that many sites use. In that case, that portion of the site would be stored outside of each of the other sites. You can link to that folder as if it were part of your Web site by creating a virtual directory. This technique shows you how to do that.

 USE IT   To add a virtual directory, right-click on the folder or the Web site where you wish to add the virtual directory and select Add | Virtual Directory. You are then welcomed to the Virtual Directory Wizard. Click the Next button.

On the second page of the wizard, you are asked for the name of the virtual directory. This is the name that visitors will enter into the browser when they wish to browse to this folder. Therefore, name the virtual directory appropriately. Click the Next button to continue.

On the third page of the wizard, you are asked to enter the path of the virtual directory. Click the Browse button and locate the desired folder. Then, click the Next button.

You should now see this dialog:

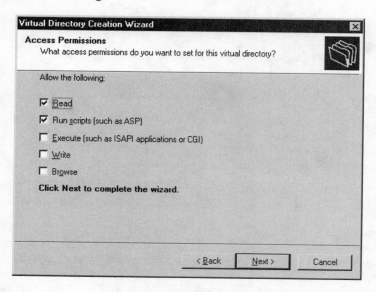

On this page of the wizard, you can set the permissions that are allowed on this virtual directory. Once you have set these properties, click the Next button followed by the Finish button. The virtual directory is now part of the site that you added it to.

Creating an ASP.NET Application

You may find that you include pages within a Web site that need to be grouped together as an application. For example, you may have a site for your online school. One part of that site may be for visitors who are just looking into your school. Another part of the site may be for students to work on their courses. The part of your site that is for the existing students is an example of an application within a Web site.

When that is the case, you may wish to distinguish the application as an ASP.NET application within IIS. When you do that, you can use a Global.asax file and can set other properties for your application. This technique shows you how to do that.

USE IT   To set a folder as an ASP.NET application, browse to that folder within IIS. Then, right-click on the folder and select Properties. Switch to the Directory tab.

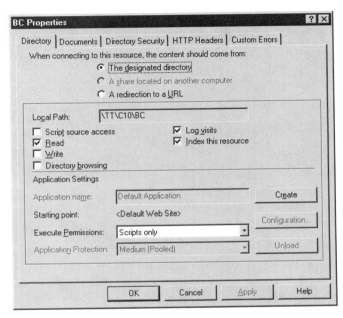

Notice the Application Settings section of the dialog. To set this folder as an ASP.NET application, click the Create button. When you do that, the Application Name text box will be activated. Enter a name into that text box and click OK. Note that the name you place into the Application Name property is for your own identification. This is not something that visitors enter into their browser or see on the page in any other way.

Setting Execute and Run Mode Properties for an ASP.NET Application

Once you create an ASP.NET application, you may need to set properties regarding how the application runs. For example, if the site is likely to fail, you may want it to run in its own application space. This technique shows you how to do that.

USE IT ▸ To set the execute and run mode for an ASP.NET application, browse to the application within IIS. Then, right-click on the application and select Properties. You should see the following dialog:

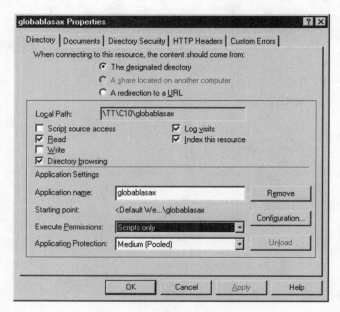

First, notice the Execute Permissions drop-down list. Since this is an ASP.NET application, you will want to set this property to at least Scripts Only. If your application includes other types of executables that visitors need to run for the functionality of the site, you need to change this property to Scripts and Executables.

Next, notice the Application Protection property. Since this is an ASP.NET application, you should set this property to at least Medium. That way, if the application fails it won't bring down IIS. It will bring down other pooled ASP.NET applications. Therefore, if this application has a high likelihood of failing, you will want to set this property to High.

Setting Application Mappings in an ASP.NET Application

When a request comes in from visitors for an ASP.NET page, that page ends with the extension .aspx. The compiler then runs the page as an ASP.NET page because it has that extension. The reason it knows to do this is because of the application mappings associated with the extension .aspx. You may find that you need to add a new application mapping so that some special pages you have created can run. You do that by using application mappings. This technique shows you how to do that.

USE IT   Application mappings map an extension to the executable that runs the page with that extension. To modify the application mappings for an ASP.NET application, open IIS and browse to that application. Right-click on the application and select Properties. Next, on the Directory tab, click the Configuration button. You should be taken to the dialog displayed in this screenshot.

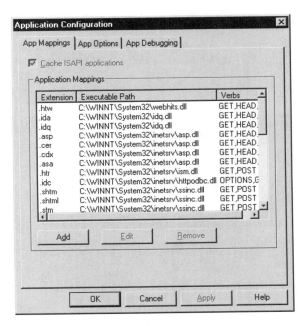

The App Mappings tab lists all the mappings associated with this ASP.NET application. If you browse through the list you should see some familiar extensions such as .aspx.

The first column in the list displays the file extensions. The second column displays the program to run when a file with that extension is requested. The third column lists the verbs that are allowed with the file extension.

Verbs are the types of action visitors take when requesting a page. For example, the verb Post is used when visitors submit a page for processing by clicking a button on a Web page. And the verb Get is used when visitors request a page that has a query string associated with it. Therefore, ASP.NET pages have both the Get and Post verbs allowed with their requests.

You can use the Add, Edit, and Remove buttons in the list to add an item, update an existing item, or to delete an item. When you click Add or Edit, you are taken to another dialog where you can enter the file extension, the executable that runs the file, and the verbs used with the file.

Enabling Session State in an ASP.NET Application

Typically, when you create an ASP.NET application, you want to keep track of visitors as they go from page to page at your site. For example, at an e-commerce site, you want to track visitors from page to page so that you can maintain their shopping cart. You do this by maintaining session state. This tip shows you how to set the Session State property.

 USE IT To use session states within an ASP.NET application, you need to open IIS and browse to the ASP.NET application. Right-click on the ASP.NET application and select Properties. Then, from the Directory tab, click the Configuration button. You are then taken to a different dialog. Switch to the App Options tab.

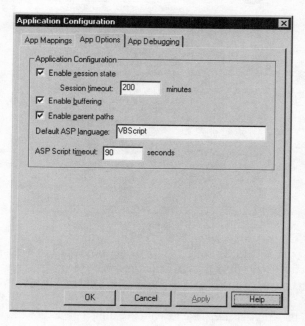

To set session state, check the Enable Session State check box. You can also set the number of minutes that can elapse between requests from visitors before their session expires. That value is set through the Session Timeout text box.

Setting a Script Timeout Value for an ASP.NET Application

For a variety of reasons, your code may start running and get stuck in a loop and be unable to complete. Or your code may get stuck waiting for some external event to occur. Therefore, you may want to set a maximum amount of time that the code on your page can run before it stops and returns an error to visitors. This technique shows you how to do that.

USE IT   To set the amount of time an ASP.NET page can run without stopping, browse to the application within IIS. Then, right-click on the application and select Properties. From the Directory tab click the Configuration button. Then, switch to the App Options tab (dialog is displayed in the previous tip).

Notice the ASP Script Timeout text box. Place into this text box the number of seconds you want your page to be able to run before it should return an error.

Removing an ASP.NET Application

You may decide after you create an ASP.NET application that it does not need to be a stand-alone application. Instead, you want it just to be a folder in the Web site that it resides in. You do this by removing it as an ASP.NET application. This technique shows you how to do that.

USE IT   To remove an ASP.NET application, open IIS and browse to the application. Then, right-click on the application and select Properties. Change to the Directory tab.

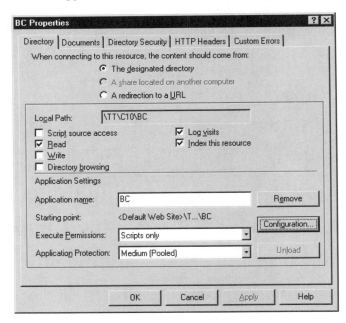

Notice the Remove button in the Application Settings section. Click that button and then click the OK button. Your ASP.NET application has now been removed.

Redirecting a File Request

You may find on occasion that you have a Web page that you need to bring down from the site. This may be because you are repairing an error or because the functionality being requested by the page is not currently available. Within IIS, you can set the page up so that when it is requested visitors are taken to a different page. This technique shows you how to do that.

 USE IT To redirect visitors to a different page when they request a page, browse to that page within IIS. Then right-click on that page and select Properties. Change to the File tab to see the dialog displayed in this screenshot.

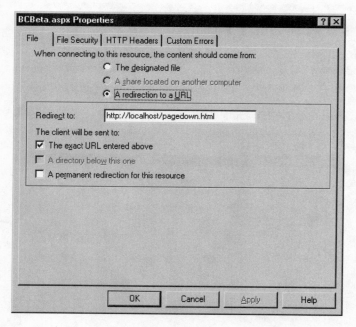

At the top of the dialog, select the Redirection to a URL radio button. You can then enter the address of the page that you want visitors to be redirected to.

Backing Up and Restoring IIS Settings

As you add sites to IIS and change settings, you quickly get to the point where you want to save the current setting so that you can revert to them if something in the configuration goes wrong. This technique shows you how to do that.

 To back-up your settings in IIS, open IIS and right-click on the server. Then select Back-up/Restore Configuration. You should see the dialog displayed in this screenshot.

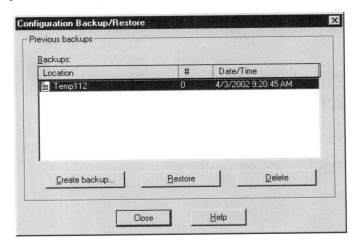

Click the Create Backup button to create a backup of all your IIS settings. When you do that, you are prompted for the name of the backup. Note though that when you backup IIS only your IIS configuration is backed up. In other words, your Web files are not backed up.

If you would like to return to your IIS settings prior to your changes, return to this dialog and select the backed-up entry that you wish to restore. Then, click the Restore button.

CHAPTER 13

Database Code

For your ASP.NET applications to really display dynamic content, they will need to be connected to a database. For example, if you have an e-commerce application, you wouldn't have much without a back-end database. Or if you have an online school, the content most likely needs to come from a database. Even if you have a simple page that allows the visitors to leave messages for each other, you will likely want to store those messages in a database.

This chapter presents tips and techniques that show you how to work with an Access or SQL Server database from your ASP.NET pages. The tips and techniques show you how to connect to those database types and retrieve and manipulate the data that they contain.

Along with the ASP.NET pages that you will find online (**http://www.osborne.com**) to go along with this chapter, you will also find an Access MDB file. That file contains the Employees table used in the tips and techniques presented in the first half of this chapter.

Also with these files you will find a SQL file. This file contains the script needed to re-create the SQL Server table as well as the stored procedures discussed in the second half of this chapter. Just run this script file from the SQL Server Query Analyzer against a new empty database to recreate these objects.

Connecting to an Access Database

When you are working with pages that contain Access database functionality, the most basic thing you need to be able to do is to connect to the database. This tip shows you what you need to do to be able to connect to an Access database.

USE IT   The ASP.NET page presented with this tip connects to an Access database. The first step
that you need to accomplish is to create the database that you are going to connect to and
note its location in relation to your ASP.NET page.

Then on your ASP.NET page you will want to import two namespaces by including these directives
at the top of the ASP.NET page:

```
<%@ Import Namespace="System.Data.OLEDB" %>
<%@ Import Namespace="System.Data" %>
```

The first namespace defines the classes you need to connect to an Access database and retrieve
data from it:

```
<%@ Import Namespace="System.Data.OLEDB" %>
```

The second namespace defines the classes you need to be able to display the data on an
ASP.NET page:

```
<%@ Import Namespace="System.Data" %>
```

Once you have imported these namespaces, you can instantiate objects of the classes that they
contain. In this tip, a connection object needs to be defined:

```
Dim DBConn as OleDbConnection
```

A connection object contains the properties and methods you need to gain access to an Access
database. Once the object has been defined, you need to indicate the connection string that is to be
used with the connection:

```
DBConn = New OleDbConnection( _
    "PROVIDER=Microsoft.Jet.OLEDB.4.0;" _
    & "DATA SOURCE=" _
    & Server.MapPath("/tt/C13/EmployeesDB.mdb;"))
```

A connection string is the information you provide when the connection is instantiated that indicates
the type of database, the location of the database, and other optional parameters such as a user name and
password to connect to the database through.

In this case, the connection string contains the name of the provider and the name of the data
source. The provider is the library that is used to connect to this particular database type. In this case,
it is set to this value:

```
PROVIDER=Microsoft.Jet.OLEDB.4.0;
```

since you are connecting to an Access database. Then the second parameter, Data Source, is set to
the physical location of the Access database. Notice that the MapPath method is used to return the
physical path to the Web root. This method is helpful when you will be placing your ASP.NET pages

on a server and you do not know ahead of time where the Web root is located, but you know that within that Web root your file will be found in the same location as the ASP.NET page.

So if the path to the Web root was this:

```
D:\WWW\Inetpub\WWWRoot
```

the MapPath method would return this full path:

```
D:\WWW\Inetpub\WWWRoot\tt\C13\EmployeesDB.mdb
```

Optionally, you can provide a connection string that contains a path like this:

```
DBConn = New OleDbConnection( _
    "PROVIDER=Microsoft.Jet.OLEDB.4.0;" _
    & "DATA SOURCE=" _
    & "c:\inetpub\wwwroot\tt\C13\EmployeesDB.mdb;")
```

Here, the full path to the database is specified. Therefore, no de-referencing is required.

Both of these connection strings have the database located within the Web root. But you could place the Access database in a location outside the Web root:

```
DBConn = New OleDbConnection( _
    "PROVIDER=Microsoft.Jet.OLEDB.4.0;" _
    & "DATA SOURCE=" _
    & "c:\EmployeesDB.mdb;")
```

If you do this, you must insure that the Web user is granted read/write access to the file in that location. You do that by right-clicking on the file in the Windows Explorer and then selecting Properties. Next, select Security and add the Anonymous user with read/write access.

Retrieving Access Data

On most of your ASP.NET pages that contain Access database connectivity, you will want to retrieve data from the database so that it can either be manipulated or displayed. For example, you may have a page that displays the locations of your company's stores. In that case, you would need to connect to your database to retrieve that data. Or maybe you have an ASP.NET page that displays current jobs offered at your company. If that is the case you would also need to retrieve data from your database.

This technique shows you how to retrieve data from an Access database.

 The ASP.NET page created for this technique retrieves three sets of data from an Access database. The data retrieved contains information from employee records.

Since you need to connect to and retrieve data from an Access database, you will need to import these two namespaces:

```
<%@ Import Namespace="System.Data" %>
<%@ Import Namespace="System.Data.OLEDB" %>
```

Then in code you can declare your data objects:

```
Dim DBConn as OleDbConnection
Dim DBCommand As OleDbDataAdapter
Dim DSPageData as New DataSet
```

The first object:

```
Dim DBConn as OleDbConnection
```

provides the connection to the database. The second object:

```
Dim DBCommand As OleDbDataAdapter
```

will contain the SQL syntax you need to retrieve the data from the database. The third object declared:

```
Dim DSPageData as New DataSet
```

will contain the data retrieved from the database.

Once you have declared your data object, you need to connect to the Access database. Here the database is located in the same folder as the ASP.NET page:

```
DBConn = New OleDbConnection( _
    "PROVIDER=Microsoft.Jet.OLEDB.4.0;" _
    & "DATA SOURCE=" _
    & Server.MapPath("/tt/C13/EmployeesDB.mdb;"))
```

Now that you have connected to the database, you instantiate the DataAdapter object:

```
DBCommand = New OleDbDataAdapter _
    ("Select LastName & ', ' & FirstName " _
    & "as EmpName, EmpID " _
    & "From Employees " _
    & "Order By LastName, FirstName", DBConn)
```

Notice that two parameters are passed into that instantiation. The first is the SQL syntax that will be used to return the desired records. In this case, the first and last name of the employees will be returned along with the ID of the employee.

The second parameter passed in is the connection object that points to the database where the data should be retrieved. In this case, the data is retrieved through the Connection object that was defined earlier in this procedure.

To run the query you call the Fill method of the DataAdapter object:

```
DBCommand.Fill(DSPageData, _
    "EmployeeNames")
```

Passed to the call are also two parameters. The first parameter is the name of the DataSet object that you want the retrieved data to be placed into. The second parameter is the name that you want to give the retrieved data in the DataSet object. That name can be whatever you want. It is simply the name that you will use later to refer to a specific set of data in the DataSet object.

But a DataSet object can contain more than one set of data. Here all the fields and records are retrieved from the Employees table:

```
DBCommand = New OleDbDataAdapter _
    ("Select * from Employees", DBConn)
```

and those records are placed into the same DataSet object into a table named EmployeesAll:

```
DBCommand.Fill(DSPageData, _
    "EmployeesAll")
```

Note that this is not a permanent table that is created nor is it even temporarily placed into a database. It is just a representation of the data retrieved that exists within the DataSet object.

Next, a third set of data is retrieved. Here the last name of the employee is retrieved, along with the month that they were born, but only for employees whose salary exceeds the amount indicated:

```
DBCommand = New OleDbDataAdapter _
    ("Select LastName, Month(BirthDate) " _
    & "as MonthBirthDate from Employees Where " _
    & "Salary > 25000", DBConn)
```

The data retrieved is placed into a third table of the DataSet object:

```
DBCommand.Fill(DSPageData, _
    "Emp3")
```

Displaying Data in a DropDownList Control

Frequently you will find that you need to display data retrieved from a database in a DropDownList control. For example, you may want to display a list of topics that come from an online help system. Or maybe you need to display the names of all the teams in a sports league whose site you run. Still again, maybe you want to display the names of books that you sell in your bookstore.

All of these sets of data could be displayed in DropDownList controls. Typically, you would display the name of the item, such as the name of the book or the name of the help topic. But internally you would store the ID for the item listed. Then when visitors selected one of the items in the DropDownList control, you would take them to another page where the full information for the item selected can be displayed.

This technique shows you how to bind data to a DropDownList.

USE IT Binding data means that you connect a control to a data source. With ASP that meant that you needed to retrieve records, then manually loop through the records and add them one at a time to a list. With ASP.NET, binding means that you connect a DataSet and a control together. The compiler then adds all the records to the list without your having to loop through them.

The ASP.NET page presented with this technique displays a list of employee names in a DropDownList control. The DropDownList control has this definition:

```
<asp:dropdownlist
    id="ddlEmps"
    datatextfield="EmpName"
    datavaluefield="EmpID"
    runat="server"
/>
```

Notice the use of the DataTextField and DataValueField properties. The values placed into these properties must match exactly the names of fields that are contained within the DataSet object that is bound to this control.

When the page loads, this procedure runs and populates the DropDownList control:

```
Sub Page_Load(ByVal Sender as Object, ByVal E as EventArgs)
```

The code should only run when the page first loads. In other words, if the page were to be submitted for processing you would not want to rebuild the list:

```
If Not IsPostBack Then
```

If the page is first loading, you need these data objects:

```
Dim DBConn as OleDbConnection
Dim DBCommand As OleDbDataAdapter
Dim DSPageData as New DataSet
```

You start by connecting to the access database:

```
DBConn = New OleDbConnection( _
    "PROVIDER=Microsoft.Jet.OLEDB.4.0;" _
    & "DATA SOURCE=" _
    & "c:\EmployeesDB.mdb;")
```

Next, you place into the DataAdapter object the SQL syntax that retrieves the employee names and their IDs:

```
DBCommand = New OleDbDataAdapter _
    ("Select LastName & ', ' & FirstName " _
    & "as EmpName, EmpID " _
    & "From Employees " _
    & "Order By LastName, FirstName", DBConn)
```

Notice that the fields returned match the names of the fields placed into the data properties of the DropDownList control.

The data is then retrieved into the DataSet object:

```
DBCommand.Fill(DSPageData, _
    "Employees")
```

Next, you indicate that the DropDownList control should be bound to the table in the DataSet object:

```
ddlEmps.DataSource = _
    DSPageData.Tables("Employees").DefaultView
```

You then bind the DropDownList control to the DataSet, effectively displaying the records in the DropDownList control:

```
ddlEmps.DataBind()
```

Displaying Access Data in a DataGrid Control

You will frequently find that you need to dump data retrieved from a database to the visitor in the form of an HTML table. A DataGrid control provides a simple way of doing that. You simply bind the DataGrid to a table in a DataSet object and that is all you have to do to have all the fields and records in the table displayed within an HTML table. This technique shows you how to bind a DataGrid to data from an Access database.

USE IT The ASP.NET page created for this technique displays information from an Employees table through two DataGrid controls. Those controls are defined within the body of the ASP.NET page:

```
<asp:datagrid
    id="dgEmps1"
    runat="server"
    autogeneratecolumns="True"
>
</asp:datagrid>
```

```
<asp:datagrid
    id="dgEmps2"
    runat="server"
    autogeneratecolumns="True"
>
</asp:datagrid>
```

When the page runs, the following code fires and populates the DataGrid controls:

```
Sub Page_Load(ByVal Sender as Object, ByVal E as EventArgs)
```

Within the procedure, these data objects are required:

```
Dim DBConn as OleDbConnection
Dim DBCommand As OleDbDataAdapter
Dim DSPageData as New DataSet
```

You start by connecting to the Access database:

```
DBConn = New OleDbConnection( _
    "PROVIDER=Microsoft.Jet.OLEDB.4.0;" _
    & "DATA SOURCE=" _
    & Server.MapPath("/tt/C13/EmployeesDB.mdb;"))
```

Then the first set of data is retrieved; in this case all the fields and records:

```
DBCommand = New OleDbDataAdapter _
    ("Select * from Employees", DBConn)
```

That data is placed into the DataSet object:

```
DBCommand.Fill(DSPageData, _
    "EmployeesAll")
```

Next, a second set of data is retrieved from the Access database and placed into the DataSet object:

```
DBCommand = New OleDbDataAdapter _
    ("Select LastName, Month(BirthDate) " _
    & "as MonthBirthDate from Employees Where " _
    & "Salary > 25000", DBConn)
DBCommand.Fill(DSPageData, _
    "Emp2")
```

You then indicate the name of the table within the DataSet object that the first DataGrid control is to use:

```
dgEmps1.DataSource = _
    DSPageData.Tables("EmployeesAll").DefaultView
```

and bind that DataGrid to the DataSet table:

```
dgEmps1.DataBind()
```

The same thing is then done to the second DataGrid control:

```
dgEmps2.DataSource = _
    DSPageData.Tables("Emp2").DefaultView
dgEmps2.DataBind()
```

Adding Access Data

Once you have a site that can display data from a database, adding data to that database can't be far behind. If you have an ASP.NET page that displays messages placed by visitors, the visitors need a way to add messages. If you have an e-commerce site, you need a way for visitors to add items to their shopping cart. If you have an ASP.NET page that describes movies currently playing in your town, you may want visitors to be able to add their own reviews.

This technique shows you how to add data to a table in an Access database.

USE IT   The ASP.NET page presented for this technique allows visitors to add a new record to an Employees table. Defined on that page are a series of TextBox controls like this one where visitors can enter the data for the new record:

```
<asp:textbox
    id="txtLastName"
    runat="Server"
/>
```

Also defined on the page is a Button control that allows visitors to submit their requests:

```
<asp:button
    id="butOK"
    text="  OK  "
    onclick="SubmitBtn_Click"
    runat="server"
/>
```

When that Button control is clicked, the procedure indicated in the OnClick property fires:

```
Sub SubmitBtn_Click(Sender As Object, E As EventArgs)
```

To add a record to an Access table, you will need two data objects. The first is a Connection object:

```
Dim DBConn as OleDbConnection
```

The second is a Command object:

```
Dim DBAdd As New OleDbCommand
```

Once these objects are defined, you need to connect to the Access database:

```
DBConn = New OleDbConnection( _
    "PROVIDER=Microsoft.Jet.OLEDB.4.0;" _
    & "DATA SOURCE=" _
    & Server.MapPath("/tt/C13/EmployeesDB.mdb;"))
```

Then, you place the text of the SQL Insert statement into the CommandText property of the Command object:

```
DBAdd.CommandText = "Insert Into Employees (" _
    & "LastName, FirstName, BirthDate, Salary, " _
    & "EmailAddress) values (" _
    & "'" & Replace(txtLastName.Text, "'", "''") _
    & "', " _
    & "'" & Replace(txtFirstName.Text, "'", "''") _
    & "', " _
    & "'" & Replace(txtBirthDate.Text, "'", "''") _
    & "', " _
    & Replace(txtSalary.Text, "'", "''") & ", " _
    & "'" & Replace(txtEmailAddress.Text, "'", "''") _
    & "')"
```

Notice that the values placed into that Insert statement come from the values entered into the TextBox controls. Also notice that the Replace function is used to convert all the """ characters to two of the same character. This is necessary because the visitor could enter a """ character into one of the fields. For example, the new employee's last name might be O'Riley. If you do not convert the """ to two of the same, the SQL statement will fail because it will see the """ as the end of the string and will not know what value Riley refers to.

Next, you indicate that the Command object will connect to the database through the Connection object:

```
DBAdd.Connection = DBConn
```

That connection is opened:

```
DBAdd.Connection.Open
```

and the SQL Insert statement is executed:

```
DBAdd.ExecuteNonQuery()
```

Updating Access Data

Updating data in an Access database is relatively painless from an ASP.NET page. It involves using a Connect object and a Command object. This technique shows you how to update data in an Access database.

 The ASP.NET page presented for this technique displays a list of employees to the visitor. The visitor selects the name of an employee, enters the employee's new salary, and clicks a Button control, saving the new salary with the employee record.

Defined on the page is a DropDownList control that will display the names of all the employees:

```
<asp:dropdownlist
    id="ddlEmps"
    datatextfield="EmpName"
    datavaluefield="EmpID"
    runat="server"
/>
```

A TextBox control is defined for entering the employee's new salary:

```
<asp:textbox
    id="txtSalary"
    runat="Server"
/>
```

and a Button control allows the change to be submitted:

```
<asp:button
    id="butOK"
    text="  OK  "
    onclick="SubmitBtn_Click"
    runat="server"
/>
```

Two procedures fire on this page. The first fires when the page loads:

```
Sub Page_Load(ByVal Sender as Object, ByVal E as EventArgs)
    If Not IsPostBack Then
        Dim DBConn as OleDbConnection
        Dim DBCommand As OleDbDataAdapter
```

```
        Dim DSPageData as New DataSet
        DBConn = New OleDbConnection( _
            "PROVIDER=Microsoft.Jet.OLEDB.4.0;" _
            & "DATA SOURCE=" _
            & Server.MapPath("/tt/C13/EmployeesDB.mdb;"))
        DBCommand = New OleDbDataAdapter _
            ("Select LastName & ', ' & FirstName " _
            & "as EmpName, EmpID " _
            & "From Employees " _
            & "Order By LastName, FirstName", DBConn)
        DBCommand.Fill(DSPageData, _
            "Employees")
        ddlEmps.DataSource = _
            DSPageData.Tables("Employees").DefaultView
        ddlEmps.DataBind()
    End If
End Sub
```

The procedure retrieves the names and IDs of the employees from the Access database. The data retrieved is bound to the DropDownList control.

The other procedure fires when the Button control is clicked:

```
Sub SubmitBtn_Click(Sender As Object, E As EventArgs)
```

When the Button control is clicked, you need to update the Salary. Therefore, you will need a Connection object and a Command object:

```
Dim DBConn as OleDbConnection
Dim DBUpdate As New OleDbCommand
```

You then need to connect to the Access database:

```
DBConn = New OleDbConnection( _
    "PROVIDER=Microsoft.Jet.OLEDB.4.0;" _
    & "DATA SOURCE=" _
    & Server.MapPath("/tt/C13/EmployeesDB.mdb;"))
```

and set the CommandText property of the Command object so that it contains the SQL Update statement that updates the salary to the value entered into the TextBox control:

```
DBUpdate.CommandText = "Update Employees Set " _
    & "Salary = " & txtSalary.Text & " Where " _
    & "EmpID = " & ddlEmps.SelectedItem.Value
```

Notice that the Where clause limits the update to the record selected in the DropDownList control. The Command object connects to the database through the Connection object:

```
DBUpdate.Connection = DBConn
DBUpdate.Connection.Open
```

The Update statement is then executed:

```
DBUpdate.ExecuteNonQuery()
```

Deleting Access Data

Once you let visitors add records to your database you will likely need to let them delete data. For example, if you let visitors add items to a shopping cart they will need to be able to delete those items. Or if you let visitors add themselves to mailing lists you offer, you will need to allow them to delete themselves from those lists. This tip shows you how to delete data in an Access database through your ASP.NET code.

 This ASP.NET page presents visitors with a list of employees in a DropDownList control. When visitors click the Button control on that page the employee selected in the DropDownList control is deleted from the database.

Within the form on the ASP.NET page, this DropDownList control is defined:

```
<asp:dropdownlist
    id="ddlEmps"
    datatextfield="EmpName"
    datavaluefield="EmpID"
    runat="server"
/>
```

Also defined within the page is a Button control:

```
<asp:button
    id="butDelete"
    text="Delete"
    onclick="SubmitBtn_Click"
    runat="server"
/>
```

Two procedures are defined on the page. The first fires when the page loads:

```
Sub Page_Load(ByVal Sender as Object, ByVal E as EventArgs)
    If Not IsPostBack Then
        Dim DBConn as OleDbConnection
        Dim DBCommand As OleDbDataAdapter
        Dim DSPageData as New DataSet
        DBConn = New OleDbConnection( _
```

```
             "PROVIDER=Microsoft.Jet.OLEDB.4.0;" _
             & "DATA SOURCE=" _
             & Server.MapPath("/tt/C13/EmployeesDB.mdb;"))
         DBCommand = New OleDbDataAdapter _
             ("Select LastName & ', ' & FirstName " _
             & "as EmpName, EmpID " _
             & "From Employees " _
             & "Order By LastName, FirstName", DBConn)
         DBCommand.Fill(DSPageData, _
             "Employees")
         ddlEmps.DataSource = _
             DSPageData.Tables("Employees").DefaultView
         ddlEmps.DataBind()
    End If
End Sub
```

This procedure populates the DropDownList control with the names and IDs for all the employee records in the database.

The other procedure fires when the Button control is clicked:

```
Sub SubmitBtn_Click(Sender As Object, E As EventArgs)
```

When that happens, you need to declare a Connection object and a Command object:

```
Dim DBConn as OleDbConnection
Dim DBDelete As New OleDbCommand
```

You then need to connect to the Access Database:

```
DBConn = New OleDbConnection( _
    "PROVIDER=Microsoft.Jet.OLEDB.4.0;" _
    & "DATA SOURCE=" _
    & Server.MapPath("/tt/C13/EmployeesDB.mdb;"))
```

Then you place the SQL Delete statement into the CommandText property of the Command object:

```
DBDelete.CommandText = "Delete From Employees " _
    & "Where EmpID = " & ddlEmps.SelectedItem.Value
```

Notice that the Where clause limits the deletion to only the record that has an ID matching the one selected in the DropDownList control.

The Command object will connect to the database through the Connection object:

```
DBDelete.Connection = DBConn
DBDelete.Connection.Open
```

and the Delete query is executed:

```
DBDelete.ExecuteNonQuery()
```

Retrieving Single Values from an Access Database

Sometimes you just need to retrieve a single value from the database and manipulate or display that piece of information. For example, you may need to retrieve the total number of products that match a search criterion. Or maybe you want to display the name of a product in the title of a page. Either way, you would need to retrieve a specific piece of information from the database. This tip shows you how to do that.

USE IT   The ASP.NET page presented for this tip displays summary information about an Employees table in an Access database. The page displays the total number of employee records in the table and it also displays the highest salary.

The summary data is displayed through this Label control:

```
<asp:label
    id="lblMessage"
    runat="Server"
/>
```

When the page loads, the following procedure runs:

```
Sub Page_Load(ByVal Sender as Object, ByVal E as EventArgs)
```

These data objects need to be declared so that the summary information can be retrieved from the database:

```
Dim DBConn as OleDbConnection
Dim DBCommand As OleDbDataAdapter
Dim DSPageData as New DataSet
```

You start by connecting to the Access database:

```
DBConn = New OleDbConnection( _
    "PROVIDER=Microsoft.Jet.OLEDB.4.0;" _
    & "DATA SOURCE=" _
    & Server.MapPath("/tt/C13/EmployeesDB.mdb;"))
```

Then the total number of employee records is retrieved:

```
DBCommand = New OleDbDataAdapter _
    ("Select Count(EmpID) as TheCount " _
    & "from Employees", DBConn)
```

That value is placed into a DataSet Table object:

```
DBCommand.Fill(DSPageData, _
    "EmpCount")
```

Also retrieved is the highest salary amount:

```
DBCommand = New OleDbDataAdapter _
    ("Select Max(Salary) as HighSal " _
    & "from Employees", DBConn)
```

which is placed into a different DataSet table:

```
DBCommand.Fill(DSPageData, _
    "HighSal")
```

Those values retrieved are placed with some fixed text into the Text property of the Label control:

```
lblMessage.Text = "Total Employees: " _
    & DSPageData.Tables("EmpCount"). _
    Rows(0).Item("TheCount") _
    & "<BR><BR>Highest Salary: " _
    & FormatCurrency(DSPageData.Tables("HighSal"). _
    Rows(0).Item("HighSal"))
```

Notice how the values are retrieved from the database table. First you refer to the correct table in the tables collection. Since the summary information returns just one record, row 0 is used. The Item collection refers to the field that contains the value in that record that you want to retrieve.

Iterating Through Records in an Access Table

Most of the time ASP.NET takes care of your having to process one record of data at a time so that you can display it in something like a DataGrid. But there are still occasions where you will need to iterate through a group of records and take some action with each record.

For example, maybe you have a page that sends out e-mail messages to a group of people in an Access database table. In that case, you need to loop through each record one at a time so that each person can be sent an e-mail. This tip shows you the structure of a code block that iterates through all the records in a DataSet table.

USE IT   The code block that demonstrates this technique fires when the sample page loads:

```
Sub Page_Load(ByVal Sender as Object, ByVal E as EventArgs)
```

Since you will be iterating through records you need these data objects:

```
Dim DBConn as OleDbConnection
Dim DBCommand As OleDbDataAdapter
Dim DSPageData as New DataSet
```

You also need a variable that will be used within a loop:

```
Dim I as Long
```

You start by connecting to the Access database:

```
DBConn = New OleDbConnection( _
    "PROVIDER=Microsoft.Jet.OLEDB.4.0;" _
    & "DATA SOURCE=" _
    & Server.MapPath("/tt/C13/EmployeesDB.mdb;"))
```

and you retrieve the data from the Employees table:

```
DBCommand = New OleDbDataAdapter _
    ("Select * from Employees", DBConn)
```

which is placed in a DataSet Table object:

```
DBCommand.Fill(DSPageData, _
    "Emps")
```

Next, you enter a loop. Notice that the loop will iterate from 0 to the total number of records minus one. That gives you the range for all the rows in the DataSet Table object:

```
For I = 0 To _
    DSPageData.Tables("Emps").Rows.Count - 1
```

Then, within that loop, you would place whatever code you needed to run for each of the records:

```
'Code to process record
```

Here, the ID of each employee record is placed in a Label control. Notice that the current row is referenced based on the iteration variable "I" that is used in this loop:

```
lblMessage.Text = lblMessage.Text _
    & "<BR>Processed Record: " _
    & DSPageData.Tables("Emps"). _
    Rows(I).Item("EmpID")
```

Because of this Next statement, the code then loops back to the For statement:

```
Next
```

Working with Transactions with an Access Database

Transactions allow you to make changes to a database as if all the changes were made as a single change. That is, they all succeed or fail together. For example, consider a bank account scenario where a customer wants to move money from one of their accounts to another. This requires a debit entry into one of the accounts and a credit entry into the other. You would not want one of these database entries to occur without the other one occurring. Thus, you need to surround the database entries within a transaction so that they will occur as a group. If one fails the other fails; if one succeeds the other succeeds.

Performing transactions within an ASP.NET page is a relatively painless coding experience. And this technique shows you how to do it.

USE IT   The ASP.NET page that demonstrates this technique attempts to delete two records from an Employees table. Each record is deleted in a separate query. But neither record is actually deleted because the transaction that the records are deleted through is not committed.

The code on this page runs when the page is loaded:

```
Sub Page_Load(ByVal Sender as Object, ByVal E as EventArgs)
```

In this case, you need to define a Connection object and a Command object:

```
Dim DBConn as OleDbConnection
Dim DBDelete As New OleDbCommand
```

But a Transaction object is also required:

```
Dim DBTrans As OleDbTransaction
```

You then set the connection string for the Access database:

```
DBConn = New OleDbConnection( _
    "PROVIDER=Microsoft.Jet.OLEDB.4.0;" _
    & "DATA SOURCE=" _
    & Server.MapPath("/tt/C13/EmployeesDB.mdb;"))
```

and open that connection:

```
DBConn.Open()
```

You then start a transaction against that connection to the database. Notice that this is done through the BeginTransaction method of the Connection object. That method returns a Transaction object:

```
DBTrans = DBConn.BeginTransaction()
```

Next, you need to indicate that the Command object will connect to the database through your Connection object:

```
DBDelete.Connection = DBConn
```

and that it is to use the Transaction object that was returned through the BeginTransaction method:

```
DBDelete.Transaction = DBTrans
```

Next, you delete one of the records from the Employees table:

```
DBDelete.CommandText = "Delete From Employees " _
    & "Where EmpID = 1"
DBDelete.ExecuteNonQuery()
```

And then a second record is deleted:

```
DBDelete.CommandText = "Delete From Employees " _
    & "Where EmpID = 2"
DBDelete.ExecuteNonQuery()
```

But neither record is deleted because the RollBack method of the Transaction object is called:

```
DBTrans.RollBack()
lblMessage.Text = "No action was taken."
```

The RollBack method takes the database back to the state it was in before any of the queries in the transaction ran.

If you do want the changes to the database to be made, you call the Commit method of the Transaction object:

```
'DBTrans.Commit()
```

In this example it is commented out so the changes to the database are not made.

Connecting to an SQL Server Database

If your ASP.NET application includes pages that utilize an SQL Server database, you will need to connect to that database. Connecting to an SQL Server database involves using a connection string that includes the name of the server, database, and login information. This tip shows you how to connect to an SQL Server database.

USE IT On most of the pages that you need to connect to an SQL Server database, you will also want to retrieve data. Therefore, you need to import these two namespaces at the top of your ASP.NET page:

```
<%@ Import Namespace="System.Data.SQLClient" %>
<%@ Import Namespace="System.Data" %>
```

The first namespace:

```
<%@ Import Namespace="System.Data.SQLClient" %>
```

provides the classes that you need to connect to an SQL Server database and run queries through.
The second namespace:

```
<%@ Import Namespace="System.Data" %>
```

allows you to instantiate a DataSet object, which can be used to display data from an SQL Server database on your page.

With these namespaces included, you can declare a Connection object:

```
Dim DBConn as SQLConnection
```

You then connect to the SQL Server database with a connection string like this one:

```
DBConn = New SQLConnection("server=localhost;" _
    & "Initial Catalog=TT;" _
    & "User Id=sa;" _
    & "Password=yourpassword;")
```

The first parameter is the name of the computer that hosts the SQL Server. In this case it is set to LocalHost, which refers to the machine that the ASP.NET page is running on.

The second parameter is the name of the database within SQL Server that you wish to connect to. The third parameter in the connection string is the name of the user that you are connecting to SQL Server as. The fourth parameter is the password for that user.

▶ | **QUICK TIP**

You can also connect to an SQL Server through its IP address. This may be helpful when the database you are connecting to is remote from the Web server. To do this, just place the IP address of the computer that hosts the SQL Server into the Server parameter.

Retrieving SQL Server Data

Once you have connected to an SQL Server database, you probably will want to retrieve data from that database. This technique shows you how to retrieve data from an SQL Server database and place it into the Table collection of a DataSet object.

 Since you need to retrieve SQL Server data, you will need a connect object:

```
Dim DBConn as SQLConnection
```

You will also need a DataAdapter object, which will allow you to run a query that retrieves data from the SQL Server database:

```
Dim DBCommand As SQLDataAdapter
```

And a DataSet object will contain the data retrieved through the DataAdapter object:

```
Dim DSPageData as New DataSet
```

You start by connecting to your SQL Server database:

```
DBConn = New SQLConnection("server=localhost;" _
    & "Initial Catalog=TT;" _
    & "User Id=sa;" _
    & "Password=yourpassword;")
```

Next, you place the Select query into the DataAdapter object that will retrieve the desired data from the database. In this case, the names and IDs of employees are retrieved:

```
DBCommand = New SQLDataAdapter _
    ("Select LastName + ', ' + FirstName " _
    & "as EmpName, EmpID " _
    & "From Employees " _
    & "Order By LastName, FirstName", DBConn)
```

The Fill method of the DataAdapter object is used to retrieve the data through that query into a DataSet object. Passed to that method is the name of the DataSet object that will store the returned records and the name of the table within the DataSet object's Tables collection that you would like to call this set of data:

```
DBCommand.Fill(DSPageData, _
    "EmployeeNames")
```

A DataSet object can hold more than one set of data. Here, all the records are returned from an Employees table:

```
DBCommand = New SQLDataAdapter _
    ("Select * from Employees", DBConn)
```

and placed into a different table of the same DataSet object:

```
DBCommand.Fill(DSPageData, _
    "EmployeesAll")
```

A third query will retrieve the month that employees were born along with their last name:

```
DBCommand = New SQLDataAdapter _
    ("Select LastName, Month(BirthDate) " _
    & "as MonthBirthDate from Employees Where " _
    & "Salary > 25000", DBConn)
```

into the same DataSet object:

```
DBCommand.Fill(DSPageData, _
    "Emp3")
```

Displaying SQL Server Data in a DropDownList Control

Frequently, you will need to display SQL Server data into a DropDownList control. This may be used to allow visitors to navigate to some other page, to select some type of category, or to answer a question on a test. The process of displaying SQL Server data in a control like a DropDownList involves binding. A DropDownList control is bound to a DataSet object.

The result is that all the records in the DataSet object are displayed in the DropDownList control. This technique shows you how to do that.

 This ASP.NET page displays a list of employees' names and also stores their IDs through a DropDownList control. Defined within the body of that page is this DropDownList control:

```
<asp:dropdownlist
    id="ddlEmps"
    datatextfield="EmpName"
    datavaluefield="EmpID"
    runat="server"
/>
```

The DataTextField property is set to the name of the field in the DataSet object that this control will be bound to, which contains the value that you want displayed in the list to the visitor. The

DataValueField property is set to the name of the field that you want passed along with the item but that is not displayed. Therefore, the visitor will see the name of the employee but the ID of the employee can be referenced in code.

Typically, when you populate a DropDownList control you want to do it once, when the page first loads. Therefore, you usually place the binding code in the Page_Load event:

```
Sub Page_Load(ByVal Sender as Object, ByVal E as EventArgs)
```

But you only want the code to run the first time the page loads. So you need to make sure the page hasn't been posted:

```
If Not IsPostBack Then
```

If it hasn't you will need these data objects:

```
Dim DBConn as SQLConnection
Dim DBCommand As SQLDataAdapter
Dim DSPageData as New DataSet
```

You start by connecting to the SQL Server database:

```
DBConn = New SQLConnection("server=localhost;" _
    & "Initial Catalog=TT;" _
    & "User Id=sa;" _
    & "Password=yourpassword;")
```

You then retrieve the data from the database. Note that the fields returned match the field names placed into the DataTextField and DataValueField properties of the DropDownList control:

```
DBCommand = New SQLDataAdapter _
    ("Select LastName + ', ' + FirstName " _
    & "as EmpName, EmpID " _
    & "From Employees " _
    & "Order By LastName, FirstName", DBConn)
```

Next, you place this data into the DataSet object:

```
DBCommand.Fill(DSPageData, _
    "Employees")
```

The DataSource property of the DropDownList control is set to the DataSet table that was just filled:

```
ddlEmps.DataSource = _
    DSPageData.Tables("Employees").DefaultView
```

and it is bound to that table, effectively displaying the data:

```
ddlEmps.DataBind()
```

Displaying SQL Server Data in a DataGrid Control

You will find that many of your data-displaying pages need to display the data in the form of an HTML table. For example, you may need to display results of sporting events from a given day. Or maybe you need to display the total amount of sales per state across the country. A DataGrid control is an excellent control through which to display this type of two-dimensional data.

 This technique shows you how to use a DataGrid to display SQL Server data. In this case the data being displayed is a list of employee records. A DataGrid control is defined on the page:

```
<asp:datagrid
    id="dgEmps"
    runat="server"
    autogeneratecolumns="True"
>
</asp:datagrid>
```

Notice that the AutoGenerateColumns property is set to True. Therefore, all the columns in the bound table will be displayed.

The code that populates the DataGrid control runs when the page loads:

```
Sub Page_Load(ByVal Sender as Object, ByVal E as EventArgs)
```

To populate the DataGrid control, you will need these data objects:

```
Dim DBConn as SQLConnection
Dim DBCommand As SQLDataAdapter
Dim DSPageData as New DataSet
```

You start by connecting to the SQL Server database:

```
DBConn = New SQLConnection("server=localhost;" _
    & "Initial Catalog=TT;" _
    & "User Id=sa;" _
    & "Password=yourpassword;")
```

Next, you retrieve the data that you want to place into the DataGrid control. Notice that the field names are returned more readable. For example, LastName is returned as Last Name. This is because the DataGrid control will display this text in the column header:

```
DBCommand = New SQLDataAdapter _
    ("Select LastName as [Last Name], " _
    & "Firstname as [First Name], " _
    & "BirthDate as [Birth Date], " _
    & "'<A HREF=""mailto:' + EmailAddress " _
    & "+ '"">' + EmailAddress + '</A>' as Email " _
    & "from Employees", DBConn)
```

Also notice that the EmailAddress field is returned as an Anchor tag. This will allow visitors to click on the Email Address field in the DataGrid to open a new e-mail to the employee that they selected.

The retrieved records are placed into a table in the DataSet object:

```
DBCommand.Fill(DSPageData, _
    "EmployeesAll")
```

The DataSource property of the DataGrid is set to that table:

```
dgEmps.DataSource = _
    DSPageData.Tables("EmployeesAll").DefaultView
```

and is bound to it:

```
dgEmps.DataBind()
```

Adding SQL Server Data

When your ASP.NET application includes SQL Server database connectivity, you often will need to add records to the database through your ASP.NET pages. For example, you may track visitors as they visit your site. With each page they visit, you may want to add a hit record to your database. Or you may allow visitors to sign themselves up for a mailing list. In that case you would need to add their information to a database. This technique shows you how to add a record to an SQL Server database table.

USE IT   The ASP.NET page presented with this technique allows visitors to add an employee record to the SQL Server database. Visitors enter information into the provided TextBox controls and click the Button control to add the new record to the database.

Defined on the page are TextBox controls like this one used to enter the new information through:

```
<asp:textbox
    id="txtLastName"
    runat="Server"
/>
```

This Button control allows visitors to submit their request:

```
<asp:button
    id="butOK"
    text="  OK  "
    onclick="SubmitBtn_Click"
    runat="server"
/>
```

When that button is clicked, this procedure fires:

```
Sub SubmitBtn_Click(Sender As Object, E As EventArgs)
```

To add a record, you will need a Connection object:

```
Dim DBConn as SQLConnection
```

and a Command object:

```
Dim DBAdd As New SQLCommand
```

The Connection object connects to the SQL Server database:

```
DBConn = New SQLConnection("server=localhost;" _
    & "Initial Catalog=TT;" _
    & "User Id=sa;" _
    & "Password=yourpassword;")
```

Next, you place into the CommandText property of the Command object the SQL Insert statement that adds the new record:

```
DBAdd.CommandText = "Insert Into Employees (" _
    & "LastName, FirstName, BirthDate, Salary, " _
    & "EmailAddress) values (" _
    & "'" & Replace(txtLastName.Text, "'", "''") _
    & "', " _
    & "'" & Replace(txtFirstName.Text, "'", "''") _
    & "', " _
    & "'" & Replace(txtBirthDate.Text, "'", "''") _
    & "', " _
    & Replace(txtSalary.Text, "'", "''") & ", " _
    & "'" & Replace(txtEmailAddress.Text, "'", "''") _
    & "')"
```

The Command object will connect to the database through the Connection object:

```
DBAdd.Connection = DBConn
```

That connection is opened:

```
DBAdd.Connection.Open
```

and the record is added to the database:

```
DBAdd.ExecuteNonQuery()
```

Updating SQL Server Data

Another type of query that you will often need to run on your ASP.NET pages that include database connectivity are Update queries. Update queries allow you to modify existing records in an SQL Server database table. This technique shows you how to run an Update query from your ASP.NET code.

USE IT The page presented with this technique allows the visitor to give all the employees in the Employees table a raise. The visitor enters the factor for the raise and every employee has their salary increased by that factor.

Defined on the ASP.NET page is this TextBox control for entering the raise amount:

```
<asp:textbox
    id="txtRaise"
    runat="Server"
/>
```

Also a Button control is defined:

```
<asp:button
    id="butOK"
    text="  OK  "
    onclick="SubmitBtn_Click"
    runat="server"
/>
```

When that Button control is clicked this code block fires:

```
Sub SubmitBtn_Click(Sender As Object, E As EventArgs)
```

Within that procedure, you will need a Connection object and a Command object:

```
Dim DBConn as SQLConnection
Dim DBUpdate As New SQLCommand
```

You start by connecting to your SQL Server database:

```
DBConn = New SQLConnection("server=localhost;" _
    & "Initial Catalog=TT;" _
    & "User Id=sa;" _
    & "Password=yourpassword;")
```

Next, you place the text of the Update query into the CommandText property of the Command object:

```
DBUpdate.CommandText = "Update Employees Set " _
    & "Salary = Salary * " & txtRaise.Text
```

The Command object will connect to the database through the Connection object:

```
DBUpdate.Connection = DBConn
DBUpdate.Connection.Open
```

The Update query can then be executed:

```
DBUpdate.ExecuteNonQuery()
```

Deleting SQL Server Data

If you have code on your ASP.NET pages that allows visitors to enter a record, or where you add records through code without their input, you will likely need to delete records from your pages. This technique shows you how to use a SQL Delete query to delete records from an SQL Server table.

USE IT This technique displays a list of employees from an SQL Server table called Employees. Visitors select a name and then click the button. When they do that the employee selected is deleted from the database.

Defined on the page is this DropDownList control that will display the employee names:

```
<asp:dropdownlist
    id="ddlEmps"
    datatextfield="EmpName"
    datavaluefield="EmpID"
    runat="server"
/>
```

and this Button control is defined:

```
<asp:button
    id="butDelete"
    text="Delete"
    onclick="SubmitBtn_Click"
```

```
        runat="server"
/>
```

When the page first loads, the following code will populate the DropDownList control:

```
Sub Page_Load(ByVal Sender as Object, ByVal E as EventArgs)
    If Not IsPostBack Then
        Dim DBConn as SQLConnection
        Dim DBCommand As SQLDataAdapter
        Dim DSPageData as New DataSet
        DBConn = New SQLConnection("server=localhost;" _
            & "Initial Catalog=TT;" _
            & "User Id=sa;" _
            & "Password=yourpassword;")
        DBCommand = New SQLDataAdapter _
            ("Select LastName + ', ' + FirstName " _
            & "as EmpName, EmpID " _
            & "From Employees " _
            & "Order By LastName, FirstName", DBConn)
        DBCommand.Fill(DSPageData, _
            "Employees")
        ddlEmps.DataSource = _
            DSPageData.Tables("Employees").DefaultView
        ddlEmps.DataBind()
    End If
End Sub
```

and this procedure fires when the Button control is clicked:

```
Sub SubmitBtn_Click(Sender As Object, E As EventArgs)
```

When that happens, you need a Connection and a Command object:

```
Dim DBConn as SQLConnection
Dim DBDelete As New SQLCommand
```

You start by connecting to the SQL Server database:

```
DBConn = New SQLConnection("server=localhost;" _
    & "Initial Catalog=TT;" _
    & "User Id=sa;" _
    & "Password=yourpassword;")
```

Then the SQL Delete statement that will delete the record selected in the DropDownList control is placed into the CommandText property of the Command object:

```
DBDelete.CommandText = "Delete From Employees " _
    & "Where EmpID = " & ddlEmps.SelectedItem.Value
```

The connection to the database for the Command object is made though the Connection object:

```
DBDelete.Connection = DBConn
DBDelete.Connection.Open
```

and the offending record is deleted:

```
DBDelete.ExecuteNonQuery()
```

Retrieving Single Values from an SQL Server Database

A Table object within the Table collection of a DataSet object contains a Rows collection. Using the Rows collection, you can reference a single value in a field in a record. This is helpful when you need to retrieve and display a single piece of information on an ASP.NET page. This technique shows you how to do that with an SQL Server database table.

USE IT   The ASP.NET page presented for this page displays the total number of employees in the Employees table as well as the highest salary in that table. That information is displayed through this Label control:

```
<asp:label
    id="lblMessage"
    runat="Server"
/>
```

When the page loads, the values are retrieved within the Page_Load event:

```
Sub Page_Load(ByVal Sender as Object, ByVal E as EventArgs)
```

In that event, you need these data objects:

```
Dim DBConn as SQLConnection
Dim DBCommand As SQLDataAdapter
Dim DSPageData as New DataSet
```

You start by connecting to the SQL Server database:

```
DBConn = New SQLConnection("server=localhost;" _
    & "Initial Catalog=TT;" _
```

```
    & "User Id=sa;" _
    & "Password=yourpassword;")
```

Then, you retrieve the total number of employees that are in the Employees table:

```
DBCommand = New SQLDataAdapter _
    ("Select Count(EmpID) as TheCount " _
    & "from Employees", DBConn)
```

That value is placed into a DataSet Table object:

```
DBCommand.Fill(DSPageData, _
    "EmpCount")
```

Next, you retrieve the highest salary from the employee records:

```
DBCommand = New SQLDataAdapter _
    ("Select Max(Salary) as HighSal " _
    & "from Employees", DBConn)
```

and place that returned value into a separate DataSet Table object:

```
DBCommand.Fill(DSPageData, _
    "HighSal")
```

Those values are placed with some fixed text into a Label control:

```
lblMessage.Text = "Total Employees: " _
    & DSPageData.Tables("EmpCount"). _
    Rows(0).Item("TheCount") _
    & "<BR><BR>Highest Salary: " _
    & FormatCurrency(DSPageData.Tables("HighSal"). _
    Rows(0).Item("HighSal"))
```

Notice how the field values are referenced. TheCount is a field in the DataSet Table object and is referenced through the Item collection. The Item collection contains all the fields. The Rows collection contains all the records returned into the DataSet object. In this case you refer to row 0, the first row. The Tables collection represents all the tables in the DataSet object. These table names were supplied in the Fill method of the DataAdapter object.

Iterating Through Records in an SQL Server Table

In many situations you no longer need to iterate through records in an SQL Server table in ASP.NET pages as you did with ASP. This is because you can now bind DataSet Tables directly to controls.

But on occasion you may still need to iterate through all the records in a DataSet Table so that they can be processed in some special way.

The DataSet Table object contains a Rows collection that allows you to iterate through each record it contains. This technique shows you how to create a loop so that you can process each record from an SQL Server table through a DataSet Table object.

USE IT The ASP.NET page presented with this technique iterates through each record in an Employees table using a For loop. The ID of each employee is placed into the Text property of this Label control as it is processed:

```
<asp:label
    id="lblMessage"
    runat="Server"
/>
```

The code that iterates through the records fires when the page loads:

```
Sub Page_Load(ByVal Sender as Object, ByVal E as EventArgs)
```

Within that procedure, these data objects are needed:

```
Dim DBConn as SQLConnection
Dim DBCommand As SQLDataAdapter
Dim DSPageData as New DataSet
```

You also need a variable that will be used in the For loop:

```
Dim I as Long
```

You start by connecting to the SQL Server database:

```
DBConn = New SQLConnection("server=localhost;" _
    & "Initial Catalog=TT;" _
    & "User Id=sa;" _
    & "Password=yourpassword;")
```

Then you retrieve all the employee records:

```
DBCommand = New SQLDataAdapter _
    ("Select * from Employees", DBConn)
```

and place them into a DataSet table object:

```
DBCommand.Fill(DSPageData, _
    "Emps")
```

Next, you initiate a For block that will go from 0 to the total number of records in the DataSet table minus 1. You retrieve the record count in the DataSet Table object through the Count property of the Rows collection:

```
For I = 0 To _
    DSPageData.Tables("Emps").Rows.Count - 1
```

Then within the loop you can process each record. You would use the variable "I" to refer to the current row within the current iteration of the loop:

```
'Code to process record
lblMessage.Text = lblMessage.Text _
    & "<BR>Processed Record: " _
    & DSPageData.Tables("Emps"). _
    Rows(I).Item("EmpID")
```

You would then move on to process the next record:

```
Next
```

Working with Transactions with an SQL Server Database

Transactions provide a way for you to group together database executions as a group so that they succeed or fail together. For example, if you had an e-commerce site you may have code that allows visitors to add a quantity of an item to their shopping cart. When you do that you also want to remove the number of items ordered from your inventory. Therefore, you have two actions that you need to execute. You want to add items to a shopping cart and you want to remove items from inventory.

These executions need to happen as a group. You don't want to add items to the shopping cart if something goes wrong with removing them from inventory. And the opposite is also true.

Therefore, the database executions need to be grouped in a Transaction. This technique shows you how to use a Transaction object with an SQL Server database.

USE IT This ASP.NET page contains SQL Delete statements that delete records from the Employees table. But the records are not deleted because they are in a transaction and the transaction is not committed to the database.

The code that performs this task fires when the ASP.NET page loads:

```
Sub Page_Load(ByVal Sender as Object, ByVal E as EventArgs)
```

Within that procedure you will need a Connection object and a Command object:

```
Dim DBConn as SQLConnection
Dim DBDelete As New SQLCommand
```

You will also need a Transaction object:

```
Dim DBTrans As SQLTransaction
```

You start by connecting to the SQL Server database:

```
DBConn = New SQLConnection("server=localhost;" _
    & "Initial Catalog=TT;" _
    & "User Id=sa;" _
    & "Password=yourpassword;")
```

and opening that connection:

```
DBConn.Open()
```

You then start a transaction by calling the BeginTransaction method of the Connection object. That method returns an open transaction, which is placed into the local Transaction object:

```
DBTrans = DBConn.BeginTransaction()
```

The Command object will connect to the database through the Connection object:

```
DBDelete.Connection = DBConn
```

It will also use the Transaction object:

```
DBDelete.Transaction = DBTrans
```

Next, two records are deleted and executed from the Employees table:

```
DBDelete.CommandText = "Delete From Employees " _
    & "Where EmpID = 1"
DBDelete.ExecuteNonQuery()
DBDelete.CommandText = "Delete From Employees " _
    & "Where EmpID = 2"
DBDelete.ExecuteNonQuery()
```

But the records are not actually deleted from the database since the RollBack method of the Transaction object is called:

```
DBTrans.RollBack()
lblMessage.Text = "No action was taken."
```

The RollBack method causes the queries that were executed within the Transaction object to be cancelled.

You could instead call the Commit method:

```
'DBTrans.Commit()
```

This method causes the pending execute statements to be executed as a group so that they fail or succeed together.

Calling a Stored Procedure

In SQL Server you create stored procedures that take some action or manipulate data in some way in your database. Once you create a stored procedure it becomes a compiled efficient set of code. You can call stored procedures from your ASP.NET pages. This tip shows you how to call a stored procedure that does not have any parameters nor does it return any value.

USE IT This ASP.NET page calls a stored procedure that adds a record to the Employees table. The stored procedure has this syntax:

```
CREATE PROCEDURE AddGarbageRecord AS
Insert Into Employees (LastName, FirstName, BirthDate,
Salary, EmailAddress) values ('Smith', 'Jane',
'12/17/1947', 55000, 'jane@na.com')
GO
```

Notice that the stored procedure does not have any input parameters and that it does not return any values.

That stored procedure is called when the ASP.NET page loads:

```
Sub Page_Load(ByVal Sender as Object, ByVal E as EventArgs)
```

You will need a Connection object:

```
Dim DBConn as SQLConnection
```

Since the stored procedure does not return a value, you will also need a Command object:

```
Dim DBSP As New SQLCommand
```

You can then connect to the database:

```
DBConn = New SQLConnection("server=localhost;" _
    & "Initial Catalog=TT;" _
    & "User Id=sa;" _
    & "Password=yourpassword;")
```

and place the SQL text that calls the stored procedure into the Command object. Notice that the call consists of the name of the stored procedure preceded by the Exec keyword:

```
DBSP.CommandText = "Exec AddGarbageRecord"
```

The Command will connect to the database through the Connection object:

```
DBSP.Connection = DBConn
DBSP.Connection.Open
```

And the stored procedure is executed:

```
DBSP.ExecuteNonQuery()
lblMessage.Text = "Stored procedure completed."
```

Retrieving Data from a Stored Procedure

Stored procedures frequently return data from a database. They can return single values, tables joined together, or all the records from a single value, and much more. You can call stored procedures that return data from your ASP.NET pages. This technique shows you how to do that.

 The page defined for this technique displays in a DataGrid control all the employees who have a birthday in the current month. The DataGrid has this definition:

```
<asp:datagrid
    id="dgEmps"
    runat="server"
    autogeneratecolumns="True"
>
</asp:datagrid>
```

The stored procedure defined in the SQL Server database has this definition:

```
CREATE PROCEDURE CurrentMonthBirthDays AS
Select * from Employees Where
Month(BirthDate) = Month(GetDate())
```

Notice that the GetDate function, which returns the current system date, is used to see if the month of that date matches the month of the birth date.

That stored procedure is called when the ASP.NET page loads:

```
Sub Page_Load(ByVal Sender as Object, ByVal E as EventArgs)
```

Within this procedure you need these database objects:

```
Dim DBConn as SQLConnection
Dim DBCommand As SQLDataAdapter
Dim DSPageData as New DataSet
```

You start by connecting to the database:

```
DBConn = New SQLConnection("server=localhost;" _
    & "Initial Catalog=TT;" _
    & "User Id=sa;" _
    & "Password=yourpassword;")
```

You then call the stored procedure:

```
DBCommand = New SQLDataAdapter _
    ("Exec CurrentMonthBirthDays", DBConn)
```

and place the matching records, if any, into the DataSet object:

```
DBCommand.Fill(DSPageData, _
    "Emps")
```

The DataGrid control is then bound to the returned data:

```
dgEmps.DataSource = _
    DSPageData.Tables("Emps").DefaultView
dgEmps.DataBind()
```

Sending Data to a Stored Procedure Through Input Parameters

If you are working towards making your ASP.NET application more efficient and that application connects to an SQL Server database, you will want to create stored procedures that do basic things like adding records, deleting records, and other such tasks. With these types of stored procedures, you need to pass data into them. This technique shows you how to call a stored procedure that needs to have parameters passed into it.

USE IT The ASP.NET page created for this technique allows visitors to add a record to the Employees table. Instead of using an Insert statement in the ASP.NET code, a stored procedure is called to add the record.

That stored procedure has this definition:

```
CREATE PROCEDURE AddEmployee
@LastName varchar(50),
```

```
@FirstName varchar(50),
@BirthDate datetime,
@Salary money,
@EmailAddress varchar(50)
AS
Insert Into Employees (LastName, FirstName, BirthDate,
Salary, EmailAddress) values (
@LastName, @FirstName, @BirthDate,
@Salary, @EmailAddress)
GO
```

Notice that the stored procedure has five input parameters. Those parameters are used in the Insert statement in the stored procedure.

On the ASP.NET page, visitors enter the values for the new employee record into TextBox control. When they click the Button control, this procedure fires, adding the new record by calling the stored procedure:

```
Sub SubmitBtn_Click(Sender As Object, E As EventArgs)
```

Within the procedure, you need these data objects:

```
Dim DBConn as SQLConnection
Dim DBAdd As New SQLCommand
```

You need to start by connecting to the SQL Server database:

```
DBConn = New SQLConnection("server=localhost;" _
    & "Initial Catalog=TT;" _
    & "User Id=sa;" _
    & "Password=yourpassword;")
```

Next, you place the SQL syntax into the Command object that calls the stored procedure:

```
DBAdd.CommandText = "Exec AddEmployee " _
    & "'" & Replace(txtLastName.Text, "'", "''") _
    & "', " _
    & "'" & Replace(txtFirstName.Text, "'", "''") _
    & "', " _
    & "'" & Replace(txtBirthDate.Text, "'", "''") _
    & "', " _
    & Replace(txtSalary.Text, "'", "''") & ", " _
    & "'" & Replace(txtEmailAddress.Text, "'", "''") _
    & "'"
```

Notice that the call passes in five parameters, the values for the new record. A comma separates each parameter.

The Command object will connect to the database through the Connection object:

```
DBAdd.Connection = DBConn
DBAdd.Connection.Open
```

and the stored procedure can be executed:

```
DBAdd.ExecuteNonQuery()
```

Using Output Parameters with a Stored Procedure

One of the ways that you can use a stored procedure is to have it return data through output parameters. Then after the call to the stored procedure you can display the values returned to you. For example, you might use a stored procedure to return summary information about a table. This could be done through output parameters. The technique presented in this section of the chapter shows you how to use output parameters.

 A Command object contains a collection of Parameter objects. These parameters are values that the stored procedure passes back to you after the call is complete. This ASP.NET page calls a stored procedure that returns values. The values returned are the total number of records in the Employees table and the name of the employee who is paid the most.

The stored procedure has this definition:

```
CREATE PROCEDURE TableInfo
@RecordCount integer OUTPUT,
@TopSalaryName varchar(100) OUTPUT
AS
Select @RecordCount = Count(EmpID) From Employees
Select @TopSalaryName = LastName + ', ' + FirstName
    From Employees Where Salary = (Select Max(Salary)
    From Employees)
GO
```

Notice that the two parameters are declared as output parameters. In the first query, one of the output parameters is set to the record count. In the second query the other parameter is set to the name of the employee who is paid the most.

That stored procedure is called when the ASP.NET page loads:

```
Sub Page_Load(ByVal Sender as Object, ByVal E as EventArgs)
```

In that procedure you will need a Connection object:

```
Dim DBConn as SQLConnection
```

that points to the SQL Server database:

```
DBConn = New SQLConnection("server=localhost;" _
    & "Initial Catalog=TT;" _
    & "User Id=sa;" _
    & "Password=yourpassword;")
```

You will need a Command object:

```
Dim DBSP As New SQLCommand
```

You also will need two Parameter objects. The first has its name match the first parameter in the stored procedure and is of the same data type:

```
Dim parRecordCount as New _
    SqlParameter("@RecordCount", SqlDbType.Int)
```

The second parameter is set to the name and type of the second output parameter in the stored procedure:

```
Dim parTopSalaryName as New _
    SqlParameter("@TopSalaryName", SqlDbType.VarChar, 100)
```

Both parameters are set to output parameters using the Direction property:

```
parRecordCount.Direction = ParameterDirection.Output
parTopSalaryName.Direction = ParameterDirection.Output
```

Next, those parameters are added to the Parameters collection of the Command object:

```
DBSP.Parameters.Add(parRecordCount)
DBSP.Parameters.Add(parTopSalaryName)
```

The CommandText property of the Command object is set to the name of the stored procedure:

```
DBSP.CommandText = "TableInfo"
```

and the command type is set to stored procedure:

```
DBSP.CommandType = CommandType.StoredProcedure
```

The Command object will connect to the database through the Connection object:

```
DBSP.Connection = DBConn
DBSP.Connection.Open
```

The stored procedure can then be executed:

```
DBSP.ExecuteNonQuery()
```

After the call to the stored procedure you can use the values in the output parameters through the Value property:

```
lblMessage.Text = "Total Employees: " _
    & parRecordCount.Value _
    & "<BR><BR>Highest Paid: " _
    & parTopSalaryName.Value
```

Visitors would then see through the Label control the total number of employees and the highest salary amount.

CHAPTER 14
Web Services

TIPS IN THIS CHAPTER

A versatile and promising feature of ASP.NET is Web services. Web services provide a way for you to create functionality that can be used on Web pages by other developers. Those developers can connect to your Web service from a variety of different systems. Web services allow this by returning data in standard XML format. In this chapter, tips and techniques are presented that show you how to create and consume a Web service.

The tips and techniques in this chapter all come from the code in a single Web service. That Web service allows developers who link to it to reference, display, add, and remove items from a Tip library. The data for that library is stored in an Access database. As with all the files from this book, you can find the Web service file, the consuming files, and the Access database online with the rest of the book's files at **http://www.osborne.com**.

Understanding Why to Create a Web Service

Web services offer a powerful way for you to encapsulate functionality that you offer through your Web server. You create Web services for a variety of reasons. This tip offers some suggestions about when you may want to create a Web service.

USE IT One of the strongest benefits of a Web service is that it encapsulates functionality in such a way that a variety of different types of end-developers could take advantage of your service. Therefore, one of the best uses of a Web service is as a way for you to provide a service to other developers.

For example, maybe you decide to create a stock service that other developers can connect to through your Web service. Through your service, you return the current price of a stock based on the stock symbol passed in. You could charge and offer a subscription for this type of Web service. The developers who use your service would need to know nothing about how your tool works. They would just need to link to your service through whatever mechanism their server supported.

Or maybe you run a site for your town. One of the items on your site is an event calendar. Other companies such as the local newspapers and television stations would like to offer the event calendar through their own site. You could implement your event calendar as a Web service, which would allow these other site owners to incorporate the event calendar into their own sites.

Another reason to create a Web service is to provide a way for novice Web developers at your own site to use more complex functionality. For example, maybe you are an expert at database manipulation and at your company you have numerous site developers who know very little about database connectivity. You could wrap into a Web service many different common database functions that the junior developers could call on to give their sites the needed functionality.

Or maybe you are an expert at developing with Exchange server. You could help out other developers who needed to provide such access by creating a Web service that made calls to Exchange server simpler.

Another reason to create a Web service is to help you organize your own development efforts. Maybe you manage many Web sites and all of those sites have a dynamic Contact Us page. You could implement the functionality of the Contact Us page within a Web service so that you could call it from all of your sites.

These are just a few of the reasons that you may find Web services helpful. As you create your ASP.NET pages, keep Web services in mind. You may find other reasons that Web services would benefit your development work.

Creating a Web Service File

A Web service can be created using any text editor. The file must contain certain tags and have a specific structure to it. This tip shows you how to create a Web service file.

 As mentioned, a Web service file can be created using a text editor. When you save the file, you must save it with the extension .asmx. That extension tells the Web server that your file is a Web service.

You can save your Web service anywhere within your Web root. Wherever you do save the file, you will need to supply that path to developers that will use your Web service. Therefore, place the file in a location that is easily addressed.

At the top of your Web service file, you need to place this tag:

```
<%@ WebService
    Language="VB"
    Class="Tips"
%>
```

The tag informs the compiler that this file is a Web service. The Language parameter indicates the name of the coding language that you are using in the Web service. The Class parameter indicates the name of the class that this service exposes. This is the name that the end-developer will use when they instantiate your service. You must include a class with that name in your Web service.

Next, you need to include this Import directive:

```
Imports System.Web.Services
```

All Web services must import this namespace, which contains the class that all Web services are based on.

After defining that tag and the Import directive, you can define the class, which has this basic definition:

```
<WebService(Namespace:="http://localhost/" _
    & "wwwroot/tt/C14/Service/")> _
Public Class Tips
'Class code.
End Class
```

Notice that you first use a WebService tag, which indicates that this class is the class that is exposed through your Web service. As a parameter within that WebService tag, you pass in the path to this file. That path must be set to the location of your ASP.NET Web service.

After that tag, you give the class Public scope and indicate its name. You then define the code in the class, which is made up of its methods. After defining those methods, you close the class' definition.

Including Namespace References and Other Directives in a Web Service

As your Web service becomes more complex, you will find that you need to import other namespaces into it. For example, if your Web service provided database functionality, you would need to import the necessary data namespaces. This tip shows you how to do that and how to use options within a Web service.

At the top of a Web service, you need to include these opening lines:

```
<%@ WebService Language="VB" Class="Tips"%>
Imports System.Web.Services
```

After those lines of code but before you define your class, you can include Option directives like these:

```
Option Strict Off
Option Explicit On
```

The first directive tells the compiler that you do not want strict data-type conversion to be enforced. Turning this directive off means that you can easily place a number variable into a string variable.

The second option indicates that you will declare all your variables. Having this option on makes it easier for you to debug your code, since an error will be thrown if you try to reference a variable that you haven't defined.

After defining your option directives, you can import other namespaces into your Web service:

```
Imports System.Data
Imports System.Data.OLEDB
```

Here, two data namespaces are added to the Web service. These allow you to connect to and retrieve data from an Access database. Notice that this is very different from the namespace directive used on an ASP.NET page.

Adding Sub Methods to a Web Service

A Web service is typically made up of many different methods. These methods can be either Subs or Functions. Functions return a value and Subs do not. This tip shows you how to define Subs in an ASP.NET Web service.

USE IT The methods created for this Web service add to the functionality of the Tips Web service. The Web service contains two Subs.

The first Sub provides the method for adding a tip to the Access database. That method has this definition:

```
<WebMethod()> Public Sub AddTip _
    (TipTitle as String, TipText as String)
    Dim DBConn as OleDbConnection
    Dim DBInsert As New OleDbCommand
    DBConn = New OleDbConnection("PROVIDER=" _
        & "Microsoft.Jet.OLEDB.4.0;" _
        & "DATA SOURCE=" _
        & "c:/inetpub/wwwroot/TT/C14/" _
        & "service/TipsDB.mdb;")
    DBInsert.Connection = DBConn
    DBInsert.Connection.Open
    DBInsert.CommandText = "Insert Into Tips " _
        & "(TipTitle, TipText) Values (" _
        & "'" & TipTitle & "', " _
        & "'" & TipText & "')"
    DBInsert.ExecuteNonQuery()
End Sub
```

You start with the WebMethod tag, which indicates that the method is exposed through your Web service:

```
<WebMethod()> Public Sub AddTip _
    (TipTitle as String, TipText as String)
```

Also on that line, you indicate that the method is a Sub and its name is AddTip. The method has two parameters that need to be passed into it. The first is the title of the tip and the second is the text of the tip. Both must be passed in as strings.

Since you need to add data to the database, you need these data objects:

```
Dim DBConn as OleDbConnection
Dim DBInsert As New OleDbCommand
```

You then connect to the Access database:

```
DBConn = New OleDbConnection("PROVIDER=" _
    & "Microsoft.Jet.OLEDB.4.0;" _
    & "DATA SOURCE=" _
    & "c:/inetpub/wwwroot/TT/C14/" _
    & "service/TipsDB.mdb;")
```

and indicate that the Command object will connect to the database through the Connection object:

```
DBInsert.Connection = DBConn
DBInsert.Connection.Open
```

Next, you add a record to the database based on the title and text passed into this method:

```
DBInsert.CommandText = "Insert Into Tips " _
    & "(TipTitle, TipText) Values (" _
    & "'" & TipTitle & "', " _
    & "'" & TipText & "')"
DBInsert.ExecuteNonQuery()
```

Lastly, you close the Sub's definition:

```
End Sub
```

The other Sub defined in this Web service allows for the deletion of a tip from the Access database:

```
<WebMethod()> Public Sub RemoveTip _
    (TipID as Long)
    Dim DBConn as OleDbConnection
    Dim DBDelete As New OleDbCommand
    DBConn = New OleDbConnection("PROVIDER=" _
        & "Microsoft.Jet.OLEDB.4.0;" _
        & "DATA SOURCE=" _
        & "c:/inetpub/wwwroot/TT/C14/" _
        & "service/TipsDB.mdb;")
    DBDelete.Connection = DBConn
    DBDelete.Connection.Open
    DBDelete.CommandText = "Delete From Tips " _
        & "Where TipID = " & TipID
    DBDelete.ExecuteNonQuery()
End Sub
```

This method needs to have a number passed into it, which is the ID of the tip that is to be deleted:

```
<WebMethod()> Public Sub RemoveTip _
    (TipID as Long)
```

For this method, you will need data objects:

```
Dim DBConn as OleDbConnection
Dim DBDelete As New OleDbCommand
```

You start by connecting to the Access database:

```
DBConn = New OleDbConnection("PROVIDER=" _
    & "Microsoft.Jet.OLEDB.4.0;" _
    & "DATA SOURCE=" _
    & "c:/inetpub/wwwroot/TT/C14/" _
    & "service/TipsDB.mdb;")
DBDelete.Connection = DBConn
DBDelete.Connection.Open
```

You then delete the record that has an ID that matches the ID that was passed into this Sub:

```
DBDelete.CommandText = "Delete From Tips " _
    & "Where TipID = " & TipID
DBDelete.ExecuteNonQuery()
```

Adding Function Methods to a Web Service

Most often, your Web services will need to return values to the consuming applications. You return values from your Web services through Functions. This technique shows you how to include Functions in your Web service.

USE IT   The code added for this technique adds three Functions to the Web service. Two of those Functions return specific values for a tip and the third returns an HTML table that displays all the tips.

The first Function returns an HTML table that contains the titles for all the tips. The titles are displayed as links, with the intention that the developer would have another page that would display the text of the tip when the link is clicked.

That Function has this definition:

```
<WebMethod()> Public Function GetTipTable _
    (RedirectPage as String, _
    QueryStringVaraibleName as String) as String
    Dim DBConn as OleDbConnection
```

```
    Dim DBCommand As OleDbDataAdapter
    Dim DSData as New DataSet
    Dim I as Long
    DBConn = New OleDbConnection("PROVIDER=" _
        & "Microsoft.Jet.OLEDB.4.0;" _
        & "DATA SOURCE=" _
        & "c:/inetpub/wwwroot/TT/C14/" _
        & "service/TipsDB.mdb;")
    DBCommand = New OleDbDataAdapter _
        ("Select TipID, TipTitle From Tips " _
        & "Order by TipTitle", DBConn)
    DBCommand.Fill(DSData, _
        "AllTips")
    GetTipTable = "<Table>"
    For I = 0 To _
        DSData.Tables("AllTips").Rows.Count - 1
        GetTipTable = GetTipTable _
        & "<TR><TD><A HREF=""" _
        & RedirectPage & "?" _
        & QueryStringVaraibleName & "=" _
        & DSData.Tables("AllTips"). _
        Rows(I).Item("TipID") _
        & """>" & DSData.Tables("AllTips"). _
        Rows(I).Item("TipTitle") _
        & "</A></TD></TR>"
    Next
    GetTipTable = GetTipTable & "</Table>"
End Function
```

Notice that two parameters need to be passed into this procedure:

```
<WebMethod()> Public Function GetTipTable _
    (RedirectPage as String, _
    QueryStringVaraibleName as String) as String
```

The first parameter is the path to the page that visitors should be taken to when they click on one of the title links. The second parameter is the name of the variable that the developer would like passed to that page when visitors click on the link. That variable is passed in the form of a query string.

In this procedure you will need these data variables:

```
Dim DBConn as OleDbConnection
Dim DBCommand As OleDbDataAdapter
Dim DSData as New DataSet
```

You will also need this variable for a For code block:

```
Dim I as Long
```

You start by connecting to the Access database:

```
DBConn = New OleDbConnection("PROVIDER=" _
    & "Microsoft.Jet.OLEDB.4.0;" _
    & "DATA SOURCE=" _
    & "c:/inetpub/wwwroot/TT/C14/" _
    & "service/TipsDB.mdb;")
```

and you retrieve all the IDs and titles of the tips:

```
DBCommand = New OleDbDataAdapter _
    ("Select TipID, TipTitle From Tips " _
    & "Order by TipTitle", DBConn)
DBCommand.Fill(DSData, _
    "AllTips")
```

You return a value from the Function by assigning a value to the Function name. Here, it is initially set to the opening HTML Table tag:

```
GetTipTable = "<Table>"
```

You then start a loop, so that you can process each of the records that have been returned:

```
For I = 0 To _
    DSData.Tables("AllTips").Rows.Count - 1
```

Within the loop, you append to the return value the title of the tip through an HTML Anchor tag:

```
GetTipTable = GetTipTable _
    & "<TR><TD><A HREF=""" _
    & RedirectPage & "?" _
    & QueryStringVaraibleName & "=" _
    & DSData.Tables("AllTips"). _
    Rows(I).Item("TipID") _
    & """>" & DSData.Tables("AllTips"). _
    Rows(I).Item("TipTitle") _
    & "</A></TD></TR>"
```

Notice that the Anchor tag links to the page name passed in through the RedirectPage parameter and that the ID of the tip is passed into that page through the link's query string.

You then move on to process the next record:

```
Next
```

After the loop, you append the closing Table tag to the return value:

```
GetTipTable = GetTipTable & "</Table>"
```

The second Function defined in this Web service would be used on a page that displays the contents of a tip. It returns the text of the tip's title:

```
<WebMethod()> Public Function GetTipTitle _
    (TipID as Long) as String
    Dim DBConn as OleDbConnection
    Dim DBCommand As OleDbDataAdapter
    Dim DSData as New DataSet
    DBConn = New OleDbConnection("PROVIDER=" _
        & "Microsoft.Jet.OLEDB.4.0;" _
        & "DATA SOURCE=" _
        & "c:/inetpub/wwwroot/TT/C14/" _
        & "service/TipsDB.mdb;")
    DBCommand = New OleDbDataAdapter _
        ("Select TipTitle From Tips Where " _
        & "TipID = " & TipID, DBConn)
    DBCommand.Fill(DSData, _
        "CurrentTip")
    If DSData.Tables("CurrentTip").Rows.Count = 0 Then
        GetTipTitle = ""
    Else
        GetTipTitle = DSData.Tables("CurrentTip"). _
            Rows(0).Item("TipTitle")
    End If
End Function
```

Passed into the method through a parameter is the ID of the tip, whose title is to be returned:

```
<WebMethod()> Public Function GetTipTitle _
(TipID as Long) as String
```

You will need these data objects:

```
Dim DBConn as OleDbConnection
Dim DBCommand As OleDbDataAdapter
Dim DSData as New DataSet
```

You start by connecting to the database:

```
DBConn = New OleDbConnection("PROVIDER=" _
    & "Microsoft.Jet.OLEDB.4.0;" _
    & "DATA SOURCE=" _
```

```
    & "c:/inetpub/wwwroot/TT/C14/" _
    & "service/TipsDB.mdb;")
```

and you retrieve from the database the title of the tip:

```
DBCommand = New OleDbDataAdapter _
    ("Select TipTitle From Tips Where " _
    & "TipID = " & TipID, DBConn)
DBCommand.Fill(DSData, _
    "CurrentTip")
```

You then check to see if a record was found based on the ID that was passed in:

```
If DSData.Tables("CurrentTip").Rows.Count = 0 Then
```

If a record wasn't found, you return an empty string:

```
GetTipTitle = ""
```

Otherwise, the title of the tip is returned:

```
GetTipTitle = DSData.Tables("CurrentTip"). _
    Rows(0).Item("TipTitle")
```

The other Function in this Web service returns the text of a tip, based on the ID of the tip passed in. That tip has this definition:

```
<WebMethod()> Public Function GetTipText _
    (TipID as Long) as String
    Dim DBConn as OleDbConnection
    Dim DBCommand As OleDbDataAdapter
    Dim DSData as New DataSet
    DBConn = New OleDbConnection("PROVIDER=" _
        & "Microsoft.Jet.OLEDB.4.0;" _
        & "DATA SOURCE=" _
        & "c:/inetpub/wwwroot/TT/C14/" _
        & "service/TipsDB.mdb;")
    DBCommand = New OleDbDataAdapter _
        ("Select TipText From Tips Where " _
        & "TipID = " & TipID, DBConn)
    DBCommand.Fill(DSData, _
        "CurrentTip")
    If DSData.Tables("CurrentTip").Rows.Count = 0 Then
        GetTipText = ""
```

```
    Else
        GetTipText = DSData.Tables("CurrentTip"). _
            Rows(0).Item("TipText")
    End If
End Function
```

Within this procedure, you connect to the Access database and attempt to retrieve the text of the tip. If a record with the ID passed in is not found, an empty string is returned. Otherwise, the text of the tip is returned.

Testing a Web Service

When you create a Web service, you will want to test it to make sure it works. One way that you can do that is by creating a page that consumes the service. But that can be more involved than you want, just so you can see if the Web service works. The other way that you can test the Web service is by opening the Web service through a browser. This technique shows you how to do that.

USE IT To debug your Web service files through a browser, open a browser window and enter the address to your page. When you do that, you should see a page displayed like the one captured in this screenshot.

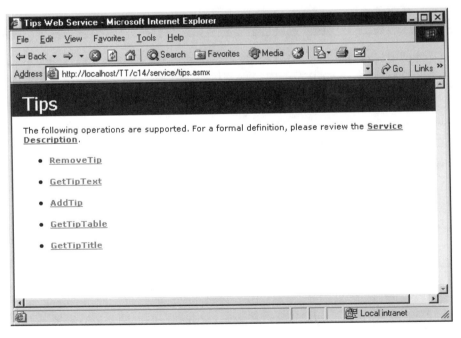

Displayed on the page are the names of all the methods that you have defined in your Web service. Each is displayed as a link. When you click on one of those links, you are taken to a page like the one displayed in this screenshot.

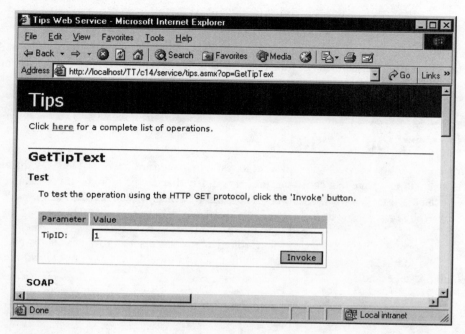

Here, the GetTipText link was selected. This page displays the name of that method along with a text box where you can enter a value for the parameter. If the method requires more than one parameter, you would see additional text boxes on this page.

This page allows you to test the method. Once you enter the parameter(s), you can click the Invoke button. That button calls the method in the Web service and passes to it the parameters you entered.

If the method has an error in it, you will see an error message. Otherwise, you will see the return value from the procedure like the one displayed in this screenshot.

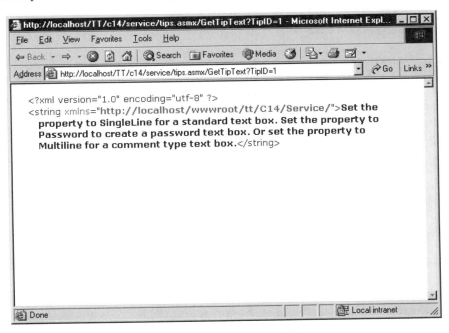

Notice that the data returned from the method call is in the form of XML tags. Here, the text from one of the tips requested from the database through the Web service is displayed.

Creating a Class File for a Web Service

When you create an ASP.NET page that uses a Web service, your page is the consumer of that Web service. Before you can consume a Web service on your ASP.NET page, you need to create a class file based on the Web service. This technique shows you how to do that.

USE IT You create a class file for your Web service by using the WSDL utility program. To use that tool, open a command prompt window and change to the folder where you will place your ASP.NET page that will consume the Web service.

Then, enter a command like this one into the command prompt window:

```
C:\Inetpub\wwwroot\TT\C14\consumer>Wsdl.exe
    /language:VB http://localhost/TT/C1
    /service/Tips.asmx?WSDL
```

Note that you must enter the line as a single line within the command prompt. When you call the WSDL utility, you pass to it the name of the programming language used in the Web service. Also, you pass to it the address of the Web service. Once you do that, you should see a .vb file in the folder where you ran this command. The file will have the same name as the Web service, just a different file extension.

▶ *QUICK TIP*

You may find that the WSDL utility is not part of the command path. If that is the case, search for the file and then copy and paste it into the folder that you are trying to use it from.

Compiling a Web Service

Once you have created a class file based on the Web service file from the location of the consuming ASP.NET page, you need to compile that class file and create a DLL. This technique shows you how to do that.

USE IT   The first step in compiling a Web service is to create a folder called "bin" in the folder where you have the ASP.NET pages that will use the Web service. After that, you need to compile the Web service into a DLL using the Visual Basic Compiler command line tool.

To use that tool, open a command prompt window and move to the folder where you have your ASP.NET pages that will use the Web service. Then run a command like this one:

```
C:\Inetpub\wwwroot\TT\C14\consumer>vbc
    /out:bin/Tips.dll /t:library
    /r:System.XML.dll,System.Web.Services.dll,System.dll
    Tips.vb
```

Note that you must enter this line as a single line in the command prompt window. In that command, you specify where you would like the DLL placed and what it is to be called:

```
/out:bin/Tips.dll
```

You also need to specify the name of the class that the compiler should compile:

```
Tips.vb
```

Once you perform this task, you should see the newly created DLL in the bin sub-folder of the current folder.

> ### QUICK TIP
>
> *You may find that the VBC utility is not part of the command path. If that is the case, search for the file and then copy and paste it into the folder that you are trying to use it from.*

Consuming a Web Service on an ASP.NET Page

Once you have compiled a Web service, you can start using it on your ASP.NET pages. This technique shows you how to do that.

USE IT   To be able to instantiate your Web service from your ASP.NET pages, the compiler needs to know where the DLL file is for the Web service. One of the places it looks is in the bin sub-folder of the current ASP.NET page. That is, if the page is in an ASP.NET application.

Therefore, after compiling the DLL into the bin folder, you need to open IIS and browse to the folder containing the ASP.NET pages that will consume the Web service. Then, right-click on the folder and select Properties. On the Directory tab of the Properties dialog, click the Create button. Apply your changes and you have created an ASP.NET application.

You can now instantiate your Web service class on your ASP.NET pages. The page created that shows you how to do that calls the Web service so that it returns an HTML table with the tips. Here is the code on that page:

```
Sub Page_Load(ByVal Sender as Object, ByVal E as EventArgs)
    Dim MyTips as New Tips()
    TempReturn = MyTips.GetTipTable("./tip.aspx", "TipID")
End Sub
```

The Web service class is instantiated like any other built-in class. Once instantiated, you can use its methods. Here, the GetTipTable method is called with two parameters passed into it.

CHAPTER 15

Mobile Internet Toolkit

TIPS IN THIS CHAPTER

443

O ne of the most interesting aspects of ASP.NET development that can be achieved is the creation of pages that are targeted for mobile devices. These devices include things like mobile phones, palm tops, and PDAs. You develop Mobile ASP.NET pages using the Mobile Internet Toolkit. This chapter presents tips and techniques for getting and using that toolkit as well as getting and using emulators.

As you are reviewing these tips and techniques and as you begin to design your Mobile ASP.NET pages, always be cognizant of the audience that you are designing for. The visitor connecting to your Mobile ASP.NET page is likely connecting through a slow connection that is displayed on a small screen and is difficult to enter data into. So anything you can do to reduce the size of the page, the elements on the page, and the input required for navigation will be most appreciated by your visitor.

Getting the Mobile Internet Toolkit

The Mobile Internet Toolkit contains the files you need on your server so that you can define the controls that it exposes. The Mobile Internet Toolkit is not a standard part of the .NET installation. Therefore, you have to download it from Microsoft. This tip tells you how to do that.

 USE IT As of the time of this writing, Microsoft has available two versions of the Mobile Internet Toolkit for a free download. One of the versions of the toolkit is intended to be installed on a server that has the release candidate version of .NET installed. The other version of the toolkit is to be installed on servers with the actual .NET product release. You can no longer download from Microsoft a version of the Mobile Internet Toolkit that can be installed on any other .NET release.

To download either of these toolkits, go to **http://msdn.microsoft.com**. From there select the link for Downloads followed by Developer Downloads. Then scroll down the list on the left and expand the Software Development Kits item followed by the Microsoft Mobile Internet Toolkit item. There you should see the two versions of the Mobile Internet Toolkit mentioned above.

If you do not see the items listed there then they likely have been moved. You should be able to find the toolkit by entering **Mobile Internet Toolkit** into the search text box.

Once you find the toolkit, download it to your server. Then simply run the downloaded EXE file and you should be able to instantiate controls in that toolkit.

Getting the Microsoft Mobile Explorer

Once you start to create your Mobile ASP.NET pages, you will want to be able to see how they look on mobile devices. One of the ways you can do that is through a mobile emulator. A mobile emulator allows you to run a mobile device like a mobile phone from your desktop.

This allows you to see what your pages look like and how they function without having to use a real mobile device. Microsoft provides such an emulator through the Microsoft Mobile Explorer. This version of the explorer emulates three different mobile phone types. This tip shows you how you can find the Microsoft Mobile Explorer.

USE IT   At the time of this writing, the Microsoft Mobile Explorer was available as a free download from Microsoft. To download this tool, go to **http://msdn.microsoft.com**. From the MSDN site select the Downloads link. Then in the list on the left side of the page, expand Windows Development | Mobility. Under Mobility you should see the Microsoft Mobile Explorer listed.

In the likely event that Microsoft moves this tool to another location, you should be able to find it by performing a search on this download page. Just enter **Mobile Explorer** into the search text box.

Once you have downloaded the tool install it on the computer that you wish to load your Mobile pages from.

▶ | **QUICK TIP**

Many companies that manufacture mobile devices produce and make available their own emulators. You can typically find these on their Web sites. For example, Motorola has a site for developers here:
http://developers.motorola.com
And Ericsson allows you to open an emulator right through a browser window here:
http://www.ericsson.com/mobileinternet/wapsimulator/index.shtml

Using the Microsoft Mobile Explorer

The Microsoft Mobile Explorer contains three different mobile phones that you can emulate. The tool also allows you to browse to any Web address. This tip shows you how to perform this functionality within the Microsoft Mobile Explorer.

USE IT   Once you install the Microsoft Mobile Explorer you can open it through the link to the program by selecting Start | Programs on your computer. When you first open the tool you will see two windows. One window displays the emulating cell phone and the other window is called the Output window. This window is useful when you are trying to diagnose a problem on your page. It lists all page and object requests and lists the status of these calls.

The emulator can display one of three cell phone types. You change the current emulation type by selecting one of the three items listed in the Devices menu, which is located under the View menu.

The XP and Large devices display a mobile phone that has 128 × 160-pixel definition. This definition can be found in many mobile phones. The other device that you can select, Small, emulates a Mobile phone with a display of 100 × 60 pixels. Such a small viewing service can be very difficult for visitors to navigate through.

This screenshot shows you what the Large emulator looks like:

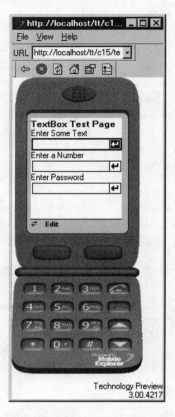

To view one of your Mobile ASP.NET pages, you simply need to enter the address to the page in the URL box.

Navigating within a page is a little different than in a standard browser. Notice the word "Edit" within the output of the page. Whenever you see text in this bottom row of the emulated output, you need to click on the phone's black button under that text to take that action.

So if you wanted to enter text into the current text box, you would need to click the button under the word "Edit." You would then be taken to a page for text input. To enter text through the emulator, you just type it directly from your keyboard.

Many of your Mobile pages will contain more than one element. Therefore, you will need to be able to tab or navigate through the items. That is what the up and down arrows are for on the keypad of the emulated phone. Just click the down arrow to be taken to the next item or the up arrow to scroll to the previous item on the page.

Creating Mobile ASP.NET Pages

To create a Mobile ASP.NET page, you need to include certain tags so that your page inherits the basic Mobile ASP.NET page definition and can define mobile controls. This technique shows you how to do that.

USE IT   On each of your Mobile ASP.NET pages you need to include a page directive like this one:

```
<%@ page
    language="VB"
    inherits="System.Web.UI.MobileControls.MobilePage"
%>
```

The Language parameter is typical of most of your ASP.NET pages. It indicates the language that the code on your page will be written in. The Inherits parameter indicates the page name of the library on which this page is based. This means that the page isn't based on a normal ASP.NET page. Instead, it inherits the MobilePage class.

You also need to include this Register tag on each of your Mobile ASP.NET pages:

```
<%@ register
    tagprefix="mobile"
    namespace="System.Web.UI.MobileControls"
    assembly="System.Web.Mobile"
%>
```

The Namespace and Assembly parameters refer to the name of the library that exposes the Mobile controls that you want to define on your Mobile ASP.NET page. You can set the TagPrefix property to whatever standard variable name you like. It is used when you define a control on your page to indicate that the control is defined in this library.

Once you define these two tags, you can begin defining Mobile controls on your page. On a standard ASP.NET page you define your controls within a Form tag. On a Mobile ASP.NET page you define your controls within a Mobile form:

```
<mobile:form
    id="Test"
    runat="server"
>
```

Notice that the text you specified in the TagPrefix property is used in the first line of the control's definition. Within the Mobile form you would define your other Mobile controls like this Label control:

```
<mobile:label
    runat="server"
    id="lblTitle"
```

```
    stylereference="title"
    text="TextBox Test Page"
/>
```

and after that you define the controls you need to close the Mobile form tag:

```
</mobile:form>
```

Working with Mobile Forms

On a standard ASP.NET page you can include at most one form. That usually works fine since your display area allows you to define numerous controls. But on a Mobile ASP.NET page the display area is much smaller. Thus, if you needed visitors to supply you with six input values, you will likely need to display these items across more than one view of the page.

You could do this by displaying multiple pages to visitors and between each page call you would store the values entered on each page. But Mobile ASP.NET pages can define more than one form. Each form is defined within the same page so it is easy to programmatically refer to all the controls. But you can display each form one at a time and let visitors navigate through the forms as they would through a wizard. This technique shows you how to do that.

USE IT The sample Mobile ASP.NET page presented with this technique defines two forms within the page. Visitors navigate to each form through Mobile Link controls.

The first form has this definition:

```
<mobile:form
    id="FirstPage"
    runat="server">
    <mobile:label
        runat="server"
        id="lbl1"
        Text="The text on the first page."
    />
    <mobile:link
        runat="server"
        id="lnkNext"
        text="View Next Page."
        navigateurl="#SecondPage"
    />
</mobile:form>
```

First notice that the form is given a name. You must give the form a name so that you can refer to it in a Mobile Link control. Within the form a Mobile Label control is defined that simply displays sample text. After that, a Mobile Link control is defined. Notice the value in the NavigateURL property. This is the name of the other form on the page concatenated with the "#" character. Therefore, when visitors click on this link, they are taken to the second form on this page.

That form has this definition:

```
<mobile:form
    id="SecondPage"
    runat="server">
    <mobile:label
        runat="server"
        id="lbl2"
        Text="The text on the second page."
    />
    <mobile:link
        runat="server"
        id="lnkPrev"
        text="View Previous Page."
        navigateurl="#FirstPage"
    />
</mobile:form>
```

Notice the name of this second form set through the ID property. This name matches the name placed in the Mobile Link control defined on the first form. Also notice that this form has a Link control. This control has the name of the first form in the NavigateURL property. Therefore, when visitors select this link they are taken back to the first form on the page.

Within these forms you would likely define other controls such as Mobile TextBox controls and a Command control. Then in your code you could refer to all the controls defined on all the forms on the Mobile page.

Referencing a Mobile Form in Code

You can define many different forms on your Mobile ASP.NET page. You often do this to break up the data entry required by the visitor. But you can also use multiple forms on a Mobile page to control the output displayed to visitors based on their choice. This technique shows you how to do that.

USE IT The Mobile ASP.NET page that demonstrates this technique asks visitors to answer a basic math question. If their answer is correct, they will see one form. And if they enter an incorrect answer, visitors will see another form.

The first Mobile form has this definition:

```
<mobile:form
    id="QuestionPage"
    runat="server">
    <mobile:label
```

```
            runat="server"
            id="lbl1"
            Text="What is 5 x 7?"
        />
        <mobile:textbox
            runat="server"
            id="txtAnswer"
        />
        <mobile:Command
            runat="server"
            id="cmdOK"
            OnClick="OK_OnSubmit"
            Text="OK"
        />
</mobile:form>
```

The form asks visitors a simple math question through a Mobile Label control. The visitors enter their answer in the Mobile TextBox control before clicking the button.

The second form has this definition:

```
<mobile:form
    id="CorrectForm"
    runat="server">
    <mobile:label
        runat="server"
        id="lbl2"
        Text="You supplied the correct answer!"
    />
</mobile:form>
```

This form will only be displayed when a correct answer is placed into the Mobile TextBox control.

The third form has this definition:

```
<mobile:form
    id="IncorrectForm"
    runat="server">
    <mobile:label
        runat="server"
        id="lbl3"
        Text="Your answer was not correct."
    />
</mobile:form>
```

This form will only be displayed when visitors enter an incorrect answer.

When visitors click the Mobile Command control the following code block fires:

```
Sub OK_OnSubmit(Sender As Object, E As EventArgs)
    If txtAnswer.Text = 35 Then
        ActiveForm = CorrectForm
    Else
        ActiveForm = IncorrectForm
    End If
End Sub
```

The If block in this procedure tests to see if visitors entered the correct answer. Notice the use of the ActiveForm property. This property can be set to the name of the form that you want displayed to visitors. Therefore, if visitors enter the correct answer the ActiveForm property is set to the name of the correct form. Similarly, if visitors enter an incorrect answer the ActiveForm property is set to the incorrect form.

Creating an AdRotator Schedule File for a Mobile AdRotator Control

If you find that you need to create a Mobile ASP.NET page that includes banner ads, you will likely want to use the Mobile AdRotator control. The Mobile AdRotator control uses a schedule file to determine the different ads that are displayed on your Mobile ASP.NET page. This technique shows you the structure of the Mobile AdRotator Schedule file.

USE IT The Mobile AdRotator Schedule file is created as an XML file. Therefore, it should be saved with an .xml extension. The file needs to have a very specific structure with balancing opening and closing tags.

Here's an example of such a file:

```
<Advertisements>
    <Ad>
        <ImageUrl>./SampleBanner.gif</ImageUrl>
        <NavigateUrl>http://www.google.com</NavigateUrl>
        <AlternateText>Cick me now!</AlternateText>
        <Impressions>700</Impressions>
    </Ad>
    <Ad>
        <ImageUrl>./AnotherSample.gif</ImageUrl>
        <NavigateUrl>http://www.microsoft.com</NavigateUrl>
        <AlternateText>Go to Microsoft Site</AlternateText>
        <Impressions>1</Impressions>
    </Ad>
</Advertisements>
```

The first line in the file needs to be an opening Advertisement tag:

```
<Advertisements>
```

That is followed by a series of Ad tags. For each ad that you want to display through the AdRotator control you need to create an Ad tag:

```
<Ad>
```

One of the properties you can set for each ad is the ImageURL property. This can be set to the location of the image that you want to have displayed through the ad:

```
<ImageUrl>./SampleBanner.gif</ImageUrl>
```

Next, you need to set the NavigateURL property:

```
<NavigateUrl>http://www.google.com</NavigateUrl>
```

This property is set to the location that you want visitors to be sent to when they select the ad.

Next, you need to set the text that you want displayed if the visitors' mobile device doesn't support graphics:

```
<AlternateText>Cick me now!</AlternateText>
```

Since this is much more likely to be the case with an ad on a Mobile device then through a browser, it is important that you set this property to something that provides the name of the site or descriptive text.

You can also include a value for the Impressions property:

```
<Impressions>700</Impressions>
```

This property is set to the frequency that you want this ad to appear compared to other ads defined in the file.

After defining these properties you can close the Ad definition:

```
</Ad>
```

And you can define another ad:

```
<Ad>
    <ImageUrl>./AnotherSample.gif</ImageUrl>
    <NavigateUrl>http://www.microsoft.com</NavigateUrl>
    <AlternateText>Go to Microsoft Site</AlternateText>
    <Impressions>1</Impressions>
</Ad>
```

Notice that this ad has a much lower number for its Impressions property then the other ad. That means that if the page that this Ad file is based on is opened 701 times, the second ad should be displayed approximately once and the first ad will be displayed the rest of the time.

At the end of the ad file you need to provide this closing tag:

```
</Advertisements>
```

Using a Mobile AdRotator Control

Once you have created an Ad file you will want to use that file on a Mobile ASP.NET page. You do this through the Mobile AdRotator control. This technique shows you how to do that.

 The Mobile ASP.NET page created for this technique contains a single Mobile form. On that form a single Mobile AdRotator control is defined. The form has this definition:

```
<mobile:form
    id="FirstPage"
    runat="server">
    <mobile:adrotator
        advertisementfile="AdRotator.xml"
        runat="server"
    />
</mobile:form>
```

Only two properties are set for the Mobile AdRotator control. The first is the AdvertisementFile property. The value in this property points to the location of the XML file that contains the ad definitions. Since no path is specified, the file must be located in the same folder as the Mobile ASP.NET page. You could supply a full path to the ad file if it was in a different location.

The other property that is set for the control is the RunAt property, which is set to Server. Therefore, the server processes the control.

Writing Code That Fires When a Mobile Ad Is Created

If you display banner ads on your Mobile ASP.NET pages you will probably want to have code that runs when an ad is created. Typically, when you display a banner ad you want to record a hit of that banner ad so that you can charge the advertiser for the ad impression. And if you don't want to charge the advertiser you will at least want to supply them with statistics about the number of times an ad was displayed.

To do this you would need code that fires whenever an ad is displayed. This technique shows you how to write code that fires when this happens.

USE IT   The Mobile ASP.NET page presented in this section displays a banner ad. When an ad is created it also displays information about the ad to the visitor through a Mobile Label control. The page contains this Mobile AdRotator control definition:

```
<mobile:adrotator
    id="ar1"
    onadcreated="AdCreated_Event"
    advertisementfile="AdRotator.xml"
    runat="server"
/>
```

Notice the use of the OnAdCreated property. This property is set to the name of the procedure that you want to run when an ad is created. If you supply a value in this property, you must create a procedure with that name in your code or an error will occur.

Also defined on the page is a Mobile Label control:

```
<mobile:label
    runat="server"
    id="lbl1"
/>
```

When an ad is created this procedure runs:

```
Sub AdCreated_Event(ByVal Sender as Object, _
    ByVal E as AdCreatedEventArgs)
    lbl1.Text = "Here is information on the ad " _
        & "currently being displayed: " _
        & " Alternate Text: " & E.AlternateText _
        & ", Image URL: " & E.ImageURL _
        & ", Navigate URL: " & E.NavigateURL
End Sub
```

Notice the parameters in the procedure's definition. When you create this procedure you must include these parameters. The second parameter, AdCreatedEventArgs, contains property that you can query to determine information about the ad being displayed.

In this case, those properties are used to display back to the visitor information on the ad being displayed. But you could modify this code so that the name of the image for the ad was added as a record to a database table to record a hit. That way, you could query that table to determine the number of times each ad had been displayed.

Creating a Basic Mobile Calendar Control

You may find that you need to allow the visitor to enter a date on one of your Mobile ASP.NET pages. You could do this through a Mobile TextBox control. But you could also supply the visitor with a Mobile Calendar control for selecting dates. Using this control makes it easier for the visitor to find a date on a Calendar instead of having to type in a date. This tip shows you how to define a basic Mobile Calendar control.

USE IT   This simple Mobile ASP.NET page displays a single Mobile Calendar control to the visitor. That control has this definition:

```
<mobile:calendar
    id="cal1"
    runat="server"
/>
```

The control is defined first with the name of the tag prefix, in this case Mobile. That is followed by a colon and the name of the control, in this case Calendar. You can then give the control a name through the ID property. You also need to indicate that the server should process the control by setting the RunAt property, as is done here.

When this page is loaded in a Mobile device, visitors may see a standard calendar, if their mobile device can render it. But more typically, visitors will see the word "Calendar." When visitors select that word they will see the page displayed in this screenshot.

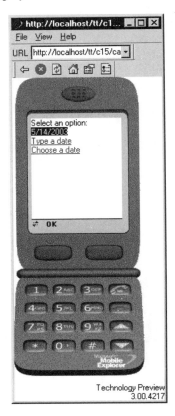

Visitors have three options. First they can simply select the current active date. That is what is displayed on the second line of the output in the mobile device. This date is initially set to the current date. But after visitors select a date, it is set to whatever date they selected.

The second option visitors have is to type in a date. If they select this option, they are presented with a Mobile TextBox control where they can enter a date directly.

Visitors can also select the "Choose a Date" option. When they select this option they are allowed to drill down to a date. First they see a month/year combination. When they select a month/year, they are presented with a list of weeks in that month/year. Once they select a week, they are presented with all the dates in that week. Visitors can then select one of those dates. The date selected becomes the current active date.

Setting and Retrieving the Selected Date in a Mobile Calendar Control

If you add a Mobile Calendar control to your Mobile ASP.NET page, you will want to read and write the selected date. This technique shows you how to do that.

USE IT This technique displays a Mobile Calendar control to visitors. When visitors first open the page, the selected date in the Mobile Calendar control is set to a year in the future. After they select a date, that date is echoed back to them through a Mobile Label control.

The Mobile Calendar control has this definition:

```
<mobile:calendar
    id="Cal1"
    runat="server"
    onselectionchanged="calSelectChange"
/>
```

Notice the use of the OnSelectionChanged property. This property is set to the name of the procedure that you want to run when visitors change the selected date in the calendar control.

Also defined on the page is this Mobile Label control:

```
<mobile:label
    id="lbl1"
    runat="server"
/>
```

When the page first loads, this code runs:

```
Sub Page_Load(ByVal Sender as Object, ByVal E as EventArgs)
    If Not IsPostBack Then
        Cal1.SelectedDate = DateAdd( _
            Microsoft.VisualBasic.DateInterval.Year, _
```

```
                1, Today())
            Cal1.VisibleDate = DateAdd( _
                Microsoft.VisualBasic.DateInterval.Year, _
                1, Today())
        End If
End Sub
```

Since the IsPostBack property is checked , the code in this procedure will only fire when the page first loads. Notice the use of the SelectedDate and the VisibleDate properties of the Mobile Calendar control. Both are set to one year in the future.

The SelectedDate property is used to set the date that has been selected in the Mobile Calendar control. The VisibleDate property also needs to be set, since this is the value that visitors see as the selected date when the calendar first loads.

This procedure runs when visitors select a date in the Mobile Calendar control:

```
Sub calSelectChange(ByVal Sender as Object, _
    ByVal E as EventArgs)
    lbl1.Text = "You selected " _
        & Cal1.SelectedDate
End Sub
```

The text in the Mobile Label control is set to the date visitors select through the Calendar control.

Allowing Selection of Multiple Dates Through the Mobile Calendar Control

The Mobile Calendar control can be used to select a range of dates such as a whole week or a whole month. This would be useful in a situation where visitors need to select a date range for a report. This tip shows you how to use the Mobile Calendar control to allow visitors to select a date range.

USE IT   The page defined for this tip displays a Mobile Calendar control to visitors. The control allows the input of a single date, a full week, or a full month. The control has this definition:

```
<mobile:calendar
    id="cal1"
    selectionmode="DayWeekMonth"
    runat="server"
/>
```

Notice the use of the SelectionMode property. This property is used to determine what date range visitors can select in the calendar. Since it is set to DayWeekMonth, visitors can choose a single date, a full week, or a month.

The default for this property is Day, which only allows visitors to select a single date. You can also set this property to DayWeek, which allows the selection of a single date or a full week. The property can also be set to None. In that case, no date selection is allowed.

Retrieving Multiple Dates Selected in the Mobile Calendar Control

If you allow visitors to select a range of dates through a Mobile Calendar control, you need to read that date range. When visitors can only select a single date, you retrieve that date through the SelectedDate property. When they can select a range of dates, you retrieve those dates by iterating through the SelectedDates collection. This technique shows you how to do that.

USE IT   The Mobile ASP.NET page presented for this technique allows visitors to select a single date, a full week, or an entire month. Once they select a date range, each date in that range is displayed back to them, through a Mobile Label control.

The Mobile Calendar control has this definition:

```
<mobile:calendar
    id="Cal1"
    selectionmode="DayWeekMonth"
    onselectionchanged="calSelectChange"
    runat="server"
/>
```

Notice that the SelectionMode property is set to DayWeekMonth. Therefore, visitors can select a single date, a full week, or an entire month. Notice also that the OnSelectionChanged property is set. That means that this procedure fires whenever visitors select a date in the control:

```
Sub calSelectChange(ByVal Sender as Object, _
    ByVal E as EventArgs)
    Dim i as Integer
    lbl1.Text = "You selected:"
    For i = 0 to Cal1.SelectedDates.Count - 1
        lbl1.Text = lbl1.Text & " " _
            & Cal1.SelectedDates(i).ToShortDateString()
    Next
End Sub
```

The procedure iterates through the collection of dates in the SelectedDates collection. Notice that the range of the variable "I" in the For loop will go from 0 to the number of dates in the collection minus 1. Therefore, within the loop, we can refer to each of the dates in the collection.

Creating a Basic PhoneCall Control

Many of your visitors to your Mobile ASP.NET pages will be connecting through a mobile phone. Since they are using such a device, they have built-in phone dialing capabilities. The Mobile PhoneCall control allows you to exploit that capability by allowing visitors to select a link on your Mobile ASP.NET page that allows them to dial a phone number. This would be helpful if you provided an online contact list service or you wanted to allow a customer who was visiting your site to call your company.

 The page created for this technique displays a PhoneCall control that visitors can click on to dial a phone number. That basic PhoneCall control has this definition:

```
<mobile:phonecall
    runat="server"
    id="Call1"
    text="Call Work!"
    phonenumber="(333) 222-2222"
/>
```

The ID property is set to the name of the control. The Text property is set to the text that you want to appear for the link on the Mobile ASP.NET page. The PhoneNumber property is set to the phone number that you want dialed if visitors select the link.

If visitors do select the link, they are presented with the phone number and are asked if they want to dial that phone number. If they choose Yes, the number is dialed. If they choose No, they are returned to the Mobile ASP.NET page.

Providing an Alternate Link Within a PhoneCall Control

The PhoneCall control can be used on your Mobile ASP.NET pages by users connecting through a mobile phone to call phone numbers. But if the visitor is connecting to your page through some other non-phone device the control becomes useless. In that case, you need to supply an alternate link for visitors to be taken to when their device does not support making a phone call. This technique shows you how to do that.

 This Mobile ASP.NET page presents visitors with a PhoneCall control. But if visitors are not using a phone device, they see a link instead of a call dialog. The PhoneCall control has this definition:

```
<mobile:PhoneCall
    runat="server"
    id="Call1"
    text="Google!"
    phonenumber="(222) 222-2222"
```

```
        alternateurl="http://www.google.com"
        alternateformat="Call Search Engine {0}
            with this number: {1}"
/>
```

Notice the use of the AlternateURL property. This property is set to the Internet location that you want visitors to go to if they are not connecting to your page through a mobile phone. Also notice the use of the AlternateFormat property. This is set to the text that visitors see if they are not connecting through a mobile phone device. Note that the "{0}" text will be replaced by the value in the Text property and that the "{1}" text will be replaced with the value in the PhoneNumber property.

So visitors connecting through a phone will see the word "Google." When they click on that word they can call the phone number set in the PhoneNumber property. Visitors connecting through a non-phone device will see the text in the AlternateFormat property. When they select that text they are taken to the page specified in the AlternateURL property.

Creating a Basic Mobile Command Control

If you have Mobile ASP.NET pages that ask visitors to supply you with information, you will often need to include a button for visitors to submit the data that they entered. On a Mobile ASP.NET page, you do that through a Mobile Command control. This tip shows you how to define the Mobile Command control and how to define a procedure that fires when the button is selected.

USE IT The Mobile ASP.NET page presented with this tip contains two forms. The first form prompts visitors for their name. When they select the Command control, they are taken to the second form where their name is echoed back to them through a Mobile Label control.

The first form has this definition:

```
<mobile:form
    id="StartForm"
    runat="server">
    <mobile:label
        runat="server"
        id="lbl1"
        Text="Enter your name:"
    />
    <mobile:textbox
        runat="server"
        id="txtName"
    />
    <mobile:Command
        runat="server"
        id="cmdOK"
        onclick="OK_OnSubmit"
```

```
        text="OK"
    />
</mobile:form>
```

Notice that the ID for the Mobile Command control is set through the ID property. In the Text property you supply the text that you want to appear on the face of the button on the outputted page.

The OnClick property needs to be set to the name of the procedure that you want to run when this button is clicked by the visitor. You must create a procedure with that name or an error will occur.

The second form on the page has this definition:

```
<mobile:form
    id="WelcomeForm"
    runat="server">
    <mobile:label
        runat="server"
        id="lbl2"
    />
</mobile:form>
```

This form contains just a Mobile Label control.

The following procedure fires when the Mobile Command control is selected:

```
Sub OK_OnSubmit(Sender As Object, E As EventArgs)
    ActiveForm = WelcomeForm
    lbl2.Text = "Welcome " & txtName.Text
End Sub
```

Notice that the name of this procedure matches the name of the procedure placed into the OnClick property of the Command control. Within this procedure the second form on the page is set as the active form, which means it is the one that will be displayed. Then the text of the Label control is set to the name visitors enter into the TextBox control.

Creating a Basic Mobile CompareValidator Control

Like ASP.NET pages, Mobile ASP.NET pages contain controls that you can use to validate the data entry visitors make. One of those controls is the Mobile CompareValidator control. The control can be used to compare a value entered in a control against a specified value or against the value in another control. This technique shows you how to use the Mobile CompareValidator control to make a comparison against a specified value.

USE IT The following mobile page prompts visitors for a whole positive number. A Mobile CompareValidator control is used to validate the visitors' input. If the number is valid, visitors see it echoed back to them. If the number is not valid, they see an error message.

```
<mobile:textbox
    runat="server"
    id="txtNumber"
/>
```

This Mobile CompareValidator control makes sure that what visitors enter is a positive whole number:

```
<mobile:comparevalidator
    id="cvCheckNumber"
    controltovalidate="txtNumber"
    valuetocompare=0
    operator="GreaterThan"
    errormessage="You must enter a positive whole number!"
    type="Integer"
    runat="server"
/>
```

The ID property is set to the name of the control. The ControlToValidate property is set to the name of the control that this control validates. The ValueToCompare property, the Type property, and the Operator property are used in tandem to validate the entry. The value entered into the TextBox control must be an integer because of the setting in the Type property. The number must be greater than zero because of the values in the Operator property and the ValueToCompare property, respectively.

The ErrorMessage property is set to the text you want displayed if the rule is violated.

Also defined on this form is a Mobile Command control:

```
<mobile:Command
    runat="server"
    id="cmdOK"
    onclick="OK_OnSubmit"
    text="OK"
/>
```

When that button is selected, the following code runs:

```
Sub OK_OnSubmit(Sender As Object, E As EventArgs)
    If cvCheckNumber.IsValid Then
        ActiveForm = FinishForm
        lbl2.Text = "You entered " & txtNumber.Text
    End If
End Sub
```

In that procedure, you check to see if the data visitors enter into the TextBox control passes validation. If it does, the second form on this page is displayed, simply echoing the number back to the visitors. If the validation fails, visitors will see the error message text specified in the CompareValidator control.

Using a Mobile CompareValidator Control to Compare the Values in Two Mobile TextBox Controls

One way that you can use a Mobile CompareValidator control is to compare a value in one control to see if it is the same as a value in another control. You often need to use this when you are asking visitors to create some kind of an account and you are prompting them for a password. When you prompt for a new password, you typically ask visitors to enter it twice so that they make sure to enter the correct value. This technique shows you how to do that.

USE IT The page presented for this technique displays two Mobile TextBox controls. Visitors must enter the same value in both controls for validation to succeed. The TextBox controls on the page have this definition:

```
<mobile:textbox
    runat="server"
    id="txt1"
/>
<mobile:textbox
    runat="server"
    id="txt2"
/>
```

A Mobile CompareValidator control is used to make sure the values entered into the TextBox controls are the same:

```
<mobile:comparevalidator
    id="cvCheckText"
    controltovalidate="txt1"
    controltocompare="txt2"
    errormessage="ENTER THE SAME TEXT TWICE!!!"
    runat="server"
/>
```

The two controls that are checked are defined through the ControlToValidate and the ControlToCompare properties. If the text in these two controls is not the same, validation fails.

Also defined on this form is a Command control that visitors can select to process their input:

```
<mobile:Command
    runat="server"
    id="cmdOK"
```

```
    OnClick="OK_OnSubmit"
    Text="OK"
/>
```

When that Command control is selected, this code block fires:

```
Sub OK_OnSubmit(Sender As Object, E As EventArgs)
    If Page.IsValid Then
        ActiveForm = FinishForm
        lbl2.Text = "You entered " & txt1.Text
    End If
End Sub
```

Within the procedure you check to see if all the validation controls on the page succeed. If they do, visitors will see a second form that displays their input. Otherwise, they see the message set in the ErrorMessage property of the Mobile CompareValidator control.

Validating a Data Type with a Mobile CompareValidator Control

The Mobile CompareValidator control can be used to compare a value in a TextBox control against the value in another TextBox control or against a value you supply in code. Additionally, you can use the Mobile CompareValidator control to make sure that what visitors type in is of a specific data type. This technique shows you how to do that.

 The page created for this technique prompts visitors to enter a date. A Mobile CompareValidator control is used to make sure that what they enter is a date. The page contains two forms. The first prompts visitors for their input through this TextBox control:

```
<mobile:textbox
    runat="server"
    id="txtDate"
/>
```

A CompareValidator control is used to make sure that what visitors enter is a date:

```
<mobile:comparevalidator
    id="cvCheckDate"
    controltovalidate="txtDate"
    operator="DataTypeCheck"
    type="Date"
    errormessage="You must enter a date!!!"
```

```
        runat="server"
/>
```

The ControlToValidate property is set to the name of the TextBox control. Notice that the Operator property is set to the special value of DataTypeCheck. This means that we are not comparing a value but instead are testing a data type. And the type that we are testing is set through the Type property. Here, it is set to Date. But you can also set this property to String, Integer, Double, or Currency.

Also defined on the first form is a Command control that visitors use to submit the page for processing:

```
<mobile:Command
    runat="server"
    id="cmdOK"
    OnClick="OK_OnSubmit"
    Text="OK"
/>
```

The second form on the page has this definition:

```
<mobile:form
    id="FinishForm"
    runat="server">
    <mobile:label
        runat="server"
        id="lbl2"
    />
</mobile:form>
```

It simply contains a Label control that is used to display the date visitors entered if the validation succeeds. The code that does that fires when the Command control is selected:

```
Sub OK_OnSubmit(Sender As Object, E As EventArgs)
    If cvCheckDate.IsValid Then
        ActiveForm = FinishForm
        lbl2.Text = "You entered " & txtDate.Text
    End If
End Sub
```

▶ **QUICK TIP**

The CompareValidator control does not perform validation if the control being tested is left blank. Therefore, if you want to make sure a value entered by the visitor is of a specific type and that it is not left blank, use a Mobile CompareValidator control with a Mobile RequiredFieldValidator control.

Notice that the code checks to see if the value entered into the TextBox control passes validation. If it does, visitors will see the second form on the page. Otherwise, they see the error message text.

Creating a Basic Mobile Image Control

You can add images to your Mobile pages. But as you develop your Mobile pages you need to always be cognizant of the fact that visitors could be looking at your page through a very small screen size and that the device they are looking through may not even support graphics. Also, the visitors' connection is likely to be much slower than the average desktop user so you need to design your pages with as few bytes as possible.

If you do decide to add images to your Mobile page you can do so through the Mobile Image control. This technique shows you how to do that.

USE IT The following Mobile ASP.NET page displays an image on a Mobile page to visitors through the Mobile Image control. The image is also a link that visitors can select to navigate to a different site.

The Mobile Image control has the following definition:

```
<mobile:Image
    runat="server"
    id="Image1"
    alternatetext="Your device does not
        support graphics!"
    alignment="right"
    navigateurl="http://www.google.com"
    imageurl="color.gif"
/>
```

The name of the control can be set through the ID property. Since some devices that are connecting to your Mobile page may not support graphics, you need to be sure to supply a value for the AlternateText property. This is what visitors will see if their device does not support graphics.

The Alignment property is used to determine the horizontal position of the image on the page. You can set this property to Left, Right, or Center.

You can make the Image control a link by supplying a value for the NavigateURL property. If you do supply a value for this property, visitors are taken to that location when they select the image on the page.

You also need to set the ImageURL property. This property is set to the location of the image file to be displayed through the image control. In this case, no path is specified so the image must be in the same folder as the Mobile ASP.NET page. Alternatively, you can supply a full path to the image if the file is in some other location.

Creating a Basic Mobile Label

One of the most basic controls that you can add to your Mobile ASP.NET page is a Mobile Label control. A Mobile Label control provides a way for you to convey to visitors textual information about the page. This tip shows you how to define Mobile Label controls.

 USE IT The page created for this tip contains three Label controls, but only two of those controls are displayed to visitors. The first Label control has this definition:

```
<mobile:label
    runat="server"
    id="lbl1"
    text="First Label"
    forecolor="Red"
    alignment="right"
    font-name="Arial"
    font-bold="True"
/>
```

You supply the name of the control through the ID property. The text that is displayed in the Label is set through the Text property. You can set the color of the text through the ForeColor property. But remember that many mobile devices don't support color so visitors may not see any color that you add.

You can set the horizontal position of the text on the page through the Alignment property. This property can be set to Left, Right, or Center. You can also set the Font properties for the Label control.

The second Label control on this page has this definition:

```
<mobile:label
    runat="server"
    id="lbl2"
    text="This text will scroll off the screen."
    forecolor="Green"
    alignment="Left"
    font-name="Times New Roman"
    font-italic="true"
    wrapping="NoWrap"
/>
```

Notice that the text in this Label control will appear differently since the style properties are set to different font and color settings. Also notice the Wrapping property. On some devices, this property will determine whether the text wraps to the next line or goes off the edge of the page. If you set the property to NoWrap, the text will not wrap to the next line.

The third Label control has this definition:

```
<mobile:label
    runat="server"
```

```
    id="lbl3"
    text="This text will not be seen."
    visible="false"
/>
```

In this Label control the Visible property is set to False. Therefore, the control will not be displayed to visitors when the page loads.

Using the StyleReference Property with a Mobile Label Control

One of the ways that you can set the style for the text in a Label control is to set the color and font properties for the controls one at a time. But if you have a style that you want to use over and over again for many controls on a Mobile page, you can use the StyleReference property. This technique shows you how to create style tags and use them in Label controls.

USE IT   This Mobile ASP.NET page displays three Label controls. Each uses its own style for its font and color settings. Two of those styles are created through a StyleSheet definition and the third uses a built-in style.

Within the Mobile ASP.NET page, the styles are defined within a StyleSheet tag:

```
<mobile:stylesheet id="ss1" runat="server">
    <Style Font-Size="Large" Font-Name="Arial"
        Font-Bold="true" ForeColor="Green"
        Font-Italic="True"  Name="BigText"/>
    <Style Font-Size="Small" Font-Name="Arial"
        ForeColor="Blue" Name="SmallText" />
</mobile:StyleSheet>
```

A style is made up of property names and values for the color and font-settings. You also give each style a name through the Name property. Once you define these styles you can use the StyleReference property of a Mobile Label control and the text in the control will be displayed according to that style.

The first Mobile Label control has this definition:

```
<mobile:label
    runat="server"
    id="lbl1"
    text="The Title"
    stylereference="title"
/>
```

This control does not use one of the styles defined in the StyleSheet tag. Instead it uses a built-in style called Title. The style is device-specific but will display the text typically in a large bold setting.

The second Label control has this definition:

```
<mobile:label
    runat="server"
    id="lbl2"
    text="Large Text"
    stylereference="BigText"
/>
```

Notice that the StyleReference property is set to one of the styles that was defined in the StyleSheet tag. The third Label references the other style in the StyleSheet tag through the StyleReference property:

```
<mobile:label
    runat="server"
    id="lbl3"
    text="Small Text"
    stylereference="SmallText"
/>
```

Creating a Basic Mobile Link Control

A Mobile Link control provides a way for visitors to select text that takes them to a different page when it is selected. This tip shows you how to define a Link control.

USE IT   The Mobile ASP.NET page presented for this tip displays two links to visitors. Both link them to the same site. The first Mobile Link control has this definition:

```
<mobile:Link
    runat="server"
    id="Link1"
    text="Click Here!"
    navigateurl="http://www.google.com"
/>
```

You place the name of the control into the ID property. The Text property is set to the text that you want to appear on the page for the link. And in the NavigateURL property you place the address of the page that visitors should be taken to if they select the link.

The second Mobile Link control has this definition:

```
<mobile:Link
    runat="server"
    id="Link2"
    text="Or Here!"
    navigateurl="http://www.google.com"
```

```
     font-bold="True"
     font-size="Large"
     alignment="Right"
/>
```

The Link control links visitors to the same site. But this control shows you that you can set font properties for the text displayed in the control. Also you can set the Alignment property, which controls the horizontal position of the link on the page.

Creating a Basic Mobile List Control

The Mobile Internet Toolkit contains a variety of controls that you can use to list information. One of those controls is the Mobile List control. The Mobile List control can be used to display a series of items in a list that can be a bulleted or numbered list. This technique shows you how to define a Mobile List control.

USE IT The page presented for this technique displays a list of colors to visitors through a Mobile List control. The items in the list are defined within the control's definition. The List control has this definition:

```
<mobile:list
    runat="server"
    id="list1"
    decoration="bulleted"
    forecolor="red"
>
```

You set the name of the List control through the ID property. Notice the use of the Decoration property. By default each item is displayed on its own line in the list without any preceding decoration, but you can set this property to Bulleted to have each item start with a bullet or you can set it to Numbered for each item to have a number.

Within the control's definition, four Item controls are added:

```
<item value="Red"/>
<item value="Green"/>
<item value="Purple"/>
<item value="Black"/>
```

The text that is displayed in the List control for the item is set through the Value property. Once you have defined the items in the control, you can close the control's definition:

```
</mobile:list>
```

Adding Items to a Mobile List Control in Code

In addition to defining the items that appear in a Mobile List control within the control's definition, you can also define the items that are to be listed in code. You do this by adding MobileListItem objects to the Items collection of the List control. This technique shows you how to do that.

USE IT   This page defines a Mobile List control without any items. But when the page is loaded, three items are programmatically added to the control.

The Mobile List control has this definition:

```
<mobile:list
    runat="server"
    id="List1"
/>
```

When the page loads, the following code fires since it is in the Page_Load procedure:

```
Sub Page_Load(ByVal Sender as Object, ByVal E as EventArgs)
    Dim MyItem1 as New MobileListItem
    Dim MyItem2 as New MobileListItem
    Dim MyItem3 as New MobileListItem
    MyItem1.Text = "Red"
    MyItem2.Text = "Gold"
    MyItem3.Text = "Orange"
    List1.Items.Add(MyItem1)
    List1.Items.Add(MyItem2)
    List1.Items.Add(MyItem3)
End Sub
```

Notice that three MobileListItem objects are created. Then the text property is set for each of those items. After that, the items are added to the List control one at a time through the Add method of the Items collection.

Removing Items from a Mobile List Control

A Mobile List control contains an Items collection that is made up of all the MobileListItem objects it displays. Once the items have been added to the List control, you can remove those items through the Remove method of the Items collection of the Mobile Label control. This technique shows you how to remove items in code from a List control.

USE IT   The Mobile ASP.NET page created for this technique displays a list of colors through a List control. Visitors can then enter a color that they want removed from the List control through a TextBox control.

The List control has this definition:

```
<mobile:list
    runat="server"
    id="List1"
/>
```

Also defined on the page is a TextBox control in which visitors enter the color they want to remove from the list:

```
<mobile:textbox
    runat="server"
    id="txtItem"
/>
```

Once visitors enter the color they want removed, they select the Command control:

```
<mobile:Command
    runat="server"
    id="cmdOK"
    onclick="OK_OnSubmit"
    text="OK"
/>
```

When they do that, this code block runs:

```
Sub OK_OnSubmit(Sender As Object, E As EventArgs)
    List1.Items.Remove(txtitem.Text)
End Sub
```

The procedure removes an item from the List control by using the Remove method of the Items collection of that control. Passed to that method is the text visitors entered, which is the color that they want to delete from the list.

Using the Mobile List Control to Display a List of Links

You may have a Mobile page that needs to list a series of links. For example, you may have a main menu page that links to other pages at your site. Or maybe you include a Links page on your Mobile site that links to sites with additional information. In these types of situations the Mobile List control may be useful. The List control can be rendered as a series of links, and this technique shows you how to use the Mobile List control in that fashion.

 This Mobile ASP.NET page lists a series of Web sites. The sites are listed as links and are displayed through a List control. That List control has this definition:

```
<mobile:list
    runat="server"
    id="list1"
    decoration="Numbered"
    itemsaslinks="True"
>
    <item
        value="http://www.google.com"
        text="Google"
    />
    <item
        value="http://www.yahoo.com"
        text="Yahoo"
    />
    <item
        value="http://www.microsoft.com"
        text="Microsoft"
    />
</mobile:list>
```

First, notice that the decoration property is used and that it is set to Numbered. That means each item in the list will be numbered in sequential order.

But more importantly, notice the ItemsAsLinks property. By default this property is set to False. But if you set the property to True, the items in a List control are displayed as links.

Take a look at how each item is defined. Values are placed in both the Value property as well as the Text property. When the ItemsAsLinks property is set to True, the Value property for each item is set to the location that visitors should be taken to if they click on the link. The Text property is set to the text that you want to appear for the link.

Binding a Mobile List Control to a Data Source

If you need to display data in a list format through a Mobile List control, you may need that data to come from a database table. For example, maybe you are displaying a list of movies playing at a movie theatre. Or maybe you need to display a list of products that match the visitors' search text. In both of those cases, the data for the List control would need to come from a database.

USE IT   This technique shows you how to bind a Mobile List control to an Access database table. The table contains a list of colors that are displayed through the List control when the control is bound to the database table.

The Mobile List control has this definition:

```
<mobile:list
    runat="server"
```

```
        id="list1"
        datatextfield="ColorName"
/>
```

Notice the use of the DataTextField property. This property is set to the name of the field in the bound table that you want to display in the List control.

The code that binds the List control to the Access table runs when the page loads:

```
Sub Page_Load(ByVal Sender as Object, ByVal E as EventArgs)
    Dim DBConn as OleDbConnection
    Dim DBCommand As OleDbDataAdapter
    Dim DSPageData as New DataSet
    DBConn = New OleDbConnection( _
        "PROVIDER=Microsoft.Jet.OLEDB.4.0;" _
        & "DATA SOURCE=" _
        & Server.MapPath("/tt/C15/C15.mdb;"))
    DBCommand = New OleDbDataAdapter _
        ("Select ColorName " _
        & "From Colors " _
        & "Order By ColorName", DBConn)
    DBCommand.Fill(DSPageData, _
        "Colors")
    List1.DataSource = _
        DSPageData.Tables("Colors").DefaultView
    List1.DataBind()
End Sub
```

Since the List control is bound to a database table, data objects are defined. After that, a connection is made to the database and then the data is retrieved into a table in the DataSet object.

Then the DataSource property of the List control is set to the data retrieved from the database. And finally, the DataBind method is used to bind the List control to that data source.

Determining the Browser Type Using the MobileCapabilities Class

As your Mobile pages become more complex you may need to provide specialized versions of your site based on the browser visitors use to view your site. In other words, if visitor were using one type of browser you would divert them to one portion of you site. And if they were using a different browser, you would send them to another section of your site. This tip shows you how to determine the type of browser that visitors are using.

USE IT   The Mobile ASP.NET page created for this tip contains a single Label control. When the page loads the name of the browser visitors are using is placed into the Label control. That Label control has this definition:

```
<mobile:label
    runat="server"
    id="Label1"
/>
```

When the page loads, the following code block fires:

```
Sub Page_Load(ByVal Sender as Object, ByVal E as EventArgs)
    Dim MyMobCaps as Mobile.MobileCapabilities
    MyMobCaps = Request.Browser
    Label1.Text = "Your browser name is: " _
        & MyMobCaps.Browser
End Sub
```

Within this procedure a MobileCapabilities object is instantiated:

```
Dim MyMobCaps as Mobile.MobileCapabilities
```

That object is set to the capabilities of the visitors' browser:

```
MyMobCaps = Request.Browser
```

The name of the browser is then retrieved through the Browser property of the MobileCapabilities object:

```
Label1.Text = "Your browser name is: " _
    & MyMobCaps.Browser
```

Using the MobileCapabilities Class to Determine Screen Size

When you are working hard to develop your Mobile pages so that they have a nice appearance in a Mobile device, you will need to determine the size of visitors' screen. Using that information, you can determine how much text to display on a page or how big to make that text. This technique shows you how to determine visitors' screen size.

USE IT   The page created for this technique displays back to visitors, through a Label control, their screen dimension in pixels. The Label control that displays that information has this definition:

```
<mobile:label
    runat="server"
    id="Label1"
/>
```

When the page loads, the following procedure runs and places the screen size into the Label control:

```
Sub Page_Load(ByVal Sender as Object, ByVal E as EventArgs)
    Dim MyMobCaps as Mobile.MobileCapabilities
    MyMobCaps = Request.Browser
    Label1.Text = "Screen Width: " _
        & MyMobCaps.ScreenPixelsWidth _
        & " Screen Height: " _
        & MyMobCaps.ScreenPixelsHeight
End Sub
```

The ScreenPixelsWidth property of the MobileCapabilities object returns the width of the screen size, and the ScreenPixelsHeight property of the MobileCapabilities object returns the height in pixels of the visitors' device.

Using the MobileCapabilities Class to Determine if the Visitor's Device Supports Color

Many mobile devices support color but many others do not. When you are trying to reduce the output of your page to the visitors' device it is helpful to know this information.

For example, if the visitors' device supports color, it would be OK to send them a color graphic. But if the device does not support color, it would be much more efficient to send a grayscale image. This tip shows you how to determine if the visitors' browser supports color.

USE IT   The following Mobile ASP.NET page checks to see if the visitors' device supports color. If it does, a color image is displayed in an Image control. If it does not, a non-color image is displayed.

The Image control has this definition:

```
<mobile:Image
    runat="server"
    id="Image1"
    AlternateText="No graphics supported!">
</mobile:Image>
```

Notice that no image is defined here. Instead, the image is set when the page loads through this procedure:

```
Sub Page_Load(ByVal Sender as Object, ByVal E as EventArgs)
    Dim MyMobCaps as Mobile.MobileCapabilities
    MyMobCaps = Request.Browser
    If MyMobCaps.IsColor Then
        Image1.ImageURL="color.gif"
    Else
        Image1.ImageURL="nocolor.gif"
    End If
End Sub
```

Here, the IsColor property is used to determine if the visitor's device supports color. If it does, one image is displayed. Otherwise, a different image is displayed.

Determining Device Type Characteristics with the MobileCapabilities Object

You may have visitors who come to your Mobile page who are not even using a Mobile device. If that were the case, you would likely want to send them to a different site that was for non-mobile devices. Also, you may want to determine specific information about the device they're using, such as the name of the device. This information may be helpful in determining how visitors are connecting to your site. The technique presented in this section shows you how to do that.

USE IT The Mobile page created for this technique displays to visitors whether or not they are using a Mobile device and the name and manufacturer of the device. That information is displayed through this Label control:

```
<mobile:label
    runat="server"
    id="Label1"
/>
```

The following procedure returns the information for that label control when the page first loads:

```
Sub Page_Load(ByVal Sender as Object, ByVal E as EventArgs)
    Dim MyMobCaps as Mobile.MobileCapabilities
    MyMobCaps = Request.Browser
    Label1.Text = "Mobile Device?: " _
        & MyMobCaps.IsMobileDevice _
        & " Mobile Device Model: " _
        & MyMobCaps.MobileDeviceModel _
```

```
          & " Mobile Device Manufacturer: " _
          & MyMobCaps.MobileDeviceManufacturer
End Sub
```

Three properties of the MobileCapabilities class are used in this procedure. The first property, IsMobileDevice, returns True if visitors are connecting through a Mobile device.

The second property, MobileDeviceModel, returns the name of the device being used. The third property, MobileDeviceManufacturer, returns the name of the company that created the device.

Creating a Basic Mobile ObjectList Control

One of the very helpful controls included in the Mobile Internet Toolkit is the Mobile ObjectList control. This control provides a way for you to easily display data that can have many fields to it.

The control renders itself with two views. In the first view, visitors see a list of items. When they select one of the items in the list, they are taken to the second view. That view shows all the fields for the item selected. This technique shows you how to create a basic Mobile ObjectList control.

USE IT The page created for this technique displays a list of employees through an ObjectList control. When visitors select one of the employees in the list, they see all the fields for the employee. The data displayed in the ObjectList control comes from an Access database table.

The ObjectList control has this definition:

```
<mobile:objectlist
    runat="server"
    id="ObjectList1"
    backcommandtext="Return to List"
/>
```

The name of the control is set through the ID property. When visitors are viewing the details of a specific record, they will see a link that will return them to the list page. The text for that link is set through the BackCommandText property.

When the page loads, the following code populates the ObjectList control:

```
Sub Page_Load(ByVal Sender as Object, ByVal E as EventArgs)
    Dim DBConn as OleDbConnection
    Dim DBCommand As OleDbDataAdapter
    Dim DSPageData as New DataSet
    DBConn = New OleDbConnection( _
        "PROVIDER=Microsoft.Jet.OLEDB.4.0;" _
        & "DATA SOURCE=" _
        & Server.MapPath("/tt/C15/C15.mdb;"))
    DBCommand = New OleDbDataAdapter _
        ("Select * " _
        & "From Emps " _
```

```
        & "Order By EmpName", DBConn)
    DBCommand.Fill(DSPageData, _
        "Emps")
    ObjectList1.DataSource = _
        DSPageData.Tables("Emps").DefaultView
    ObjectList1.DataBind()
End Sub
```

Since the ObjectList control is bound to an Access database, database objects need to be defined. Once they are defined, you connect to the Access database and retrieve data into the DataSet object:

```
DBCommand.Fill(DSPageData, _
    "Emps")
```

The ObjectList control is then bound to that DataSet object:

```
ObjectList1.DataSource = _
    DSPageData.Tables("Emps").DefaultView
ObjectList1.DataBind()
```

When visitors first open the page, they see the following screenshot.

Notice that visitors see a list of names. The field that is used on this first page of the ObjectList control is the first field in the DataSet object that it is bound to.

Notice that all the employee names are links. If visitors select one of those links they will see all the employee's information as is displayed in this screenshot.

Notice the link text at the bottom of this page. This is the text that was set through the BackCommandText property. When visitors select that link, they are returned to the first page of the control.

Creating Your Own Fields Within a Mobile ObjectList Control

By default the ObjectList control will use all the fields that are in the DataSet Table that it is bound to. It will also display the name of the field for the title within the ObjectList control. You can override this behavior by defining your own fields within the Object list control. This technique shows you how to do that.

USE IT   The Mobile ASP.NET page created for this technique displays a list of employees with their information. But instead of letting the ObjectList control automatically generate the columns, they are defined within the control.

The ObjectList control has this definition:

```
<mobile:objectlist
    runat="server"
    id="ObjectList1"
    autogeneratefields="False"
    backcommandtext="Return to List"
>
    <field name="EmpName" datafield="EmpName" title="Name"/>
    <field name="EmpPhone" datafield="EmpPhone" title="Phone"/>
    <field name="EmpEmail" datafield="EmpEmail" title="Email"/>
</mobile:objectlist>
```

Notice that the AutoGenerateFields property is set to False. This is how you tell the compiler not to generate the fields within the control.

Then in the middle of the control's definition, three Field controls are defined. This is how you specify the fields that you want included in the list. The DataField property for each field is set to the name of the field in the database that you want to bind to. The Title property is set to the text that you want to precede the field value with.

When the page loads, the ObjectList control is populated through this code:

```
Sub Page_Load(ByVal Sender as Object, ByVal E as EventArgs)
    Dim DBConn as OleDbConnection
    Dim DBCommand As OleDbDataAdapter
    Dim DSPageData as New DataSet
    DBConn = New OleDbConnection( _
        "PROVIDER=Microsoft.Jet.OLEDB.4.0;" _
        & "DATA SOURCE=" _
        & Server.MapPath("/tt/C15/C15.mdb;"))
    DBCommand = New OleDbDataAdapter _
        ("Select * " _
        & "From Emps " _
        & "Order By EmpName", DBConn)
    DBCommand.Fill(DSPageData, _
        "Emps")
    ObjectList1.DataSource = _
        DSPageData.Tables("Emps").DefaultView
    ObjectList1.DataBind()
End Sub
```

The procedure defines data objects, connects to the access database, and retrieves the employee information. The ObjectList control is then bound to that data.

Adding a Mobile Panel Control to a Mobile Form

A Mobile Panel control provides a mechanism for you to group controls together. This often helps to make your pages easier to read, to provide for functionality flow, or to define style characteristics for a group of controls. This technique shows you how to define a basic Panel control on a Mobile page.

USE IT   The following page displays raw text and HTML tags, as well as a Label control, through a Panel control. Since these items are defined within a Panel control, the items will inherit the style properties of the Panel control.

The Panel control has this definition:

```
<mobile:panel
    id="Pan1"
    runat="server"
    forecolor="Red"
    font-name="Arial"
    alignment="right"
>
```

The name of the control can be set through the ID property. You can use the ForeColor property to determine the color of the text for the items defined within the Panel control. The Panel control also has Font properties that will be used by subordinate controls. The Alignment property determines the horizontal position of the controls within the Panel control. You can set this property to Left, Right, or Center.

Within the opening and closing tags of the Panel control, the items are defined:

```
Raw text
    <BR>
    <B>More raw text</B>
    <BR>
    <mobile:label
        id="lbl1"
        runat="server"
        text="Hello"
    />
```

Notice that raw text can be placed within a Panel control as well as basic HTML tags and other Mobile controls. All of these items will inherit the style properties of the Panel control.

After defining the controls that the Panel contains, you need to supply a closing tag for the Panel control:

```
</mobile:panel>
```

Adding Controls to a Mobile Panel Control Through Code

You may find that you need to create a Mobile page, but you don't know ahead of time the exact number of TextBox controls that you need to display. For example, maybe you have a dynamic survey page that prompts visitors for questions, but the number of questions as well as the content for the questions comes from a database and you don't know ahead of time how many questions will be on the survey. Therefore, you need code that adds controls to a page when the page loads. You can add controls in this fashion through a Mobile Panel control. This technique shows you how to do that.

USE IT This page defines a Panel control without any subordinate controls. Instead, when the page loads, controls are added to the Panel control through the Controls collection of the Panel control.

The Panel control has this basic definition:

```
<mobile:panel
    id="Pan1"
    runat="server"
/>
```

Then when the page loads, the following procedure adds the controls to that Panel control:

```
Sub Page_Load(ByVal Sender as Object, ByVal E as EventArgs)
    Dim MyLabel = New System.Web.UI.MobileControls.Label
    Dim MyTB = New System.Web.UI.MobileControls.TextBox
    MyLabel.ID = "lbl1"
    MyLabel.Text = "The first label."
    Pan1.Controls.Add(MyLabel)
    MyTB.ID = "txt1"
    MyTB.Text = "Enter some text!"
    Pan1.Controls.Add(MyTB)
End Sub
```

Notice that two controls are defined. One is a Mobile Label control and the other is a Mobile TextBox control. The properties for each control are set before they are added to the Panel control. The controls are added to the Panel control using the Add method of the Controls collection of the Panel control.

Using a Mobile Panel Control as a Wizard Interface

When you have a complex Mobile form that asks visitors for a variety of information, you need to break that information up so that it can be displayed a page at a time. You need a wizard interface where you display a few fields at a time before proceeding.

One of the ways that you can do that is through the Mobile Panel control. The Mobile Panel control makes it easy for you to show only parts of a Mobile page based on the functionality of the page. This technique shows you how to do that.

USE IT The Mobile ASP.NET page created for this technique defines three Panel controls. One of the Panel controls prompts visitors to answer a question. Then when they submit an answer, they see one of two other Panels based on whether or not they answered the question correctly. The first Panel control has this definition:

```
<mobile:panel
    id="PanQuestion"
    runat="server"
    visible="True"
>
    What is 7 x 7?
    <mobile:textbox
        id="txtAnswer"
        runat="server"
    />
    <mobile:Command
        runat="server"
        id="cmdOK"
        OnClick="OK_OnSubmit"
        Text="OK"
    />
</mobile:panel>
```

Within the Panel control visitors are presented with a simple math question, a TextBox control to enter their answer, and a Command control so that they can submit their response.
The second Panel control is only displayed if visitors answer the question correctly:

```
<mobile:panel
    id="PanCorrect"
    runat="server"
    visible="False"
>
    You are correct!
</mobile:panel>
```

and the third Panel control is displayed only if visitors answer the question incorrectly:

```
<mobile:panel
    id="PanWrong"
    runat="server"
    visible="False"
```

```
>
    You are wrong!
</mobile:panel>
```

When visitors submit their answer to the question, this code block fires:

```
Sub OK_OnSubmit(Sender As Object, E As EventArgs)
    PanQuestion.Visible = False
    If txtAnswer.Text = 49 Then
        PanCorrect.Visible = True
    Else
        PanWrong.Visible = True
    End If
End Sub
```

The procedure first hides the Question Panel control. Then if visitors entered a correct answer, the Correct Panel control is displayed. Otherwise, visitors will see the Incorrect Panel control.

Using the Mobile RangeValidator Control

Frequently, you need to verify that the data entered by visitors into a field falls into an expected range. For example, if visitors can enter a quantity of product to order, you would want to make sure that the number entered was at least 1 and that it wasn't above an expected value. Or if visitors were entering the number of their exemptions for a tax form, you would also want to limit this range. To provide that type of data validity check, you can use the Mobile RangeValidator control.

USE IT   The page created for this technique prompts visitors to enter a number and a date. RangeValidator controls are used to make sure that the data entered falls within the specified range.

Visitors are first asked to enter a number:

```
<mobile:label
    runat="server"
    id="lbl1"
    Text="Enter a number from 1 to 5:"
/>
<mobile:textbox
    runat="server"
    id="txtNumber"
/>
<mobile:rangevalidator
    id="rngNumber"
    controltovalidate="txtNumber"
    type="Integer"
```

```
    minimumvalue=1
    maximumvalue=5
    runat="server"
    errormessage="Number not in correct range!!!"
/>
```

The number is entered through a TextBox control but is validated through the RangeValidator control. The name of the RangeValidator control is set through the ID property. You place the name of the control that this validation control validates into the ControlToValidate property. The Type property is set to the data type of the value being tested. And the MinimumValue and MaximumValue properties are set to the range of the control. Finally, the ErrorMessage property is set to the text that visitors see if they violate the error message.

Visitors then enter a date:

```
<mobile:textbox
    runat="server"
    id="txtDate"
/>
<mobile:rangevalidator
    id="rngDate"
    controltovalidate="txtDate"
    type="Date"
    minimumvalue="1/1/2005"
    maximumvalue="12/31/2005"
    runat="server"
    errormessage="Date not in correct range!!!"
/>
<mobile:Command
    runat="server"
    id="cmdOK"
    OnClick="OK_OnSubmit"
    Text="OK"
/>
```

Again, a RangeValidator control is used to verify that the date falls into the specified range. That range is set through the MinimumValue and MaximumValue properties of the RangeValidator control. Notice that the Type property is set to Date. Therefore, the control validates that visitors enter a date.

▶ ### QUICK TIP

The RangeValidator control does not perform its validity check if visitors leave the field blank. To make sure visitors enter a value that falls into a range, use a RangeValidator control with a RequiredFieldValidator control.

When visitors submit the page for processing, the following code block fires:

```
Sub OK_OnSubmit(Sender As Object, E As EventArgs)
    If Page.IsValid Then
        ActiveForm = FinishForm
        lbl2.Text = "You entered " & txtNumber.Text _
            & " and " & txtDate.Text
    End If
End Sub
```

In the procedure you make sure that the date entered passes the validity checks. If it does, visitors see a second form on this Mobile page that echoes their entries through a Label control.

Using a Mobile RequiredFieldValidator Control

Many of your pages will include TextBox controls in which visitors must enter a value before continuing. For example, if you have a Login page, visitors would have to enter a name and their password. The Mobile RequiredFieldValidator control provides an easy way to make sure that visitors enter a value into a TextBox control. This technique shows you how to do that.

USE IT The page created for this technique displays a TextBox control to visitors and asks them to enter any value. A RequiredFieldValidator control is used to make sure that they do enter a value.

The TextBox control on this page has this definition:

```
<mobile:textbox
    runat="server"
    id="txt1"
/>
```

This RequiredFieldValidator control makes sure visitors enter something into the control:

```
<mobile:requiredfieldvalidator
    id="rfv1"
    controltovalidate="txt1"
    runat="server"
    errormessage="This field is required!!!"
/>
```

Notice that the ControlToValidate property is set to the name of the TextBox control. Also notice that the ErrorMessage property is set to the text that will appear if visitors do not enter a value into the field.

The form also contains a Command control:

```
<mobile:Command
    runat="server"
```

```
        id="cmdOK"
        OnClick="OK_OnSubmit"
        Text="OK"
/>
```

When visitors click that control, the following code block fires:

```
Sub OK_OnSubmit(Sender As Object, E As EventArgs)
    If Page.IsValid Then
        ActiveForm = FinishForm
        lbl2.Text = "You entered " & txt1.Text
    End If
End Sub
```

In this procedure, you check to see if the validation succeeded. If it did, a second form on the page shows visitors the entry that they made.

Checking Against an Initial Value with a Mobile RequiredFieldValidator Control

In some circumstances, you may need visitors to enter a value into a control that is different than the value already in the control. For example, you may have a TextBox control that initially contains the text, "Enter your name." Visitors would then need to change that text to their own name. You can use the RequiredFieldValidator control to make sure that visitors do change this text and this technique shows you how to do that.

USE IT   This page prompts visitors for their name directly though this TextBox control:

```
<mobile:textbox
    runat="server"
    id="txt1"
    text="Enter Your Name"
/>
```

Notice that the TextBox control has an initial value. Visitors are required to change that value because of this RequiredFieldValidator control:

```
<mobile:requiredfieldvalidator
    id="rfv1"
    controltovalidate="txt1"
    runat="server"
    initialvalue="Enter Your Name"
```

```
        errormessage="This field is required!!!"
/>
```

Notice the use of the InitialValue property. It is set to the same text that is initially placed into the TextBox control. That means visitors must change that value or they will see the error message when the page is tested.

▶ | **QUICK TIP**
_____

When you use the RequiredFieldValidator control with the InitialValue property set, the control does not check to see if visitors leave the field blank. To make sure that they do not leave the control blank and that they change the control from an initial value, use two RequiredFieldValidator controls.

Creating a DropDownList Mobile SelectionList Control

The Mobile Internet Toolkit contains a variety of controls that you can use to list information. One of the most versatile is the Mobile SelectionList control. It can display a list of items for selection in different formats. One of those formats is as a DropDownList control. This technique shows you how to define a Mobile SelectionList control as a DropDownList.

USE IT   This page lists different departments through a SelectionList control. The items are displayed in a drop-down list and visitors can select one of the items.
   The SelectionList control has this definition:

```
<mobile:selectionlist
    runat="server"
    id="sl1"
    selecttype="DropDown"
>
    <item text="Sales"/>
    <item text="Marketing"/>
    <item text="MIS"/>
</mobile:selectionlist>
```

The name of a SelectionList control is set through the ID property. Notice that the SelectType property is set to DropDown. That means that the control will be rendered as a DropDownList control. Between the opening and closing tags of the control, you define the items that you want to appear in the list. Then, once you have completed the definition of the items, you supply the closing tag for the SelectionList control.

Creating a ListBox Mobile SelectionList Control

A ListBox control differs from a DropDownList control in that the list is expanded in a ListBox control. If you wish to render a ListBox control on your Mobile ASP.NET page, you can use a SelectionList control to accomplish that task. This technique shows you how to do that.

USE IT The following page presents visitors with a list of departments. The list is presented in the form of a ListBox through a SelectionList control. That SelectionList control has this definition:

```
<mobile:selectionlist
    runat="server"
    id="sl1"
    selecttype="ListBox"
    rows=5
>
    <item text="Sales"/>
    <item text="Marketing"/>
    <item text="MIS"/>
</mobile:selectionlist>
```

Notice that the SelectType property is set to ListBox. That is how you indicate that you want the items to appear in a list as opposed to a drop-down list. Notice also the use of the Rows property. This property is set to the number of items you want to appear in the list at one time so that visitors will not have to scroll down.

Creating a Radio Mobile SelectionList Control

If you wish to add radio buttons to your Mobile form, you can do so through the Mobile SelectionList control. That control renders each item in its definition as a separate radio button. This tip shows you how to define a SelectionList control as radio buttons.

USE IT The page created for this technique presents a list of departments. Each one is rendered as a radio button through a SelectionList control. That SelectionList control has this definition:

```
<mobile:selectionlist
    runat="server"
    id="sl1"
    selecttype="Radio"
>
    <item selected text="Sales"/>
    <item text="Marketing"/>
    <item text="MIS"/>
</mobile:selectionlist>
```

Notice that the SelectType property is set to Radio. This is how you indicate that you wish to have each item displayed as a radio button. Also notice that the Sales item is marked as Selected. This means that when the page initially loads, the radio button for this item appears checked.

Binding a Mobile SelectionList Control to a Data Source

If you use a Mobile SelectionList control to display a list of items, you will frequently need to have that list populated from a data source. This technique shows you how to do that.

USE IT   The Mobile ASP.NET page created for this technique displays a list of colors to visitors through a SelectionList control. The data comes from an Access table. When visitors select an item, it is echoed back to them through a Label control.

The SelectionList control has this definition:

```
<mobile:selectionlist
    runat="server"
    id="sl1"
    selecttype="DropDown"
    datatextfield="ColorName"
/>
```

Notice that the SelectType property is set to DropDown. Therefore, the items will appear in the list as a drop-down list. The DataTextField property needs to be set to the name of the field that you wish to display in the list.

Once visitors make their selection, they can submit their choice through this Command control:

```
<mobile:Command
    runat="server"
    id="cmdOK"
    OnClick="OK_OnSubmit"
    Text="OK"
/>
```

The other form on this page simply contains a Label control:

```
<mobile:form
    id="FinishForm"
    runat="server">
<mobile:label
    runat="server"
    id="lbl1"
/>
</mobile:form>
```

Two procedures are defined on this page. The first fires when the page loads. It populates the SelectionList control:

```
Sub Page_Load(ByVal Sender as Object, ByVal E as EventArgs)
    If Not IsPostBack Then
        Dim DBConn as OleDbConnection
        Dim DBCommand As OleDbDataAdapter
        Dim DSPageData as New DataSet
        DBConn = New OleDbConnection( _
            "PROVIDER=Microsoft.Jet.OLEDB.4.0;" _
            & "DATA SOURCE=" _
            & Server.MapPath("/tt/C15/C15.mdb;"))
        DBCommand = New OleDbDataAdapter _
            ("Select ColorName " _
            & "From Colors " _
            & "Order By ColorName", DBConn)
        DBCommand.Fill(DSPageData, _
            "Colors")
        sl1.DataSource = _
            DSPageData.Tables("Colors").DefaultView
        sl1.DataBind()
    End If
End Sub
```

Notice that the code only runs the first time the page loads. If it is the first loading of the page, data objects are defined and data is retrieved from the database. The SelectionList control is bound to that data.

The other procedure fires when the Command control is selected:

```
Sub OK_OnSubmit(Sender As Object, E As EventArgs)
    ActiveForm = FinishForm
    lbl1.Text = "You selected " _
        & sl1.Selection.ToString()
End Sub
```

That procedure shows the second form and displays the item selected by visitors. Notice that the text of the item selected is retrieved through the Selection object of the SelectionList control.

Creating a Basic Mobile TextBox Control

You can't create a very defined Mobile ASP.NET page without using a TextBox control. Whether visitors need to enter their name, a search string, their address, or the start date for a report, you are likely to use a TextBox control in all these situations. This tip shows you the basic structure of a TextBox control.

The simple page created for this technique displays a single TextBox control to visitors. That control has this definition:

```
<mobile:textbox
    runat="server"
    id="txtSomeText"
    text="Enter some text"
    maxlength=25
    size=6
/>
```

You place the name of the control in the ID property. The Text property can be optionally set to an initial value. This is the property you use to check and see what the text was that visitors entered.

The MaxLength property is set to the maximum number of characters that visitors can type in. Typically, you set this to the size of the database field that the text entered will be stored in.

The Size property is used to determine the width of the control, across a line in the mobile device.

Creating a Mobile TextBox Control That Only Allows Numeric Entry

One of the ways that you can use a Mobile TextBox control is to use it as an input source for numeric data from visitors. For example, maybe you have a quantity field or a years of education field; both of those fields should contain only numbers. One of the ways you can limit the input is through a Mobile TextBox control. This technique shows you how to do that.

> ### QUICK TIP
>
> *Limiting the input of a TextBox control to only numeric characters works only on some devices. It is not supported through HTML. Therefore, this technique may not work for you if your target audience may be connecting through a standard browser. If that is the case, consider using one of the validation controls.*

 The page created for this technique defines a single Mobile TextBox control. That control has this definition:

```
<mobile:textbox
    runat="server"
    id="txtNumber"
    numeric="True"
/>
```

Notice the use of the Numeric property. By default, this property is set to False. If it is set to True, on devices that support this tag visitors can only enter numbers into the field.

Creating a Mobile TextBox Control for Password Entry

If visitors have to enter a password to gain access to your mobile site, they expect that as they type the password, the characters cannot be read on their screen. Instead, they expect to see the "*" character or the "#" character. This tip shows you how to use the Mobile TextBox control to meet that expectation.

USE IT The following Mobile ASP.NET page displays a single TextBox control to visitors. The TextBox control is used for the entry of passwords. The TextBox control has this definition:

```
<mobile:textbox
    runat="server"
    id="txtPassword"
    password="True"
/>
```

Notice the use of the Password property. By default, it is set to False. When it is set to True, visitors' input is not seen as they type. Instead, mask characters like the "#" or "*" appear.

Creating a Basic Mobile TextView Control

If you need to display text on your Mobile page that contains basic HMTL tags such as a line break or a paragraph tag, you cannot do that through a Label control. Instead, you need to use a TextView control. Although a TextView control sounds more like a TextBox control, it is really more like a Label control that is designed to display a greater quantity of text with basic mark-up tags. This technique shows you how to define a Mobile TextView control.

USE IT The Mobile ASP.NET page presented in this technique defines a Label control and a TextView control. The output of the control demonstrates the difference between the two. The Label control has this definition:

```
<mobile:label
    runat="server"
    id="lblError"
    alignment="Center"
    text="The word <B>bold</B> is not in bold."
/>
```

Notice the HTML Bold tag placed in the Text property. That tag will not be processed. Instead, visitors will see the raw text "<B>" and "</B>" without the word "bold" in bold.

Take a look at the definition of the TextView control:

```
<mobile:textview
    runat="server"
    id="tvTextr"
    text="The word<BR><B>bold</B><BR>is in bold."
/>
```

Here, the Text property also contains basic HTML elements. These elements will be processed since they are used in a TextView control. Therefore, the word "bold," will appear in bold with line breaks before and after the control. In addition to supporting the <B> tag and the <BR> tag, the control also supports the <P>, <I>, and <A> HTML tags.

Using the Mobile ValidationSummary Control

On Mobile devices, the screen space can be very small. Therefore, you may not have the room for error messages if visitors violate the validation rules on your page, especially if they violate a couple of those rules. That is where the Mobile ValidationSummary control can be useful. The ValidationSummary control allows you to display all the error messages on a separate form on your page. Visitors see the error messages and the ValidationSummary control provides them with a link, so they can return to the data entry form. This technique shows you how to use this control.

USE IT The page created for this technique prompts visitors for a number and a date. RangeValidator controls are used to make sure the data entered falls into an expected range. If visitors violate the validation rules, they are taken to an error page where a ValidationSummary control displays all the error messages. Otherwise, visitors see the data they entered echoed through a Label control.

The page contains three forms. The first form prompts visitors for their input:

```
<mobile:form
    id="StartForm"
    runat="server">
    <mobile:label
        runat="server"
        id="lbl1"
        Text="Enter a number from 1 to 5:"
    />
    <mobile:textbox
        runat="server"
        id="txtNumber"
    />
    <mobile:rangevalidator
```

```
            id="rngNumber"
            controltovalidate="txtNumber"
            type="Integer"
            minimumvalue=1
            maximumvalue=5
            runat="server"
            errormessage="Number not in correct range!!!"
    />
    <mobile:label
        runat="server"
        id="lbl1b"
        Text="Enter a date in 2005:"
    />
    <mobile:textbox
        runat="server"
        id="txtDate"
    />
    <mobile:rangevalidator
        id="rngDate"
        controltovalidate="txtDate"
        type="Date"
        minimumvalue="1/1/2005"
        maximumvalue="12/31/2005"
        runat="server"
        errormessage="Date not in correct range!!!"
    />
    <mobile:Command
        runat="server"
        id="cmdOK"
        OnClick="OK_OnSubmit"
        Text="OK"
    />
</mobile:form>
```

Notice the use of the RangeValidator controls to limit visitors' input into the TextBox controls. The ErrorMessage text will not be displayed next to the TextBox controls. Instead, it will be displayed through the ValidationSummary control.

The second form on the page has this definition:

```
<mobile:form
    id="FinishForm"
    runat="server">
    <mobile:label
        runat="server"
        id="lbl2"
```

```
    />
</mobile:form>
```

This form is viewed if the data visitors entered is correctly validated.

The third form contains the ValidationSummary control:

```
<mobile:form
    id="ErrorForm"
    runat="server">
    <mobile:validationsummary
        id="vsAllErrors"
        runat="server"
        headertext="For these reasons,
            your data could not be processed:"
        formtovalidate="StartForm"
    />
</mobile:form>
```

This form is only displayed when the data entry rules are violated. The HeaderText property is set to whatever text you want to appear in the control before the error messages. After the header text is displayed, visitors will see a bulleted list of all the violated rule error messages.

The FormToValidate property needs to be set to the name of the form on this page that this validation summary uses. In this case, it is the first form.

The following code fires when visitors click the Command control:

```
Sub OK_OnSubmit(Sender As Object, E As EventArgs)
    If Page.IsValid Then
        ActiveForm = FinishForm
        lbl2.Text = "You entered " & txtNumber.Text _
            & " and " & txtDate.Text
    Else
        ActiveForm = ErrorForm
    End If
End Sub
```

If the validation rules can be enforced, visitors will see the FinishForm. Otherwise, they will see the ErrorForm that contains the ValidationSummary control.

CHAPTER 16

Page Samples

TIPS IN THIS CHAPTER

Throughout this book, tips and techniques have been presented that show you how to use the numerous aspects of ASP.NET development so that they can be added to your ASP.NET pages. In this chapter, tips and techniques that were presented throughout the book are combined to create ASP.NET pages that might be included on a variety of sites.

As you review these ASP.NET pages, think about how you could alter the functionality to suit your needs. Remember that an efficient developer builds ASP.NET pages by borrowing and enhancing pages that they have already created.

If you find that you enjoy the offerings in this chapter, you may want to explore another book of mine called *Instant ASP.NET Applications* (McGraw-Hill/Osborne, 2001). In that book, I present full ASP.NET pages and applications that can be directly used in a variety of situations.

Creating a Login Page

If you have a site that you wish to secure and prevent unauthorized visitors from entering, you will need a Login page. Maybe you require visitors to log in before shopping at your e-commerce site. Or maybe visitors must log in before viewing your site's extensive content. This technique shows you how to create a basic Login page.

USE IT Two pages are defined for this technique. One page shows you how to log visitors in against the data in an Access database. The other page verifies visitors have logged in before displaying its content.

The first page contains a TextBox control where visitors enter their user name:

```
<asp:textbox
    id="txtUserName"
    columns="25"
    maxlength="50"
    runat=server
/>
```

Visitors must enter something into that field because of the RequiredFieldValidator control linked to it:

```
<asp:requiredfieldvalidator
    id="rfvUserName"
    controltovalidate="txtUserName"
    display="Dynamic"
    font-name="tahoma"
    font-size="10pt"
    runat=server>
    User Name is Required!
</asp:requiredfieldvalidator>
```

A second TextBox control is defined for the visitors' password:

```
<asp:textbox
    id="txtPassword"
    columns="25"
    maxlength="50"
    runat=server
    textmode="password"
/>
```

Notice that the TextMode property is set to Password. Therefore, visitors will see the "*" character as they type.

A value must be entered into this field because of this RequiredFieldValidator control:

```
<asp:requiredfieldvalidator
    id="rfvpassword"
    controltovalidate="txtpassword"
    display="dynamic"
    font-name="verdana"
    font-size="10pt"
    runat=server>
    password is required!
</asp:requiredfieldvalidator>
```

When visitors are ready to log into the site, they can click on this Button control:

```
<asp:button
    id="butok"
    text="  ok  "
    onclick="submitbtn_click"
    runat="server"
/>
```

Since the page connects to an Access database and retrieves data, you need to import two data namespaces:

```
<%@ Import Namespace="System.Data" %>
<%@ Import Namespace="System.Data.OLEDB" %>
```

When visitors click the OK button, the following code block fires:

```
Sub SubmitBtn_Click(Sender As Object, E As EventArgs)
    Dim DBConn as OleDbConnection
    Dim DBCommand As OleDbDataAdapter
    Dim DSLogin as New DataSet
    DBConn = New OleDbConnection("PROVIDER=" _
```

```
        & "Microsoft.Jet.OLEDB.4.0;" _
        & "DATA SOURCE=" _
        & Server.MapPath("/TT/C16/Login/" _
        & "LogIn.mdb;"))
    DBCommand = New OleDbDataAdapter _
        ("Select UserID from " _
        & "Users Where " _
        & "UserName = '" & txtUserName.Text _
        & "' and Password = '" & txtPassword.Text _
        & "'", DBConn)
    DBCommand.Fill(DSLogin, _
        "UserInfo")
    If DSLogin.Tables("UserInfo"). _
        Rows.Count = 0 Then
        lblMessage.Text = "The user name and password " _
            & "were not found. Please try again."
    Else
        Session("UserID") = DSLogin.Tables("UserInfo"). _
            Rows(0).Item("UserID")
        Session("UserName") = txtUserName.Text
        Response.Redirect("./welcome.aspx")
    End If
End Sub
```

Within the procedure, you connect to the Access database and retrieve the users' ID based on the user name and password that was entered. You then check to see if a record with the user name and password entered is found. If it is not found, the record count would be 0 and you prompt visitors to try again. Otherwise, you store the visitors' name and ID in session variables and send them to the Welcome page.

The code on the Welcome page makes sure that visitors have logged in before displaying its content. Defined on that page is a single Label control:

```
<asp:Label
    id="lblMessage"
    Font-Size="12pt"
    Font-Name="Tahoma"
    runat="server"
/>
```

When the page loads, this code block fires:

```
Sub Page_Load(ByVal Sender as Object, ByVal E as EventArgs)
    If Len(Session("UserID")) = 0 Then
        Response.Redirect("./login.aspx")
    End If
```

```
        lblMessage.Text = "Welcome: " & Session("UserName")
End Sub
```

The code checks to see if visitors have logged in by looking for the UserID Session variable. If it is empty, visitors are sent back to the Login page. Otherwise, they see this page.

Displaying a Phone Directory

If you manage a site for the company that you work for or are asked to develop for, you may need to have a page that lists contact phone numbers for employees. This technique creates such a page. It displays employee names and phone numbers from an Access database and allows visitors to filter the records that they see.

 The employees' names, departments, and phone numbers are displayed on the page through the DataGrid control:

```
<asp:datagrid
    id="dgEmps"
    runat="server"
    autogeneratecolumns="True"
/>
```

Notice that the AutoGenerateColumns property is set to True. Therefore, the columns in the DataGrid will come directly from the bound DataSet table.

Also defined on this page is a DropDownList control that displays the different departments in the Employees Table:

```
<asp:dropdownlist
    id="ddlDepartments"
    datatextfield="Department"
    autopostback="True"
    onselectedindexchanged="ddl1_Changed"
    runat="server"
/>
```

Visitors use this DropDownList control to filter the records that are displayed. They select a department, the page reloads, and they see only the employees from that department.

When the page first loads, this procedure runs:

```
Sub Page_Load(ByVal Sender as Object, ByVal E as EventArgs)
    If Not IsPostBack Then
```

That procedure connects to the Access database and retrieves all the employee records:

```
Dim DBConn as OleDbConnection
Dim DBCommand As OleDbDataAdapter
Dim DSPageData as New DataSet
DBConn = New OleDbConnection( _
    "PROVIDER=Microsoft.Jet.OLEDB.4.0;" _
    & "DATA SOURCE=" _
    & Server.MapPath _
    ("/tt/C16/Phone/PhoneDir.mdb;"))
DBCommand = New OleDbDataAdapter _
    ("Select EmpName as [Employee Name], " _
    & "Department, PhoneNumber as " _
    & "[Phone Number] From Emps " _
    & "Order By EmpName", DBConn)
```

The DataGrid control is bound to that data:

```
DBCommand.Fill(DSPageData, _
    "Employees")
dgEmps.DataSource = _
DSPageData.Tables("Employees").DefaultView
    dgEmps.DataBind()
```

Next, you need to retrieve all the departments for the DropDownList control:

```
DBCommand = New OleDbDataAdapter _
    ("Select Distinct Department From Emps " _
    & "Order By Department", DBConn)
DBCommand.Fill(DSPageData, _
    "Departments")
ddlDepartments.DataSource = _
    DSPageData.Tables("Departments").DefaultView
        ddlDepartments.DataBind()
```

The other procedure on this page fires when visitors change the selection in the DropDownList control:

```
Sub ddl1_Changed(Sender As Object, E As EventArgs)
    Dim DBConn as OleDbConnection
    Dim DBCommand As OleDbDataAdapter
    Dim DSPageData as New DataSet
    DBConn = New OleDbConnection( _
```

```
            "PROVIDER=Microsoft.Jet.OLEDB.4.0;" _
            & "DATA SOURCE=" _
            & Server.MapPath _
            ("/tt/C16/Phone/PhoneDir.mdb;"))
        DBCommand = New OleDbDataAdapter _
            ("Select EmpName as [Employee Name], " _
            & "Department, PhoneNumber as " _
            & "[Phone Number] From Emps " _
            & "Where Department = '" _
            & ddlDepartments.SelectedItem.Text _
            & "' Order By EmpName", DBConn)
        DBCommand.Fill(DSPageData, _
            "Employees")
        dgEmps.DataSource = _
            DSPageData.Tables("Employees").DefaultView
        dgEmps.DataBind()
End Sub
```

When that happens, the DataGrid control is repopulated. But this time, visitors only see the employees who work in the department that they selected.

Creating a Store Location Page

If you need to design a site for a company that has numerous stores, their customers will appreciate a page that helps them find the company's stores. The page created for this technique allows visitors to drill down the stores displayed by selecting a state and then a city within that state. Visitors then see all the stores in the location selected.

USE IT The ASP.NET page displays data from an Access database through two DropDownList controls and a DataGrid control. The first DropDownList control displays the states where a store is located:

```
<asp:dropdownlist
    id="ddlStates"
    datatextfield="State"
    autopostback="True"
    onselectedindexchanged="ddlState_Changed"
    runat="server"
/>
```

The second DropDownList control displays all the cities within the selected state:

```
<asp:dropdownlist
    id="ddlCities"
```

```
        datatextfield="City"
        autopostback="True"
        onselectedindexchanged="ddlCity_Changed"
        visible="False"
        runat="server"
    />
```

Notice that this control is initially invisible. That is because you don't want visitors to see a city list until they have selected a state.

The DataGrid control has this definition:

```
<asp:datagrid
    id="dgStores"
    runat="server"
    autogeneratecolumns="True"
/>
```

It will display all the stores in the city/state visitors selected.

The page has three procedures defined. The first procedure fires when the page loads:

```
Sub Page_Load(ByVal Sender as Object, ByVal E as EventArgs)
    If Not IsPostBack Then
        Dim DBConn as OleDbConnection
        Dim DBCommand As OleDbDataAdapter
        Dim DSPageData as New DataSet
        DBConn = New OleDbConnection( _
            "PROVIDER=Microsoft.Jet.OLEDB.4.0;" _
            & "DATA SOURCE=" _
            & Server.MapPath _
            ("/tt/C16/StoreLocation/StoresDB.mdb;"))
        DBCommand = New OleDbDataAdapter _
            ("Select Distinct State From Stores " _
            & "Order By State", DBConn)
        DBCommand.Fill(DSPageData, _
            "States")
        ddlStates.DataSource = _
            DSPageData.Tables("States").DefaultView
        ddlStates.DataBind()
    End If
End Sub
```

This procedure populates the first DropDownList control with all the states in the Access database.

The second procedure fires when visitors select one of the states in the first DropDownList control:

```
Sub ddlState_Changed(Sender As Object, E As EventArgs)
    Dim DBConn as OleDbConnection
```

```
    Dim DBCommand As OleDbDataAdapter
    Dim DSPageData as New DataSet
    DBConn = New OleDbConnection( _
        "PROVIDER=Microsoft.Jet.OLEDB.4.0;" _
        & "DATA SOURCE=" _
        & Server.MapPath _
        ("/tt/C16/StoreLocation/StoresDB.mdb;"))
    DBCommand = New OleDbDataAdapter _
        ("Select Distinct City From Stores " _
        & "Where State = '" & ddlStates.SelectedItem.Text _
        & "' Order By City", DBConn)
    DBCommand.Fill(DSPageData, _
        "Cities")
    ddlCities.DataSource = _
        DSPageData.Tables("Cities").DefaultView
    ddlCities.DataBind()
    ddlCities.Visible = True
    lblMessage3.Visible = True
End Sub
```

The procedure populates the second DropDownList control with all the cities in the state that visitors selected. Notice that the second DropDownList control, as well as a Label control, are made visible. This is required since they were initially hidden.

The third procedure fires when visitors select an item in the Cities DropDownList control:

```
Sub ddlCity_Changed(Sender As Object, E As EventArgs)
    Dim DBConn as OleDbConnection
    Dim DBCommand As OleDbDataAdapter
    Dim DSPageData as New DataSet
    DBConn = New OleDbConnection( _
        "PROVIDER=Microsoft.Jet.OLEDB.4.0;" _
        & "DATA SOURCE=" _
        & Server.MapPath _
        ("/tt/C16/StoreLocation/StoresDB.mdb;"))
    DBCommand = New OleDbDataAdapter _
        ("Select StoreName as [Store Name], " _
        & "Address From Stores " _
        & "Where City = '" _
        & ddlCities.SelectedItem.Text & "' " _
        & "And State = '" _
        & ddlStates.SelectedItem.Text & "' " _
        & "Order By StoreName", DBConn)
    DBCommand.Fill(DSPageData, _
        "Stores")
```

```
    dgStores.DataSource = _
        DSPageData.Tables("Stores").DefaultView
    dgStores.DataBind()
End Sub
```

This procedure populates the DataGrid control with records from the Stores table. Notice that only the stores with the city and state that visitors selected are displayed.

Making a Contact Us Page

Regardless of the size of your site, you will likely want to provide a way for visitors to submit a question or comment to you. This type of page is sometimes called a Contact Us page. The technique in this section shows you how to create a Contact Us page.

USE IT   The ASP.NET page created for this technique asks visitors for information about themselves and provides an input area for their question or comment. Visitors can submit their query, which is inserted into a table in an Access database.

One TextBox control is defined on the page for the visitors' name:

```
<asp:textbox
    id="txtContactName"
    columns="25"
    maxlength="50"
    runat=server
/>
```

That field must have a value placed into it because of this RequiredFieldValidator control:

```
<asp:requiredfieldvalidator
    id="rfvContactName"
    controltovalidate="txtContactName"
    display="Dynamic"
    font-name="Tahoma"
    font-size="10pt"
    runat=server>
    User Name is Required!
</asp:RequiredFieldValidator>
```

Next, visitors enter their e-mail address through a TextBox control:

```
<asp:textbox
    id="txtContactEmail"
    columns="25"
```

```
    maxlength="50"
    runat=server
/>
```

That field is also required:

```
<asp:requiredfieldvalidator
    id="rfvContactEmail"
    controltovalidate="txtContactEmail"
    display="Dynamic"
    font-name="Tahoma"
    font-size="10pt"
    runat=server>
    User Name is Required!
</asp:RequiredFieldValidator>
```

Through a DropDownList control, visitors then select a topic for the question or comment that they are submitting:

```
<asp:dropdownlist
    id="ddlTopic"
    runat=server
>
    <asp:listitem>Web Site</asp:listitem>
    <asp:listitem>Order Status</asp:listitem>
    <asp:listitem>Other</asp:listitem>
</asp:dropdownlist>
```

An additional TextBox control allows visitors to enter their message:

```
<asp:textbox
    id="txtTheMessage"
    columns="25"
    rows=5
    textmode="multiline"
    runat=server
/>
```

Notice that the TextMode property is set to MultiLine. Therefore, visitors will see a TextBox control that allows many lines of input.

A Button control is also defined on the page, which allows visitors to submit their query:

```
<asp:button
    id="butOK"
```

```
        text="  OK  "
        OnClick="SubmitBtn_Click"
        runat="server"
/>
```

When that button is clicked, the only code block on the page fires:

```
Sub SubmitBtn_Click(Sender As Object, E As EventArgs)
    Dim DBConn as OleDbConnection
    Dim DBAdd As New OleDbCommand
    DBConn = New OleDbConnection( _
        "PROVIDER=Microsoft.Jet.OLEDB.4.0;" _
        & "DATA SOURCE=" _
        & Server.MapPath _
        ("/tt/C16/ContactUs/ContactDB.mdb;"))
    DBAdd.CommandText = "Insert Into Contacts " _
        & "(ContactName, ContactEmail, Topic, " _
        & "TheMessage, DateTimeEntered) values (" _
        & "'" & Replace(txtContactName.Text, "'", "''") _
        & "', " _
        & "'" & Replace(txtContactEmail.Text, "'", "''") _
        & "', " _
        & "'" & ddlTopic.SelectedItem.Text & "', " _
        & "'" & Replace(txtTheMessage.Text, "'", "''") _
        & "', Now)"
    DBAdd.Connection = DBConn
    DBAdd.Connection.Open
    DBAdd.ExecuteNonQuery()
    lblMessage.Text = "Your request has been submitted."
End Sub
```

In that procedure, you connect to the Access database and insert a record into the Access table, based on the data visitors entered on the form. Notice that a time stamp is also inserted in the record through the DateTimeEntered field. This field is set to the current date and time through the Access Now method.

Displaying a Survey Page

A fun element that you can add to your site or to a page is a Survey page. This type of page or element goes under different names but it basically allows visitors to answer a question and then they see the results of the survey question. This type of quick vote interface often changes on a daily basis. The technique presented in this section shows you how to create a Survey page.

USE IT The page created for this technique displays a question to visitors. They select an answer from a DropDownList control. When they submit their response, they see the current tally of all responses to the question.

An Access database is used for this page. One table in that database contains questions. A second table contains responses to those questions. Since the questions and answers come from the database, it is very easy to use the page for different questions. When visitors submit their response to the question, it is stored in a third table.

The page defines two Panel controls. The first Panel control displays the possible responses and the second Panel control displays the summary of all the responses to the question.

Before either Panel control is defined a Label control appears:

```
<asp:label
    id="lblQuestion"
    font-size="10pt"
    font-name="Lucida Console"
    runat="server"
/>
```

This control will display the text of the question regardless of which panel is being viewed.

Within the first Panel control, a DropDownList control is defined:

```
<asp:dropdownlist
    id="ddlAnswers"
    datatextfield="SurveyAnswer"
    runat="server"
/>
```

That control will display all the possible responses to the current question.

A Button control is also defined within this Panel control:

```
<asp:button
    id="butOK"
    text="  OK  "
    OnClick="SubmitBtn_Click"
    runat="server"
/>
```

The other Panel control only has a DataGrid control defined within it:

```
<asp:datagrid
    id="dgResponses"
    runat="server"
    autogeneratecolumns="True"
/>
```

That DataGrid control will display the summarized results of all the respondents.

Two procedures are defined on this page. The first procedure fires when the page loads:

```
Sub Page_Load(ByVal Sender as Object, ByVal E as EventArgs)
```

The first thing done in this procedure is to set the ID of the current survey question. This number needs to match one of the questions in the database. Storing the ID of the question like this makes it easy for you to switch to another question:

```
Application("CurrentQuestion") = 2
```

The rest of the code only runs when the page first loads:

```
If Not IsPostBack Then
```

If that is the case, you need database objects:

```
Dim DBConn as OleDbConnection
Dim DBCommand As OleDbDataAdapter
Dim DSPageData as New DataSet
```

You then connect to the Access database and retrieve the current question:

```
DBConn = New OleDbConnection( _
    "PROVIDER=Microsoft.Jet.OLEDB.4.0;" _
    & "DATA SOURCE=" _
    & Server.MapPath _
    ("/tt/C16/Survey/SurveyDB.mdb;"))
DBCommand = New OleDbDataAdapter _
    ("Select SurveyQuestion From " _
    & "SurveyQuestions Where SurveyQuestionID = " _
    & Application("CurrentQuestion"), DBConn)
DBCommand.Fill(DSPageData, _
    "TheQuestion")
```

The text retrieved from the database is placed into the Label control:

```
lblQuestion.Text = _
    DSPageData.Tables("TheQuestion"). _
    Rows(0).Item("SurveyQuestion")
```

You also need to retrieve the responses to this question:

```
DBCommand = New OleDbDataAdapter _
    ("Select SurveyAnswer From " _
    & "SurveyAnswers Where SurveyQuestionID = " _
    & Application("CurrentQuestion"), DBConn)
```

```
DBCommand.Fill(DSPageData, _
    "TheAnswers")
```

The DropDownList control is bound to those response records:

```
ddlAnswers.DataSource = _
    DSPageData.Tables("TheAnswers").DefaultView
ddlAnswers.DataBind()
```

The other procedure fires when visitors click the Button control:

```
Sub SubmitBtn_Click(Sender As Object, E As EventArgs)
```

In that case, you need to define these data objects:

```
Dim DBConn as OleDbConnection
Dim DBAdd As New OleDbCommand
Dim DBCommand As OleDbDataAdapter
Dim DSPageData as New DataSet
```

You then connect to the database:

```
DBConn = New OleDbConnection( _
    "PROVIDER=Microsoft.Jet.OLEDB.4.0;" _
    & "DATA SOURCE=" _
    & Server.MapPath _
    ("/tt/C16/Survey/SurveyDB.mdb;"))
```

and add the visitors' response to the Responses table in the Access database:

```
DBAdd.CommandText = "Insert Into Responses " _
    & "(SurveyQuestionID, Response) values (" _
    & Application("CurrentQuestion") & ", " _
    & "'" & ddlAnswers.SelectedItem.Text & "')"
DBAdd.Connection = DBConn
DBAdd.Connection.Open
DBAdd.ExecuteNonQuery()
```

Next, you need to run an aggregate query that retrieves the total number of each response that has been selected by visitors to the current question:

```
DBCommand = New OleDbDataAdapter _
    ("Select Response, " _
    & "Count(ResponseID) as [Hit Count] " _
    & "From Responses " _
    & "Where SurveyQuestionID = " _
```

```
        & Application("CurrentQuestion") _
        & " Group By Response", DBConn)
DBCommand.Fill(DSPageData, _
    "TheResponses")
```

The DataGrid control displays those aggregate results:

```
dgResponses.DataSource = _
    DSPageData.Tables("TheResponses").DefaultView
dgResponses.DataBind()
```

You also need to hide the question Panel control:

```
PanelQuestion.Visible = False
```

but display the other Panel control:

```
PanelResponse.Visible = True
```

Making an Employee of the Month Page

Many companies honor the hard work of an employee by making the employee an Employee of the Month. A great way to highlight that achievement would be to create an ASP.NET page that displays information about the current Employee of the Month. This technique shows you how simple that can be.

USE IT To retrieve the employee data, the ASP.NET page created for this technique uses an Access database. That database contains a table with employee information. A field in that table denotes the employee who is the current Employee of the Month.

Defined in the body of the ASP.NET page is a single Label control:

```
<asp:label
    id="lblEmpInfo"
    font-size="10pt"
    font-name="Lucida Console"
    runat="server"
/>
```

The text in that control is set when the page loads:

```
Sub Page_Load(ByVal Sender as Object, ByVal E as EventArgs)
    Dim DBConn as OleDbConnection
    Dim DBCommand As OleDbDataAdapter
    Dim DSPageData as New DataSet
```

```
DBConn = New OleDbConnection( _
    "PROVIDER=Microsoft.Jet.OLEDB.4.0;" _
    & "DATA SOURCE=" & Server.MapPath _
    ("/tt/C16/EmpOfTheMonth/EmpDB.mdb;"))
DBCommand = New OleDbDataAdapter _
    ("Select * From " _
    & "Emps Where EmpOfTheMonth = 1", DBConn)
DBCommand.Fill(DSPageData, _
    "TheEmployee")
If DSPageData.Tables("TheEmployee"). _
    Rows.Count = 0 Then
    lblEmpInfo.Text = "There is no current employee " _
        & "of the month. Please try again."
Else
    lblEmpInfo.Text = "Congratulations to " _
        & DSPageData.Tables("TheEmployee"). _
        Rows(0).Item("FirstName") & " " _
        & DSPageData.Tables("TheEmployee"). _
        Rows(0).Item("LastName") & " who is the " _
        & "current Employee of the month.<BR>Call " _
        & DSPageData.Tables("TheEmployee"). _
        Rows(0).Item("FirstName") & " at " _
        & DSPageData.Tables("TheEmployee"). _
        Rows(0).Item("Phone") & " to say how " _
        & "proud you are!"
    End If
End Sub
```

Within that procedure, you need data objects. You start by connecting to the Access database and retrieving the data on the current Employee of the Month. You then check to see if an Employee of the Month was found. If one wasn't found, you display a message stating that fact. Otherwise, data on the current employee is mixed with fixed text and an HTML tag to produce the page output.

Creating a What's New Page

One way to inform your visitors of new content on your site is through a What's New page. Such a page would contain articles describing what is new at your site or company. The technique presented in this section shows you how to do that.

 The page created for this technique displays the most recent news item to visitors through a Label control. The data that is displayed comes from an Access database.

The page also allows visitors to view old news items by selecting the date of the old news from a DropDownList control.

Defined within the body of the ASP.NET page is this Label control:

```
<asp:label
    id="lblTheNews"
    font-size="12pt"
    font-bold="True"
    font-name="Lucida Console"
    runat="server"
/>
```

That control will display the currently viewed news item. Also defined on this page is a DropDownList control:

```
<asp:dropdownlist
    id="ddlNews"
    datatextfield="DateEntered"
    datavaluefield="NewsID"
    autopostback="True"
    onselectedindexchanged="ddlNews_Changed"
    runat="server"
/>
```

The control allows visitors to navigate to an old news item by selecting its date in this control.

Two procedures are required to produce the needed functionality. The first procedure runs when the page first loads:

```
Sub Page_Load(ByVal Sender as Object, ByVal E as EventArgs)
    If Not IsPostBack Then
```

If that is the case, you need to define data objects:

```
Dim DBConn as OleDbConnection
Dim DBCommand As OleDbDataAdapter
Dim DSPageData as New DataSet
```

and connect to the Access database:

```
DBConn = New OleDbConnection( _
    "PROVIDER=Microsoft.Jet.OLEDB.4.0;" _
    & "DATA SOURCE=" _
    & Server.MapPath _
    ("/tt/C16/WhatsNew/WhatsNewDB.mdb;"))
```

You then retrieve the latest news item in the News table:

```
DBCommand = New OleDbDataAdapter _
    ("Select Top 1 TheNews From News " _
    & "Order By DateEntered Desc", DBConn)
DBCommand.Fill(DSPageData, _
    "News")
```

The text of that news item is placed into the Text property of the Label control:

```
lblTheNews.Text = _
    DSPageData.Tables("News").Rows(0). _
    Item("TheNews")
```

You also need to select all the news item dates along with their IDs to display into the DropDownList control:

```
DBCommand = New OleDbDataAdapter _
    ("Select NewsID, DateEntered From News " _
    & "Order By DateEntered DESC", DBConn)
```

The DropDownList control is bound to that data:

```
DBCommand.Fill(DSPageData, _
    "NewsDates")
ddlNews.DataSource = _
    DSPageData.Tables("NewsDates").DefaultView
ddlNews.DataBind()
```

The other procedure fires when visitors select a date from the DropDownList control:

```
Sub ddlNews_Changed(Sender As Object, E As EventArgs)
    Dim DBConn as OleDbConnection
    Dim DBCommand As OleDbDataAdapter
    Dim DSPageData as New DataSet
    DBConn = New OleDbConnection( _
        "PROVIDER=Microsoft.Jet.OLEDB.4.0;" _
        & "DATA SOURCE=" _
        & Server.MapPath _
        ("/tt/C16/WhatsNew/WhatsNewDB.mdb;"))
    DBCommand = New OleDbDataAdapter _
        ("Select TheNews From News " _
        & "Where NewsID = " & ddlNews.SelectedItem.Value _
        , DBConn)
    DBCommand.Fill(DSPageData, _
        "News")
```

```
        lblTheNews.Text = _
            DSPageData.Tables("News").Rows(0). _
            Item("TheNews")
End Sub
```

The procedure connects to the database and retrieves the text of the news item visitors selected.

Displaying a New Products Page

If you have an e-commerce site, you want to make it easy for returning customers to find products that you have recently added to your catalog. One way you can do that is through a New Products page. This technique shows you how to create a New Products page.

USE IT   The page created for this technique connects to an Access database that contains product information. One of the fields for each product is the date that it was added to the database. That date is used to return all the products that were added to the catalog in the last month. Those items are displayed on the page through a DataGrid control.

The DataGrid control has this definition:

```
<asp:datagrid
    id="dgNewProducts"
    runat="server"
    autogeneratecolumns="True"
/>
```

The only code on the page runs when the page is loaded:

```
Sub Page_Load(ByVal Sender as Object, ByVal E as EventArgs)
    Dim DBConn as OleDbConnection
    Dim DBCommand As OleDbDataAdapter
    Dim DSPageData as New DataSet
    DBConn = New OleDbConnection( _
        "PROVIDER=Microsoft.Jet.OLEDB.4.0;" _
        & "DATA SOURCE=" _
        & Server.MapPath _
        ("/tt/C16/NewProducts/ProductsDB.mdb;"))
    DBCommand = New OleDbDataAdapter _
        ("Select ProductName as [Name], " _
        & "ProductDescription as [Description], Price " _
        & "From Products Where " _
        & "Datediff(""d"",DateAdded,Now) <= 31 " _
        & "Order by ProductName", DBConn)
    DBCommand.Fill(DSPageData, _
        "NewProducts")
```

```
dgNewProducts.DataSource = _
    DSPageData.Tables("NewProducts").DefaultView
dgNewProducts.DataBind()
End Sub
```

The code first connects to the Access database. Notice the query that returns new products. The DateDiff function returns all the products that have a DateAdded date that is within 31 days of the current system date. The products returned through this query are bound to the DataGrid control.

Creating a Tip of the Day Page

A nice way to enhance your site is through a Tip of the Day page. This type of page usually displays a brief helpful piece of advice related to the type of content you offer at your site. Sometimes a Tip of the Day page is created as a stand-alone page. But more often it appears as added content to another page. This technique shows you how to create a Tip of the Day page.

USE IT   The page created for this technique reads tips from an Access database. Those tips are displayed on an ASP.NET page. The page displays the same tip for a day. A new tip is displayed when the server date changes. A sequence number field in the database table is used to determine the sequence in which the tips are displayed from day to day. The field must have a record with a sequence number of 1 and all others must be incremented by one.

Defined on the page is one Label control that will display the title of the tip:

```
<asp:label
    id="lblTipTitle"
    font-size="10pt"
    font-name="Lucida Console"
    runat="server"
/>
```

and a second Label control that will display the text of the tip:

```
<asp:label
    id="lblTipText"
    font-size="10pt"
    font-name="Lucida Console"
    runat="server"
/>
```

The only procedure on the page fires when the page first loads:

```
Sub Page_Load(ByVal Sender as Object, ByVal E as EventArgs)
```

In this event, you will need data objects:

```
Dim DBConn as OleDbConnection
Dim DBCommand As OleDbDataAdapter
Dim DSPageData as New DataSet
```

You start by checking to see if the date has changed since the last tip was displayed:

```
If Application("TipDate") <> Today() Then
```

If it has, you store the current date in the tip date variable:

```
Application("TipDate") = Today()
```

You also need to increment the tip number so that the next tip will be used:

```
If Not Isnumeric(Application("TipNumber")) Then
    Application("TipNumber") = 1
Else
    Application("TipNumber") = _
        Application("TipNumber") + 1
End If
```

You then need to connect to the Access database:

```
DBConn = New OleDbConnection( _
    "PROVIDER=Microsoft.Jet.OLEDB.4.0;" _
    & "DATA SOURCE=" _
    & Server.MapPath _
    ("/tt/C16/Tip/TipDB.mdb;"))
```

You then retrieve the tip:

```
DBCommand = New OleDbDataAdapter _
    ("Select TipTitle, TipText From Tips " _
    & "Where SequenceNumber = " _
    & Application("TipNumber"), DBConn)
DBCommand.Fill(DSPageData, _
    "TheTip")
```

But the sequence number may have been set beyond the range of the tips in the database. Therefore, here, you make sure a record was found:

```
If DSPageData.Tables("TheTip").Rows.Count = 0 Then
```

If it wasn't, you retrieve the first tip in the database:

```
Application("TipNumber") = 1
DBCommand = New OleDbDataAdapter _
    ("Select TipTitle, TipText From Tips " _
    & "Where SequenceNumber = " _
    & Application("TipNumber"), DBConn)
DBCommand.Fill(DSPageData, _
    "TheTip")
```

Then, the title of the tip is placed into one Label control:

```
lblTipTitle.Text = _
    DSPageData.Tables("TheTip").Rows(0). _
    Item("TipTitle")
```

and the text of the tip is placed in another:

```
lblTipText.Text = _
    DSPageData.Tables("TheTip").Rows(0). _
    Item("TipText")
```

Displaying Query Results on an ASP.NET Page

If you have advanced users who are accessing data through your site, you may want to provide them a way of entering their own ad hoc query. For example, maybe you have a site on your intranet that mangers connect to to view summary sales information. These advanced users may know enough about databases to be able to run their own SQL statement. This technique shows you how to create a page that allows that.

USE IT   The ASP.NET page created for this technique prompts visitors for parts of an SQL Select statement. Visitors then submit their query. The results of running the query are displayed in a DataGrid control.

This sample use of the page connects to a database that contains employee information. But you could point the page to some other database by changing the connect string.

Within the body of the page, a TextBox control is defined that allows visitors to enter the fields that they want returned through the query:

```
<asp:textbox
    id="txtFieldList"
    runat="server"
/>
```

That TextBox control must have a value because of this RequiredFieldValidator control:

```
<asp:requiredfieldvalidator
    id="rfvFieldList"
    controltovalidate="txtFieldList"
    display="Dynamic"
    font-name="Tahoma"
    font-size="10pt"
    runat=server>
    Field list is required!
</asp:requiredfieldvalidator>
```

Next, visitors enter the name of the table that they want to retrieve data from:

```
<asp:textbox
    id="txtTableName"
    runat="server"
/>
```

That field is also required:

```
<asp:requiredfieldvalidator
    id="rfvTableName"
    controltovalidate="txtTableName"
    display="Dynamic"
    font-name="Tahoma"
    font-size="10pt"
    runat=server>
    Field list is required!
</asp:requiredfieldvalidator>
```

Visitors can also supply a Where clause for the query:

```
<asp:textbox
    id="txtWhere"
    runat="server"
/>
```

as well as an Order By clause:

```
<asp:textbox
    id="txtOrder"
    runat="server"
/>
```

Also defined on the page is a Button control that visitors click when they want to submit their query:

```
<asp:button
    id="butOK"
    text="  OK  "
    OnClick="SubmitBtn_Click"
    runat="server"
/>
```

After the query runs, the results of the query are placed into this DataGrid control:

```
<asp:datagrid
    id="dgQuery"
    runat="server"
    autogeneratecolumns="True"
/>
```

The only code on the page fires when visitors click the Button control:

```
Sub SubmitBtn_Click(Sender As Object, E As EventArgs)
```

In this procedure, you will need data objects:

```
Dim DBConn as OleDbConnection
Dim DBCommand As OleDbDataAdapter
Dim DSPageData as New DataSet
```

You also need to declare a String variable that will store the text of the query as it is being constructed:

```
Dim TheQuery as String
```

Next, you connect to the Access database:

```
DBConn = New OleDbConnection( _
    "PROVIDER=Microsoft.Jet.OLEDB.4.0;" _
    & "DATA SOURCE=" _
    & Server.MapPath _
    ("/tt/C16/Query/EmpDB.mdb;"))
```

You build the query from the field list and the table name visitors enter:

```
TheQuery = "Select " & txtFieldList.Text _
    & " From " & txtTableName.Text
```

If visitors supply a Where clause, that is also added to the query:

```
If txtWhere.Text <> "" Then
    TheQuery = TheQuery & " Where " _
        & txtWhere.Text
End If
```

The same is done for the Order By clause:

```
If txtOrder.Text <> "" Then
    TheQuery = TheQuery & " Order By " _
        & txtOrder.Text
End If
```

Next, you run the query:

```
DBCommand = New OleDbDataAdapter(TheQuery, DBConn)
DBCommand.Fill(DSPageData, _
    "QueryResults")
```

and bind the returned data to the DataGrid control:

```
dgQuery.DataSource = _
    DSPageData.Tables("QueryResults").DefaultView
dgQuery.DataBind()
```

Visitors then see the results of running their query.

Creating a Help Desk Page

Web sites serve their visitors well when visitors are able to have their questions answered without contacting an employee directly. Often, answering visitors' questions requires a hierarchical approach to their questions. You start by asking visitors a top-level question. Then, based on the answer visitors supply, you ask them another question. The process is repeated until they select an answer to a question that does not lead to another question. Instead, visitors are offered a resolution to their problem. This technique shows you how to create this type of Help Desk page.

USE IT   The page created for this technique asks visitors to answer questions. They continue to answer questions until a possible resolution is reached. The data for the questions, responses, and answers comes from an Access database. In this case, the data presented with the page helps visitors solve a problem with their VCR. But you could change the data in the database so that it helped visitors solve some other problem.

Defined within the body of the ASP.NET page is a Label control that displays the title of the question being asked:

```
<asp:Label
    id="lblTitle"
    runat="server"
/>
```

A second Label control is used to display the text of the current question or the possible resolution if visitors reach that point:

```
<asp:Label
    id="lblQuestion"
    runat="server"
/>
```

Another control displayed on this page is a DropDownList control that displays the possible responses to the current question:

```
<asp:dropdownlist
    id="ddlAnswers"
    runat=server
    DataTextField="TheChoice"
    DataValueField="QuestionID">
</asp:dropdownlist>
```

and a Button control is defined that allows visitors to submit their response:

```
<asp:button
    id="butOK"
    text="OK"
    Type="Submit"
    OnClick="SubmitBtn_Click"
    runat="server"
/>
```

Two procedures are defined on this page. The first procedure fires when the page loads:

```
Sub Page_Load(ByVal Sender as Object, ByVal E as EventArgs)
```

The code should only run the first time that page loads:

```
If Not IsPostBack then
```

If that is the case, you need these data objects:

```
Dim DBConn as OleDbConnection
Dim DBCommand As OleDbDataAdapter
Dim DSPageData as New DataSet
```

You start by connecting to the Access database:

```
DBConn = New OleDbConnection( _
    "PROVIDER=Microsoft.Jet.OLEDB.4.0;" _
    & "DATA SOURCE=" _
    & Server.MapPath _
    ("/tt/C16/HelpDesk/HelpDeskDB.mdb;"))
```

You then retrieve the top-level question from the Help Desk database. Notice that the top-level question is denoted with a 0 in the ParentID field:

```
DBCommand = New OleDbDataAdapter _
    ("Select QuestionID, TitleText, TheMessage " _
    & "From HelpDesk Where ParentID = 0", DBConn)
DBCommand.Fill(DSPageData, _
    "Question")
```

The database contains a single table. In that table, the records relate to each other through the ParentID field. One question will have many questions that it can lead to. These questions that it can lead to are linked to the question through the ParentID field.

Next, you retrieve the possible responses to the current question by looking for the records that have the same ParentID as the current top-level question:

```
DBCommand = New OleDbDataAdapter _
    ("Select QuestionID, TheChoice " _
    & "From HelpDesk " _
    & "Where ParentID = " _
    & DSPageData.Tables("Question"). _
    Rows(0).Item("QuestionID") _
    ,DBConn)
DBCommand.Fill(DSPageData, _
    "Choices")
```

The title and text of the current question are placed into Label controls:

```
lblTitle.Text = "Help Desk - " _
    & DSPageData.Tables("Question"). _
        Rows(0).Item("TitleText")
lblQuestion.Text = _
    DSPageData.Tables("Question"). _
        Rows(0).Item("TheMessage")
```

And the DropDownList control is bound to the possible responses to the current question:

```
ddlAnswers.DataSource = _
    DSPageData.Tables("Choices").DefaultView
ddlAnswers.DataBind()
```

The second procedure fires when visitors select an answer to the current question. When that happens either another question or a possible resolution is displayed:

```
Sub SubmitBtn_Click(Sender As Object, E As EventArgs)
```

Within this procedure, you need these data objects:

```
Dim DBConn as OleDbConnection
Dim DBCommand As OleDbDataAdapter
Dim DSPageData as New DataSet
You start by connecting to the database:
DBConn = New OleDbConnection( _
    "PROVIDER=Microsoft.Jet.OLEDB.4.0;" _
    & "DATA SOURCE=" _
    & Server.MapPath _
    ("/tt/C16/HelpDesk/HelpDeskDB.mdb;"))
```

You then retrieve the title and text of the next question, or the resolution, based on the response visitors select:

```
DBCommand = New OleDbDataAdapter _
    ("Select QorA, TitleText, TheMessage " _
    & "From HelpDesk Where QuestionID = " _
    & ddlAnswers.SelectedItem.Value,DBConn)
DBCommand.Fill(DSPageData, _
    "Question")
```

The title Label will display the text of the title for the item retrieved:

```
lblTitle.Text = "Help Desk - " _
    & DSPageData.Tables("Question"). _
    Rows(0).Item("TitleText")
```

And the Question Label control will either display the text of the question or the resolution:

```
lblQuestion.Text = _
    DSPageData.Tables("Question"). _
    Rows(0).Item("TheMessage")
```

Next, you check to see if the current item is a question or a resolution. If it is a question, the QorA field will be set to "Q":

```
If DSPageData.Tables("Question"). _
    Rows(0).Item("QorA") = "Q" Then
```

If that is the case, you need to retrieve the responses to that question:

```
DBCommand = New OleDbDataAdapter _
    ("Select QuestionID, TheChoice " _
    & "From HelpDesk " _
    & "Where ParentID = " _
    & ddlAnswers.SelectedItem.Value, DBConn)
DBCommand.Fill(DSPageData, _
    "Choices")
```

and place them into the DropDownList control:

```
ddlAnswers.DataSource = _
    DSPageData.Tables("Choices").DefaultView
ddlAnswers.DataBind()
```

Otherwise, the item is a resolution and you need to hide the DropDownList control and the Button control:

```
Else
    ddlAnswers.Visible = False
    butOK.Visible = False
End If
```

Displaying a Links Page

Many sites make it easier for visitors to find other helpful sites through a Links page. Such a page typically lists other sites with descriptions and allows visitors to click on the name of the site to navigate to it. This technique shows you how to create such a page.

USE IT The page created for this technique displays a list of links through a DataGrid control. The data for the links comes from an Access database.

The DataGrid control has this definition:

```
<asp:datagrid
    id="dgLinks"
```

```
    runat="server"
    autogeneratecolumns="True"
/>
```

That DataGrid control is populated through the Load event of the page:

```
Sub Page_Load(ByVal Sender as Object, ByVal E as EventArgs)
```

In that event, you need these data objects:

```
Dim DBConn as OleDbConnection
Dim DBCommand As OleDbDataAdapter
Dim DSPageData as New DataSet
```

You start by connecting to the database and retrieving all the Link records:

```
DBConn = New OleDbConnection( _
    "PROVIDER=Microsoft.Jet.OLEDB.4.0;" _
    & "DATA SOURCE=" _
    & Server.MapPath _
    ("/tt/C16/Links/LinksDB.mdb;"))
DBCommand = New OleDbDataAdapter _
    ("Select '<A HREF=""' & TheLink & '"">' " _
    & "& LinkTitle & '</A>' as [Link], " _
    & "LinkDescription as [Description] From Links " _
    & "Order By LinkTitle", DBConn)
```

Notice that the first field returned is the concatenation of the title of the link, along with the URL of the link, within an HTML Anchor control. This will allow visitors to click on the title in the DataGrid control to be taken to the site they selected.

The data is retrieved and bound to the DataGrid control:

```
DBCommand.Fill(DSPageData, _
    "Links")
dgLinks.DataSource = _
    DSPageData.Tables("Links").DefaultView
dgLinks.DataBind()
```

Adding a Link to a Links Page

If you have a Links page, it is probably offered in one of two ways. Either you provide the data for it directly through the database or you allow visitors to add links to the list. This technique builds on the last technique by showing you how to create a page that allows visitors to add a link to your Links page.

USE IT   The page presented in this section allows visitors to add a link to a Links page. Visitors enter information about the link and the link is added to the database. Visitors are then returned to the Links page.

The page defines this TextBox control for entering the title of the Link:

```
<asp:textbox
    id="txtLinkTitle"
    columns="25"
    maxlength="50"
    runat=server
/>
```

A second TextBox control allows visitors to enter in the address of the link:

```
<asp:textbox
    id="txtTheLink"
    columns="25"
    maxlength="100"
    runat=server
/>
```

And a third TextBox control allows visitors to supply a description for the link:

```
<asp:textbox
    id="txtLinkDescription"
    columns="25"
    maxlength="255"
    runat=server
/>
```

A Button control is defined that allows visitors to submit their link:

```
<asp:button
    id="butOK"
    text="  OK  "
    OnClick="SubmitBtn_Click"
    runat="server"
/>
```

The only code on the page fires when visitors click the Button control:

```
Sub SubmitBtn_Click(Sender As Object, E As EventArgs)
    Dim DBConn as OleDbConnection
    Dim DBAdd As New OleDbCommand
    DBConn = New OleDbConnection( _
        "PROVIDER=Microsoft.Jet.OLEDB.4.0;" _
```

```
              & "DATA SOURCE=" _
              & Server.MapPath _
              ("/tt/C16/Links/LinksDB.mdb;"))
      DBAdd.CommandText = "Insert Into Links " _
              & "(LinkTitle, TheLink, LinkDescription) " _
              & "values (" _
              & "'" & Replace(txtLinkTitle.Text, "'", "''") _
              & "', " _
              & "'" & Replace(txtTheLink.Text, "'", "''") _
              & "', " _
              & "'" & Replace(txtLinkDescription.Text, "'", "''") _
              & "')"
      DBAdd.Connection = DBConn
      DBAdd.Connection.Open
      DBAdd.ExecuteNonQuery()
      Response.Redirect("./links.aspx")
End Sub
```

In that event, you connect to the Access database and add the record visitors entered. Then you send the visitors back to the Links page.

Recording Page Activity

As you start to build traffic to your site, you will quickly want to know how much traffic you are getting. In other words, you will want to know how many hits you are getting to each of your pages. One of the ways that you can monitor your page activity is to add a record to a database table every time a visitor enters one of your pages. This technique shows you how to do that.

USE IT   Three pages were created to demonstrate this technique. Each of the pages has almost identical code. That code adds a record to an Access database table every time one of the pages is viewed. Into that record the name of the page that was hit is recorded, as is the date and time of the hit.

The code that records the hit fires on these pages when they load:

```
Sub Page_Load(ByVal Sender as Object, ByVal E as EventArgs)
```

> ▶ **QUICK TIP**
>
> *This type of recording will record a page hit every time the page is opened. That means if the page is returned to the server for processing, another page hit will be recorded. If you just want to record a hit the first time the page is opened, surround the code with an IsPostBack If block.*

Within the procedure, you need data objects:

```
Dim DBConn as OleDbConnection
Dim DBAdd As New OleDbCommand
```

You start by connecting to the Access database:

```
DBConn = New OleDbConnection( _
    "PROVIDER=Microsoft.Jet.OLEDB.4.0;" _
    & "DATA SOURCE=" _
    & Server.MapPath _
    ("/tt/C16/PageActivity/PADB.mdb;"))
```

You then add a record to the database:

```
DBAdd.CommandText = "Insert Into PAs " _
    & "(PageName, DateTimeEntered) " _
    & "values ('Home', Now)"
DBAdd.Connection = DBConn
DBAdd.Connection.Open
DBAdd.ExecuteNonQuery()
```

Notice that the name of this page is "Home." You would change that name on each page so that each page had an accurate account of the number of hits to it. Also, notice that the function "Now" is used to place the current date and time into the DateTimeEntered field of the record.

Displaying Page Activity

If you are recording hit activity to your Web site, you probably would want a page that you could use to quickly see the number of hits each page had received. This technique shows you how to do that.

USE IT The page created for this technique connects to an Access database and retrieves the total number of times each page has been viewed. When the page first loads, the total page activity across all dates is displayed. But visitors can enter a start and end date to limit the hit count to a date range.

Within the body of the page, this DataGrid control displays the hit counts:

```
<asp:datagrid
    id="dgHits"
    runat="server"
    autogeneratecolumns="True"
/>
```

If visitors wish to filter the hit count to a date range, they enter the start date into the following TextBox control.

```
<asp:textbox
    id="txtStartDate"
    runat=server
/>
```

Visitors must enter a value into the field because of this RequiredFieldValidator control:

```
<asp:requiredfieldvalidator
    id="rfvStartDate"
    controltovalidate="txtStartDate"
    display="Dynamic"
    font-name="Tahoma"
    font-size="10pt"
    runat="server">
    You must enter a date!
</asp:requiredfieldvalidator>
```

What they enter must be a date because this CompareValidator control is linked to it:

```
<asp:comparevalidator
    id="cvStartDate"
    controltovalidate="txtStartDate"
    operator="DataTypeCheck"
    type="Date"
    runat="server"
>
    You must enter a date!
</asp:CompareValidator>
```

A second TextBox control, RequiredFieldValidator control, and CompareValidator control allows visitors to enter an end date.

Also defined on the page is a Button control that visitors can click to submit their date range:

```
<asp:button
    id="butOK"
    text="  OK  "
    OnClick="SubmitBtn_Click"
    runat="server"
/>
```

When the page first loads, this code block fires:

```
Sub Page_Load(ByVal Sender as Object, ByVal E as EventArgs)
    If Not IsPostBack Then
        Dim DBConn as OleDbConnection
        Dim DBCommand As OleDbDataAdapter
```

```
        Dim DSPageData as New DataSet
        DBConn = New OleDbConnection( _
            "PROVIDER=Microsoft.Jet.OLEDB.4.0;" _
            & "DATA SOURCE=" _
            & Server.MapPath _
            ("/tt/C16/PageActivity/PADB.mdb;"))
        DBCommand = New OleDbDataAdapter _
            ("Select PageName as [Page Name], " _
            & "Count(PAID) as [Count] " _
            & "From PAs " _
            & "Group By PageName", DBConn)
        DBCommand.Fill(DSPageData, _
            "TheResults")
        dgHits.DataSource = _
            DSPageData.Tables("TheResults").DefaultView
        dgHits.DataBind()
    End If
End Sub
```

The code connects to the database and retrieves the count of all the page hits without specifying a date range. The DataGrid is bound to this data.

The other procedure fires when the Button control is clicked:

```
Sub SubmitBtn_Click(Sender As Object, E As EventArgs)
    Dim DBConn as OleDbConnection
    Dim DBCommand As OleDbDataAdapter
    Dim DSPageData as New DataSet
    DBConn = New OleDbConnection( _
        "PROVIDER=Microsoft.Jet.OLEDB.4.0;" _
        & "DATA SOURCE=" _
        & Server.MapPath _
        ("/tt/C16/PageActivity/PADB.mdb;"))
    DBCommand = New OleDbDataAdapter _
        ("Select PageName as [Page Name], " _
        & "Count(PAID) as [Count] " _
        & "From PAs " _
        & "Where DateTimeEntered >= #" _
        & txtStartDate.Text & "# and " _
        & "DateTimeEntered <= #" & txtEndDate.Text _
        & "# Group By PageName", DBConn)
    DBCommand.Fill(DSPageData, _
        "TheResults")
    dgHits.DataSource = _
        DSPageData.Tables("TheResults").DefaultView
```

```
    dgHits.DataBind()
End Sub
```

This procedure is very similar to the last procedure. It connects to the database and binds the DataGrid control to the returned data. But it limits the data returned to the date range entered into the TextBox controls.

Creating a Quiz Page

Whether you have an online school or offer totally different content, you may find for a variety of reasons that you want to quiz your visitors on some topic. This technique shows you how to create a basic Quiz page.

USE IT The page created for this technique displays three questions to visitors as well as possible answers to each of those questions. When visitors submit the quiz it is scored and they see their result.

Each question displayed is a combination of raw text for the question:

```
How is the new version of "C" pronounced"?
<BR>
```

along with a DropDownList control that displays the possible answers to the question:

```
<asp:dropdownlist
    id="ddlAnswer1"
    runat=server
>
    <asp:listitem>C Pound</asp:listitem>
    <asp:listitem>C Triple Plus</asp:listitem>
    <asp:listitem>C Plus Plus Plus</asp:listitem>
    <asp:listitem>C Sharp</asp:listitem>
</asp:dropdownlist>
```

When visitors are through answering the questions, they submit their answers by clicking the Button control:

```
<asp:button
    id="butOK"
    text="  OK  "
    OnClick="SubmitBtn_Click"
    runat="server"
/>
```

When they do click that button, the following code block fires:

```
Sub SubmitBtn_Click(Sender As Object, E As EventArgs)
    Dim TotalCorrect as Integer
    If ddlAnswer1.SelectedItem.Text = "C Sharp" Then
        TotalCorrect = TotalCorrect + 1
    End If
    If ddlAnswer2.SelectedItem.Text = "Visual Basic" Then
        TotalCorrect = TotalCorrect + 1
    End If
    If ddlAnswer3.SelectedItem.Text = "SelectedItem" Then
        TotalCorrect = TotalCorrect + 1
    End If
    lblMessage.Text = "You scored " & TotalCorrect _
        & " correct."
End Sub
```

Within this procedure, you compare the visitors' answer with the correct answer. If they answer the question correctly, you add one to the TotalCorrect variable. After checking each answer, you display the total number of correct answers back to the visitors.

Index

INTERNATIONAL CONTACT INFORMATION

AUSTRALIA
McGraw-Hill Book Company Australia Pty. Ltd.
TEL +61-2-9417-9899
FAX +61-2-9417-5687
http://www.mcgraw-hill.com.au
books-it_sydney@mcgraw-hill.com

CANADA
McGraw-Hill Ryerson Ltd.
TEL +905-430-5000
FAX +905-430-5020
http://www.mcgrawhill.ca

**GREECE, MIDDLE EAST,
NORTHERN AFRICA**
McGraw-Hill Hellas
TEL +30-1-656-0990-3-4
FAX +30-1-654-5525

MEXICO (Also serving Latin America)
McGraw-Hill Interamericana Editores S.A. de C.V.
TEL +525-117-1583
FAX +525-117-1589
http://www.mcgraw-hill.com.mx
fernando_castellanos@mcgraw-hill.com

SINGAPORE (Serving Asia)
McGraw-Hill Book Company
TEL +65-863-1580
FAX +65-862-3354
http://www.mcgraw-hill.com.sg
mghasia@mcgraw-hill.com

SOUTH AFRICA
McGraw-Hill South Africa
TEL +27-11-622-7512
FAX +27-11-622-9045
robyn_swanepoel@mcgraw-hill.com

**UNITED KINGDOM & EUROPE
(Excluding Southern Europe)**
McGraw-Hill Education Europe
TEL +44-1-628-502500
FAX +44-1-628-770224
http://www.mcgraw-hill.co.uk
computing_neurope@mcgraw-hill.com

ALL OTHER INQUIRIES Contact:
Osborne/McGraw-Hill
TEL +1-510-549-6600
FAX +1-510-883-7600
http://www.osborne.com
omg_international@mcgraw-hill.com

Complete References

Herbert Schildt
0-07-213485-2

Jeffery R. Shapiro
0-07-213381-3

Chris H. Pappas & William
H. Murray, III
0-07-212958-1

Herbert Schildt
0-07-213084-9

Ron Ben-Natan & Ori Sasson
0-07-222394-4

Arthur Griffith
0-07-222405-3

For the answers to everything related to your technology, drill as deeply as you please into our Complete Reference series. Written by topical authorities, these comprehensive resources offer a full range of knowledge, including extensive product information, theory, step-by-step tutorials, sample projects, and helpful appendixes.

OSBORNE
www.osborne.com

For more information on these and other Osborne books, visit our Web site at www.osborne.com